Consciences and the Reformation

OXFORD STUDIES IN HISTORICAL THEOLOGY

Series Editor
Richard A. Muller, Calvin Theological Seminary

Founding Editor
David C. Steinmetz †

Editorial Board
Robert C. Gregg, Stanford University
George M. Marsden, University of Notre Dame
Wayne A. Meeks, Yale University
Gerhard Sauter, Rheinische Friedrich-Wilhelms-Universität Bonn
Susan E. Schreiner, University of Chicago
John Van Engen, University of Notre Dame
Robert L. Wilken, University of Virginia

THE UNACCOMMODATED CALVIN
Studies in the Foundation of a Theological Tradition
Richard A. Muller

THE CONFESSIONALIZATION OF HUMANISM IN REFORMATION GERMANY
Erika Rummell

THE PLEASURE OF DISCERNMENT
Marguerite de Navarre as Theologian
Carol Thysell

REFORMATION READINGS OF THE APOCALYPSE
Geneva, Zurich, and Wittenberg
Irena Backus

WRITING THE WRONGS
Women of the Old Testament among Biblical Commentators from Philo through the Reformation
John L. Thompson

THE HUNGRY ARE DYING
Beggars and Bishops in Roman Cappadocia
Susan R. Holman

RESCUE FOR THE DEAD
The Posthumous Salvation of Non-Christians in Early Christianity
Jeffrey A. Trumbower

AFTER CALVIN
Studies in the Development of a Theological Tradition
Richard A. Muller

THE POVERTY OF RICHES
St. Francis of Assisi Reconsidered
Kenneth Baxter Wolf

REFORMING MARY
Changing Images of the Virgin Mary in Lutheran Sermons of the Sixteenth Century
Beth Kreitzer

TEACHING THE REFORMATION
Ministers and Their Message in Basel, 1529–1629
Amy Nelson Burnett

THE PASSIONS OF CHRIST IN HIGH-MEDIEVAL THOUGHT
An Essay on Christological Development
Kevin Madigan

GOD'S IRISHMEN
Theological Debates in Cromwellian Ireland
Crawford Gribben

REFORMING SAINTS
Saint's Lives and Their Authors in Germany, 1470–1530
David J. Collins

GREGORY OF NAZIANZUS
ON THE TRINITY AND THE
KNOWLEDGE OF GOD
In Your Light We Shall See Light
Christopher A. Beeley

THE JUDAIZING CALVIN
*Sixteenth-Century Debates over the
Messianic Psalms*
G. Sujin Pak

THE DEATH OF SCRIPTURE AND
THE RISE OF BIBLICAL STUDIES
Michael C. Legaspi

THE FILIOQUE
History of a Doctrinal Controversy
A. Edward Siecienski

ARE YOU ALONE WISE?
*Debates about Certainty in the Early
Modern Church*
Susan E. Schreiner

EMPIRE OF SOULS
*Robert Bellarmine and the Christian
Commonwealth*
Stefania Tutino

MARTIN BUCER'S DOCTRINE OF
JUSTIFICATION
*Reformation Theology and Early Modern
Irenicism*
Brian Lugioyo

CHRISTIAN GRACE AND
PAGAN VIRTUE
*The Theological Foundation of
Ambrose's Ethics*
J. Warren Smith

KARLSTADT AND THE ORIGINS OF
THE EUCHARISTIC CONTROVERSY
A Study in the Circulation of Ideas
Amy Nelson Burnett

READING AUGUSTINE IN THE
REFORMATION
*The Flexibility of Intellectual Authority in
Europe, 1500–1620*
Arnoud S. Q. Visser

SHAPERS OF ENGLISH CALVINISM,
1660–1714
Variety, Persistence, and Transformation
Dewey D. Wallace, Jr.

THE BIBLICAL INTERPRETATION
OF WILLIAM OF ALTON
Timothy Bellamah, OP

MIRACLES AND THE PROTESTANT
IMAGINATION
*The Evangelical Wonder Book in
Reformation Germany*
Philip M. Soergel

THE REFORMATION OF
SUFFERING
*Pastoral Theology and Lay Piety in Late
Medieval and Early Modern Germany*
Ronald K. Rittgers

CHRIST MEETS ME EVERYWHERE
Augustine's Early Figurative Exegesis
Michael Cameron

MYSTERY UNVEILED
*The Crisis of the Trinity in Early Modern
England*
Paul C. H. Lim

GOING DUTCH IN THE
MODERN AGE
*Abraham Kuyper's Struggle for a Free
Church in the Netherlands*
John Halsey Wood, Jr.

CALVIN'S COMPANY OF PASTORS
*Pastoral Care and the Emerging
Reformed Church, 1536–1609*
Scott M. Manetsch

THE SOTERIOLOGY OF
JAMES USSHER
The Act and Object of Saving Faith
Richard Snoddy

HARTFORD PURITANISM
*Thomas Hooker, Samuel Stone, and Their
Terrifying God*
Baird Tipson

AUGUSTINE, THE TRINITY, AND THE CHURCH
A Reading of the Anti-Donatist Sermons
Adam Ployd

AUGUSTINE'S EARLY THEOLOGY OF IMAGE
A Study in the Development of Pro-Nicene Theology
Gerald Boersma

PATRON SAINT AND PROPHET
Jan Hus in the Bohemian and German Reformations
Phillip N. Haberkern

JOHN OWEN AND ENGLISH PURITANISM
Experiences of Defeat
Crawford Gribben

MORALITY AFTER CALVIN
Theodore Beza's Christian Censor and Reformed Ethics
Kirk M. Summers

THE PAPACY AND THE ORTHODOX
A History of Reception and Rejection
A. Edward Siecienski

DEBATING PERSEVERANCE
The Augustinian Heritage in Post-Reformation England
Jay T. Collier

THE REFORMATION OF PROPHECY
Early Modern Interpretations of the Prophet & Old Testament Prophecy
G. Sujin Pak

ANTOINE DE CHANDIEU
The Silver Horn of Geneva's Reformed Triumvirate
Theodore G. Van Raalte

ORTHODOX RADICALS
Baptist Identity in the English Revolution
Matthew C. Bingham

DIVINE PERFECTION AND HUMAN POTENTIALITY
The Trinitarian Anthropology of Hilary of Poitiers
Jarred A. Mercer

THE GERMAN AWAKENING
Protestant Renewal after the Enlightenment, 1815–1848
Andrew Kloes

THE REGENSBURG ARTICLE 5 ON JUSTIFICATION
Inconsistent Patchwork or Substance of True Doctrine?
Anthony N. S. Lane

AUGUSTINE ON THE WILL
A Theological Account
Han-luen Kantzer Komline

THE SYNOD OF PISTORIA AND VATICAN II
Jansenism and the Struggle for Catholic Reform
Shaun Blanchard

CATHOLICITY AND THE COVENANT OF WORKS
James Ussher and the Reformed Tradition
Harrison Perkins

THE COVENANT OF WORKS
The Origins, Development, and Reception of the Doctrine
J. V. Fesko

RINGLEADERS OF REDEMPTION
How Medieval Dance Became Sacred
Kathryn Dickason

REFUSING TO KISS THE SLIPPER
Opposition to Calvinism in the Francophone Reformation
Michael W. Bruening

FONT OF PARDON AND NEW LIFE
John Calvin and the Efficacy of Baptism
Lyle D. Bierma

THE FLESH OF THE WORD
The extra Calvinisticum *from Zwingli to Early Orthodoxy*
K. J. Drake

JOHN DAVENANT'S HYPOTHETICAL UNIVERSALISM
A Defense of Catholic and Reformed Orthodoxy
Michael J. Lynch

RHETORICAL ECONOMY IN
AUGUSTINE'S THEOLOGY
Brian Gronewoller

GRACE AND CONFORMITY
The Reformed Conformist tradition and the Early Stuart Church of England
Stephen Hampton

MAKING ITALY ANGLICAN
Why the Book of Common Prayer Was Translated into Italian
Stefano Villani

AUGUSINE ON MEMORY
Kevin G. Grove

UNITY AND CATHOLICITY IN CHRIST
The Ecclesiology of Francisco Suarez, S.J.
Eric J. DeMeuse

RETAINING THE OLD EPISCOPAL DIVINITY
John Edwards of Cambridge and Reformed Orthodoxy in the Later Stuart Church
Jake Griesel

CALVINIST CONFORMITY IN POST-REFORMATION ENGLAND
The Theology and Career of Daniel Featley
Gregory A. Salazar

BEARDS, AZYMES, AND PURGATORY
The Other Issues That Divided East and West
A. Edward Siecienski

BISSCHOP'S BENCH
Contours of Arminian Conformity in the Church of England, c. 1674–1742
Samuel David Fornecker

JOHN LOCKE'S THEOLOGY
An Ecumenical, Irenic, and Controversial Project
Jonathan S. Marko

CONSCIENCES AND THE REFORMATION
Scruples over Oaths and Confessions in the Era of Calvin and His Contemporaries
Timothy R. Scheuers

Consciences and the Reformation

Scruples over Oaths and Confessions in the Era of Calvin and His Contemporaries

TIMOTHY R. SCHEUERS

OXFORD
UNIVERSITY PRESS

Oxford University Press is a department of the University of Oxford. It furthers
the University's objective of excellence in research, scholarship, and education
by publishing worldwide. Oxford is a registered trade mark of Oxford University
Press in the UK and certain other countries.

Published in the United States of America by Oxford University Press
198 Madison Avenue, New York, NY 10016, United States of America.

© Oxford University Press 2023

All rights reserved. No part of this publication may be reproduced, stored in
a retrieval system, or transmitted, in any form or by any means, without the
prior permission in writing of Oxford University Press, or as expressly permitted
by law, by license, or under terms agreed with the appropriate reproduction
rights organization. Inquiries concerning reproduction outside the scope of the
above should be sent to the Rights Department, Oxford University Press, at the
address above.

You must not circulate this work in any other form
and you must impose this same condition on any acquirer.

CIP data is on file at the Library of Congress
ISBN 978-0-19-769214-1

DOI: 10.1093/oso/9780197692141.001.0001

Printed by Integrated Books International, United States of America

*To my parents,
the Reverend Ronald Scheuers
and Faye [Mulder] Scheuers*

and

*to my wife Amanda—
as Calvin said of his beloved Idelette,
singularis exempli femina,
a woman of matchless type.*

Contents

Acknowledgments — xiii
Abbreviations — xv
Notes on Translation and Texts — xvii

Introduction — 1

SECTION I: CALVIN AND THE REFORMERS' INHERITED LEGAL TRADITION

1. Before Calvin: Oaths, Religious Coercion, and the Freedom of Conscience from the Medieval Church to the Reformation — 15

SECTION II: ANSWERING CONSCIENTIOUS OBJECTORS: CALVIN AND THE REFORMERS AGAINST RADICAL DISSENT AND RELIGIOUS COMPROMISE

2. Conscience, Confession, and the Consolidation of Early Public Reform in Strasbourg, 1530–1535 — 49

3. "Vera pietas veram confessionem parit": Confession, Conscience, and Charity in the Anti-Nicodemism of Calvin and the Reformers — 73

4. Confession, Conscience, and Christian Freedom in the Later Anti-Nicodemite Writings of Calvin and the Reformers, 1540–1562 — 104

SECTION III: OATHS, CONFESSIONAL SUBSCRIPTION, AND THE BINDING OF THE CONSCIENCE IN REFORMATION GENEVA

5. Citizen's Oath and Confession of Faith in Reformation Geneva, 1536–1538: Necessary, Indifferent, or a *Tertium Quid*? — 139

6. "Make Them Afraid of Bearing False Witness": Oaths, Conscience, and Discipline in the Registers of the Genevan Consistory, 1541–1564   166

7. After Calvin: Oaths, Subscription, Conscience, and Compromise in the Genevan Academy, 1559–1612   202

Conclusion   228

Bibliography   239
Index   251

Acknowledgments

At the completion of this project, I am left with a debt of gratitude to many individuals whose help and inspiration I am happy to acknowledge.

Since this book first saw life as my PhD dissertation, initial gratitude belongs to those who facilitated my overall progress in the pursuit of this degree: library staff at the David Allan Hubbard Library at Fuller Theological Seminary; staff and administrators at Fuller's Center for Advanced Theological Studies; fellow students and colleagues in seminars and post-class discussions; and professors who modeled the very standards of scholarly excellence they sought to inculcate in their students. My work was also made possible by the generous provision of a sizable academic merit grant offered through the seminary.

An early iteration of this material was presented at the Sixteenth Century Society Conference, where Karin Maag at the H. Henry Meeter Center for Calvin Studies gave an encouraging assessment of my research, while also suggesting areas of further study. Her willingness to provide access to Genevan archival materials is greatly appreciated.

I owe a special debt of thanks to the faculty of Mid-America Reformed Seminary, including J. Mark Beach and Cornelis Venema, who first encouraged me to pursue doctoral studies, as well as Mark Vander Hart, who introduced me to the rigors of Latin.

I am very thankful to several other scholars whose advice and resources proved immensely beneficial to my research. Anthony Perron of Loyola Marymount University was very kind to oversee my work in medieval canon law. Jeffrey and Isabella Watt graciously provided unpublished transcriptions of the Genevan Consistory Records and, along with Karen Spierling, assisted my translation of some obscure entries. Michael Bruening, Grayson Carter, Jason Zuidema, as well as Oliver Crisp and Herman Selderhuis, my secondary readers, also deserve credit for their friendly counsel and availability to discuss research materials.

I owe a unique debt of thanks to the staff at Oxford University Press for overseeing the preparation and publication of this volume: to editors Tom Perridge and Rachel Ruisard, as well as to the anonymous readers at OUP who initially reviewed my manuscript and offered generous comments and constructive suggestions. I am particularly grateful to Richard Muller for his warm and insightful correspondence, and for initially agreeing to publish this book in the Oxford Studies in Historical Theology series while he was the editor.

My principal gratitude for the completion of this project goes to my doctoral mentor, John L. Thompson, whose scholarly erudition is matched only by his tireless commitment to his students. John significantly broadened my understanding of the texts and contexts of the Reformation and facilitated ample opportunities for me to hone my teaching and writing abilities while working as his teaching and research assistant. He always took great interest in my work and helped me to frame my thoughts in clearer, more cogent and interesting ways. It has been a privilege and an honor to study under Dr. Thompson, and I will forever appreciate his assistance and encouragement, as well as his delightful wit, warm hospitality, and pastoral patience. I only hope to inherit a small portion of his unequaled spirit.

I want to express heartfelt appreciation to my brothers and sisters in Christ at First United Reformed Church of Chino, California, where I currently serve as Associate Pastor. Many of these dear saints took an invested interest in my work and supported me through countless prayers and uplifting words. Special thanks belong to my pastor, colleague, and friend, Rev. Bradd Nymeyer, who enjoyed experiencing doctoral studies "vicariously" through me as we met each week for conference and prayer. The staff, faculty, and trustees of Providence Christian College, where I serve as an Adjunct Assistant Professor of History, also deserve credit for supporting my research endeavors.

Finally, I am grateful to all of my precious family members for their loving support, faithful prayers, and steady encouragement while I worked on this project. I am particularly thankful to my parents, Rev. Ronald and Faye Scheuers, for modeling the godly virtues of creativity, excellence, and humility, and for instilling these same values in me. I am also grateful to my parents-in-law, Scott and Kim Schelbauer, for their support of and interest in my work.

Singular appreciation is reserved for my dear wife Amanda and our lovely daughter Scottlynn. Over the course of this project, they have been a constant source of encouragement, blessing, and inspiration. They exhibited unparalleled patience with me as I sometimes wrote from dawn to dusk—this, despite many demands upon my wife's own professional and domestic life. Mere words cannot express my gratitude for their enduring love and firm commitment to me and my work.

Soli Deo Gloria

Abbreviations

AEG	Archives d'Etat de Genève
AEG, Jur. Pen.	Repertoire du Registres du Conseil des causes criminelles et consistoriales
AEG, R.Consist.	Registres du Consistoire de Genève (archival manuscripts)
BOL	*Martini Buceri Opera Latina.* Leiden: Brill, 1982–.
Bonnet	John Calvin. *Letters of John Calvin.* Edited by Jules Bonnet. 4 vols. Philadelphia: Presbyterian Board of Publication, 1854.
CO	John Calvin. *Joannis Calvini Opera Quae Supersunt Omnia.* Edited by G. Baum, E. Cunitz, E. Reuss. 59 vols. Brunswick, 1863–1900.
COR 4/4	John Calvin. *Ioannis Calvini Opera* Omnia. Series 4: *Scripta Didactica et Polemica.* Volume 4: *Epistolae Duae (1537), Deux Discours (Oct. 1536).* Edited by Erik Alexander de Boer and Frans Pieter van Stam. Geneva: Droz, 2009.
Crottet	Alexandre Crottet, ed. *Correspondance française de Calvin avec Louis du Tillet, chanoine d'Angoulême et curé de Claix: Sur les questions de l'église et du ministère évangélique.* Geneva: Cherbuliez, 1850.
CTS	John Calvin. *Tracts and Treatises* (Calvin Translation Society). 3 vols. Translated by Henry Beveridge. 1851; Grand Rapids, MI: Eerdmans, 1958.
CTSOT/CTSNT	John Calvin. *Old Testament and New Testament Commentaries* (Calvin Translation Society). 23 vols. Translated by Henry Beveridge. Reprint. Grand Rapids, MI: Baker Books, 2009.
ET	English Translation
Herminjard	A. L. Herminjard, ed. *Correspondance des réformateurs dans les pays de langue française.* 9 vols. Geneva; Paris: 1866–1897.
Institutes 1536	John Calvin. *Institutes of the Christian Religion* [1536 edition]. Translated by Ford Lewis Battles. Grand Rapids, MI: H. H. Meeter Center for Calvin Studies/Eerdmans, 1986.
LCC 20–21	John Calvin. *Institutes of the Christian Religion.* Edited by John T. McNeill. Translated by Ford Lewis Battles. The Library of Christian Classics. Vols. 20–21. 1960; Louisville, KY: Westminster John Knox Press, 2006.
LCC 22	John Calvin. *Theological Treatises.* Edited by J. K. S. Reid. Philadelphia: Westminster Press, 1954.

LW	Martin Luther. *Luther's Works* ("American Edition"). Edited by Jaroslav Pelikan and Helmut T. Lehmann, et al. 56 vols. St. Louis; Concordia; Philadelphia: Fortress Press, 1955–1986.
OS	John Calvin. *Calvini Opera Selecta*. Edited by Peter Barth and Wilhelm Niesel. 5 vols. München: Kaiser, 1926–1952.
QGT	*Quellen zur Geschichte der Täufer. Elsaß* I–II. Teil: Stadt Straßburg, 1522–1535. Edited by Manfred Krebs and Hans Georg Rott. Vols. 7–8. Heidelberg: Gütersloher Verlagshaus Gerd Mohn, 1959–1960.
RC	Registres du Conseil
R.Consist.	Registres du Consistoire de Genève à l'époque de Calvin (published editions)
RCP	*Registres de la Compagnie des Pasteurs au temps de Calvin*. Edited by Robert M. Kingdon and Jean-François Bergier. 2 vols. Geneva, 1962–1964. English translation by Philip C. Hughes. *The Register of the Company of Pastors of Geneva in the Time of Calvin*. Grand Rapids, MI: Eerdmans, 1966 (cited as Hughes ed.).
SCJ	*Sixteenth Century Journal*
ST	Thomas Aquinas. *Summa Theologica*. Vols. 2–3. In *Doctoris angelici divi Thomae Aquinatis opera omnia*. Edited by Stanislai Eduardi Fretté and Pauli Maré. 34 vols. Paris: Ludovicum Vivés, 1871.
WA	Martin Luther. *Martin Luthers Werke: Kritische Gesamtausgabe*. Weimar: H. Boehlaus Nachfolger, 1883–.

Medieval Legal Texts

Dist. 1, c. 1	*Decretum Gratiani*, Distinctio 1, canon 1
C. 1, q. 1, c. 1	*Decretum Gratiani*, Causa 1, quaestio 1, canon 1
Dig. 1.1.1	*Digestum Justiniani*, book 1, tit. 1, lex 1
Cod. 1.1.1	*Codex Justiniani*, book 1, tit. 1, lex 1
Inst. 1.1.1	*Institutiones Justiniani*, book 1, tit. 1, lex 1
Nov.	*Novellae* (Justinian)

Notes on Translation and Texts

Translations are mine unless otherwise noted. In all cases where a modern translation is used, I also include references to the Latin, French, or German editions that I have consulted.

I have modernized the spelling and punctuation of the early modern English editions of several treatises (except for the titles) by conforming the use of "u" and "v" to modern conventions, removing redundant consonants and antiquated vowel combinations, as well as inserting or removing commas where appropriate.

Introduction

Was the Reformation "a success story" or "the tale of a failure"? Gerald Strauss's decades-old question continues to stimulate scholarship on the tactics and trajectories of moral reform in Protestant urban centers during the Reformation.[1] The controversial conclusion of Strauss's article, that early optimism gave way to disillusionment and discontent among the reformers as their disciplinary tactics failed to bring about the desired reform, has sparked diverse responses since its publication in 1975.[2] Yet despite its mixed reception, the impressive corpus of textual evidence unearthed by Strauss clearly demonstrates that no study of the Reformation can expect to judge the success or failure of that movement without accounting for the reformers' assessment of their own labors—the success or failure of which was often measured by the responses of the laity and civil magistrates to the reformers' sometimes controversial measures for reform.

This monograph examines the complex relationship between oath-taking, confessional subscription, and the binding of the conscience in John Calvin's reform in light of an important but still unresolved question raised by Strauss's article, namely: "Had anything changed in the consciences and minds of men as a result of the Reformation?"[3] Scholars of this period generally acknowledge that, within the historiography of religious tolerance and claims to freedom of conscience, "the Reformation era has always been considered of paramount importance for the developments which led to the achievement of 'a liberal and tolerant society.'"[4] The Reformation effectively broke up the monolithic edifice of medieval Catholic Christianity, spawning a diversity of reformist groups enamored with the possibility of newfound

---

[1] Gerald Strauss, "Success and Failure in the German Reformation," *Past & Present* 67 (1975): 30–63.

[2] For a more positive assessment of the Reformation and its consequences for European society, including its effect upon general literacy, individual conscience, and moral discipline, see Philip Benedict, *Christ's Churches Purely Reformed: A Social History of Calvinism* (New Haven, CT, and London: Yale University Press, 2002), 429–546.

[3] Strauss, "Success and Failure in the German Reformation," 42.

[4] Ole Peter Grell, Introduction to *Tolerance and Intolerance in the European Reformation*, ed. Ole Peter Grell and Bob Scribner (Cambridge: Cambridge University Press, 1996), 1.

religious liberties. When Luther's conscientious objection to the alleged spiritual abuses of the Roman Church went public in 1517 with his Ninety-Five Theses, his bold invective sparked renewed passion for and appeals to the freedom of conscience among reform-minded clergy and laity in sixteenth-century Germany and its surrounding lands. The combined effect of Luther's later emphasis on the principles of *sola scriptura* and *sola fide* was to assert that believers were utterly free in matters not explicitly commanded by Scripture. The individual conscience—a person's innate knowledge of God's judgment—was now "man's highest court of appeal." This message proved to be a refreshing change for laypeople languishing under a bevy of Catholic human traditions and burdensome regulations.[5]

Although it is well established that appeals to conscience played a prominent and public role in theological, civil, and social discussions during the Reformation, Strauss's question nonetheless poses unique challenges to the historian, in no small part because it calls for an assessment of people's *thoughts* about conscience based upon an often-fragmentary record of their words and actions under diverse historical circumstances. Notwithstanding the daunting nature of this task, Reformation historians have regularly chimed in on the matter—some praising the reformers for rescuing the sacredness of the private conscience, and others expressing belief that the reformers' failure to build their entire movement according to the pattern initially set by its cornerstone of freedom of conscience effectively "tarnished the tremendous legacy of the Protestant Reformation."[6] Bob Scribner, for example, has argued that the reformers allowed three of their core principles—freedom of conscience, separation of secular and spiritual authority, and protection of weaker brothers and sisters—to be "compromised or overridden

---

[5] Harry Loewen, *Luther and the Radicals* (Waterloo, ON: Wilfrid Laurier University Press, 1974), 14–15. Steven E. Ozment argues that the Reformation gained such a wide and (largely) immediate acceptance in the cities of medieval Germany, not so much because it restored methods of order and regulation to the cities, but because it sought to unburden the laity from excessive regulations and the troubling overreach of clerical abuses. See Ozment, *The Reformation in the Cities: The Appeal of Protestantism to Sixteenth-Century Germany and Switzerland* (New Haven, CT: Yale University Press, 1975), 36–77, 44–46. For a helpful overview of Calvin's theology of conscience in relation to divine and human law, see Herman J. Selderhuis, "Calvin's Views on Conscience and Law," in *Das Gewissen in den Rechtslehren der protestantischen und katholischen Reformationen*, ed. Michael Germann and Wim Decock (Leipzig: Evangelische Verlagsanstalt, 2017), 33–50. As will be seen, although my volume addresses the theory of conscience, it mainly focuses on the *practice* of the conscience (that is, private appeals to conscience in the context of public moral life) amidst various Reformation-era controversies.

[6] Ganoune Diop, "The Sixteenth Century Reformation's Context and Content: Highlighting the Pivotal Role of Freedom of Conscience," *Scientia Moralitas: International Journal of Multidisciplinary Research* 2, no. 1 (2017): 8.

in the course of the early Reformation. The imperative demands of the Word of God took precedence over claims of individual conscience; ... the urgent need to organise new evangelical churches led to implicit (and often explicit) abandonment of the separation of secular and spiritual authority; and the urgency to effect immediate reform overrode love of neighbor and concern for weaker brethren."[7]

In light of such claims, this study's choice of Calvin as a primary interlocutor seems appropriate, not simply because of persistent caricatures of Calvin as one of the Reformation's most notorious and tyrannical authoritarians, but also because Calvin and his Reformed colleagues were not spared from having to deal with objections leveled against their own brand of confessional Christianity even in their own day.[8] Indeed, two driving principles of the Reformation, *sola Scriptura* and individual freedom of conscience, occasionally produced unintended consequences for Calvin and the other

---

[7] Bob Scribner, "Preconditions of Tolerance and Intolerance in Sixteenth-Century Germany," in *Tolerance and Intolerance in the European Reformation*, 34–35. In his introduction to the above volume, Grell argues that although the early humanists like Desiderius Erasmus and Thomas More headlined a period of tolerance, "this brief interlude was then followed by the bigotry and intolerance of the first decades of the Reformation, especially by reformers such as Calvin, Knox and Beza" (1). It is necessary to recognize, however, that "toleration" has a rather complex historical meaning that may well complicate any indictment of the reformers for their alleged bigotry. Philip Benedict reveals that "tolerance" is a very complex attribute whose historical meaning was always "bound up with prevailing ideas about the particular matter at stake and the larger nature of the political community, with practical considerations of power, and with the extent and character of the personal contacts between those who might do the persecuting and those who might be persecuted." Very few sixteenth-century clerics and civil authorities actually conceived of toleration as a good thing, as it roughly denoted the willing accommodation of some evil or impure belief. From a historical perspective, then, the charge of "intolerance" is not an easy one to make without first understanding the ideological issues at stake in a given context. Likewise, "freedom of conscience"—a phrase arising from the Reformation itself—referred "not to the freedom that individuals might enjoy from having their deepest religious convictions subject to government constraint and punishment, but to the conscience's liberation through faith from the fear and doubt that were its fate for those still mired in the errors of Catholicism." See Benedict, "*Un roi, une loi, deux fois*: Parameters for the History of Catholic-Reformed Coexistence in France, 1555–1685," in *Tolerance and Intolerance in the European Reformation*, 65–67.

[8] Opposition to Calvin's doctrinal and ecclesiastical reforms arose from various sectors of French evangelicalism in the sixteenth century, as explained by Michael W. Bruening in his very recent book, *Refusing to Kiss the Slipper: Opposition to Calvinism in the Francophone Reformation* (Oxford: Oxford University Press, 2021). From his study of Calvin's severest critics, Bruening shows how Calvin's own reform strategies sometimes took shape as defensive reactions to the challenges of his opponents. The portrayal of Calvin as the tyrant of Geneva persists still today in both popular and academic writings, despite its convincing refutation by leading Calvin scholars: Roland Bainton famously quipped, "If Calvin ever wrote anything in favor of religious liberty, it was a typographical error," in his "Preface" to *Concerning Heretics: Whether they are to be persecuted and how they are to be treated. A collection of the opinions of learned men both ancient and modern [an anonymous work attributed to Sebastian Castellio]* (1935; New York: Octagon Books, 1965), 74. See also Molly Worthen, "Who Would Jesus Smack Down?" *New York Times Magazine*, January 6, 2009; and Roger Olson, *The Story of Christian Theology: Twenty Centuries of Tradition and Reform* (Downers Grove, IL: Intervarsity Press, 1999), 21.

reformers, especially when it came to organizing and enforcing reform in sixteenth-century Geneva and its local regions. The reformers faced the challenge of distinguishing what they believed were "impious constitutions" of the Roman Church—human traditions claiming to bind the consciences of the faithful—and "legitimate church observances," such as oaths and formal subscription to Reformed confessions of faith.[9] Organizing reform in the cities became somewhat precarious when friends and foes alike accused Calvin and his partners of burdening their consciences with extra-Scriptural statements of faith composed by human authorities—a claim that, if true, would necessarily shape our assessment of the integrity of the Reformation during Calvin's lifetime.

The principal goal of this study is to offer a close reading and evaluation of the texts and controversies surrounding Calvin's struggle for reform, especially as they reveal some of the unique challenges Calvin and his pastoral colleagues encountered in their attempts to employ oath-swearing and formal confession of faith as a necessary means to consolidate the reformation of church and society. This study aims to provide a more nuanced understanding of how the reformers navigated the often-complex relationship between exegesis, theory, and practice in Reformed communities during Calvin's lifetime. Some biblical commentators from Calvin's inherited tradition—as well as Anabaptist interpreters in his own day—believed that Scripture taught a complete prohibition of any and all oaths and vows, and typically appealed to Matthew 5:34–37 as evidence for the complete abrogation of all "external ceremonies" that cruelly bound the consciences of believers.[10] Such claims often forced Calvin and his colleagues to defend the occasional necessity of sworn oaths and confessional subscription, not only by distinguishing their opponents' reading of Scripture from their own, but also by contending for a modified form of individual liberty on the basis of a highly nuanced conception of the relationship between conscience and

---

[9] John Calvin, *Institutes of the Christian Religion* (1559) 4.10.28 (LCC 21:1206; CO 2:887–88).

[10] One notable example is St. John Chrysostom, who believed that sworn oaths were "altogether forbidden" and that it was wrong "to impose the necessity of swearing on anyone." Chrysostom, *Discourses Against Judaizing Christians* (Fathers of the Church, vol. 68), trans. Paul W. Harkins (1979; repr., Washington, DC: Catholic University of America Press, 1988), Hom. 1.3.4, p. 12. Although Calvin tended to favor Chrysostom's exegesis over that of Augustine, he departs from Chrysostom's reading of Matthew 5 and sides with Augustine on the matter of sworn oaths. On Matthew 5:34, Calvin writes that, while the Scriptures do not forbid the swearing of oaths *simpliciter*, Christ does want us "to refrain from allowing ourselves the liberty of unnecessary swearing: for, when there are just reasons to demand it, the law not only permits, but expressly commands us to swear." Calvin, *Commentary on the Harmony of the Evangelists*, CTSNT 1:295 (CO 45:182).

tradition. Nonetheless, the matter of oath-swearing provides a fascinating example of how pragmatism and the practical concerns of reform directly influenced the conclusions to which the reformers' exegesis brought them. At times, Calvin's ideas about a well-ordered society were challenged and needed to be altered in order to accommodate the often-messy reality of life in Reformed cities, in which justice, truth, and order did not always prevail, and in which individual consciences—including Calvin's—were not always appeased, but rather acclimated to the overarching cause of personal and communal reform. Thus, the collateral goal of this project is to discover what such accommodations reveal about Calvin as a *pastoral* theologian, in that they help us distinguish the beliefs and practices he believed were essential to the Reformed faith and life from those that, in the end, belonged to the periphery and were far more negotiable or malleable. The principal aim of this study, then, is to demonstrate how oaths and vows were used to shape confessional identity, secure social order, forge community, and promote faithfulness in public and private contracts, as well as to illustrate the complex and difficult task of simultaneously protecting the individual conscience as part of bringing a new take on Christian freedom to Reformed communities.

I.1. State of the Question

In addition to R. H. Hemholz's comprehensive study of classical canon law, which describes the various types of oaths used in ecclesiastical courts, the general topic of oaths and vows has received several historical treatments in recent decades.[11] Works by Paolo Prodi, Giorgio Agamben, Stefania Tutino, and Jonathan Grey address the historical development and use of oaths in late medieval and early modern Europe—albeit with only limited attention to Calvin's Geneva—by exploring the religious, legal, and linguistic roots of oaths in the human experience.[12] Tutino acknowledges that, whereas in the Western tradition the oath was normally seen as a powerful tool for

---

[11] R. H. Hemholz, *The Spirit of Classical Canon Law* (Athens: University of Georgia Press, 2010).

[12] Paolo Prodi, *Il sacramento del potere: Il giuramento politico nella storia constituzionale dell'Occidente* (Bologna: Società editrice il Mulino, 1992); Giorgio Agamben, *The Sacrament of Language: An Archeology of the Oath*, trans. Adam Kotsko (Stanford, CA: Stanford University Press, 2011); Stefania Tutino, *Shadows of Doubt: Language and Truth in Post-Reformation Catholic Culture* (Oxford: Oxford University Press, 2014). See especially chapter 5, "The Sacrament of Language and the Curse of Speech"; and Jonathan Michael Gray, *Oaths and the English Reformation* (Cambridge: Cambridge University Press, 2013).

connecting humans with God and with each other, the "ways in which the oath connects the sphere of the sacred and that of the law, however, are still very much in dispute among scholars from a variety of disciplines, from anthropologists to philosophers to historians to jurists."[13] By focusing attention on Calvin's use of oaths and vows as charitable bonds to promote social order and to protect the purity of consciences, my intention is to shed greater light on the value and importance of oaths in early modern Reformed communities, especially Calvin's Geneva, where conflicts between the "sphere of public authority" and the "sphere of private conscience" were often expressed through the practice of oath taking.[14]

As this study will also explore, Calvin and the reformers repeatedly faced the difficult question of how the realm of private judgment should relate to the governance of ecclesiastical and civil rulers. With respect to Calvin's ethical legacy, several prominent works have explored the concepts of justice, human rights, and liberties in early modern Protestant thought, including Calvin's views on the relation between church and state, the two kingdoms, and the law-gospel distinction. Works by Josef Bohatec, Andre Bieler, John Witte, and most recently, Matthew Tuininga, provide helpful background for assessing Calvin's widely applied principles of equity and charity, which informed his views on truthful speaking and living—essential concerns underlying the use of oaths and vows in society.[15] Nevertheless, these works do not deal specifically or at length with the matter of oaths and confessional subscription in Genevan society, and have tended to deal with Calvin's theoretical thought to the exclusion of his own practice amid complex moral situations (as revealed in the Genevan city and church records).

There is also a growing body of scintillating literature devoted to understanding life, worship, and discipline in sixteenth-century Geneva. The

---

[13] Tutino, *Shadows of Doubt*, 150.

[14] Prodi, *Il sacramento del potere*, 150, argues that oaths functioned as "sacraments of power" in late medieval and early modern Europe: "the institution, theory, and practice of oaths as they evolved over time are important lenses through which we can understand the development of the concepts of power and authority" during this period. Similarly, see Keith P. Luria, *Sacred Boundaries: Religious Coexistence and Conflict in Early-Modern France* (Washington, DC: Catholic University of America Press, 2005).

[15] Josef Bohatec, *Calvins Lehre von Staat und Kirche* (Breslau, 1937); Bohatec, *Budé und Calvin* (Graz: Herman Böhlaus, 1950); Bohatec, *Calvin und das Recht* (Aalen: Scientia Verlag, 1991); André Biéler, *Calvin's Economic and Social Thought*, ed. Edward Dommen and trans. James Greig (Geneva: World Council of Churches Publications, 2005); John Witte, *The Reformation of Rights: Law, Religion and Human Rights in Early Modern Calvinism* (Cambridge: Cambridge University Press, 2010); and Matthew J. Tuininga, *Calvin's Political Theology and the Public Engagement of the Church: Christ's Two Kingdoms* (Cambridge: Cambridge University Press, 2017).

translation, editing, and transcription efforts of Robert Kingdon, Jeffrey and Isabella Watt, Thomas Lambert, and M. Wallace McDonald have made the *Registers of the Consistory of Geneva* more accessible to students of Calvin's pastoral ministry. In addition to work done by Witte and Kingdon on marriage and the family, major studies by William Naphy, Scott Manetsch, Karen Spierling, as well as a very recent work by Jeffrey Watt, have contributed greatly to our understanding of the consolidation of Reformed doctrine and life in Geneva through the disciplinary oversight of the Genevan consistory. My study will hopefully enhance this ongoing study by demonstrating how the practices of oath-swearing and confessional subscription also proved to be an integral concern for those striving to cultivate social order and purity of conscience among Geneva's residents during Calvin's lifetime.[16]

Finally, this study aims to shed light on Reformation-era notions about the individual conscience. It is not a survey of the philosophy of conscience leading up to the Reformation period—such studies are already in print.[17] Although this study accounts for the different theories of conscience that shaped the reformers' general thought, as a work of intellectual history it primarily seeks to identify and assess various personal appeals to conscience within the context of late-medieval and Reformation-era conflicts over doctrine and piety. Several recent articles by John L. Thompson have begun to explore the complexity of Calvin's views on conscience, natural law, and adiaphora as they came to expression in his pastoral ministry.[18] In a similar

---

[16] John Witte, Jr., and Robert M. Kingdon, *Sex, Marriage, and Family in John Calvin's Geneva*, Vol. 1: *Courtship, Engagement, and Marriage* (Grand Rapids, MI: Eerdmans, 2005); William G. Naphy, *Calvin and the Consolidation of the Genevan Reformation*, 2nd ed. (Louisville, KY: Westminster John Knox, 2003); Scott M. Manetsch, *Calvin's Company of Pastors: Pastoral Care and the Emerging Reformed Church, 1536–1609* (Oxford: Oxford University Press, 2013); Karen E. Spierling, *Infant Baptism in Reformation Geneva: The Shaping of a Community, 1536–1564* (Louisville, KY: Westminster John Knox Press, 2005); Spierling, "'Il faut éviter le scandale': Debating Community Standards in Reformation Geneva," *Reformation & Renaissance Review* 20, no. 1 (2018): 51–69; and Jeffrey R. Watt, *The Consistory and Social Discipline in Calvin's Geneva* (Rochester, NY: University of Rochester Press, 2020).

[17] See, especially, Timothy C. Potts, *Conscience in Medieval Philosophy* (Cambridge: Cambridge University Press, 1980); Douglas C. Langston, *Conscience and Other Virtues: From Bonaventure to MacIntyre* (University Park: Pennsylvania State University Press, 2001); and Alexander Murray, *Conscience and Authority in the Medieval Church* (Oxford: Oxford University Press, 2015).

[18] John L. Thompson, "Second Thoughts about Conscience: Nature, the Law, and the Law of Nature in Calvin's Pentateuchal Exegesis," in *Calvinus Pastor Ecclesiae*, ed. Herman J. Selderhuis and Arnold Huijgen (Göttingen: Vandenhoeck & Ruprecht, 2016), 123–47; Thompson, "Confessions, Conscience, and Coercion in the Early Calvin," in *Calvin and the Early Reformation*, ed. Brian C. Brewer and David M. Whitford (Leiden: Brill, 2019), 155–79; and Thompson, "Reforming the Conscience: Magisterial Reformers on the Theory and Practice of Conscience," in *Christianity and the Laws of Conscience: An Introduction*, ed. Jeffrey B. Hammond and Helen M. Alvaré (Cambridge: Cambridge University Press, 2021), 132–51.

way, this work attempts to add nuance to our assessment of the reformers' understanding of the freedom of conscience as illustrated by their attempts to enforce Reformation-era creeds, confessions, and prudent regulations for church and state, despite the crisis of conscience that such efforts provoked in those under their care.

I.2. Significance of the Topic

As of yet, no full-length academic study on the history of oaths and conscience has given specific attention to the unique circumstances and controversies surrounding Calvin's own promotion of oath-swearing in Geneva. Moreover, works focused on Calvin's legal background have not taken a thorough look at how his views on justice, charity, and the freedom of conscience played into his theory and utilization of oaths in the service of the public confession of faith. As a work of social and intellectual history, this project contributes not only to a more complete understanding of the historical development and significance of oaths and vows in late-medieval and early-Reformation society, but also to a better grasp of Calvin's social ethics.

This study will also contribute modestly to the ongoing assessment of Calvin's exegetical legacy. Although it is not a work on Reformation exegesis per se, this study does take ample consideration of relevant exegetical issues by elucidating the sometimes complex relationship between the interpretation of Scripture and the ecclesiastical, political, and social concerns of reform. Past studies on oaths in the thought of Calvin and his Reformed peers have tended to treat the exegetical question from mainly one of two angles, either as an issue of biblical interpretation (hermeneutical)[19] or as a matter of struggle for authority in Geneva (political).[20] In contrast, this study is conducted on the principle that these two elements are best studied in an integrated fashion. Calvin's pastoral and civic leadership in Geneva was guided by his interpretation of Scripture. We also observe that his pastoral concerns occasionally had an effect upon his exegesis, prompting him to place special emphasis on certain parts of Scripture more than others. As our study will show, this integration of exegesis and social praxis, in particular, accounts for Calvin's prevalent use of Scripture to justify his own tactics for reform, while

---

[19] Willem Balke's main assertion throughout *Calvin and the Anabaptist Radicals*, trans. William J. Heynen (Grand Rapids, MI: Eerdmans, 1981).
[20] Quirinus Breen, *John Calvin: A Study in French Humanism* (Hamden, CT: Archon Books, 1968).

also appealing to his own conscience as a type of secondary confirmation of what he believed to be biblical courses of action.

By further mining the wealth of information contained in the official records of the Genevan consistory and Company of Pastors, this study will also illustrate how doctrine and theory were implemented in the city with respect to oaths and vows, and how concerned members of Genevan society challenged and shaped those ideas. This will contribute to a fuller understanding of the unique history of Geneva itself, as a bastion of early Reformed thought and practice; it will also shed light on the delicate relationship between political and religious freedom experienced in other Reformed communities during this time period. Indeed, the nature of the controversial exchanges between independent-minded Genevans and the local civil and ecclesiastical authorities is not yet fully understood. Only a few scholars, for example, have attempted to sort out the potential incongruity of Calvin and Guillaume Farel's repeated demands for confessional uniformity in Geneva by means of swearing an oath to a human document (*The Genevan Confession of Faith*, 1537).[21] This study acknowledges that the apparent binding of consciences through a socially sanctioned practice like oath-swearing could create the appearance, at least, of incongruity between several Reformation mainstays—namely, the doctrine of *sola Scriptura*, the absolute freedom of the believer's conscience from all "spiritual commands" of the Roman Church, and the *sola fide, sola gratia* nature of salvation and sanctification—and the occasional demands of consistories and city councils that all citizens should swear oaths as a necessary pledge of their commitment to Reformed doctrine and lifestyle. This apparent incongruity did in fact produce controversy and confusion among various segments of Genevan society, and raises important questions that this study attempts to answer. For example: What could be said—what were Calvin and his Company of Pastors willing to say—about those who resisted swearing an oath or making public confession of faith *as a matter of conscience*, even though swearing was deemed beneficial for them by the civil and spiritual leaders of the city? And how far were the pastors willing to go to promote the proper use of vows and oaths, while weeding out the kinds of frivolous and insincere vows that were believed to threaten social unity and purity of doctrine and life in Geneva?

---

[21] This issue has begun to be explored—but is not yet fully mined—by Kingdon, "Confessionalism in Calvin's Geneva," *Archiv für Reformationsgeschichte* 96 (2005): 109–16; Herman A. Speelman, *Calvin and the Independence of the Church* (Göttingen: Vandenhoeck & Ruprecht, 2014), 57–102; and Thompson, "Confessions, Conscience, and Coercion in the Early Calvin," 155–79.

In the following chapters, I evaluate and appraise these untapped issues, reassess and challenge the prevalent idea that Calvin's mature ecclesiology represents a radical expansion of church law and authority that effectively compromised his early belief in the freedom of conscience, and raise new questions for further study.

Finally, assessing Calvin's understanding of the relation between oaths, confession, and the freedom of conscience will contribute to a retrieval and reassessment of historic confessional Christianity. The history of Protestantism is inextricably tied to the value and importance of creeds, confessions of faith, and formal subscription, all of which have played a significant role in the church's fidelity, unity, and global witness. Likewise, the principle of freedom of conscience has occupied a central place in the Protestant understanding of the gospel. How these matters relate in the history of the church, and whether they can coexist meaningfully today, are questions that will inevitably shape contemporary theology and praxis. Perhaps especially in this anticonfessional age, the modern church would do well to become reacquainted with its theological tradition and hone its ability to read the Bible constructively alongside Christian thinkers of the past. Achieving this goal will require a "methodologically constructed and controlled objectivity" that neither lionizes one's theological tradition uncritically nor absolutizes the pressing concerns of the Christian church today at the expense of traditional doctrinal reflection.[22] This study operates on the assumption that retrieving the history of theology and applying it to contemporary issues in the church will, at very least, spare modern Protestants from suffering the dismal consequences of a myopic and self-absorbed ecclesiology.

I.3. Method

This study employs a historical method that seeks to navigate the complex relationship between human ideas and social life by exploring their mutual effect. As a work of intellectual and social history, it approaches the topic of oaths, confession, and conscience by tracing lines of continuity and discontinuity between key historical figures—including the inherited texts shaping their ideas—and the implementation of their thought in a specific social and

---

[22] I take this phrase from James E. Bradley and Richard A. Muller, *Church History: An Introduction to Research Methods and Resources* (1995; Grand Rapids, MI: Eerdmans, 2016), 47.

historical context. In order to accomplish this goal, this study follows a threefold track.

The first section locates Calvin and his Reformed contemporaries within their inherited legal tradition—a tradition that frequently dealt with the interrelated matters of sworn oaths, the problem of religious coercion, and freedom of conscience (Chapter 1). The following section examines several medieval and Reformation-era cases in which ecclesiastical and civil leaders faced conscientious objections to their oath-driven tactics for reform. The type of confessional Christianity espoused by Calvin and some of his Reformed allies faced particularly staunch opposition from Anabaptists and spiritualists (Chapter 2), as well as certain "Nicodemite" Christians (Chapters 3–4) who were tempted to escape Catholic persecution by avoiding public confession of faith. The struggles that ensued between the reformers and these various religious dissidents reveal that the Protestant leaders were especially sensitive to claims that their strategies for reform were injurious to the spiritual freedom of the private conscience. Their responses to such complaints reveal the reformers' pastoral concern not only to maintain the purity of conscience—of their subjects, as well as their own—but also to distinguish legitimate and illegitimate claims to conscience based on their own interpretation of Scripture.

The third section of this study concentrates on the practice of oath-swearing and confessional subscription among diverse sectors of Calvin's Geneva through the early seventeenth century. As the focal point of this study, this section explores some of the unique controversies and discipline cases that troubled Calvin, the Genevan Consistory, and the civil magistrates as they sought to reform the political, social, and academic facets of Geneva's public life. Such controversies were distinctively marked by problems associated with the link between oaths, formal confession of faith, and the binding of the conscience. This portion of the study begins in Chapter 5 with an examination of Calvin and Farel's contentious use of oath-swearing as their chosen means to obtain confessional uniformity in the early years of Genevan reform, an event that raises important questions about the conscience-binding power of church traditions reflected in several early Reformed statements of faith. Following this, our focus turns in Chapter 6 to the use of oaths and vows in Genevan social and ecclesiastical life. We will explore and assess cases of moral discipline, sacramental abuse, as well as controversies surrounding engagement and marriage vows, which often required the intervention of church overseers to distinguish between legitimate (binding) and frivolous (non-binding) oaths. Several important cases that sparked a conflict of conscience between ecclesiastical and civil leaders in Geneva will also be assessed. Finally, Chapter 7 offers a description and analysis of how academic oaths and formal subscription were employed during a critical period of institutional development for the Genevan Academy—a period in which matriculation oaths waxed and waned in importance, eventually giving way to conscientious objections and practical concerns for institutional viability. In addition to consulting prominent secondary works on the development of political, social, and academic reform in Geneva, the latter portions of this study make ample use of the Registers of the Company of Pastors and Consistory in Geneva, as well as the *Annales*, records demonstrating the wide range of advisory and disciplinary matters touching all segments of Genevan society. By examining a diverse selection of Reformation texts and contexts illustrating the critical relationship between confessionalism and conscience, then, this study will show that Calvin and his colleagues' relative success at transforming consciences according to God's word could often be ascribed to their willingness to adjust their own expectations and tactics to the ever-changing circumstances of reform.

SECTION I
CALVIN AND THE REFORMERS' INHERITED LEGAL TRADITION

1
Before Calvin

Oaths, Religious Coercion, and the Freedom of Conscience from the Medieval Church to the Reformation

We see Calvin most clearly—as a person and as a theologian—against the backdrop of his late medieval context. Older portrayals of Calvin as a father of modern doctrinal systems—popularized in early nineteenth- and twentieth-century accounts of the reformer's life and thought—have been soundly rebuffed, and for good reason. Calvin was, as a point of fact, thoroughly unaware of certain dogmatic patterns that we now recognize as being "modern."[1] He was no more the father of modern critical exegesis than he was the original visionary of modern liberal democratic societies.[2] That is to say, Calvin could not have considered himself a forerunner of something that lay entirely outside his historical purview. Likewise, the young Calvin was, in most respects, a man of his times. And his times were driven by the effort to promulgate and practice the authoritative teachings of the medieval Christian Church. Moreover, Calvin did not utterly disown the intellectual inheritance of his youth following his conversion to the evangelical religion in the early 1530s. Later in life, as a seasoned reformer of the church, Calvin continued to apply with great fervency many of the legal principles and theological methods he had acquired at an early age while studying in Paris,

---

[1] For an enlightening rebuttal to modern dogmatic accommodations of Calvin, see "An Approach to Calvin: On Overcoming Modern Accommodations," chapter 1 in Richard A. Muller, *The Unaccommodated Calvin: Studies in the Foundation of a Theological Tradition* (Oxford: Oxford University Press, 2000), 3–17.

[2] On Calvin's—and his Reformed colleagues'—exegetical dependence on the Church Fathers and medieval doctors, see Muller, "Biblical Interpretation in the Era of the Reformation: The View from the Middle Ages," in *Biblical Interpretation in the Era of the Reformation*, ed. Richard A. Muller and John L. Thompson (Grand Rapids, MI: Eerdmans, 1996), 3–22; and John L. Thompson, "Calvin's Exegetical Legacy: His Reception and Transmission of Text and Tradition," in *The Legacy of John Calvin* (Calvin Studies Society Papers 1999), ed. David Foxgrover (Grand Rapids, MI: Calvin Studies Society, 2000), 31–56. For a recent evaluation of various interpretations of Calvin's sociopolitical thought and legacy, see Matthew J. Tuininga, *Calvin's Political Theology and the Public Engagement of the Church: Christ's Two Kingdoms* (Cambridge: Cambridge University Press, 2017), 10–19.

Orléans, and Bourges, albeit with an ever-critical eye toward the need for church reform.

In order to trace out some of the theories and practices that lay behind Calvin's views on oaths, church constitutions, and the conscience, then, some reconstruction of his native intellectual world is required. The following pages set Calvin and the reformers against the backdrop of their inherited medieval and Renaissance legal tradition by identifying diverse voices—ancient, medieval, and humanist—that were instrumental in establishing principles and regulations for the swearing of oaths and vows. The aim of this initial section is to acquire some understanding of the traditionally foundational principles of justice and equity that oaths were intended to promote and preserve in medieval society under various circumstances. It does not aim to provide an exhaustive recounting of the diverse types of oaths that were common to medieval canon and civil law, but rather to identify the unique contexts and controversies that the taking of oaths sometimes occasioned. This section of the study will also show how the reformers' inherited legal tradition allowed for a use of oaths, vows, and other church ceremonies as binding agents whose power could be mitigated by circumstantial prudence, permissive natural law, and a charitable concern for the protection of weaker consciences.

1.1. Oaths, Vows, and the Freedom of Conscience in the *Ius Commune*: Contexts and Controversies

The swearing of oaths pervaded medieval life. The classical bodies of canon law and secular law expressed a common faith that the binding quality of oaths could promote truthfulness in the courts, protect the well-being of social institutions, and restrain the pernicious crime of perjury.[3] Oaths played an especially central role in ecclesiastical and civil courts as the primary means for ensuring lawful proceedings and procuring truthful testimony from witnesses and litigants. Within medieval church courts, canon law administered an "oath-dominated" kind of justice that employed the sworn oath as the "institutional glue par excellence" for solving legal dilemmas.[4]

---

[3] R. H. Hemholz, *The Spirit of Classical Canon Law* (Athens: University of Georgia Press, 2010), 173.

[4] Paolo Prodi, *Il sacramento del potere: Il giuramento politico nella storia constituzionale dell'Occidente* [The Sacrament of Power: The Political Oath in the Constitutional History of the West] (Bologna: Società editrice il Mulino, 1992), 161, quoted in Hemholz, *The Spirit of Classical Canon Law*, 145.

The *Corpus Iuris Civilis* assigned a similarly prominent role to oaths in the civil courts. Justinian's *Digest* stated, "The greatest remedy for the swift disposal of litigation has come into use, namely, the conscientiousness of oathtaking, by means of which disputes are settled either by the agreement of the litigants themselves or by the authority of the judge."[5]

From this, we might be tempted to conclude that formal oaths were taken and received in all cases as inviolable and unquestionable guarantees of the veracity of all that followed a sworn oath. But in fact, the binding quality of oaths was a frequent point of contention in medieval society. Debates over what distinguished a licit, efficacious oath from an illicit, impotent one commonly arose in the ecclesiastical and civil courts, and the varied circumstances that occasioned such debates are reflected in the legal texts that were in use during this period.[6] The standard texts of Roman and canon law acknowledge a variety of such moral and legal predicaments, either occasioned by the swearing of an oath or remedied by the same. Just how oaths and vows are treated in such cases gives us insight into the place, purpose, and permanence of these instruments of justice in late medieval society. Moreover, a close study of the documents reveals something of the complex relationship that existed between three important aspects of the medieval concept of justice: the diverse contexts in which oaths were taken; the prevailing commitment to the absolute sanctity of the sworn oath; and the principles of justice that oaths ideally promoted.

1.1.1. Oaths and Scripture

Prior to defining regulations for the proper formation of oaths, the common law first sought to address the exegetical question of whether oaths and

---

[5] Dig. 12.2.1 (Gaius, *Ad Edictum Provinciale* 5): "Maximum remedium expediendarum litium in usum venit iurisiurandi religio, qua vel ex pactione ipsorum litigatorum vel ex auctoritate iudicis deciduntur controversiae."

[6] Several studies have traced the prominent place that oaths occupied in ecclesiastical and civil courts. R. H. Hemholz's classic work on the spirit of canon law elucidates the common classification of oaths by the medieval canonists, describing the various kinds of oaths used in ecclesiastical court procedure. See chapter 6, "Religious Principles and Practical Problems: The Canon Law of Oaths," in Hemholz, *The Spirit of Classical Canon Law*, 145–73. See also the classic study of oaths by James Endell Tyler, *Oaths: Their Origin, Nature, and History* (London: John W. Parker, 1834), 235–315. A similar study by French historian Robert Fossier illuminates the varied types and functions of oaths in daily life and in civil courts during the middle ages. See especially chapter 5, "Man in Himself," in Fossier, *The Axe and the Oath: Ordinary Life in the Middle Ages* (Princeton, NJ: Princeton University Press, 2010), 223–91.

vows were even legitimate on the basis of Holy Scripture. Several prominent church fathers, upon reading passages like Matthew 5:34, 37, and James 5:12, had concluded that Jesus either forbade all forms of swearing or at least highly discouraged its regular practice. Patristic opinion commonly dictated that it was better for believers to speak plainly and truthfully, rather than resort to the use of human ceremonies that threatened to bind one's conscience to potentially rash decisions and actions.[7]

Nonetheless, following Augustine, the medieval church agreed en masse that oaths and vows of a proper form were lawful and also uniquely helpful—occasionally even necessary—for promoting the virtues of fairness and truthfulness in society. Theologians, canonists, and civil jurists were of one mind concerning the legitimacy of oaths, although these voices of legal authority sometimes arrived at the same conclusion by disparate means. Gratian's *Decretum* acknowledged the small pedigree of those who rejected oaths based on a literal reading of Matthew 5 and James 5. In an attempt to harmonize differing Patristic voices with the practice of the apostles, however, Gratian demonstrated that oaths are in fact not forbidden according to the majority tradition. The apostles, knowing the command of the Lord, nevertheless appear to have sworn oaths.[8] And the old law (*veteri lege*) clearly implied that swearing oaths was allowed when it distinguished between true and false swearing.[9] Thus, drawing on the instruction of Augustine, Jerome, and Isidore of Seville, the *Decretum* ruled that Scripture did not forbid oaths *simpliciter*, but only the immoderate use of oaths that could result in swearing falsely. Thus, on one hand, a person ought to avoid the love of oaths, as though they were "a good to be sought after," since the custom or habit of

---

[7] E.g., Cyprian of Carthage, *De Lapsis*, c. 6, decried those who made a practice not only of swearing rashly but also lying under oath. The general rule of Chrysostom, whose judgment Gratian reproduces in the *Decretum*, C. 22, q. 5, c. 12, is that there should be no difference between an oath and plain, trustworthy speech: "Inter iuramentum et locutionem fidelium nulla debet esse differentia." The canon law, although it gave a far more prominent place to oaths, still expressed great concern for protecting the *salus animarum* of oath takers, thus reflecting Chrysostom's concern over immoderate oaths. The *Decretum* cites Chrysostom's concern that both perjury and lying were deserving of divine judgment, and that "the mouth that lies shall kill the soul": "et periurium et mendacium, divini iudicii pena dampnatur, dicente scriptura: Os, quod mentitur, occidit animam." Thirteenth-century canonist Bernard of Compostella (the elder) expressed a similar opinion that the command of Christ and his apostles intended to prohibit all immoderate and spontaneous forms of swearing, and to teach that the words of one's mouth should coincide with the intentions of the heart. See Bernardus Compostellanus antiquus, *Compilatio Romana (1208)*, 14.7, in *Die Dekretalensammlung des Bernardus Compostellanus antiquus*, ed. Heinrich Singer (Vienna: Alfred Holder, 1914), 64–68. For additional commentary on church fathers that appear to have denied the validity of oaths altogether, see Tyler, *Oaths*, 17–34.

[8] C. 22, q. 1, c. 2; and Bernard of Compostella, *Compilatio Romana*, 14.7, p. 67.

[9] C. 22, q. 1, c. 14.

swearing oaths (*consuetudine iurandi*) made one prone to slip into the sin of perjury. Nevertheless, oaths often served the useful purpose of promoting truth and assuaging feelings of uncertainty.[10]

Having established that oaths and vows were in fact lawful, the remaining problem was how to distinguish between licit and illicit oaths, as well as to provide some commentary on the appropriate use of oaths in various circumstances. Over time, the canon law tradition settled on three "companions" (*comites*) of oaths that were required to render oaths licit and binding. It was determined that the virtues of "truth (*veritatem*), judgment (*iudicium*), and justice (*iusticiam*) must accompany oaths."[11] When these virtues were lacking, a person's oath amounted to no oath at all, but rather perjury—a false oath.[12] Thus, the common law ruled that illicit oaths—that is, oaths falsely sworn either in ignorance or ill intent—were non-binding and powerless.[13]

Navigating the terrain between licit and illicit oaths, however, would prove to be yet another instance of practice being more complex than theory, as the standard legal texts in use during the late medieval period attest.[14] These codices reflect the challenging task of protecting the sanctity of oaths in church and society, while also seeking to mitigate the misuse of oaths, as well as to curb overconfidence in their binding quality. A give-and-take relationship prevailed between the common legal tradition and the everyday practice of oath-taking. Sometimes old laws were changed or rewritten in order to protect the sanctity of the oath. Other times, the binding power of oaths was softened to accommodate unusual contexts and controversies, both in court and in daily life.

---

[10] C. 22, q. 1, d. p. c. 14: "non tamen tamquam bonum est appetendum, ne consuetudine iurandi labamur in periurium." See chapter 3, "Christian Oaths: A Case Study in Practicality over Doctrine," in Kevin Uhalde, *Expectations of Justice in the Age of Augustine* (Philadelphia: University of Pennsylvania Press, 2007), 77–104, for a helpful study of how oath-swearing served as an important tool for mitigating doubt and uncertainty in the early medieval church.

[11] C. 22, q. 2, c. 2.

[12] C. 22, q. 4, d. p. c. 23, §1: "ubi autem ista defuerint, non est iuramentum, sed periurium;" C.22, q. 2, d. a. c. 1: "periurium sit falsum iurare." Inst. 1.1.3 similarly states that the fundamental precepts of the law (*Iuris praecepta*) are "to live honorably, not to injure another, and to render to each person that which is his (*honeste vivere, alterum non laedere, suum cuique tribuere*)."

[13] C. 22, q. 4, c. 18: "illicitum iuramentum non est servandum ... nullam habens virtutem."

[14] On the casuistic situations surrounding lying and perjury in medieval thought, as well as in canon law, see Emily Corran, *Lying and Perjury in Medieval Practical Thought: A Study in the History of Casuistry* (Oxford: Oxford University Press, 2018). See especially chapter 2, "The Early Casuistry of Lying and Perjury," 44–65.

1.1.2. *Intentio* and the Moral Dilemma of Infelicitous Oaths

Perhaps the most important factor in determining the legitimacy and efficacy of oaths was the notion of *intentio*.[15] Common law placed a high value on the conscious motivation underlying the act of swearing an oath. In most cases, a person's intentions when taking an oath had more weight than the content or form of the oath itself, and intentions were routinely considered when evaluating potential cases of perjury. Generally speaking, only oaths taken "in good faith" (*bona fide*) would avoid the charge of perjury, even if such oaths were deemed invalid for other reasons.[16]

Canon law was particularly careful about delineating the difference between a false oath and a deceptive oath in terms of the intention of the one swearing. It ruled, for example, that a person had not committed the sin of perjury when he swore to the truth of something that was, in fact, apart from his knowledge, false, since he did not intend to swear falsely but was deceived.[17] The intention to swear an oath from a heartfelt conviction (*ex animo*) of its truth enabled one to avoid the sin of perjury, even though that to which he swore was, in fact, a falsehood. On the other hand, the person who swore that something was true, knowing all the while that it was not true, clearly perjured himself by acting in such a detestable manner.[18] The general principle at work here was that the guilt of perjury depended on "the manner in which a word proceeds from the will [rational soul]. The tongue is not reckoned guilty unless the mind is guilty." A person's intentions when swearing an oath, rather than the wording of the oath itself, were determinative for the assignment of guilt or innocence in the case of perjury, since God is the witness and judge of a person's conscience.[19]

---

[15] See James A. Brundage, *Medieval Canon Law* (1995; New York: Routledge, 2013), 171.

[16] Dig. 12.2.30.3 (Paulus, *Ad Edictum* 18).

[17] C. 22, q. 2, c. 3: "Fac illum iurare, qui verum putat esse pro quo iurat; verum putat esse, et tamen falsum est; non ex animo iste periurat, fallitur."

[18] C. 22, q. 2, c. 3: "Scit falsum esse, et dicit verum esse, et iurat tamquam verum sit quod scit falsum esse. Videtis, quam ista detestanda sit belua, et de rebus humanis exterminanda?" This principle, that swearing falsely was a serious form of dissimulation or deception, formed the basis for lawfully sworn oaths in the minds of sixteenth-century Catholics and Protestants alike. See Jonathan Michael Gray, *Oaths and the English Reformation* (Cambridge: Cambridge University Press, 2013), 37–44.

[19] C. 22, q. 2, c. 3: "Interest, quemadmodum verbum procedat ex animo. Ream linguam non facit nisi rea mens." See also C. 22, q. 5, c. 9–d. p. c. 13. Likewise, the canon law made a distinction between lying and uttering a falsehood: "Non enim omnis, qui falsum dicit, mentitur; sicut nec omnes, qui mentitur, falsum dicit" (C. 22, q. 2, d. p. c. 3). On the prevailing medieval theory that oaths linked humanity to God as the "witness" of the human conscience—a theory also embraced by civil and ecclesiastical courts during the Reformation—see Gray, *Oaths and the English Reformation*, 17–30.

The *Decretum* invoked a few standard Scriptural examples to illustrate this principle that the mind or intention, rather than the tongue, makes a person guilty of perjury. One example was King Saul's foolish oath, recorded in I Samuel 14:24–15:35. At war with the Philistines, Saul laid an oath on the fighters of Israel, saying, "cursed is the man who eats bread until it is evening and I am avenged of my enemies." His son Jonathan, not having heard the oath, later sought to revive his strength by eating some wild honey. Against Saul's will, Jonathan's life was nevertheless spared from the penalty of the oath because of the people's intervention on his behalf. Commenting on this biblical case, the canon law ceded that Jonathan was not actually guilty of perjury for breaking his father's vow, for he was entirely unaware of it, and could not have purposefully intended to commit an injustice by violating the oath. In this case, it was better that the penalties appended to Saul's oath remained dormant.[20]

Saul's ill-advised oath, and other Scriptural examples like it, raised the problem of how to treat "rash vows" as well as oaths made by incompetent persons.[21] Oaths sworn rashly, that is, without careful thought or good intention, posed a serious moral dilemma: Was it better for a person to fulfill what he had vowed to do, however foolish, in order to protect the sanctity of the oath? Or should he break his oath in order to avoid committing another, potentially worse kind of sin? Moreover, the common legal tradition disputed whether the foolish intention behind such rash oaths automatically rendered them invalid in all cases. Civil law was decidedly more direct and harsher in dealing with rash vows than the canon law. The *Digest* ruled that someone who had perjured himself by failing to fulfill a hasty, ill-spoken vow should be "sent away to be chastised by flogging under the notice, 'Do not swear rashly!'"[22]

---

[20] C. 22, q. 2, d. p. c. 22, §2.

[21] No doubt the most scandalous example of a rash vow in Scripture is that of Jephthah (Judges 11:29–40), which *Decretum* C. 22 does not touch. For an extended treatment of this passage in the history of biblical commentary, see John L. Thompson's chapter, "Jephthah's Daughter and Sacrifice," in his *Writing the Wrongs: Women of the Old Testament among Biblical Commentators from Philo through the Reformation* (Oxford: Oxford University Press, 2001), 100–78.

[22] Dig. 12.2.13.6 (Ulpianus, *Ad Edictum* 22): Here I borrow S. P. Scott's translation of a rather difficult Latin phrase; in Samuel Parsons Scott, ed., *The Civil Law*, 17 vols. (Cincinnati: Central Trust, 1931), 4:113–26. Ecclesiastical and civil courts utilized an additional resource for preserving the sanctity of the oath, which also served to protect parties in a court case from the ill-intentioned use of oaths and vows. In particular, the law protected oaths and those who swore them by instituting yet another oath. This special type of oath, the "oath of calumny" (*juramentum calumniae*), promised that all subsequent oaths would be taken in good faith, devoid of the intention to cause annoyance, harass other parties, or stymie legal proceedings. Dig. 12.2.34.4 (Ulpianus, *Ad Edictum* 26): "Anyone who tenders an oath ought first to swear the oath of calumny, if it is demanded of him, after which time his intended oath will be sworn" (*Qui iusiurandum defert, prior de calumnia debet iurare, si hoc*

22 CONSCIENCES AND THE REFORMATION

The canon law was more deliberative about the moral dilemmas occasioned by making a rash vow. Such deliberation grew out of a long history of dealing with the dilemma of morally conflicting choices. Medieval philosophers and theologians commonly acknowledged and discussed the ancient problem of *perplexitas*, that is, the bewildering condition of "being trapped by conflicting moral obligations."[23] Among the medieval canonists who acknowledged that genuine moral dilemmas actually existed in natural law, appeals were commonly made to the long-standing principle that one should always seek to minimize evildoing by choosing the lesser of two evils.[24] The *Decretum* applied this principle in its commentary on two well-known Scriptural accounts of rash vows: Herod's foolish vow that resulted in the beheading of John the Baptist, and David's imprudent vow to kill the wicked Nabal. In both cases, the canon ruled that it was better not to fulfill a foolish promise sworn by oath than to commit a greater crime, such as the shedding of human blood.[25] Thus, in the case of a moral dilemma created by a rash vow, in which it was evil both to keep and break one's oath, the canon law traditionally ruled that "it is necessary to choose from among the

---

exigatur, deinde sic ei iurabitur). See also Cod. 4.1.9 (Diocletian & Maximian 294): "Delata condicione iurisiurandi reus (si non per actorem, quominus de calumnia iuret, steterit) per iudicem solvere vel iurare, nisi referat iusiurandum, necesse habet."

The oath *de calumnia* was particularly prominent in civil court proceedings. All parties, without exception, were to take this one-time oath at the beginning of a formal suit, in order to promote the "respect of the litigants" (*reverentia litigantium*). Nov. 49.3.1 (537): "generaliter semel [iusiurandum] huiusmodi." The calumny oath required plaintiffs to swear that they would not attempt to cause annoyance (*calumniantes*) by proceeding with their suit; it also required the defendants to swear that they did not intend "to make controversy [*facere . . . non causa contentionis*]." Nov. 49.3 (537). Both parties also pledged to abstain from delaying the proceedings in order to obstruct justice. Nov. 49.3.1 (537). Civil law even ruled that it was partly the responsibility of the party tendering an oath to the defendant to demand that the oath of calumny be sworn. If a party tendered an oath without first requesting the oath of calumny, then he is only to blame if an act of calumny is later committed. See Dig. 12.2.37 (Ulpianus, *Ad Edictum* 33). In tendering the calumny oath, both parties agreed upon the following stipulations, as in the case of contracting documents: "That none of his allegations have been prompted by malice; that he has not acted fraudulently in having a comparison of handwriting made; and that he will act in such a way that nothing whatever may remain concealed; and that no subterfuge of any description will, under any circumstances, be employed." See Nov. 73.7 (538). Here I borrow Scott's translation of the Latin in *The Civil Law* 16:277: "etiam iusiurandum inicere proferenti, quia nihil maligni conscious in eo quod a se profertur nec quandam artem circa collationem fieri praeparans sic utitur eo, quatenus neque perimatur quicquam omnino et per omnia munitio in rebus fiat." See, likewise, Nov. 73.7.3 (538): In the case of proving the genuineness of legal documents, one should swear an oath of calumny to prove his intention not to conceal the truth (*veritate abscondere*). In short, the oath *de calumnia* served as an added buffer to protect the sanctity of oaths from their infelicitous use by unjust agents in a court of law.

[23] M. V. Dougherty, *Moral Dilemmas in Medieval Thought: From Gratian to Aquinas* (Cambridge: Cambridge University Press, 2011), 7.
[24] Dougherty, *Moral Dilemmas*, 2–8.
[25] C. 22, q. 4, c. 1.

lesser of two evils." It was better to renege one's vow than to accrue the greater shame of keeping it.[26]

In his study of moral dilemmas in medieval thought, M. V. Dougherty identifies some of the pragmatic considerations that led to mitigating the binding quality of infelicitous oaths. Dougherty raises several examples from the *Decretum* (dist. 13) that show that the cumulative effect of an oath—whether kept or broken—was often most determinative in choosing "the lesser evil." One of these cases involved the moral dilemma of an agent who had sworn an oath to commit a crime. In the wake of his rash oath, the agent must choose either to keep his vow and break the law, or violate his oath in order to avoid injuring others. In either case, he has bound himself to perform a "morally impermissible act." The pragmatic ruling of the *Decretum* was as follows: Because by fulfilling his vow to commit a crime the agent would injure his entire community and not just himself, he should therefore choose the lesser evil and renege his vow. Upon violating his oath, the agent would perjure himself and offend God. Were he to fulfill the tenets of his rash vow, however, he would also do harm to his neighbors—clearly the greater evil.[27] Thus, although the legal tradition routinely ruled that sworn oaths should be strictly upheld, the moral dilemmas occasioned by rash and ill-intentioned vows required that a more deliberative approach be taken. Gratian's Gregorian view in the *Decretum* therefore conceded, "there are situations where the best an agent can hope for is the avoidance of a more serious moral failure, and the agent must at times be content with the commission of less grave offences."[28]

---

[26] C. 22, q. 4, c. 7: "De duobus malis minus eligi oportet."

[27] Dougherty, *Moral Dilemmas*, 25–26.

[28] Dougherty, *Moral Dilemmas*, 31. The *Decretum* (dist. 13) contains several other examples of foolish, worldly vows considered to be lacking in obligatory force due to the improper intentions underlying them. These examples, though highly unusual and likely speculative, reveal much about the moral dilemmas envisioned by the medieval jurists. It is also worthy to note that Gratian's commentators, whose glosses on Gratian are contained in the *Glossa ordinaria*, typically disagreed with Gratian and denied that true moral perplexity was possible. They argued, instead, that moral dilemmas had no objective existence but were merely epistemic, being the product of subjective moral beings acting or thinking in foolish ways: "Perplexity cannot be caused by the order of things (*res*), but simply occurs in a mind (*animus*) that holds an opinion that is foolish (*stulta*).... According to the glossator, the moral order is always consistent and the natural law can always be viewed as issuing observable precepts." Thus, in the case of someone caught between perjury and another crime, the error lies not with the natural law but with the agent, whose feelings of perplexity are merely the result of holding the foolish idea that a rash vow is actually binding. The *Glossa ordinaria* simply stated that no one is no obliged to fulfill a rash or foolish vow. See Dougherty, *Moral Dilemmas*, 34–39. See also Brian Tierney, chapter 2, "Canonistic Jurisprudence," in his *Liberty and Law: The Idea of Permissive Natural Law, 1100–1800* (Washington, DC: Catholic University of America Press, 2014), 15–47.

1.1.3. Oaths, the *Mitigatio legis*, and Concern for the *Salus Animarum*

Because of the medieval legal tradition's great reverence for oaths as strict sources of duty, one is tempted to conclude that oaths had too much power. It might seem that the binding character of oaths was so absolute that they could easily be wielded as a means to disenfranchise others or even promote perjury, thus compromising the very virtues of truth, judgment, and justice that, ideally, should always accompany the swearing of oaths. In reality, however, canonists and civil jurists alike sought all sorts of ways to protect people from the sin of perjury, reflecting a high valuation of the sanctity of oaths, on one hand, as well as a controlling desire to protect vulnerable citizens from the potential danger of injury by the immoderate use of oaths.[29] "The *ius commune* in many regions also incorporated principles of 'canonical equity' as well, which allowed judges to adjust the rules to fit the circumstances of a particular situation where justice seemed to require departure from strict law." The civil law, in particular, reflects a variety of ways in which jurists tried to protect oaths and the *salus animarum* (health of the souls) of those who swore them, either by enacting new laws or reinterpreting old ones, in order to solve moral dilemmas occasioned by the taking of an oath. The following two cases will illustrate this phenomenon.[30]

1.1.3.1. Oaths and Ignorant Judges

One fairly common complaint heard by civil jurists involved the regrettable oath to abide by decisions of unqualified and ignorant arbiters. As was common practice, litigants swore an oath that they were content with the judges chosen to try their case (*iurant . . . se iudicibus . . . suadent*) and would abide by their decision. Situations arose, however, in which parties that were "ignorant with respect to the law" (*ignorantes leges*) took an impetuous oath to abide by the decisions of judges who, unbeknownst to them, had "neither an observance of what is just nor understood how to decide what is right."[31] Realizing their error only after the oath had been sworn and the

---

[29] E.g., it was the opinion of Julius Paulus that "it is not customary to look simplistically into the perjury of one who has sworn an oath under the compulsion of law" (*De periurio eius, qui ex necessitate iuris in litem iuravit, quaeri facile non solere*). Dig. 12.3.11 (Paulus, *Responsorum* 3).

[30] Brundage, *Medieval Canon Law*, 61. On the importance of the *salus animarum* in ecclesiastical courts, see Hemholz, *The Spirit of Classical Canon Law*, 133, 169–72.

[31] Nov. 82.11 (539).

injury committed, litigants often sought to have their cases reheard, thereby rejecting the tenets of their initial oath and perjuring themselves in the process.

Deciding that such experiences required a change to the law, jurists decreed that arbiters would no longer be appointed by virtue of the oath taken by the parties in a case. This alteration of existing law would protect people from falling into perjury against their will on account of the ignorance of their judges (*in periurium invitum incidant... propter iudicum ignorantiam*). Instead, litigants who wished to choose their own judges would be required to pay a price (*poena*), prompting a decision that was consensual, responsible, and final. Jurists went even further by pronouncing the judgment of God upon anyone who failed to take refuge under the protection of this new law: Litigants who chose their arbiters anyway, considering the proviso of a sworn oath itself to be sufficient, would have the penalty of perjury (*poenas periurii*) conferred upon them by God. The jurists also declared that the law would be equitable to those who had suffered on account of the ignorance of their arbiters; their oath would not disadvantage them or inflict penalty for perjury. Litigants would no longer be subject to injury on account of the ignorance of judges through the respect due to an oath (*propter iudicantium ignorantiam citra iurisiurandi reverentiam*).[32] In this case, then, jurists sought to protect the sanctity of the oath as well as the *salus animarum* of the oath taker by rewriting existing laws to mitigate the potential for injustice and perjury.

1.1.3.2. Oaths and Filial Law

Another case presented to the civil jurists raised the question of whether someone could, by reneging their vow, take advantage of the legal system to disenfranchise vulnerable persons. This case involved the rights of a certain Martha, a woman of noble birth (*femina clarissima maiestati*) who petitioned the courts for the restoration of her rightful patrimony. The details of her situation, as recounted by Emperor Justinian, were these: Following the death of Martha's father Sergius while she was of a very tender age (*tenera admodum aetate*), her mother Auxentia took an oath that she would never again enter into marriage (*testatione ... se nuptias non venturam*). On the basis of her vow, Auxentia was granted sole guardianship of Martha, including the right to administer her patrimony. Soon after, however, just as

---

[32] Nov. 82.11 (539).

if she had not taken any oath (*quasi neque iusiurandum ullum*), Auxentia remarried, abandoned the administration of Martha's inheritance, and appointed her second husband guardian over her young daughter. Having no care for Martha's interests, Auxentia took advantage of her daughter's youthful ignorance by forcing her to relinquish (*renuntiaret*) all rights of action concerning the property left to her by her father. Martha's mother then appealed to the Imperial Law (*praetendisse legem*), which ruled that it is impossible for someone to claim restitution in opposition to his own action (*qua contineatur non posse se contra ipsam restitutionis iure uti*), making it legally impossible for her daughter to reclaim the patrimony that was originally hers. Upon reaching an age at which she could comprehend the injustice committed against her, Martha petitioned the courts for an explanation: Could Auxentia take advantage of her broken vow to gain authority over her daughter's rightful property?

The civil jurists responded to this legal dilemma by proving their desire to protect vulnerable citizens from injury inflicted through the ill-intentioned or manipulative use of oaths. After consideration of Martha's petition, this pragmatic decree was issued (*sacram pragmaticam formam*): Because Auxentia had contracted a second marriage and treated her oath contemptibly (*contempt*), she would not be granted recourse to the Imperial Law to which she had earlier appealed, and Martha would be permitted to sue her mother for complete restitution of her property. It was also ruled that, due to the unique nature of the case, Auxentia could not invoke the constitution that forbade children from claiming restitution against their parents (*non posse liberos contra parentes suos ... restitutionis iure uti*). The purpose of this constitution had been that children should render to their parents the respect, honor, and deference (*reverentia ... honor et cultus*) that they deserve. But the jurists expressed the desire that this rule should also serve to protect children from parents who would do them harm (*dummodo nullum ab ipsis damnum illis inferatur*). Case law ruled, then, that due to Auxentia's abusive vow, the law should be mitigated to protect Martha from injustice against her and her rightful patrimony. An immoderate oath attempting to take advantage of legal loopholes could not be used as a means for disenfranchising the most vulnerable members of society.[33]

---

[33] Nov. 155 (533).

1.2. Religious Coercion and Freedom of Conscience among Scholastic Theologians, Renaissance Humanists, and Lutheran Reformers

Medieval common law's innate concern for the just and felicitous use of sworn oaths and vows is indicative of the church's vigorous pursuit of religious harmony during this period in its history. Catholic theologians and canonists believed they could restore the church's unity by disciplining the doctrinally rebellious and by conforming them to their teachings and traditions. Occasionally, however, the ceremonies and religious duties prescribed by ecclesiastical authorities provoked genuine crises of conscience in lay members who were able to voice their complaints in good faith. In such cases, jurists and theologians sometimes felt compelled to reconsider the binding effect of human laws and traditions, and theorized about how such laws might be prudently mitigated to protect the sacredness of the private conscience. The following summary makes strategic use of primary texts and secondary research to construct a brief account of how the tentative relationship between religious coercion and the freedom of conscience was developed in the minds of scholastic, humanist, and Reformed theologians before Calvin arrived on the scene.

1.2.1. Medieval Scholasticism

From our contemporary Western perspective, medieval scholasticism—simply on account of its affinity for maintaining a fixed doctrinal tradition and for tackling general philosophical puzzles—does not strike us as representing a particularly accommodating or tolerant period of the church. One might assume that the leaders of the medieval church were far too preoccupied with the coercion of religious obedience to be concerned with the practical moral dilemmas that might require a mitigation of positive law for the sake of conscience. In fact, however, concerns about religious tolerance and the protection of the individual conscience occupied the minds of ecclesiastical authorities quite regularly during this period. It is well-known, for example, that the medieval canonists generally adopted a policy of toleration (*tolerantia*) toward Jews and other non-Christians by permitting—though nevertheless disapproving of—their errant beliefs in order to promote the greater good of societal peace and order.[34] The prevailing opinion was that little would be accomplished from trying to coerce pagans to profess belief against their independent desires.

Among those already professing the Christian faith, however, far less tolerance existed for the doctrinally deviant.[35] Thomas Aquinas, the "Prince of Scholastics," likened the public profession of the Christian faith to the obligation of keeping a sworn vow. Appealing to Augustine, he argued that "to accept the faith is a matter of the will (*voluntatis*), but to keep what has already been received is a necessity (*necessitatis*). Wherefore heretics should be compelled to keep the faith"—even to the point of being pressed to fulfill their promise under "bodily compulsion (*corporaliter compellendi*)."[36] Although the church could not compel unbelievers to embrace Christianity against their consciences, in the case of professing believers, however, ecclesiastical authorities had a divine commission to "coerce the baptized precisely on the basis of their baptismal obligations."[37]

From this position rose the specter of a related problem: Could the church, either by its formal constitutions and religious ceremonies, or by the exercise of discipline, compel anyone to act or believe against their conscience, even when someone was acting in good faith against the instruction of the church? In theory, it appeared that no such freedom could exist. In practice, however, the canonists and scholars of the medieval era were deeply concerned about the occasional need to adjust the regulations of civil and church law in order to protect individual rights of conscience—albeit without threatening communal harmony. Thomistic scholars, for example, agreed that violating certain human laws endangered the soul, but they were generally willing to compromise when determining which traditions were essential and which

---

[34] Ian Christopher Levy, "Liberty of Conscience and Freedom of Religion in the Medieval Canonists and Theologians," in *Christianity and Freedom*, Vol 1: *Historical Perspectives*, ed. Timothy Samuel Shah and Allen D. Hertzke (Cambridge: Cambridge University Press, 2016), 150–51. On medieval Christianity's attitude toward non-believers, also see Joseph A. Lecler's classic study, *Toleration and the Reformation*, 2 vols, trans. T. L. Westow (New York: Association Press, 1960), 1:71–79.

[35] See Lecler, *Toleration and the Reformation*, 1:79–92.

[36] Thomas Aquinas, ST 3, II.IIae, q. 10, a. 8: "ita accipere fidem est voluntatis, sed tenere jam acceptam est necessitatis. Et ideo haeretici sunt compellendi ut fidem teneant." Aquinas held the generally accepted view that to espouse heretical beliefs was a worse sin than holding pagan commitments, because of the failure to keep what one has promised. See ST 3, II.IIae.10.6.

[37] Levy, "Liberty of Conscience," 160. Twelfth-century theologian Ivo of Chartres made a similar declaration concerning marriage vows: celibacy or marriage remain "a matter of free choice before a vow was made, [but] once the vow has been made they become a matter of necessity, and have their own restrictions and regulations." See the prologue to Ivo of Chartres's *Decretum*, in Eugene R. Fairweather, ed., *A Scholastic Miscellany: Anselm to Ockham* [LCC 10] (1956; Louisville, KY: Westminster John Knox Press, 2006), 241–42.

were not.[38] Some canonists warned that acting against the certitude of one's conscience was a mortal sin and should be avoided, even if it meant defying ecclesiastical rule.[39] Thus,

> notwithstanding coercive tactics adopted under some circumstances, there remained a consistent recognition of religious freedom secured by both divine and natural law. The personal exercise of that freedom could indeed be curtailed for the sake of the common good, but any such curtailment would be held to standards of due process that guaranteed the rights of Christians and non-Christians alike. Within the confines of the medieval universities, or in the episcopal courts . . . there always remained a sphere of freedom within which the individual Christian could pursue the truth. Canonists would speak of "natural right," while theologians coupled this with an "evangelical freedom" that could not be infringed by any human law.[40]

But the medieval theologians did not all agree on the question of whether the conscience always binds. This question became especially relevant in cases when the conscience was in error and when individuals claimed they could not obey ecclesiastical regulations—believed by the church to be manifestly beneficial and (allegedly) above correction—due to a personal crisis of conscience. Among the medieval doctors, two main schools of thought existed on the question of the "erroneous conscience": the Augustinian (Franciscan) school, and the Abelardian (Thomistic) school.

A key principle of the Augustinian tradition was that the private conscience, regarded as a fallible and changing guide, must always submit to the objective order of God's law as it is interpreted and enforced by ordained officers of the church. Alexander of Hales and St. Bonaventure, for example, declared that only when a person's conscience matches the fixed standard of the divine law does it actually bind or instruct the believer in a meaningful way.[41] Bonaventure assigned *synderesis*—what medieval theologians

---

[38] On disputes among late medieval Catholics and English Protestants over the relationship between human law and the coercion of conscience, see Richard J. Ross, "Binding in Conscience: Early Modern English Protestants and Spanish Thomists on Law and the Fate of the Soul," *Law and History Review* 33, no. 4 (November 2015): 803–37.
[39] See Alexander Murray, *Conscience and Authority in the Medieval Church* (Oxford: Oxford University Press, 2015), chapter 5, "Excommunication and Conscience in the Middle Ages," 161–97.
[40] Levy, "Liberty of Conscience," 150.
[41] For the differences between the Augustinian (Franciscan) and Abelardian (Thomistic) views on conscience and moral responsibility, see Takashi Shogimen, *Ockham and Political Discourse in the Late Middle Ages* (Cambridge: Cambridge University Press, 2007), 124–30. For various theories of conscience in medieval philosophy, as well several relevant texts in translation from this period,

generally considered to be the "higher part of reason" naturally directing a person toward the good—to the realm of the human will. A person is obligated to follow this innate habit of the soul, but only as long as one's *conscientia*, that is, one's inborn moral knowledge or intellectual apprehension of the natural law, is applied practically in ways that are consistent with the unchanging standard of divine law.[42] Conversely, to follow an erroneous conscience that conflicts with divine law is to commit a mortal sin that "places a man outside the state of salvation." Bonaventure concluded, "it is thus clear that *conscientia* always either binds us to do what it tells us, or binds us to change it. *Conscientia* does not, however, always bind us to do what it tells us, e.g., a *conscientia* which tells us that we are not obliged to do something to which a man would, otherwise, be bound. Such a *conscientia* is called 'mistaken.'"[43] Practically, this means that when a layperson is perplexed about his or her religious duty, one's conscience may require "additional education" from ecclesiastical authorities in order to apprehend one's moral obligation under particular circumstances.[44] In such cases, Bonaventure, along with Hales, argued that the faithful are obliged to defer to the wisdom of their superiors: "If he does not know how to judge it by himself, he must consult someone wiser, or to turn to God in prayer, if human consultation is not available.... It is also clear that the command of a prelate is to be preferred to conscience, especially when the prelate commands what he can and ought to command.'" For the Franciscans, then, in the case of an objective moral obligation issued by a divinely appointed church official, every believer was obligated to abide by that decree, regardless of their conscience. Prelates should nevertheless be cautious about commanding the faithful's consciences in respect to indifferent acts.[45]

In contrast to the Augustinian school, Dominicans like Albert the Great, as well as Aquinas after him, adopted a view of the conscience that bore some similarity to the ideas of twelfth-century theologian Peter Abelard. Abelard's

consult Timothy C. Potts, *Conscience in Medieval Philosophy* (Cambridge: Cambridge University Press, 1980). In his early thirteenth-century treatise on conscience, *Summa de Bono*, 3, Philip the Chancellor argued, "*conscientia* is sometimes mistaken, sometimes right. But in whatever power there is any mistake over what is to be done, in that power there is sin" (text and translation in Potts, 102).

[42] Bonaventure, *Commentarius in secundum librum sententarium*, dist. 39, a. 2, q. 1 (Potts trans., 115–16).
[43] Bonaventure, *Commentarius*, dist. 39, a. 1, q. 3 (Potts trans., 114–15).
[44] Bonaventure, *Commentarius*, dist. 39, a. 1, q. 2 (Potts trans., 114).
[45] Bonaventure, *Commentarius*, dist. 39, a. 1, q. 3, quoted in Shogimen, *Ockham and Political Discourse in the Late Middle Ages*, 126.

moral treatise, *Scito te Ipsum*, proposed that one's actions—whether good or bad—should be judged on the basis of a person's intentions while making decisions under various circumstances. Anyone who set out to commit sin was obviously without excuse before God's law; those acting in good faith but with erroneous intention (ignorance), however, could not be accused of having committed a sin, since they genuinely intended to glorify God through their actions, however mistakenly.[46] Aquinas embraced some of Abelard's notions regarding the subjective character of human moral actions while developing his own understanding of the erroneous conscience in his *Summa Theologica*. Aquinas—and later William of Ockham—considered the conscience to be a faculty of human intellect or reason. For Aquinas, both synderesis and conscience belong to what he called the "practical intellect" (*intellectus practicus*), which he distinguished from the "speculative intellect" (*intellectus speculativus*), the realm of the intellect that deals with the truth in and of itself. As part of the practical intellect, the conscience has as its object "the good directed to operation, under the aspect of truth."[47] From this perspective, Aquinas determined that the conscience "binds" whenever it applies judgment to an individual case. Such a judgment might be right—if correctly applying knowledge to some decision—or wrongly deduced, resulting in an erroneous conscience. Though an erroneous conscience might not excuse someone's misbehavior, nevertheless, because the conscience is the subjective means by which any action is presented to a person as either good or bad, acting against one's conscience is always a sin. According to Aquinas, then, the conscience always binds, even if it is mistakenly convinced by erring reason to believe or act in a way contrary to God's command.[48]

In contrast to the Franciscan school, then, Aquinas and Ockham believed that the obligation of one's conscience was much more absolute, and thus they were more open to the idea that a subordinate could dissent from his or her superior on the basis of their conscience—even an erroneous conscience. Nevertheless, Aquinas generally assigned the superiority of the erroneous

---

[46] Peter Abelard, *Ethica seu Liber Dictus Scito te Ipsum*, chapter 11, col. 652C, in J.-P Migne, ProQuest Information and Learning Company, ProQuest (Firm), and Chadwyck-Healy, Patrologia Latina Database (vol. 178), accessed April 23, 2021, http://pld.chadwyck.com/.: "Bonam quippe intentionem, hoc est, rectam in se dicimus; operationem vero, non quod boni aliquid in se suscipiat, sed quod ex bona intentione procedat. Unde et ab eodem homine cum in diversis temporibus idem fiat, pro diversitate tamen intentionis ejus operatio modo bona modo mala dicitur, et ita circa bonum et malum variari videtur." See also chapter 13.

[47] ST 2, I, q. 79, a. 11, ad. 2. An English translation of this section is available in Anton C. Pegis, ed., *Basic Writings of Saint Thomas Aquinas*, 2 vols. (New York: Random House, 1945), 1:763–64.

[48] ST 2, I, q. 79, a. 13 (Pegis trans., 1:766–67).

conscience over the authority of church prelates to matters that are in themselves indifferent, suggesting that Aquinas's practical sense of the relationship between conscience and human law was not altogether different than the Franciscans'.[49] Aquinas's rather circumscribed notion of the freedom of conscience with regard to human law is reflected in his *Summa Theologica*. On the topic of whether human laws bind the conscience, Aquinas argues that, if human laws are just and clearly derive from God's eternal law, they do in fact bind the conscience. Such laws that "are just and binding in conscience, and are legal laws" are those that have been ordained for the common good and can be applied with "equality of proportion."[50] Although Aquinas leaves the interpretation of the law's intention to the authorities in most cases, he does indicate, however, that unusual cases of necessity might require a softening of the law's letter in order to fulfill the intended purpose of the law to promote the common welfare and prevent scandal.[51]

Aquinas's views on the natural mitigation of positive law reflect his inherited canonical tradition. Medieval canonists generally acknowledged that the natural law contained an inborn principle of permissiveness that allowed for the preservation of human freedom under circumstances in which the strict application of obligatory law might harmfully bind the conscience in unjust ways. In his expansive study on the idea of permissive natural law, Brian Tierney reveals that, among early decretists such as Hugh of St. Victor and Ivo of Chartes, there was an understanding that "the intrinsic nature of law included the idea that law could be permissive and that it could define an area of voluntary behavior where individuals were free to act as they chose, though some choices might be more commendable than others."[52] The notion of permissive natural law emphasized that proper courses of human action were often determined by assessing prevailing circumstances, rather than by following the strict application of doctrine or theory. Thus, another prominent canonist, Bernard of Compostella, argued that the permissiveness of natural law could "allow for alternative or even opposing courses of action, either of which could be counseled or prohibited in different circumstances."[53]

---

[49] Shogimen, *Ockham and Political Discourse in the Late Middle Ages*, 126–29.
[50] ST 3, II, q. 96, a. 4 (Pegis trans., 2:794–95).
[51] ST 3, II, q. 96, a. 6 (Pegis trans., 2:797–99).
[52] Tierney, *Liberty and Law*, 18.
[53] Bernardus Compostellanus, *ad Dist.* 38, c. 8., cited in Tierney, *Liberty and Law*, 37.

As we saw above in the case of infelicitous oaths, this type of permissiveness often included the obligation to choose between the lesser of two evils, and could mitigate the penalty for individuals caught in the act of swearing a frivolous oath.[54] Reflecting Abelard's influence upon medieval canon law, permissive natural law theorists contended that someone's actions were best judged on the basis of their good-faith intentions—however miscalculated their actions might be. And like Aquinas, canonists also held the notion of Christian prudence in high regard when dealing with complex moral situations: "Prudence was defined as right reason applied to practical action. Because it included an understanding of both universal principles and particular cases it could guide humans to choose wisely in all the contingent circumstances that would arise in the course of human affairs."[55] By closely linking prudence to the conscience—when viewed as the practical intellect—many canonists envisioned a significant measure of independence for the conscience. Though generally regarded as fallible and in need of occasional correction, the canonists also considered private conscience to be a worthy moral compass capable of determining the best course of action under various and sometimes complex circumstances—even to the point of requiring a prudent mitigation of ecclesiastical and civil law.

On a practical level, Aquinas's theory about the erroneous conscience, combined with the decretists' notion of the law's permissiveness, complicated matters when it came to handling conscientious complaints against the authority and doctrines of the church. Ian Christopher Levy points out that, in the medieval universities, for example, instructors censured for purportedly teaching against canon law faced a troubling crisis of conscience. In their own minds, they had not sought to contravene, but simply stimulate discussion about, the spirit of the canons. To recant meant going against their own consciences; to refuse meant facing the discipline of the church. When university masters appealed to their own consciences in support of their position, however, they were nevertheless corrected by the chancellor on account of the sworn oaths they had taken before lecturing on Lombard's *Sentences*, by which they had promised not to contravene in any way the official teachings of the Catholic faith. "We see, therefore, that while the free and creative exchange of ideas was indeed the lifeblood of the medieval university,

---

[54] E.g., see Dougherty, *Moral Dilemmas*, 25–26.
[55] Tierney, *Liberty and Law*, 77. On Aquinas's lengthy treatment of prudence—which he generally defined as the ability to choose wisely between the best and worst courses of action under diverse circumstances—see ST 3, II.IIae, q. 47.

parameters had to be established for the general welfare of the corporation. In this sense the university was a microcosm of the larger society; masters had a responsibility to the scholarly community to which they belonged—an allegiance that took precedence over the public expression of their own individual speculations"—and over their consciences.[56] Thus, although medieval theologians accepted that common law could be mitigated for the sake of private conscience—at least in theory—it was equally the case that not all conscientious dissent would be tolerated, especially if the authority of the church and communal harmony were in jeopardy.

The complex relationship between obligatory law, freedom of conscience, and Christian prudence dovetailed with yet another perplexing issue that would occupy jurists and theologians well into the Protestant Reformation—namely, that of indifferent matters or adiaphora. Regarding issues of proper worship, moral obligation toward one's neighbors, and the observance of human traditions, natural law and case law theorists strained to answer a basic question: "were practices not mandated in scripture implicitly permitted or implicitly forbidden?"[57] Furthermore, who were authorized to define whether the traditions or constitutions of the church counted as either indifferent or obligatory? The Augustinian tradition generally regarded indifferent matters as falling outside the scope of the freedom of conscience. Whether such matters would be required or forbidden of believers was a question best answered by ordained church officials, whom God had instilled with the authority and wisdom to decide whether some indifferent acts might be required for maintaining ecclesiastical and communal order.[58]

Aquinas placed the issue of adiaphora squarely within the context of the critical relationship between scandal and neighbor-love or charity. His *Summa Theologica* (Pars Secunda Secundae) contains a treatise on the theological virtues of faith, hope, and charity, along with their opposing vices. In this section, he identifies a particular threat to Christian charity, namely, the vice of scandal. Aquinas specifically deals here with the problem of the so-called *Scandalum infirmorum*—"offense of the weak"—which is the occasioning of someone's "spiritual downfall" (*ruinam spiritualem*) through immoderate words or deeds. He affirmed that, even in matters indifferent, someone might create an environment in which another person is encouraged to sin or act against conscience. Causing scandal might occur

---

[56] Levy, "Liberty of Conscience," 164–65.
[57] Tierney, *Liberty and Law*, 160.
[58] Lecler, *Toleration and the Reformation*, 1:96.

directly, as "when someone either intends, by his evil word or deed, to lead another person into sin, or, if he does not so intend, when his deed is of such a nature as to lead another into sin" (*scandalum activum*). One might also cause another's sin in an indirect or unintentional way (*scandalum passivum*) due to the weakness of the one affected.[59] Aquinas argued that, while someone might not be directly guilty in the case of a passive scandal—since his or her actions are of themselves indifferent and therefore a matter of freedom—they are not therefore at liberty to exercise their freedom of conscience to the detriment of a weaker neighbor. Rather, it may be necessary for laypersons and clerics to give up or abstain temporarily from (non-salvific) "spiritual goods" (such as excommunication and fraternal correction to avoid church schism) as well as "temporal goods" (such as food, drink, or private property) as a prudent means of instructing the weak and ignorant who are prone to stumble.[60] Thus, Aquinas and the late medieval tradition asserted that, although the requirements of strict law could be softened on occasion to protect even erroneous consciences, nevertheless, no person's conscience was so sacrosanct—even in matters indifferent—that it could supersede the higher law of charity or neighbor-love.

1.2.2. Christian Humanism

Unlike medieval scholasticism, the Christian humanist tradition of the late fifteenth century was not preoccupied with developing new theories of conscience. Inspired by the intellectual and philological developments of the Renaissance, Christian humanists were generally far more interested in adapting medieval models of conscience to their rhetorical, social, and ecclesiastical aims.[61] In part, this entailed a heightened desire to preserve the

---

[59] ST 3, II.IIae, q. 43, a. 1: "Per se quidem, quando aliquis suo malo verbo vel facto intendit alium ad peccandum inducer; vel etiamsi ipse hoc non intendat, ipsum factum est tale quod de sui ratione habet quod sit inductivum ad peccandum."

[60] ST 3, II.IIae, q. 43, a. 7–8. For a more detailed examination of *Scandalum informorum* in Aquinas's thought, see Nelson Deyo Kloosterman, *Scandalum Infirmorum et Communio Sanctorum: The Relation between Christian Liberty and Neighbor Love in the Church* (Neerlandia, AB: Inheritance Publications, 1991), 45–49. Several of my later chapters will also assess the prevalence of this concern amid several Reformation controversies.

[61] Rudolf Scheussler, "Conscience, Renaissance Understanding of," in *Encyclopedia of Renaissance Philosophy*, ed. Marco Sgarbi (New York: Springer, 2018), 1–7, accessed April 15, 2021, https://doi.org/10.1007/978-3-319-02848-4_602-1. On the close relationship between conscience and rhetoric among Christian humanists, see Gary Remer, *Humanism and the Rhetoric of Toleration* (University Park: Pennsylvania State University Press, 1996).

freedom of conscience against the excessive or untempered application of canon and civil law. Joseph Lecler notes that, unlike the medieval doctors who sought to acquire spiritual unity through the discipline of heretics, humanists were generally known for their "irenic" pursuit of common ground in matters of religious and moral debate. The humanist ideal—exemplified in the pacifism of Nicholas of Cusa—was "not so much tolerance as the reducing of religious differences by a loyal attempt at conciliation."[62]

Among the voices speaking in favor of religious accommodation during this period, the most influential by far was that of Desiderius Erasmus, "prince of the humanists." A pacifist like Cusa, Erasmus became a vocal opponent of the militaristic conquest of surrounding pagan nations by advocating a policy of toleration toward unbelievers and certain types of heretics. In true humanist form, he argued that the Catholic Church's hope for doctrinal renewal and increased unity resided not in military strength or in clerical grandeur, but in a restored commitment to reading the Bible through the interpretive lens of the classical Christian (Patristic) tradition (*ad fontes*). It was this reformist ideal, at least in part, that stirred up Erasmus's patience toward the young Luther—despite the rogue monk's tumultuous influence upon the church.[63] When dealing with doctrinal deviants like Luther, Erasmus advocated the rhetorical principle of "persuasion, not force," preferring that the church play an instructive rather than disciplinary role in convincing heretics to desist in their rebellion.[64] On several occasions, when speaking of Luther, Erasmus expressed the need for patience: "I prefer that he should be cured, not broken." Even later, as Lutheranism caught fire and began to spread rapidly through the Holy Roman Empire, Erasmus called for a temporary policy of tolerance, contending that the Protestants "should be left to their consciences" until such time as some common ground could be found. Erasmus argued that, at very least, this strategic accommodation of the Lutheran sect was preferable to the greater evil of a destructive civil war.

---

[62] Lecler, *Toleration and the Reformation*, 1:105. Lecler notes that Nicholas of Cusa's *De concordantia catholica* (1433) was written because "he was concerned with preserving harmonious relations between the body and the soul of the Church, the Empire, and the priesthood," at a time when the growing independence of the States were beginning to break up the monolithic control of the papacy (107).

[63] Scholastic theologians occasionally tried to invalidate the humanist movement by linking it to the "heretical" Lutheran Reformation. See Daniel Ménager, "Erasmus, the Intellectuals, and the Reuchlin Affair," in *Biblical Humanism and Scholasticism in the Age of Erasmus*, ed. Erika Rummel (Leiden: Brill, 2008), 39–54.

[64] Remer, *Humanism and the Rhetoric of Toleration*, 45–50.

Not surprisingly, however, his policy was not embraced by Rome's leaders with any seriousness, even as a temporary solution for unity.[65]

Concerning the church's authority to regulate personal piety by means of religious ceremonies, including public professions of faith, Erasmus could be somewhat innovative. In the preface to his *Paraphrase on Matthew* (1522), Erasmus makes the controversial suggestion that adolescents baptized as children should be formally examined (*interrogentur*) by priests in order to demonstrate an adequate understanding of their baptism's meaning and importance. He proposes a new kind of confirmation ceremony that would require youths to "publicly renew their baptismal profession of faith . . . with ceremonies that are solemn, fitting, chaste, serious and grand, and appropriate to a profession that is the most sacred of all."[66] In other writings, however, Erasmus conveys palpable disdain for the uncritical acceptance of human traditions, including sworn vows. In his *Paraphrase on Mark* (1523), for example, Erasmus mocks King Herod for feeling "conscience bound by his most foolish oath" to deliver the head of John the Baptist to Herodias (Mark 6), since, as an adulterer, he was a man already skilled in the practice of "breaking the bonds of all treaties and solemn vows." Erasmus concludes his summary of this biblical event with a scornful tone: "O faith and religious observance, O civility and humanity worthy to be recorded in chronicles!"[67] One wonders whether Erasmus's closing words are meant merely to censure Herod for his misguided oath and conscience, or whether a more general application to the overuse of religious oaths and ceremonies is intended.

Regardless, Erasmus's conciliatory vision for church reform mainly emphasized the importance of charity and the liberty of conscience. In contrast to the Scholastics, Erasmus believed that, in most cases, the requirement of charity and mutual good will trumped even the importance of doctrinal fidelity—including the church's regulation of religious observances. In the preface to his paraphrase of Matthew's gospel, for example, Erasmus settles a case involving an imaginary crisis of conscience. Having offered the opinion that adolescents might profit from being made to reaffirm the promises conferred in their baptisms by means of a formal vow, he raises a potential

---

[65] Lecler, *Toleration and the Reformation*, 1:116–20.

[66] Desiderius Erasmus, *Paraphrasis in Evangelium Matthaei* (Nürnberg, 1525), B 3ʳ-4ᵛ; ET in *Collected Works of Erasmus: Paraphrase on Matthew* (Vol. 45), ed. Robert D. Sider, trans. Dean Simpson (Toronto, ON: University of Toronto Press, 2008), 20.

[67] Erasmus, *Paraphrasis in Evangelium Marci* (Köln, 1524), I [8]ʳ; ET in *Collected Works of Erasmus: Paraphrase on Mark* (Vol. 49), ed. Robert D. Sider, trans. Erika Rummel (Toronto, ON: University of Toronto Press, 1988), 82 (Mark 6:24–29).

problem: what if a young man refuses to be compelled to renew his baptismal vows? Erasmus's solution to this hypothetical problem stresses the need for accommodation: "If [backsliding from one's profession] cannot be prevented, perhaps it will be more expedient if such a person is not compelled, but is left to his own inclination until he returns to his senses and repents."[68] Erasmus's willingness to leave obstinate non-conformists to the judgment of their own consciences for correction is striking, especially for his day. Perhaps even more striking, however, is his occasional lack of patience for certain types of religious dissidents, such as the Anabaptists, whose refusal to obey Christian magistrates and whose attempts to set up their own divine kingdom on earth were considered to be direct violations of Scripture and of the Patristic tradition, and could not be tolerated.[69]

Despite apparent inconsistencies in his practical application of the freedom of conscience to different groups, Erasmus advocated a truly liberal theory of doctrinal accommodation, even going beyond his medieval forebears in considering all religious non-essentials to be negotiable rather than incumbent upon believers. He regarded much of Catholic ritual to be matters of adiaphora, including pilgrimages, bowing before statues of saints, dietary restrictions, as well as other man-made ceremonies that are not essential to the Christian faith. Erasmus not only recognized the realm of "ceremonial adiaphora;" he also observed a kind of "doctrinal adiaphora." In his view, even certain doctrines of the faith are essentially indifferent—in whole or in part—and therefore not obligatory beliefs. The sum of true religion, according to Erasmus, could be boiled down to "peace and concord." To ensure these elements remained the focus of the church's life and worship, clerics should avoid defining too many points of doctrine and instead leave as many matters as possible to the judgment of the individual, including intellectual questions surrounding the nature of the Trinity and the character of the Sacraments. Nevertheless, while Erasmus—and much of the humanist tradition with him—assigned matters of outward ceremony and even doctrine to the realm of private judgment (conscience), it was determined that such

---

[68] Erasmus, *Paraphrasis in Evangelium Matthaei*, B 4ʳ (Simpson trans., 22).

[69] In an undated letter, presumably meant for Charles V, Erasmus declares, "Anabaptists must not be tolerated," because they teach their people to disobey the civil magistrates, be they Christian or pagan. See *Life and Letters of Erasmus*, ed. James Anthony Froude (London: Longmans, Green, 1894), 344–45. For examples of sixteenth-century Anabaptists and spiritualists attempted to appropriate Erasmus's views on religious toleration for their own radical agendas, see Peter G. Bietenholz, *Encounters with a Radical Erasmus: Erasmus' Work as a Source of Radical Thought in Early Modern Europe* (Toronto, ON: University of Toronto Press, 2009), especially chapter 3, "Peace and War According to Erasmus and Sebastian Franck," 69–93.

accommodations should never come at the expense of Christian morality or the practical manifestation of charity for the sake of the weak.[70]

1.2.3. Lutheran Reformation

In *Law and Protestantism*—a study of the Lutheran Reformation's strategic appropriation of medieval common law—John Witte, Jr. writes, "the Reformation that Martin Luther unleashed in Germany in 1517 began as a loud call for freedom—freedom of the church from the tyranny of the pope, freedom of the laity from the hegemony of the clergy, freedom of the conscience from the strictures of canon law." And while it is generally true that the freedom of conscience quickly became the "rallying cry" of the Lutheran Reformation, it is a less-acknowledged fact that Luther's thoughts about conscience underwent various and strategic changes in the early years of reform, as Witte goes on to show.[71] Indeed, the concept of freedom of conscience took on different forms within Luther's thought and practice over the course of his life. A closer look at the contexts and controversies that shaped Luther's (and other early reformers') understanding of the relationship between conscience, law, and charity bear witness to this reality.

It is undisputed that Luther's falling-out with the Church of his youth was precipitated by a fundamental concern for the Christian conscience—his own conscience, as well as the consciences of laity who he perceived "were being misled to place their trust not in Christ alone but in adherence to spurious laws, human traditions, and false teachings."[72] Luther saw the Catholic penitential system as an abusive violation of believers' spiritual freedom in Christ, and he arrived at this belief not only through observing the empty strictures of his own Augustinian order, but also in reaction to his inherited theological tradition, which was shot through with the influence of late medieval nominalism represented by the thought of Gabriel Biel. Biel's theology emphasized the necessity of developing a genuine love for God—concomitant with the infusion of grace—that would manifest itself through penance and good works in the Christian's life. Those who summoned their natural capacity

---

[70] Remer, *Humanism and the Rhetoric of Toleration*, 51–53.
[71] John Witte, Jr., *Law and Protestantism: The Legal Teachings of the Protestant Reformation* (Cambridge: Cambridge University Press, 2002), 1.
[72] John L. Thompson, "Reforming the Conscience: Magisterial Reformers on the Theory and Practice of Conscience," in *Christianity and the Laws of Conscience: An Introduction*, ed. Jeffrey B. Hammond and Helen M. Alvaré (Cambridge: Cambridge University Press, 2021), 135.

and did their best to please God would (certainly) be rewarded for the sake of Christ and on account of his available merits (*facientibus quod in se est Deus non denegat gratiam*). This system of partial merit kept believers' consciences suspended in permanent uncertainty, however, wondering whether they had sufficiently pleased God through external manifestations of love to warrant this special dispensation of meritorious grace.[73]

In his 1519 commentary on Paul's letter to the Galatians, Luther publicly opposed the idea that believers could attain any assurance of justification by observing the moral law, arguing instead that full justification is obtained only by faith in Christ. Speaking on Galatians 2:11–13—where the Apostle contends that relying on the law in any part for a person's salvation places one under a curse—Luther claims that the laws of the pope subvert the gospel, faith, and charity, and "introduce tortures of conscience (*carnificinas conscientarum*) in the assembly of the ignorant."[74] That same year, in his *Sermon on the Sacrament of Penance*, Luther argues that only those who have received God's full remission of sin and guilt through faith in Christ's work on the cross can approach God with "happy hearts and a good conscience."[75] True peace of conscience entailed freedom from the condemnation of sin as well as liberty from the vain attempt to obtain righteousness through obedience to the law. Indeed, Luther had discovered that the "righteousness of God," of which Paul wrote in Romans 1:17, is not that righteousness by which God punishes the sinner, but rather the alien righteousness of Christ conferred upon wretched sinners who trust in Christ and his merits alone by faith.[76]

Luther's exposition of the spiritual freedom of the believer against the spiritual bondage of Catholicism was never intended, however, to promote a form of rabid individualism that would justify the removal of all external

---

[73] On Biel's nominalist soteriology, see Heiko Oberman, *The Harvest of Medieval Theology: Gabriel Biel and Late Medieval Nominalism* (Durham, NC: Labyrinth Press, 1983), especially chapter 6, "The Process of Justification," 146–84.

[74] Martin Luther, *In Epistolam Pauli ad Galatas M. Lutheri Commentarius* (1519), in *Martin Luthers Werke: Kritische Gesamtausgabe* (Weimar: H. Boehlaus Nachfolger, 1883–) [hereafter WA], 2:487, 16–17: "Heu quot carnificinas conscientarum in ecclesiam invexit ignorantia ista legis dei et legum hominum!"

[75] Luther, *Ein Sermon von dem Sakrament der Buße* (1519), WA 2:715, 8–9: "frölichem hertzen und gutem gewissen."

[76] Commenting on Romans 1:17 in his 1520 treatise, "The Freedom of a Christian," Luther writes, "For the word of God cannot be received or honored by any works but by faith alone. Therefore, it is clear that the soul needs the word alone for life and righteousness, because if the soul could be justified by anything else, it would not need the word and, consequently, would not need faith." ET in Timothy J. Wengert, ed., *The Freedom of a Christian (1520): The Annotated Luther Study Edition*, Vol. 1: *The Roots of Reform* (Minneapolis: Fortress Press, 2016), 492; WA 7:51.

obligations upon the faithful—much less to play down the authority and moral imperatives of God's word.[77] In his defense before the Holy Roman emperor at the Diet of Worms on April 18, 1521, Luther maintained that his conscience was still "captive" to God's word, which compelled him to resist the false rulings of the Catholic Church. His Worms defense is well-attested:

> Unless I am convinced by the testimony of Scriptures or by clear reason (for I do not trust either in the pope or in councils alone, since it is well known that they have often erred and contradicted themselves), I am bound by the Scriptures I have quoted and my conscience is captive to the word of God. I cannot and I will not retract anything, since it is neither safe nor right to go against conscience.[78]

Instead of championing his own conscience above all, as if it were an independent source of moral authority untethered to the instruction of Scripture, Luther was rather "defending the utter priority of the word of God not only to guide his teachings and writings but also, first and foremost, as the only possible way to know that he, still confessedly a sinner, was loved and saved by God."[79] And although Charles V responded that Luther was obviously in error in his reading of God's word—since it conflicted with the Pope's allegedly infallible interpretation—and that he could not justly appeal to his conscience for support, Luther nevertheless held that his conscience was sound because it conformed to the objective standard of divine Scripture that he himself could understand. Thus, Luther's position at Worms, and later in his *On Secular Authority* (1523), was not that the conscience should be free from any and all compulsion, but that a conscience *captive to God's word* should not be transgressed, even when going against the governing authorities.[80]

---

[77] This point is stated and argued in Michael G. Baylor, *Action and Person: Conscience in Late Scholasticism and the Young Luther* (Leiden: Brill, 1977). Baylor's study offers a thorough comparison of Luther's conception of conscience against the backdrop of medieval theories of conscience, including Aquinas's.

[78] WA 7:838, 4–9: "Nisi convictus fuero testimoniis scripturarum aut ratione evidente (nam neque Papae neque conciliis solis credo, cum constet eos et errasse sepius et sibi ipsis contradixisse), victus sum scripturis a me adductis et capta conscientia in verbis dei, revocare neque possum nec volo quicquam, cum contra conscientiam agree neque tutum neque integrum sit." ET in Baylor, *Action and Person*, 1.

[79] Thompson, "Reforming the Conscience," 137.

[80] In *On Secular Authority: To What Extent It Should Be Obeyed* (1523), Luther writes, "it is therefore the height of folly when they command that one shall believe the Church, the Fathers, and the Councils, though there be no word of God for it. It is not the church but the Devil's apostles who command such things, for the church commands nothing unless it knows for certain that it is God's word.... No one shall or can command the soul unless he is able to show it the way to heaven; but this no human being can do, only God alone. Therefore, in matters that concern the salvation of souls,

It was this position, in particular, that had fostered Luther's earlier harangue against Catholic canon law. On December 10, 1520, with his students and fellow professors of theology at the University of Wittenberg standing by, Luther gleefully burned the books of canon law, including Gratian's *Decretum*.[81] Canon law had turned Christianity into a religion of merit, Luther believed. It encouraged papal tyranny, fostered greed, and enabled the exploitation of the weak, utterly contradicting the virtues of Scripture. By managing every facet of the Christian life through specious human ordinances and a complicated system of sacraments, canon law "tyrannized the Christian's conscience," made Christianity a religion of law instead of grace, and "destroyed the spiritual love and freedom of the Gospel." Based on his critical assessment of Catholic canon law in the early 1520s, Luther argued that all "legal authority" should be removed from abusive clerics and relegated to the civil magistrates. The church was to be "a community of faith and love, not a corporation of law and politics. The consciences of its members are to be guided by Scripture and the Spirit, not governed by human traditions and priestly injunctions."[82] The Lutheran break from medieval canon law was to be swift and all-encompassing.

In the wake of Luther's thoroughgoing rejection of canon law, however, an unexpected plague of lawlessness broke out among the evangelical churches of Germany that challenged the very foundations of civil and ecclesiastical authority. The Peasants' War of 1525 constituted a shocking display of civil disobedience, ostensibly in the name of the freedom of conscience. Luther initially urged the protestors to pursue their cause "with good conscience and justice" (*mit gutem gewissen und recht*), albeit without the use of force

---

nothing but God's word shall be taught and accepted." ET in Hans J. Hillerbrand, ed., *The Annotated Luther*, Vol. 5: *Christian Life in the World* (Minneapolis: Fortress Press, 2016), 109; WA 11:262.

[81] Witte, *Law and Protestantism*, 53. Witte notes that Melanchthon and Agricola were the ones who coordinated this public bonfire. Initially, even Aquinas's works were destined for the blaze, only to be spared by the reluctance of faculty members who refused to give up their copies of his works (53). Other evangelical theologians were vocally opposed to canon law, including Martin Bucer and his reformist partner in Strasbourg, Wolfgang Capito. Certain Catholic teachers, such as Wittenberg jurist Justus Jonas, as well as Johann Freiherr von Schwarzenburg, were also critical (60–62). Reflecting the impact of the first-generation reformers upon his own thought, Calvin could be rather selective in his appeals to common law. Muller notes that Calvin made "very unsystematic and polemical use of Lombard and Gratian," and was more inclined to offer biblical and practical arguments in favor of church constitutions, including oaths and vows, instead of appealing to human authorities. See Muller, *The Unaccommodated Calvin*, chapter 10, "The Study of Calvin: Contexts and Directions," 174–88.

[82] Witte, *Law and Protestantism*, 56–58.

against God's ordained magistrates.[83] At least at first, he was confident that the peasants' consciences—now free from the burden of false religion—would properly direct them to act in a way consistent with the rule of charity and with respect for God's appointed rulers. As the revolt grew more unwieldly and fatalities rose, however, Luther saw the need to step in and condemn the peasants' behavior as unbecoming of their spiritual freedom in Christ. In early May 1525, Luther wrote *Against the Storming Peasants*, in which he sharply criticized the peasants for acting with a "bad conscience" (*boese gewissen*). Unwilling to justify their violence, he instead came to the defense of the German princes, calling them to put down the lawless revolt "with good conscience" as God's appointed servants tasked with punishing the wicked.[84]

Problems also arose within the young churches of the Reformation: clerics and congregants alike were appealing to their newfound freedom from canon law to justify spiritual, doctrinal, and liturgical "laxness"; church members were exercising their spiritual liberty in ways contrary to the rule of love and charity, to the detriment of their neighbors; clerics had lost credibility and authority to enact and enforce laws in the church; and the dissoluteness of morals and life was growing rampant.[85] Luther's insistence on the complete freedom of the Christian seemed the logical culprit of all these problems.

Luther remained certain that he held a biblical understanding of the spiritual freedom won for believers through Christ. He was nevertheless forced to reassess how that same freedom should relate to Christian public life and to the order of the visible church. From this point on, Luther and his Reformed colleagues offered a more circumscribed definition of the freedom of conscience by clarifying that a believer's spiritual freedom did not always entail absolute freedom from all human rule, be it civil or ecclesiastical. A Christian would always be free in Christ from injurious human traditions (a "completely free lord of all, subject to none") but should nevertheless be willing to bear the yoke of the civil magistrates by living "under law" for the sake of one's unbelieving neighbors and for the greater good of social order

---

[83] Luther, *Ermahnung zum Frieden auf die zwölf Artikel der Bauerschaft in Schwaben* (1525), WA 18:300, 5: "Nichts weniger ist euch auch wol furzusehen, das yhr ewr sachen mit gutem gewissen und recht furnemet."

[84] Luther, *Widder die stürmenden bawren* (1525), WA 18:360, 12–15: "So soll nu die oberkeit hie getrost fort dringen und mit gutem gewissen dreyn schlahen, weyl sie eyne ader regen kan, Denn hie ist das vorteyl, das die bawren boese gewissen und unrechte sachen haben, und wilcher bawr darueber erschlagen wird, mit leyb und seele verluren und ewig des teuffels ist."

[85] The civil and ecclesiastical unrest that arose in the wake of Luther's reforms are nicely summarized in Witte, *Law and Protestantism*, 65–69.

and tranquility (a "completely dutiful servant of all, subject to all").[86] This modified conception of Christian freedom also required that some form of centralized authority should be restored to the evangelical churches—through the work of ordained ministers, church officers, and the prudent use of church ordinances—and that some of the most insightful parts of medieval canon law should be reappropriated to serve the overall goals of reform.[87] In this way, some of Luther's early and radical notions regarding the freedom of conscience needed to be mitigated on account of the more pressing need to organize and unite the fledgling evangelical church under its true leader—not Luther, but Jesus Christ himself.

Luther's controlling desire to rescue believers' consciences from the excessive regulations and burdensome traditions of the Catholic Church, as well as to restore the primacy of Scripture and the rule of Christ over his church, has occasionally led some scholars to suggest that Luther, by teaching a doctrine of justification by faith alone, believed that everything but faith is indifferent—that is, strictly a matter of Christian freedom (adiaphora). In reality, although Luther's understanding of sanctification was not as robust as Calvin's would be, his vision of Christian freedom was not so radical as to do away with all ethical instruction or the necessity of Christian progress in godliness. Even though believers have been transferred to the kingdom of Christ and rule with him over all—and thus subject to none—Luther nevertheless insists that the Christian is still obliged (out of gratitude for salvation) to observe God's commandments, to abstain from those things forbidden in them, and to act for the good of one's neighbor—thus, being servants of all. Though Luther preferred not to use the word "law" to denote the Christian's ongoing duty before God and the world, preferring to speak of God's moral "commands," and although he was more hesitant than Calvin to ascribe a pedagogical role to the conscience, preferring to speak of good works arising spontaneously as free "works of grace," nevertheless, Luther held that Christians are called to work out their love for God and neighbor in practical and visible ways.[88]

---

[86] Luther's two main propositions in *The Freedom of a Christian* (1520), Wengert ed., 488; WA 7:21, 1–4: "Eyn Christen mensch ist eyn freyer herr ueber alle ding und niemandt unterthan. Eyn Christen mensch ist eyn dienstpar knecht aller ding und yderman unterthan."

[87] On the evangelical conversion of medieval canon law, see Witte, *Law and Protestantism*, 70–83.

[88] Although Luther never used the phrase "the third use of the law (*tertius usus legis*)," he nevertheless affirmed its functional use. Luther not only recognized the law's theological use—in pointing sinners to Christ—but also its use as a standard to instruct Christians in the cultivation of good works. See Paul Althaus, *The Theology of Martin Luther* (Philadelphia: Fortress Press, 1970), 266–73.

Thus, the adiaphoristic freedom advocated by Luther, as well as by his chief ally Philip Melanchthon, was not a simplistic rejection of all traditions and ceremonies lacking explicit Scriptural command. Their view of indifferent matters was carefully circumscribed by the rule of charity, which required that personal freedom of conscience be exercised not in an immoderate or reckless manner—opposing all human laws and traditions simply because one has the freedom to do so—but out of love for church order and the protection of the church's weaker members. Both Luther and Melanchthon therefore acknowledged that "some of the human traditions had been established precisely for the sake of unity and order, and for that reason could still serve a very useful purpose."[89] Indeed, such useful ceremonies—especially those suited for the confession of sins and public profession of faith—should be observed due to their manifest benefit for the church. From this it is clear that the German Reformers did not believe Christians were totally exempt from the control of civil and ecclesiastical leaders, including themselves! In 1522, while writing his *Invocavit* sermons, Luther complained that the Protestant leaders had not sought *his counsel* when things became violent and disorderly under the radical leadership of Andreas Karlstadt. Bernard Verkamp notes, "this was not merely the cry of a hurt ego, but rather was indicative of Luther's conviction that even in matters indifferent one must proceed orderly, which in turn implied going through the proper channels of authority, including the secular authorities, whose decrees regarding religious services should be obeyed to the extent that they make for orderly life and do not contradict the gospel."[90] Thus, while Luther and Melanchthon continued to reject the blasphemous notion that human laws and spurious traditions could bind a Christian's conscience—if required as conditions of salvation—they did

---

[89] Bernard J. Verkamp, "The Limits upon Adiaphoristic Freedom: Luther and Melanchthon," *Journal of Theological Studies* 36, no. 1 (1975): 71.

[90] Verkamp, "The Limits upon Adiaphoristic Freedom," 72. Luther would occasionally apply his views on conscience and Christian freedom in inconsistent ways, as when, in 1524, he sparked controversy by allowing Prince Philip of Hesse to take a second wife on account of his adulterous relationship with another woman. In this peculiar case, Luther argued that it was more necessary for Philip to assuage his conscience by marrying his lover than to apply the Scriptures too rigidly to cases of polygamy—a decision that would be widely criticized, even by Calvin. A helpful summary of this situation is found in Thompson, "Reforming the Conscience," 146–47. Following Luther's death in 1546, Melanchthon also felt compelled to accommodate his own views on conscience and adiaphora to the pressing need to maintain the essential truths of the gospel against Catholic pressures. Melanchthon's willingness to accept the imposition of certain church ceremonies brought down the criticism of Flacius Illyricus, a colleague in Wittenberg, who argued that Melanchthon's concession compromised the Christian faith: although certain aspects of Catholic tradition and ceremony were indifferent in and of themselves, because they were being forced upon Protestants as a necessary element of divine worship, it was a violation of conscience. For a helpful examination of this adiaphorist proposal, known as the "Leipzig interim," see Tierney, *Liberty and Law*, 160–65.

not deny that civil and ecclesiastical leaders retained the right and authority to enact legislation with regard to indifferent matters. For the sake of communal harmony and charity, believers could be made to observe church ordinances that were deemed beneficial to the right ordering of the church.

***

From our brief examination of medieval, humanist, and Reformation voices on the topic of religious coercion and the freedom of conscience, it is evident that late medieval concepts of tolerance were extremely circumscribed. The faithful were never at liberty to practice the Christian faith simply as they wished; nor were they ever free to reject the external obligations and religious rites that state and church officials deemed necessary for them. No one was allowed to hold beliefs or act in ways that would disrupt social and ecclesiastical harmony, or trouble the consciences of weaker members of society. Indeed,

> the leading principle of securing the common good, which necessarily curtailed the sort of individual liberties that the modern West has grown accustomed to, meant that thoughts and feelings cherished deep within the human heart might have to remain there unexpressed. The church did not judge what was in secret, and in that way honored the sacred interior sphere of conscience, but it was obligated to protect fellow Christians when dangerous ideas entered the public realm.[91]

At the same time, canonists and natural law theorists, as well as the early reformers, demonstrated a willingness to protect the souls and consciences of their parishioners from the sharp edges of the law. This was done, in part, by recognizing that canon and civil law could be applied in softer ways under morally ambiguous circumstances. A freer application of the law—particularly in cases involving oaths, confession of faith, and complaints about conscience—was intended to fulfill the intention of common law, yet without burdening souls in the process. Luther himself seems to have applied this accommodated perspective to his own evangelical conversion of canon and civil law, setting the stage for later reformers, like Calvin, to appropriate these principles for their own use.

---

[91] Levy, "Liberty of Conscience," 171.

SECTION II
ANSWERING CONSCIENTIOUS OBJECTORS

Calvin and the Reformers against Radical Dissent and Religious Compromise

2
Conscience, Confession, and the Consolidation of Early Public Reform in Strasbourg, 1530–1535

From the general history of the early Reformation, we observe that the movement sparked by Luther's conscientious stance quickly encountered problems of its own. Civil and ecclesiastical authorities began to face a host of practical problems brought on by an emerging "confessionalization"—the late sixteenth-century proliferation of doctrinal confessions that precipitated an ecclesial, political, and social restructuring in the centuries that ensued— as well as wide-reaching appeals to the freedom of conscience. But the diverse movements spawned by Luther's revolt were not harmonious when it came to deciding *which* appeals to conscience were justifiable and therefore valid. Many of Luther's "spiritual children," though they cheered his defiant break from Rome, opposed several key theological and moral positions of the reformer. Religious dissenters—including various stripes of Anabaptists, Spiritualists, and fanatical visionaries—were convinced by their own consciences and interpretations of the Bible that Luther's reforms were insufficiently radical.[1] Over time, the Wittenberg reformer developed a palpable disdain for these bothersome groups, although he had been an early supporter of religious freedom, even to the point of opposing state punishment of religious dissidents. Luther came to believe that the principle of Christian freedom of conscience could never justify impure doctrine or impious actions, which would only threaten social harmony.[2] Though he granted each and every Christian the right of Scriptural interpretation, he could not grant validity to the interpretations of all supposedly reform-minded Christians, even if they claimed to hold their beliefs in good conscience. The conscience

---

[1] Harry Loewen, *Luther and the Radicals* (Waterloo, ON: Wilfrid Laurier University Press, 1974), 27.

[2] John S. Oyer, *Lutheran Reformers against Anabaptists: Luther, Melanchthon and Menius and the Anabaptists of Central Germany* (The Hague, Netherlands: Martinus Nijhoff, 1964), 114–39 (chap. 4).

proved effective and profitable only for those whose consciences actually conformed to the plain teaching of Scripture—albeit as variously defined by Luther and the other reformers. Thus, from the records of the early reform period we note the existence of diverse and sometimes conflicting appeals to freedom of conscience, complicating our ability to gauge the successes and failures of the Reformation's defense of this important principle.

This conflict is perhaps no more evident than in urban centers of the Reformation, where competing claims to authority—and conscience— emerged among three primary sectors of society: laity, clergy, and civil magistrates. The south German city of Strasbourg offers a primary example of how this dynamic played out. Reformation historians count Strasbourg among the most tolerant Protestant cities of the sixteenth century. Magisterial concern for protecting the freedom of conscience and religion made the city a reputable safe haven for Anabaptists and related dissident groups until the late 1520s. Nevertheless, as the need for consolidating public moral reform grew more urgent, the Reformed preachers' tolerance for religious dissidents and conscientious objections to governance wore thin. As will be seen, the early period of reform in Strasbourg witnessed frequent appeals to conscience among the general populace, as religious dissenters, magistrates, and clerics jockeyed for their respective interests—often appealing to conscience as a means to other ends.[3] Indeed, the documentary traces available to us especially reveal that the Strasbourg reformers struggled—often with great frustration—to clarify the place that civic duty and moral discipline should occupy in an evangelical religion principally committed to Christian freedom of conscience.

2.1. Conscientious Discontent in Strasbourg on the Eve of the Reformation

The city of Strasbourg on the eve of its Reformation was a microcosm of the general milieu of discontent that characterized late-medieval German

---

[3] Standard works on the history of the Strasbourg Reformation (regularly consulted here) include François Wendel, *L'Église de Strasbourg: Sa constitution et son organisation, 1532–1535* (Paris: Presses Universitaires de France, 1942); Miriam Usher Chrisman, *Strasbourg and the Reform: A Study in the Process of Change* (New Haven, CT: Yale University Press, 1967); Lorna Jane Abray, *The People's Reformation: Magistrates, Clergy, and Commons in Strasbourg, 1500–1598* (Ithaca, NY: Cornell University Press, 1985); and James Kittelson, *Toward an Established Church: Strasbourg from 1500 to the Dawn of the Seventeenth Century* (Mainz: Philipp Von Zabern, 2000).

society. Decades before the city began its turn toward reform in 1521, government officials, Catholic clergy, and city elites heard complaints from the general populace concerning the host of unbearable encroachments upon their liberties and private consciences.[4] One common grievance addressed the centuries-long abuse of clerical power and privilege. From the early Middle Ages, canon law had granted special exemptions to clerics that underlined their separateness from the laity and citizenship duties. Medieval Catholic ecclesiastics enjoyed "a twofold immunity of the religious from secular jurisdiction: an *immunitas localis*, exempting ecclesiastical properties from taxes and recognizing the right of asylum in holy places, and an *immunitas personalis*, exempting clergy from the jurisdiction of civil courts."[5] Many priests removed themselves from the lived existence of the people, literally dwelling on the outskirts of town—some even outside the city walls. That the city clerics should claim such spiritual power over the consciences of the laity, all the while benefiting from a civic community in whose responsibilities they refused to share, severely vexed the general populace.[6] At the root of discontent stemming from the supervisory failures of their clerics lay the people's anxiety over the burdensome array of church traditions, obligatory ceremonies, and penitential rites that dominated notions of medieval Catholic piety. By the early 1500s, the Strasbourgeois had become deeply

---

[4] Wendel, *L'Église de Strasbourg*, 25, shows that Strasbourg's initial embrace of Protestant worship, as well as the ascendancy of evangelical preachers in the city, began already in 1521 following Charles V's Edict of Worms. A year later the Magistrates indicated their preference for Protestant doctrine when they granted Matthew Zell, a Lutheran minister, freedom to preach from the cathedral pulpit. Conscientious discontent also pervaded Strasbourg's commercial sphere leading up to the Reformation; e.g., craft guild masters were engaged in a decades-long conflict with their journeymen over the right to establish confraternities—quasi-religious, self-regulated organizations having set rules and obligations for their artisan members. Whereas the journeyman furriers of Strasbourg believed it was their right to establish such confraternities as a means to hone and govern their craft and elevate citizenship status—a right they had enjoyed since the turn of the prior century (1404)—guild masters and city magistrates became convinced that such associations would gradually erode their own economic, social, and political authority. The city's *Knechteordnung* of 1465 intended to remove all bargaining power from the journeymen and place the authority to negotiate conditions of employment squarely in the hands of the guild masters. All journeymen were then forced to "swear an oath of obedience to masters and council, pledging themselves to advance the interest and honor of the city and do nothing to cause it harm or injury as long as they shall serve this city and reside in it" (The *Knechteordnung* of Strassburg, Art. 2, in *Manifestations of Discontent in Germany on the Eve of the Reformation*, trans. Gerald Strauss [Bloomington: Indiana University Press, 1971], 134). Early Protestant leaders—and later, the clerics and magistrates of Geneva—were also deeply critical of lay-religious confraternities, believing they threatened the notion of the priesthood of believers embodied in the local church. Ozment notes, "in Protestant eyes, confraternities were only lay efforts to imitate clergy, to create separate and allegedly superior religious groups" (Ozment, *The Reformation in the Cities*, 84). Thus, confraternities faced opposition from civil and ecclesiastical leaders alike—albeit for different reasons.

[5] Ozment, *The Reformation in the Cities*, 36.

[6] Chrisman, *Strasbourg and the Reform*, 34–35.

suspicious of the clerics' constant efforts to "extend monastic ideals of fasting, prayer, and confession to ordinary Christians," surmising that moral reform was but a means of extracting payment from the laity to enrich the convents.[7] Nevertheless, at century's turn, the winds of change had already started to shift in Strasbourg as the civil authority began to place limits on the ecclesiastics' power by "drawing ecclesiastical institutions under its supervision and direction; rights of jurisdiction had been established over clerical persons in certain cases, and some of the old tension diminished as far as the city was concerned."[8]

Remarkably, it was as the prevailing winds of conscientious discontent began to carry reformist ideas into Strasbourg that the political and social instability of previous centuries gave way to a period of calm. By 1480, the city had finalized its new constitution, adding three supervisory councils to the existing political bodies, the *Ammeister* (administrative elite) and the *Rat* (legislators).[9] Miriam Usher Chrisman notes the surprising fact that the political and social stability of this period was achieved without a popular uprising or a complete reconfiguring of the political and social hierarchy. Inherent political, social, and economic inequalities persisted as remnants of past centuries, but relative peace and contentment prevailed among Strasbourg's inhabitants because "the desire for order was greater than the desire for change." Although the common people had complained of economic and spiritual overreach, the native desire for order and the general respect for rule of law fostered the prevailing belief that "political authority should be placed in the hands of the superior classes."[10] Thus, each year, citizens (male household leaders) from every sector of society gathered in January, together with the city magistrates, to make a communal vow of mutual responsibility and respect (*Schwörbrief*).[11] Most swore without dissent, but some objected out of suspicion that the oath was a power play to maintain the social status quo.[12]

---

[7] Abray, *The People's Reformation*, 29. On the trend toward "anticlericalism" in Strasbourg at the turn of the century, see pp. 25–31.

[8] Chrisman, *Strasbourg and the Reform*, 36–42. By as early as 1480, "the civil authority had appropriated important rights of appointment, had forced the chapters to pay a fee in return for the protection of the city, and could tax the ecclesiastical courts" (42).

[9] Chrisman, *Strasbourg and the Reform*, 24–26.

[10] Chrisman, *Strasbourg and the Reform*, 27.

[11] Kittelson, *Toward an Established Church*, 16. This oath, regularly refused by Anabaptists, was sworn every year at the beginning of January. See, e.g., QGT 8:300, #534 (April 11, 1534). See n. 11.4.

[12] Edmund Pries, "Anabaptist Oath Refusal: Basel, Bern and Strasbourg, 1525–1538" (PhD diss., University of Waterloo, 1995), accessed February 23, 2018, ProQuest Dissertations & Theses, 26–27, 162–213.

When Martin Bucer, Wolfgang Capito, Caspar Hedio, and Jacob Sturm—the ministers who would take the lead of the reform movement—were welcomed by the city around the year 1523, the Catholic leaders realized they were no longer safe in Strasbourg.[13] The magistrates had firmly decided for the Reformation. Seeking the means best suited to maintain civil peace, they threw their support behind the Protestant vision of order that would "preserve the liberated from a reimposition of the burdens of what was unnecessary and untrue."[14] This shift toward a Protestant order manifested itself in various ways. For one, the Reformed clergy, in stark contrast to their Catholic predecessors, lived like the rank and file of Strasbourg—they married and established households, purchased citizenship and swore the annual burgher's oath, sought guild connections, and had the approval of the majority of the city's politicians.[15] The reformers immersed themselves in the life of the city, urgently seeking to stock its pulpits with qualified ministers whose gospel preaching would spark moral reform in every sector of society. The ministers' primary emphasis on "the absolute power of the Word of God" signaled to everyone in Strasbourg—the magistrates, laity, and religious refugees alike—that the ministry of the church was to have a central role in society as the principal agent of redemption and renewal.[16] The civil magistrates were also called upon to fulfill their duty to promote true religion and godly discipline.

Thus, the arrival of the reformers indicated that a different type of order was emerging—one that, while it emphasized the sacred freedom of the conscience as a corollary to the doctrine of salvation by faith alone, also sought to implement the yoke of Christ over all of life, albeit in sometimes unfamiliar ways. An initial problem faced by the Reformed clergy, however, was how to relate civic righteousness to the Reformation cornerstone of the freedom of conscience without creating the suspicion that their tactics for moral reform were just alternative versions of the coercive practices of their Catholic predecessors. That task would prove to be most difficult amid heightened appeals to conscience during the consolidation of public reform in the early 1530s.

---

[13] Wendel, L'Église de Strasbourg, 25.
[14] Ozment, The Reformation in the Cities, 159.
[15] Kittelson, Toward an Established Church, 23. Kittelson notes that Capito even married into a family that held a seat on one of the city's most influential governing councils, the Council of Fifteen, which Chrisman explains was a sort of "watchdog committee for administration" (Chrisman, Strasbourg and the Reform, 25). For more on the Strasbourg reformers' path to citizenship, see Ozment, The Reformation in the Cities, 86–89.
[16] Chrisman, Strasbourg and the Reform, 85–86.

2.2. Conscience and the Consolidation of Public Reform in Strasbourg: 1530–1535

Appeals to conscience began to proliferate in Strasbourg as opposition to the efforts of magistrates and clergy to consolidate social and moral reform intensified. From the earliest stages of the Reformation in Strasbourg, the ministers of the city and its government shared a joint vision that true religion ought to manifest itself publicly—it was not solely the property of the individual soul or mind. The Reformation was to exert a visible and pervasive influence on all levels of society.[17] But this ideal faced significant challenges during the period of the early 1530s. The pastors painted a bleak picture for the Grand Council in the fall of 1532: much of the city's residents led lax religious lives and held questionable moral standards. Their contempt for the preached word was no doubt due to the dearth of doctrinal training among the pastors.[18] Efforts to improve the situation were only hindered by the rival influence of religious dissidents, including Anabaptists Melchior Hoffman, Balthasar Hubmaier, and Michael Sattler, and spiritualists like Sebastian Franck and Caspar Schwenckfeld, which collectively threatened the spiritual and public order of the city. Perhaps most threatening to the civil and ecclesiastical leaders' conscientious commitment to broad reform in the city was the spiritualists' incessant vocal rejection of the notion that true religion could be enforced by any external authority—a position they defended with ample appeals to the freedom of conscience. This argument would prove to be a most serious obstacle to the authorities' plans, for by it, Anabaptists and their mystic-spiritualist sympathizers "negated the very grounds upon which the pastors and the government agreed and that formed the foundation for every additional building block in the city's Reformation to date."[19]

---

[17] Arriving in Strasbourg in 1523, Bucer and Capito found the magistrates largely, but not entirely, cooperative with their vision of building a Christian society through the proper use of discipline. As Amy Burnett explains in her article, "Church Discipline and Moral Reformation in the Thought of Martin Bucer," *SCJ* 22, no. 3 (1991): 440, Bucer's proposed system of discipline—at least in its later, most mature form—included four primary elements: "religious instruction for both children and adults; a public confession of faith and obedience, especially as part of a confirmation ceremony; fraternal admonition combined with the oversight of morals by pastors and lay elders; and in cases of grave sin, the imposition of public penance and, if necessary, excommunication." During Bucer's time in Strasbourg, however, the magistrates retained control over the power of church discipline.

[18] Wendel, *L'Église de Strasbourg*, 53.

[19] Kittelson, *Toward an Established Church*, 29.

The principle of Christian freedom had, of course, become a sort of watchword of the Reformed movement, responsible for much of the early and widespread enthusiasm for the Reformation within urban centers of the period. But the large and diverse body of Luther's followers was hardly of one mind when it came to applying this principle to matters of doctrine and piety. Some of the more radical sects spawned by the Lutheran Reformation were so motivated by notions of freedom of conscience that they were suspicious of any and all external yokes, be they evangelical rulers, ordained ministers, or even Scripture itself. Joseph Lecler, in his classic study of toleration during the Reformation, notes that such ideas, expressing in seed form "the fundamental tenets of religious individualism," resulted less from popular movements, such as the sudden rise of Anabaptism, and were mostly circulated by "isolated individuals," such as Franck, or by "small, formless groups," like Schwenckfeld and his followers.[20] And indeed, it was the teachings of Franck and Schwenckfeld that most seriously threatened to derail the agenda for holistic reform in Strasbourg, especially because they argued that all external means of spiritual instruction and discipline were not only superfluous but also harmful to the private conscience and the free working of God's Spirit.[21]

---

[20] Lecler, *Toleration and the Reformation*, 1:165.

[21] The Strasbourg preachers had heard similar attacks from prominent Anabaptist teachers Wilhelm Reublin and Jakob Kautz. In January 1529, the ministers formally condemned the teachings of the two men, who were preaching that the true church of Christ is solely invisible and internal. In their address to the Rat concerning these two men, the preachers argued on the basis of Scripture that, although the church is invisible only to the degree that those who belong to it enjoy eternal life by an inward faith in the invisible God, nevertheless, the church is properly called a "body," having an outward, tangible existence as the visible people of God: "Hieruff sagen wir, das solche theilung der kirchen und gemeyne gottes die geschrifft niergendt hatt, redet auch von keyner innerlichen kirchen uff die weyse, wie yetz auß Kautzen wortten erzelet ist. Die geschrifft redt nur von einer kirchen, die ein leib, gespons und rich Christi ist, und das sind fromme, gottselige leutte, deren neues und ewiges leben wol inwendig durch den glauben alleyn in gott stätt und deßhalb unsichtbar ist." QGT 7:201, #171 (January 23, 1529). The ministers were also forced to defend the necessity of preaching against the claim that, since the time of the apostles, the secret call of God abrogated all external forms of spiritual authority—even the Scriptures. See QGT 7:204–205, #171.

Schwenckfeld's persistent criticism of the clergy was especially threatening to early reform efforts in Strasbourg. Kittelson notes that his proactive arguments "struck at the heart of developments in Strasbourg far more profoundly than did the actions of more overt dissidents (such as Melchior Hoffman) who flatly opposed infant baptism and sought to found churches of genuine believers. Schwenckfeld's spiritualizing of everything raised questions about whether anything that the reformers and the government were doing was of any importance whatsoever" (Kittelson, *Toward an Established Church*, 32).

2.2.1. Franck and Schwenckfeld

In a 1530 treatise, Franck announced the emergence of a purer branch of the Reformation, one that, in contrast to Lutheranism, Zwinglianism, and Anabaptism,

> will discard all outward preaching, ceremonies, sacraments, excommunications, and pastoral counsel as unnecessary, seeking only to form an invisible spiritual Church, gathered from all over the world in the unity of the Spirit and the faith, and governed not by external means but only by the eternally invisible word of God, as the Apostolic Church was governed following the death of the Apostles.[22]

Franck's essential problem with Luther and the other reformers was that their religious movement, although it had begun with the goal of freeing believers from a corrupt Roman Church preoccupied with exterior ceremonies, rites, and confessions of faith, had now merely traded this Catholic yoke for an evangelical bridle. In place of the Roman papacy, the reformers had substituted a "new papacy"—the established church and its external regulation of the faith in league with the secular magistrates.[23] And for the Catholic idols of ceremony and tradition, they had substituted a new idolatrous "god"—the "paper papacy" (*papieren Papst*) of the Scriptures.[24] Franck contended that the reformers placed too much emphasis on the written Scriptures (the "letter") as the standard for judging belief, further arguing that the true and pure meaning of Scripture, and of Divine Revelation in

---

[22] Sebastian Franck, *Chronica und Beschreibung der Türkei* (Nürnberg, 1530), sig. K iii^r: "das man alle ausserlich predig, ceremoni, sacrament, ban, beruss, als unnotig wil auss dem weg raumen und glat ein unsichtpar geistlich kirchen in ainigleit des geist und glauben versamlet unter allen voldern und allein durchs ewig unsichtbar wort von Got on ainich eusserlich mittel regiert wil anrichte als seidie Apostolisch kirch bald nach der Apostel abgang." Franck would argue similarly in his 1531 *Letter to John Campanus*: "I believe that the outward church of Christ, including all its gifts and sacraments, because of the breaking in and laying waste by Antichrist right after the death of the apostles, went up into heaven and lies concealed in the Spirit and in truth." ET in *Spiritual and Anabaptist Writers*, ed. George H. Williams and Angel M. Mergal [LCC 25] (The Westminster Press, 1958), 149. Franck's epistle was published in Latin but survives only in German and Dutch translations.

[23] Franck, *Letter to Campanus*, LCC 25:151. Vigilantly opposed to the Reformers' Old Testament argument for the validity of a Christian civil magistrate, Franck wrote to his colleague, "but this remains a firm sentence: If the priesthood cannot be re-established out of the old law, neither can [Christian] government and outward government be established according to the law of Moses. Yet the Evangelicals at court are now fashioning for the princes another [rule] and nicely press the sword into their hands and, as the proverb has it, pour oil into the fire."

[24] In the same letter, Franck accused the evangelicals of "crowding the Spirit" into the text of the Bible, making Scripture their "god" (LCC 25:159).

general, is spiritual and is communicated to the Christian conscience by the immediate operation of God's Spirit.[25] Writing from Strasbourg to John Campanus—a radical Lutheran turned Anabaptist—in 1531, Franck urged his friend and colleague to avoid the temptation to be "addicted to the letter of Scripture," but instead "interpret the Scripture as a confirmation of your conscience, so that it testifies to the heart and not against it." For Franck, the conscience—"God in [the] heart"—supersedes the authority of the Scriptural text.[26] Included in Franck's spiritualism was a rejection of Old Testament figures as exemplars for Christian behavior. The Old Testament is, as a whole, consumed with law, shadows, and external ceremonies—an "empty quiver."[27] The New Testament, by contrast, is consumed by the freedom of the Spirit and "a good conscience" that resists all outward displays of piety and forms of discipline and rests only in the "righteousness of heart" that exists "in the Spirit."[28]

Schwenckfeld, a mystic-spiritualist sharing many of Franck's ideas, also excoriated the evangelical movement for its perceived lack of moral acuity. Arriving in Strasbourg in 1529 to seek asylum in the reputably tolerant city, Schwenckfeld quickly attracted the critical attention of Bucer, due in part to his vocal opposition toward the external ministry and discipline of the church.[29] In a manner similar to Franck, Schwenckfeld resisted all forms of outward regulation of Christian faith and conduct, insisting that true religion is guided by the inner word of the Spirit rather than the transitory, external letter of Scripture. "The Word of God is free," he had written in his 1527 *De Cursu Verbi Dei*; it "does not cling to visible things, nor to the official ministry," but belongs to a separate, invisible order.[30] His emphasis on the invisible character and immediate action of the word of God sharply contrasted

---

[25] Lecler, *Toleration and the Reformation*, 1:168–69. In his *Letter to Campanus*, Franck's virulent opposition to evangelical preaching and the external ministry of the gospel is unmistakable: "They preach without any fruit, for they are not sent of God but instead retch out the Word solely according to the letter, soiled with human filth, not according to the divine sense. For they also don't know another word to say but what is Scriptural, and of no other teachers except their evangelists" (LCC 25:158).

[26] Franck, *Letter to Campanus*, LCC 25:159.

[27] Franck, *Letter to Campanus*, LCC 25:151.

[28] Franck, *Paradoxa ducenta octoginta* (Rabe, 1558), *Paradoxa* 89, p. 116: "ein gut gwissen ... gerechtigkeit dess hertzen ... im geist."

[29] Lecler, *Toleration and the Reformation*, 1:178.

[30] Caspar Schwenckfeld, *De Cursu Verbi Dei* (Basel: Thomas Wolff, 1527), sig. A [vi]ʳ: "Cursus verbi dei vivi, liber est, non haeret in visibilibus ... sed totus in invisibilibus quiescit." On Franck and Schwenkfeld's radical spiritualism, see also Emmet McLaughlin, "Spiritualism: Schwenckfeld and Franck and the Early Modern Resonances," in *A Companion to Anabaptism and Spiritualism, 1521–1700*, ed. John D. Roth and James M. Stayer (Leiden: Brill, 2007), 119–62.

the reformers' insistence on the Pauline assertion that faith came through the audible proclamation and reception of the gospel.[31] But, like Franck, Schwenckfeld argued that the reformers' appeal to Scripture as the principal authority for faith and life merely confused the spirit of the gospel with its letter, squelching the free work of the Spirit upon the believer's conscience by the external regulation of religion. To be of "good conscience," according to Schwenckfeld, was not to bind oneself to the biblical script, as Luther and the other reformers taught, but rather to have one's carnal conscience purified by Christ's blood and renewed by the Spirit.[32]

Franck's and Schwenckfeld's withering critiques of the evangelicals immediately called into question the legitimacy of the Strasbourg reform project. Their arguments signaled, moreover, that a clash of consciences had ensued, having wide-ranging implications for the doctrinal, social, and political Reformation of the city. The fragmentary records available from these critical early years of reform indicate a variety of ways that the civil and church leaders navigated the challenging terrain of reform carved out by frequent and often-conflicting appeals to conscience. They show that the reformers and magistrates alike sought ways to protect what they believed in their own consciences to be their God-ordained prerogatives, while also seeking to dispel a rising suspicion that they were attempting to establish a "new papacy" in the city, including the re-institution of practices that some claimed were an unwarranted burden on the consciences of its inhabitants.[33]

2.2.2. The General Synod of 1533 and Its Aftermath

The initial steps taken by ecclesiastical leaders to combat the objections of Franck, Schwenckfeld, and many like-minded citizens reflect something of the delicate balance they were seeking to achieve. They remained focused on the necessary task of organizing and enforcing the Reformation in the city, while at the same time explicitly trying to avoid the troubling

---

[31] Schwenckfeld, *De Cursu Verbi Dei*, sig. A [vi]ʳ: "Age probemus nunc exemplis scripturae operatio nem dei, sive doctrinam spiritus semper praecedere. Et fidem non esse ex audita externo tantum."

[32] In his treatise on the good and evil conscience, entitled *Bom guten und bosen gewissen, anzeigun ge auss heileger Schrifft* (1529), Schwenckfeld declares that a person with a "good conscience" has "a heart above all external things." Since one's conscience "knows how to act for God" by the direct witness of the Spirit, all externals are irrelevant to the Christian life, including outward religious obligations. See *Corpus Schwenckfeldianorum* (CS), ed. Chester David Hartranft (Leipzig: Breitkopf & Härtel, 1913), 3:459.28–31. For the entire treatise, see pp. 440–69 (#82).

[33] Wendel, *L'Église de Strasbourg*, 72.

accusation that they were injuring consciences by forcing people to hold certain beliefs. Thus, shortly before November 30, 1532, the preachers and the *Kirchenpfleger*—a lay committee tasked with overseeing the doctrinal and personal fidelity of the parish pastors—petitioned the city council to call a synod where they might offer various suggestions for improvement in the city, including establishing doctrinal and administrative standards for the church, addressing diaconal matters, and—of greatest concern—dealing with the disruption of religious dissidents.[34] Arguing that bringing the holy gospel to fruition in the city required visible statutes for organizing and judging true religion, Bucer and Capito's appeal for a general synod of the Strasbourg church nevertheless attempted to diffuse the complaint that they were forcing beliefs on its inhabitants' consciences. In calling for the synod, they insisted that its efforts to establish commands and ordinances for the church intended "not at all, as quite a few assert, to force [people] to believe, but to abolish the blatant abuse" of holy Scripture as well as to protect the divine rights of the Christian magistrates.[35]

The city council approved the preachers' request, stipulating that a presynod should first convene in order to approve the final draft of the *Articles of Faith* (1533) that Bucer had earlier composed. This statement of faith specifically conveyed the notion that the magistrates were instilled with the divine authority to regulate the conduct of its citizens, punish false worship, and promote the ministers' preaching of sound doctrine in accord with God's commandments.[36] The articles also reflected the traditional Cyprianic theme that forgiveness of sins is conveyed, at least normatively, through the ministry of the visible church. Thus, by means of an "associative relationship," Strasbourg's ecclesiastical and lay civil leaders moved forward with their plans to define in a public way what was to be accepted as true religion in the city.[37] Yet—as we will see—they did so cautiously, sensitive to how their reforms appeared to the public eye, and all the while vying for their

---

[34] QGT 7:575-77, #348 (shortly before November 30, 1532). The *Kirchenpfleger* was instituted by an ordinance passed on October 30, 1531, which assigned parish overseers to supervise the proclamation of sound doctrine and control good order in church and society. For more information about the *Kirchenpfleger* and its tasks during this period, see Wendel, *L'Église de Strasbourg*, 45; and Chrisman, *Strasbourg and the Reform*, 209-32.

[35] QGT 7:575, #348: "Soliche gepot vnnd ordnung machen... ist gar nicht, als etliche aussgiessen, zum glauben zwingen, sonder offenlich ergernüss."

[36] QGT 8: 4-8, #358 (April 1533) contains a record of Bucer sending his rough draft of the *Articles*—originally comprised of twenty-two articles, then later trimmed to sixteen—to Capito, Hedio, and Zell. The *Glaubensartikel* eventually approved at the general synod are recorded in QGT 8:25-32, #371 (shortly before May 31, 1533).

[37] Chrisman, *Strasbourg and the Reform*, 212.

own institutional prerogatives in the struggle for doctrinal, social, and political order.

By the time the general synod commenced on June 10, 1533, the *Articles* had been thoroughly dissected, in no small measure, by Anton Engelbrecht, a parish pastor who attacked proposals regarding the rights of the magistrate to punish heresy and bind consciences to certain beliefs. During his participation in the pre-synod, Engelbrecht complained that the preachers' tactics for acquiring doctrinal uniformity would simply confuse the Strasbourgeois. His remarks contained an explicit charge: the people would notice the blatant contradiction between the preachers' initial message of the freedom of conscience and their now papist-like attempts to enforce the obligation of faith by employing the arm of the magistrates.[38] Engelbrecht specifically accused Bucer of allowing "the government to encroach upon individual freedom of conscience, thus expanding the realm of the *externa* at the cost of the individual's personal convictions."[39] The Articles were nevertheless approved by the synod after only a brief period of debate.[40]

Although resistance to the city's statement of faith had proved unsuccessful at halting its ratification, the accusations of Engelbrecht, Schwenckfeld, and others apparently disrupted the internal peace of the Reformed ministers. The synodical records show that in the months surrounding the general assembly, the Strasbourg preachers repeatedly felt the need to defend their ministry and interpretation of Scripture in the face of their opponents' attacks—notably, on the basis of their own "good conscience." In August 1533, the preachers responded to Schwenckfeld directly by letter, insisting on the faithfulness and fruitfulness of their gospel ministry. They were convinced, on account of the certainty of conscience granted by the Spirit of God, that they had proclaimed the singular truth of Christ.[41] A few months later,

---

[38] QGT 8:57, #374 (June 3–6, 1533): "Die Prediger, die zuerst für die Freiheit des Glaubens gepredigt haben, können nicht jetzt das Gegenteil lehren: das Volk würde den Widerspruch zu sehr merken; auch würde man damit das Papsttum bestätigen."

[39] Marijn de Kroon, "Martin Bucer and the Problem of Tolerance," *SCJ* 19, no. 2 (1988): 165. Later in the pre-synod deliberations, Engelbrecht voiced his own conscientious fear that he would be forced to affirm something contrary to his own words and confessions. See QGT 8:58, #374 (June 3–6, 1533).

[40] QGT 8:70, #384 (June 10–14, 1533; Protokoll der Haupttagung der Synode: Zensur der Landgemeinden und Annahme der Glaubensartikel durch dieselben). Following the formal approval of the Articles on June 10, the synod proceeded to hear the arguments of the sectarian radicals during June 11–14. See also Chrisman, *Strasbourg and the Reform*, 217, and Wendel, *L'Église de Strasbourg*, 72, 76, which identify Engelbrecht's driving concern that the *papaut* would be reinstated in Strasbourg if the Articles failed to distinguish adequately between the magistrate's external authority and the spiritual government of the church.

[41] QGT 8:126, #418 (August 1533; Schreiben der Straßburger Prediger an Schwenckfeld): "der geist gottis in vnseren gewissenn zeugniß gibt."

in October, the ministers submitted a counter-answer to Schwenckfeld's recent *Schutzschrift* (letter of defense). In it they reiterated to their opponent, "we know that we preach the Word of God," standing firm with a good conscience [*mit guten gewißenn*] against his erroneous teachings that manifestly divide the church.[42] In the same response, after acknowledging their commitment to the principle of acting freely according to one's own conscience, the Strasbourg preachers effectually denied that Schwenckfeld's own appeals to conscience were valid because he could not prove to them on the basis of the Holy Scriptures that they were wrong and he was right, and because his teachings only served to destroy the churches and the work of God. Conversely, the preachers insisted, "we could bear witness with divine Scripture and our good conscience... that we were preaching the gospel."[43] Quite evidently, the Reformed preachers did not believe that all arguments made on the basis of individual freedom were necessarily made in "good conscience." Rather, the proof of a good conscience was inextricably tied to a person's conformity to Holy Scripture and the apparent fruitfulness of one's ministry.

The Strasbourg preachers' defense of their ministry—partly on the basis of conscience—reflects the conclusions of the synod itself, which closed on June 14 after four days of lengthy debate between Bucer and several leading religious dissidents, including—in addition to Schwenckfeld—the Anabaptists Clement Ziegler, Melchior Hofmann, Claus Frey, and Martin Stor.[44] The overwhelming verdict of Bucer and the general assembly was that the sectarians had not proved from Scripture that anything the Reformers and magistrates had mandated for the city was wrong. The prevailing complaint that the magistrate's role in overseeing religious order and discipline was a harmful imposition on the freedom of conscience simply could not be substantiated on a scriptural basis, for the conscience did not exist as its own seat of authority apart from or in contradiction to the word of God. The Strasbourg authorities insisted that the dissidents' divisive stance was, in fact,

---

[42] QGT 8:163–64, #435a (between October 10 and 19, 1533): "Wir wissen, das wir das ... wort gottes predigen."
[43] QGT 8:165, #435a (between October 10 and 19, 1533): "Vnnd das könden wir also zeugen mit zeugnus göttlicher schrifft vnnd vnseres gutten gewisses ... das wir das war euangeli warlich predigen."
[44] Chrisman, *Strasbourg and the Reform*, 218. After the four-day back-and-forth between Bucer and his Anabaptist opponents, the articles remained fixed, and Capito closed the session. See QGT 8:70, #384 (June 1–4, 1533; Verhör der Sektierer).

manifestly *unbiblical*, especially due to its blatant lack of conformity to the rule of love that establishes a good conscience.

Several things were thus accomplished almost immediately after the general synod of 1533, at least from the perspective of the ecclesiastical leaders. The meeting drew clear lines of demarcation between those who were committed to orthodox doctrine and social concord, and those who willingly fostered division by exalting personal conviction. A new church order (*Kirchenordnung*) for managing the doctrinal beliefs and personal conduct of clerics and laity alike emerged in seed-form from the proceedings.[45] In the immediate aftermath of the synod, the Reformed preachers were also constructing a common defense of their own ministries on the basis of conscience and the word of God. In so doing, they worked against the idea that someone could legitimately appeal to the private conscience in order to justify a freewheeling and divisive spirit. The clergy were convinced that Holy Scripture should judge all appeals to conscience, and from their perspective the synod had, at least in part, achieved the goal of distinguishing orthodox appeals to conscience from unorthodox ones.

Nevertheless, to the reformers' great frustration, the synod left some critical matters unsettled. Chrisman notes that, in the end, the synod "only partially achieved its aim. An orthodox doctrine had been agreed upon, but no provisions had been made to preserve and protect it beyond the very general statement with regard to the powers of the magistrates."[46] And in the meantime, Schwenckfeld continued to protest what he believed to be violations of conscience committed by the religious "tyranny . . . of the secular government," a complaint he voiced in several letters to Leo Jud during the spring of 1533, in which he argued that magisterial judgment over religious matters harmfully blurred the distinction between the "two kingdoms"—that of Christ and this world.[47] Anabaptist activism also continued unabated following the general synod, and Bucer complained to his colleague, Heinrich Bullinger, that the attacks of the "Catabaptists" against the officials of the church proved they were enemies of the truth.[48]

---

[45] Kittelson, *Toward an Established Church*, 40.

[46] Chrisman, *Strasbourg and the Reform*, 218. QGT 8:91–92, #387 (June 16, 1533) records that several prominent sectarians, including Hoffman, Schwenckfeld, Claus Frey, and Martin Stor, initially resisted questions posed by the synod, although the Council determined that they should nevertheless come to address the body. The conclusion of the general assembly by no means quelled vocal opposition to the synod's decisions.

[47] For Schwenckfeld's letters to Leo Jud, see Lecler, *Toleration and the Reformation*, 1:181–82, and CS 4:413–44 (#125), 4:752–53 (#135).

[48] QGT 8:201–202, #447 (October 29, 1533; Bucer an Bullinger—Lange Ausführungen über die Pflichten der Obrigkeit in Religionssachen).

During the unsettling months that followed the close of the synod, the reformers appealed to the magistrates by stressing the urgent need for official control over the implementation of the synodical decisions. Various proposals for the consolidation of religious instruction and moral discipline were presented to the city council, but at year's close the magistrates had taken no real action to carry them out.[49] Worse still—from the vantage point of most (though not all) of the preachers—was the growing sense of caution (perhaps second thoughts) among government leaders about their own role in the establishment and regulation of public religious norms. The preachers were accustomed to hearing the voices of Engelbrecht and Schwenckfeld protesting lay and clerical oversight of religion in Strasbourg, but now a "vague and undefined resistance to the new order" was arising from within "the government itself."[50] A precedential sentiment among the Strasbourg magistrates—conveyed as early as 1525—was circulating among the lay rulers, namely, the belief that their commitment to Holy Scripture did not necessarily permit them to constrain other people's consciences.[51] Even during the autumn session of the 1533 synodal assembly—a meeting largely aimed at establishing orthodox doctrine and orderly church polity— the magistrates urged patience and told the clergy, "the council does not want to force anyone's conscience."[52] Indeed, the Strasbourg political leaders were so hesitant to acquiesce to the reformers' calls for an official establishment of the synodical decrees that they dragged their feet in granting formal approval and publication of the proposed church order until late 1534.[53]

By January 1534 the clergy became so impatient with what they saw as inexcusable inactivity on the part of the magistrates that they acted on their own. During the formal seating of the new Rat officers, subsequent to their annual oath of service, Hedio rose to preach a lively sermon (*Ratspredigt*)

---

[49] Chrisman, *Strasbourg and the Reform*, 219.

[50] Kittelson, *Toward an Established Church*, 40. Kittelson reveals that, even Matthew Zell, one of the earliest Reformed preachers in Strasbourg, expressed occasional ambivalence toward confessions of faith and demands for subscription—as did his wife Katherina, who defended Schwenckfeld and others against the reformers' "tyranny" (p. 41).

[51] *Politische Correspondenz der Stadt Strassburg im Zeitalter der Reformation*, vol. 1 (1517–1530), ed. Hans Virck. Urkunden und Akten der Stadt Strassburg, 2. Abt. Strasbourg, 1882, #225 (April 27, 1525). State records indicate that, already in 1525, the Strasbourg rulers were holding sympathetic conversations with the public over expressed concerns that the people were being forced to observe certain "words" and "letters" set forth by the civil authorities.

[52] QGT 8:178, #441 (October 23 and 29, 1533): "so dan ein ersamer rath nit willens, jemans sein gmüt zwingen, hat mans bey demselben bleiben lassen." ET in Abray, "Confession, Conscience and Honour," 98–99.

[53] Kittelson, *Toward an Established Church*, 40. For a thorough summary and interpretation of these events, also see Chrisman, *Strasbourg and the Reform*, 201–31.

from the cathedral lectern, in which he strongly urged the civil authorities to fulfill their God-given religious duties on behalf of the city and its people. Hedio's sermon reflected the reformers' original conception of a united, godly society, wherein preachers (*Predigern*), schoolmasters (*Schulmeistern*), and civil authorities (*Obrigkeit*) worked side by side to foster a society knit together by a commitment to sound doctrine and the Christian rule of love and charity. At the height of his sermonic appeal—and with clear reference to the sectarians' complaint that the preachers were forcing belief upon them—Hedio declared, "indeed, that is why there is the harmful, toxic opinion that Satan is driving . . . [when] he says, the civil authorities should not burden themselves with matters of religion."[54] His call to the lay magistrates could not have been more direct: they had been charged by God with the authority and the duty to protect the faithful ministry of the word, establish religious standards for the city, and act swiftly against any dissident group whose ideas and behavior disrupted the church's peace and purity. But the sermon elicited no response from its hearers, and in the weeks that followed, the reformers threatened from their pulpits to censure the magistrate's dereliction of duty.[55]

Palpable feelings of exasperation were conveyed by the Reformed ministers during this time, in no small measure due to the magistrate's reluctance to fulfill its religious duties based on a rather ambiguous understanding of the freedom of conscience. As we have seen, the reformers were neither insensitive to complaints that they were "new papists"—they specifically sought ways to alleviate fears associated with that charge—nor did they disagree with the principle that it was wrong to compel someone to believe something against his or her will. They did, nevertheless, make an important distinction between the coercion of consciences and the necessary regulation of doctrine and practice in a deliberately Reformed society.[56] In an earlier exchange with Bullinger, dated October 29, 1533, Bucer acknowledged the widely circulated objection that "no one ought to be compelled to faith, since faith cannot be governed by the sword." Indeed, "what they are saying is true," he conceded, "but not to the point." Contrary to the explicit claims of Franck, Schwenckfeld, and the Strasbourg Anabaptists, and in further contradiction

---

[54] For Hedio's *Ratspredigt uber die Pflichten der Obrigkeit*, see QGT 8:262–63, #492 (January 14, 1534): "darumb ists ja ein schedliche, giftige, geschwinde meynung, die sathan ytzund treybt . . . so er sagt, die oberkeit soll sich der religionsachen nit beladen" (p. 263).
[55] Chrisman, *Strasbourg and the Reform*, 221.
[56] As Hedio's *Ratspredigt* also emphasized to the sitting magistrates. See QGT 8:262, #492 (January 14, 1534): "*Die Prediger haben nichts unterlassen um die notwendigen Reformen anzuregen. . . .*" Emphasis original.

to the suspicions of some pastors and politicians, the reformers did "not wish to push faith" on the people, "but rather the doctrine of the faith; that is, not to be coercive in instances of faithlessness but of blasphemy. Faith and faithlessness are matters of the soul, which no person can judge."[57] In this respect, the important distinction between the "inner" person and "external matters"—so prominently featured in the arguments of the sectarians—was not absent from the reformers' own vocabulary. Indeed, a central feature of sixteenth-century Protestant thought was the insistence that one's faith and conscience were impervious to the judgments of all human authority. God was the sole witness and judge of the individual conscience.[58]

What Bucer and his colleagues could not abide, however, was the idea that the private conscience held absolute sovereignty over matters of doctrine and public life. No one, they argued, could justly appeal to the freedom of conscience in order to validate holding unbiblical, blasphemous beliefs. Thus, while personal faith remained the property of the individual conscience alone, enforcing "the doctrine of the faith" and establishing good order were altogether different matters. Coexistent with the free, internal domain of faith and conscience is the realm of temporal authority—"the area of the community, with its economic, social, political, juridical, and religious aspects."[59] The reformers generally acknowledged that this kingdom of law, order, and duty, albeit temporal and passing away, was nevertheless ordained by God as a means to restrain vice and promote virtue in society, as well as to protect (ideally) the sacred ministry of the gospel and the church's care of souls.[60] Within the framework of these "two kingdoms," therefore, the reformers

---

[57] QGT 8:201–202, #447 (October 29, 1533; Bucer an Bullinger—Lange Ausführungen über die Pflichten der Obrigkeit in Religionssachen): "Obijctur et illud: ad fidem neminem debere compelli, fidem non posse regi gladio. Quae vera sunt, sed nihil ad rem dicta. Non fidem, sed doctrinam fidei promoueri volumus, ita non perfidiam, sed blasphemias coerceri. Fides et perfidia cordium sunt, quae nemo hominum iudicare potest" (p. 202).

[58] See, e.g., the poetic "exhortation to spiritual judgment" composed by Strasbourg pastor, Wolfgang Schultheiß, which expresses concern for freedom of conscience and peace amid religious disputes, in QGT 7:291–97, #236a (1530). De Kroon notes that "this area [internal freedom from all human authority], it seems, was in the sixteenth century a realm of personal freedom of conscience acknowledged and respected by all, within which religious tolerance was de facto possible and realizable" ("Martin Bucer and the Problem of Tolerance," 161).

[59] De Kroon, "Martin Bucer and the Problem of Tolerance," 161.

[60] In his small treatise, *Concerning the True Care of Souls* (1538), Bucer would later argue that "orderly punishment" could be used well as a means to compel the doctrinally lax to amend their ways for the good of church and society: "our kind God bestows his grace and success as much on orderly punishment and force to urge people to forsake evil lusts and desires and turn to sound doctrine and thus to conscientious well-doing, as he does on other words and works which he has ordained for the salvation of mankind." ET in Martin Bucer, *Concerning the True Care of Souls*, trans. Peter Beale (East Peoria, IL: The Banner of Truth Trust, 2009), 83.

understood that civil peace and order could not strictly be divorced from one's internal faith and service of God and neighbor.[61]

In his 1530 dedication to the University of Marburg for the second edition of his commentary on the gospels, Bucer had commented on the extent to which doctrinal deviance could be tolerated among the Christian churches in the name of freedom of conscience. He found his answer in "Paul's words in I Tim. 1:5, where Paul encourages love, which comes from a pure heart, a good conscience, and sincere faith." Faith in Christ and love for fellow Christians are essential to the "doctrina pietatis."[62] The final draft of the *Glaubensartikel* likewise addressed Anabaptist resistance to civil responsibility by explaining the communal nature of the "True Church." Bucer emphasized that, because the church is composed of Christians united to Christ and one another by the body and blood of their Savior, true believers ought to live in harmony, with their first concern being not for the individual but for the admonition and spiritual betterment of the whole—a message he had earlier propounded in his 1523 treatise, "One Should Not Live for Oneself Alone but for Others, and How to Go About It."[63] The reformers were convinced that beliefs and practices violating the rule of love and charity could not be justly claimed to be made in "good conscience."

Shortly after 1530, Johannes Brenz, a colleague and reformer of Württemberg, had also questioned whether religious dissidents could justly appeal to conscience in their opposition to secular and ecclesiastical

---

[61] For recent summaries of the prevalence of "two kingdoms" thought among the early modern reformers, consult William J. Wright, *Martin Luther's Understanding of God's Two Kingdoms: A Response to the Challenge of Skepticism* (Grand Rapids, MI: Baker Academic, 2010); Witte, *Law and Protestantism*, chapter 3, "A Mighty Fortress: Luther and the Two Kingdoms Framework," 87–117; and Matthew J. Tuininga, *Calvin's Political Theology and the Public Engagement of the Church: Christ's Two Kingdoms* (Cambridge: Cambridge University Press, 2017), chapter 1, "Two Swords, Two Powers, or Two Kingdoms: Spiritual and Political Authority in Early Modern Europe," 23–60.

[62] De Kroon, "Martin Bucer and the Problem of Tolerance," 158.

[63] QGT 8:28, #371 (1533; Die der Synode Vorgelegten Glaubens artikel). For a summary of Bucer's 1523 treatise on the Christian's communal responsibilities, see Ozment, *The Reformation in the Cities*, 63–67. This same concern for the rule of love and charity pervades the Tetrapolitan Confession (see Chapter 5 in this volume). Paul P. Peachey, "The Radical Reformation, Political Pluralism, and the Corpus Christianorum," in *The Origins and Characteristics of Anabaptism: Proceedings of the Colloquium Organized by the Faculty of Protestant Theology of Strassburg*, ed. Marc Lienhard (The Hague, Netherlands: Martinus Nijhoff, 1977), 21, notes that much of the conflict between the reformers and their sectarian opponents stemmed from their divergent social models. Whereas the reformers held a "holistic" view of society, in which each segment of society served the good of the whole, Anabaptists and other radical groups followed an "elementarist" vision that saw "reality vested in the units," which jeopardized the integrity of the larger social construct. To the extent that the reformers in Strasbourg were building on centuries of precedence for the construction of their social model, whereas sectarians were searching for a social model that did not yet exist, the Anabaptists and related groups seemed genuinely "radical" to most of the Strasbourgeois.

authorities. The title of his treatise puts this question in proper focus: "Do secular authorities oppress a man's conscience when they uproot false doctrine, and can this same authority force dissenters to change their belief against their conscience?" Brenz's answer, not surprisingly, was that "no violence is done to the conscience when punishments are imposed on" religious sectarians, even if they "believe that their teachings are consistent with the Word of God." Like Bucer and the Strasbourg preachers, Brenz agreed that "it is no doubt wrong for a man to oppress, upset or afflict the conscience of anyone," since "nobody but God knows the heart and conscience of man . . . and can rule and order them." Nevertheless, Brenz insisted that appeals to conscience must be judged by the standard of truth. He went so far as to say, "there is . . . no conscience without truth." Those who hold unorthodox and blasphemous ideas are "deceived by the devil" and thus "have no conscience properly speaking, but only a fictitious and degraded conscience." He concluded, therefore, that whenever an erroneous person obstinately presumes to "bring up his conscience as a pretext for refusing to listen or to receive the wholesome teaching of the divine truth," godly authorities are compelled to "punish or expel" that person. In doing so, they do not actually oppress the conscience; rather, their correction "helps man to acquire that straight and good conscience, to wipe off the mark or stigma of the beast, and to attain the truth." Brenz's comments closely resemble the thoughts of Luther, who argued that without the normative truth of Holy Scripture on one's side, a "good conscience" was not possible.[64] Thus, for the reformers, freedom of the conscience, however much it was meant to be liberated from external, human coercion, did not entail freedom to believe and practice whatever religion one wished, or to act in ways that violated the rule of love and charity. Moreover, Christian doctrine and practice "as taught in pulpit and classroom"—and codified in the creeds and confessions—"were matters

---

[64] *Ob eine Obrigkeit wenn sie falsche Lehre ausrottet, darum uber die Gewissen herrsche, und ob von der Obrigkeit die Irrigen wider ihr Gewissen tönnen zu anderen Glauben gezwungen werden.* The section of Brenz's treatise dealing with the magistrates and conscience is found in F. Bidenbach, *Consiliorum Theologorum Decas 3, Consilium 9* (Frankfurt, 1611), 196–202. ET in Lecler, *Toleration and the Reformation*, 1:250–53. Likewise, in his *On Secular Authority: To What Extent It Should be Obeyed* (1523), Luther argues that a person is in error if his beliefs and practice lack clear scriptural warrant: "Whoever believes something to be right that is wrong or uncertain is denying the truth, which is God himself. He is believing in lies and errors, and counting as right that which is wrong." ET in Hans J. Hillerbrand, ed., *The Annotated Luther: Vol. 5, Christian Life in the World* (Minneapolis, MN: Fortress Press, 2016), 109; WA 11:262. These comments by Luther and then Brenz reflect discussions about the so-called erroneous conscience stretching back to Augustine and Abelard.

for public agreement; consequently, they were rightfully a concern of the Christian magistrates."[65]

Eventually, on March 4, 1534, the Strasbourg civil leaders took formal action in response to the ministers' overtures for ecclesiastical organization. They approved what the synod had recommended, that the Tetrapolitan Confession and the *Articles*—mostly the products of Bucer's pen—be received as the city's official doctrinal standards. The Rat also required that anyone not complying with these articles should leave the city within eight days.[66] Although acceding to the ministers' appeals for an official confession, the magistrates nevertheless vacillated on the extent to which these articles should be the standard for judging the religious life of the city's inhabitants. Members of government remained sensitive to the lay complaint that the Reformation was creating a new papacy, and repeatedly expressed its hesitancy to bind anyone's conscience to what the preachers taught.[67] When the Tetrapolitan Confession came under the review of the council, its members insisted that copies be distributed so they could study it at their own pace, "because it is very long, so that we could hardly hear it in a day at the Council or nobody would sit until the end [of the Confession], and when we reach the end, we would have forgotten the beginning."[68] Later that March, as various councilors voiced their opinion of the proposed articles of faith, one city official, Carl Mieg, conveyed his suspicion—albeit not outright dislike—of the Tetrapolitan, saying that as a layman, he hoped that he would not be trapped into that which he did not understand and then forced to believe and confess it.[69] State records indicate that several other council members remained

---

[65] Kittelson, *Toward an Established Church*, 41. For a corroborating conclusion, see Jordan J. Ballor, "Discipline, Excommunication, and the Limits of Conscience: Magisterial Protestant Perspectives on Church and Civil Authority in the Era of the Reformation," in *Das Gewissen in den Rechtslehren der protestantischen und katholischen Reformationen*, ed. Michael Germann and Wim Decock (Leipzig: Evangelische Verlagsanstalt, 2017),119–23.

[66] Chrisman, *Strasbourg and the Reform*, 221–22; QGT 8:301, #535 (April 13, 1534).

[67] Chrisman, *Strasbourg and the Reform*, 222, reveals that, although the Rat established an official requirement that civil officials should attend weekly Sunday sermon, while also encouraging church attendance among the guilds, they did so "hesitantly, since it smacked of a new papacy." Burnett, "Church Discipline," 441, also notes that, in 1535, the senators expressed hesitation to grant the pastors authority to mandate catechism attendance. The rulers "acknowledged that it certainly was desirable that everyone attended the quarterly catechisms along with wife, children and servants, but they were convinced that such attendance could not be compelled."

[68] Wendel, *L'Église de Strasbourg*, 112, quoting Sébastien Brant's *Annales*. Wendel shows that, although the Council decided with a majority vote to maintain the Strasbourg Confession (Tetrapolitan) and the XVI Articles, the body also heard a number of opposing voices (pp. 109–111).

[69] QGT 8:294, #523 (March 20, 1534; Verschiedene Ratsherren sagen ihre Meinung betr. der Tetrapolitana und der 16 Glaubensartikel der Synode): "Carl Mieg will dem, so m. h. h. erkennen, nicht zuwider seyn, hoff aber doch nicht, daß er gefangen sei als ein lai, was er nicht verstände, daß ers eben also glauben und bekennen muss."

personally ambivalent about the Tetrapolitan, including one who favored resistance to it, as well as another who complained that a later confession, the Formula of Concord, was "over his head and [he] hoped his conscience would not be bound to it."[70] A year later, in 1535—as Schwenckfeld and the Anabaptists remained firmly insistent that Christian freedom in the Spirit was directly opposed to the imposition of articles of faith—the Strasbourg Ammeister (chief oligarchs)[71] felt obligated to change the wording of an oath due to the misunderstanding of some who claimed that the magistrates were forcing them to "swear to believe what the preachers teach."[72]

As the above records show, the civil authorities remained "conservative and cautious" in their approach to the organization of the church all throughout the process of public reform in Strasbourg during the early 1530s. On matters of conscience, including forcing public confession of faith and disciplining unorthodox beliefs, the magistrate always made sure to retain its authoritative advantage over the ecclesiastical leaders. In the end, the ordinance of 1534 again failed to quell the ministers' disappointment in the regime's reluctance to embrace their far-reaching methods and aspirations for reform. During the decades that followed, the reformers would occasionally resort to subterfuge as an alternative way of accomplishing their vision of church discipline—including forming secret committees and holding lay interviews without the magistrate's approval—but these methods were quickly discovered and the clergy reprimanded.[73] As Chrisman notes, the magistrate was

---

[70] See Appendix A in Abray, *The People's Reformation*, 229–41, which records some of the activities and confessional opinions of the *Ratscherren*. E.g., Philips von Kageneck admitted of having no opinion on the Tetrapolitan Confession in 1534 (p. 235); as did Jacob Meyer, although he favored resistance in 1547 (p. 237). Barthel Keller expressed concern in 1577 that he could not bind his conscience to a confession (the Formula of Concord) beyond his comprehension (p. 235). Abray's summary is largely based on the Ratsprotokolle, minutes of the Senate and XXI, Archives municipales de Strasbourg, and the study of Thomas A. Brady, Jr., *Ruling Class, Regime and Reformation at Strasbourg, 1520–1555* (Leiden: Brill, 1978).

[71] For more on the Strasbourg oligarchy and its political hierarchy, see Brady, *Ruling Class*, 163–96 (chap. 5).

[72] QGT 8:439, #647 (March 12, 1535): "sie sollten schwören zu glauben wie die prädikanten lehren...." The reformers' efforts to convince the magistrates of their sacred duty faced near-constant opposition during the second half of the decade. Schwenckfeld continued his onslaught against Bucer at the colloquy at Tubingen in 1535, on May 28, where he again accused him of looking to the empty letter of the Old Law to justify using the arm of civil authority to coercively establish religion—in particular, through binding articles of faith (Lecler, *Toleration and the Reformation*, 179).

[73] Chrisman, *Strasbourg and the Reform*, 222, 229–30. Both Chrisman and Abray, *The People's Reformation*, 199–201, show that, between 1544 and the early 1570s, the Reformed clergy employed several tactics to enact an orderly system of discipline behind the magistrates' back. Such plans included calling secret meetings for the preaching ministers to discuss matters of church discipline, as well as pre-communion lay interviews to examine parishioners' worthiness to partake of the eucharist. This latter practice was perhaps most suspect, given its similarity to the obligatory "papist confession" (even the ministers worried that the laity would fail see the subtle difference and

simply "unwilling to give the clergy the authority to maintain pure doctrine and was even less willing to give them the right to discipline the lay congregation."[74] Not to be circumvented by the reformers, the civic leaders kept their closest watch on the Strasbourg clerics: the preachers' ambitions for the church would remain subject to the magistrates' overpowering concern for lay consciences and, indeed, for their own.[75]

* * *

From the piecemeal records examined above, we now undertake "the precarious jump" from specific texts and contexts to advance some general observations about the diverse appeals to conscience during the early years of Strasbourg's Reformation.[76] We have seen that the project of consolidating reform in Strasbourg began as a mostly harmonious effort by the civil officials and clerics. The city's initial turn toward Protestant doctrine and worship in the early 1520s was largely of the magistrates' doing, and when Bucer and Capito arrived in 1523 to take leadership over the movement, it came with the immediate support of civil leaders who believed that sound preaching would go a long way toward establishing social peace and unity. The Reformed preachers likewise believed that the magistrates could help them create a well-ordered confessional church in the city. Temporal regents, they believed, had been granted the divine task of protecting true religion by enacting certain regulatory measures to establish a godly society under the authority of God's word. From the very beginning, then, the magistrates and reformers agreed on the general principle that Christian piety—the observance of true religion—was a matter of public importance and not something relegated to the individual conscience alone.

The proliferation of sectarian groups during the 1520s severely challenged this relative harmony. In addition to the radical civil views of the

---

become distressed of heart). In the end, the magistrates thoroughly rejected the ministers' proposal, reprimanded them for making their idea public before gaining the Rat's approval, and required all the preachers to "swear on their burgher's oath to do nothing until the regime authorized them to proceed" (Abray, *The People's Reformation*, 200). This matter of reformation-by-subterfuge raises interesting questions about whether the reformers could justly commit such trickery in "good conscience"—a topic for another study.

[74] Chrisman, *Strasbourg and the Reform*, 222, 224. QGT 8:354, #577 (June 19, 1534) records the magistrates' defense of the ministers, while also stressing that matters of faith should remain voluntary.

[75] Chrisman, *Strasbourg and the Reform*, 222–32.

[76] Heiko A. Oberman, "The Travail of Tolerance: Containing Chaos in Early Modern Europe," in Grell and Scribner, eds., *Tolerance and Intolerance*, 29.

Anabaptists, religious dissenters like Franck and Schwenckfeld called into question the very theological foundations upon which the agenda for holistic reform in Strasbourg had been constructed. Their adamant rejection of all external regulation of religion seriously challenged the notion that God had invested civil magistrates with the task of defending true religion and punishing heresy, while also disputing the legitimacy of the reformers' own calling and ministry. Perhaps most troubling of all was their proactive charge that the chosen methods for acquiring moral reform and urban peace were injurious to the individual conscience and contrary to the liberating work of God's Spirit. This form of argument, in no small measure because it dealt with the internalization of religion, signaled to the civil and church authorities that their initial decision to tolerate sectarian groups in Strasbourg—if left unchecked—would normalize conflicts between the desire for confessional uniformity and the adjoining impulse to conserve civic tranquility. All sides understood that the social and theological stakes were high, and that their dispute had direct implications for the freedom of conscience, the authoritative claims of God and Scripture, and the threat of social upheaval.

What the records of 1530–1535 reveal is that the disruption caused by sectarian appeals to conscience gradually polarized the civil and ecclesiastical leaders by pushing them toward their respective visions for reform. In their appeal to the magistrates for the general synod of 1533, the reformers attempted to make clear what were the necessary procedures for ensuring doctrinal conformity and spiritual discipline in the city. They fervently defended the coercive use of civil authority to promote reform by urging the magistrates to fulfill their God-ordained duties, all the while dismissing the complaint that this arrangement was at all injurious to the consciences of their opponents. Appealing to their own "good conscience," the preachers reminded everyone—laity and civil authorities alike—that all earthly courts of appeal, including that of the private conscience, were subject to the word of God that *they* preached. On the other hand, the same records reveal that the magistrates were far less willing than the reformers to dismiss claims that the coercive regulation of the doctrine of faith did harm to the private conscience, and more inclined to appeal to the supposedly troubled consciences of the laity as a cautionary means of staving off suspected attempts by the clergy to overstep their bounds of authority in the church and city. Indeed, in the aftermath of the synod, the civil authorities repeatedly expressed worry over the possibility of forcing people's consciences to do anything, albeit less from a concern for protecting doctrinal deviants and more out of an interest in preserving the social and political hierarchy by stamping out flames of religious tension in Strasbourg.

All of these competing interests and appeals complicate our ability to perceive an easy answer to the question of whether the Strasbourg pastors had succeeded at convincing the laity that their reform measures were not in conflict with the freedom of conscience. For the reformers, freedom of conscience mainly entailed personal liberation from the burdensome regulations of Catholicism, which they believed left people in a state of fear and uncertainty about one's eternal security. But this internal freedom certainly did not absolve a person from his or her responsibility as a member of an earthly community. The reformers insisted that one could be bound to certain regulations externally, for the good of the community, and yet be free spiritually from bondage to sin. Godly regulations—such as those proposed by the clergy and civil leaders—did not bind consciences if they were necessary for reform. Some of the means proposed for acquiring confessional uniformity might properly be indifferent in and of themselves, but once manifestly proved to be good for the unity and purity of the church, no cause for disobedience to the ordained authorities could remain. The reformers believed, fundamentally, that it was biblical preaching that quieted the conscience, and at least in this role they had succeeded at being faithful.

Nevertheless, the Strasbourg ministers expressed great frustration that religious dissidents, along with certain magistrates and laypeople, refused to yield to the formal regulation of sound doctrine on the basis of rather vague and obscure appeals to private conscience. For their own part, the preachers were convinced—on the basis of their own conscience under the direction of God's word, they claimed—that a good conscience existed only where someone had truly embraced the gospel. Only when true religion and right discipline had been accepted could good consciences truly exist and thrive. But the magistrates had not fulfilled their duty to create such a society; instead, they made ill-defined appeals to the freedom of conscience to avoid embracing the Reformed confessions to the extent demanded by the clergy. Thus, in the end, the profound misunderstandings about the nature of the conscience and its relation to God's word that permeated the earliest years of Strasbourg reform left the reformers dissatisfied and seeking alternative—sometimes clandestine—means of accomplishing their goals.

3

"Vera pietas veram confessionem parit"

Confession, Conscience, and Charity in the Anti-Nicodemism of Calvin and the Reformers

In the previous chapter we observed that Bucer and Capito's efforts to consolidate public reform in Strasbourg were driven by the idea that true religion should not be relegated to the individual soul or mind. Responding to complaints voiced by certain city magistrates and concerned citizens, as well as various stripes of Anabaptist and Spiritualist radicals, the reformers rejected the idea that the private conscience held total jurisdiction over matters of doctrine and communal life. The conscience, though free from the burden of false religion, remained ever-subject to the word of God, and might also be regulated by prudent means determined by civil and religious leaders to be necessary for enforcing sound doctrine in a well-ordered society. The Strasbourg reformers insisted, therefore, that genuine piety was not simply a private matter but should manifest itself externally through the public confession of faith.

The question of whether religious "externals"—oaths and vows, or any ceremonies relating to corporate worship and the public profession of faith—could be imposed upon Christians without doing injury to the conscience became especially significant to French Protestants living in territories not yet committed to the cause of the Reformation. The situation for sixteenth-century French Protestants was comparable to the challenges faced by early Christians languishing under Roman imperial rule. Protestants living in Catholic France faced rampant hostility to their newfound faith, including sporadic persecution that fostered the ever-present temptation to compromise or conceal their Reformed beliefs. Some feared that if they criticized the worship of Rome or made themselves scarce at Mass, the religious and civil authorities would strip them of their social position or, worse still, exact physical punishment upon them for rejecting Catholic worship. In response to such fears, certain Protestants sought to avoid suffering by simulating outward conformity to Catholic ceremonies, arguing that it was permissible to participate in the externals of popish worship as long as they did not embrace them internally. Since the Christian conscience has liberty concerning all religious ceremonies, some argued, feigning outward adherence to false religion was a matter of indifference, and therefore lawful. Such claims quickly caught the attention of the reformers, especially John Calvin, and it was not long before these French Protestants were labeled "Nicodemites" after the biblical Nicodemus, a Pharisee by day, follower of Jesus by night (John 3).[1]

When it came to the substance of Catholic worship, Calvin and his closest colleagues were of one mind: the worship of Rome—especially the Mass— was fraught with doctrinal error, pernicious superstition, and blasphemous idolatries. All agreed and stated in no uncertain terms that Catholic worship was "of Satan." Precisely how to advise French Protestants languishing under Catholic rule, however, became a matter of some disagreement between them. Must French Protestants, for the sake of the purity of conscience, completely extricate themselves from the Catholic Church and maintain true piety by advertising their Protestant beliefs through public confession, come what may? Or were they allowed to veil their Protestant sympathies for a time while continuing to participate in the externals of Romish worship? Indeed, was it more pious to flee persecution and remain "unstained by the world" (Jas. 1:27), or could the French Christians better serve the Lord by enduring the courts of "Babylon" in order to proselytize the lost, becoming "all things to all people"—to echo the Apostle Paul (I Cor. 9:22)—so that some might be won over to the pure gospel?[2] The reformers could not all agree on an answer, but their dispute was not for lack of familiarity with the Nicodemite predicament.

The plight of French believers in Catholic lands, including the temptation to avoid public confession of faith, was not uncharted ground for reformers like Guillaume Farel, Pierre Viret, Calvin, Bucer, and Capito. Each had known the life of a religious refugee, however briefly. Each understood the

---

[1] There has been a recent expansion of interest in matters surrounding the topic of Nicodemism. In addition to the works cited in this chapter, see David F. Wright, "Why Was Calvin So Severe a Critic of Nicodemism?," in *Calvinus Evangelii Propugnator: Calvin Champion of the Gospel; Papers Presented at the International Congress on Calvin Research, Seoul, 1998*, ed. Wright, A. N. S. Lane, and Jon Balserak (Grand Rapids, MI: CRC, 2006), 66–90; Jane K. Wickersham, *Rituals of Prosecution: The Roman Inquisition and the Prosecution of Philo-Protestants in Sixteenth-Century Italy* (Toronto: University of Toronto Press, 2012); M. Anne Overell, *Nicodemites: Faith and Concealment between Italy and Tudor England* (Leiden: Brill, 2019); and Kenneth J. Woo, *Nicodemism and the English Calvin, 1544–1584* (Leiden: Brill, 2019).

[2] Anti-Nicodemite writings regularly speak about the Catholic church as a place of exile or slavery—a "Babylon" or "Egypt"—for Protestant believers. See section 3.2.2, below.

excruciating ambiguity of a life torn between familiar Catholic observances and a growing suspicion and crisis of conscience that Roman doctrine and worship had become corrupt beyond repair. Now, squarely settled in Reformed lands and tasked with advising their French brothers and sisters in the matter of their public profession, the reformers faced the challenge of deciding whether to follow a hard-line approach, defending the pure worship of God against every deviation, or to let compassion and patience rule the day.

This chapter examines the reformers' dilemma by reconstructing the timeline of events that precipitated the anti-Nicodemite position of Calvin and several of his key allies against religious compromise in the 1530s. As will be seen, Calvin's strong position against Nicodemite behavior, including his equally strong demand for public confession of faith, did not develop in a vacuum. On the contrary, Calvin's staunch position and firm rhetoric were significantly shaped by personal interactions with Reformed mentors, especially Farel and Bucer, as well as by tense exchanges with erstwhile friends and fellow refugees at a time when his own Protestant beliefs were still in their infancy. Specifically, this chapter examines a critical question that contributed to the dilemma faced by Calvin and the reformers, namely, whether the choice of Nicodemism represented a valid type of spirituality that deemed all external forms of religion "indifferent," and therefore a matter of private interpretation, or whether the "dissimulation" of one's internal commitments necessarily violated the dictates of conscience and was thus a violation of genuine piety. This chapter will illustrate how this critical question pervaded the reformers' discussions and disagreements surrounding the issue of Nicodemism, producing distinctive conceptions of the important relationship between confession, conscience, and the rule of charity.

3.1. Confession, Conscience, and the Emerging Anti-Nicodemite Polemic

Over the span of his life and ministry, Calvin composed a significant number of treatises and open letters to friends and opponents alike on the topic of Nicodemism.[3] These were mostly written in French for a general audience and were especially intended to benefit Protestants residing in French

---

[3] Calvin's anti-Nicodemite writings were produced and published between 1536 and 1562. The majority of these will be examined in Chapter 4.

Catholic territories.[4] Throughout his correspondence, Calvin acknowledged that his French brothers and sisters faced a truly harrowing situation that he in no way wished upon them. Their options were nevertheless very clear, at least from where he stood. They could flee the Catholic Church quietly and live in voluntary exile, somewhere where pure worship is practiced, or stay and resist idolatry even to the point of death.[5] Feigning Catholicism, however, was not an acceptable alternative to persecution. Thus, Calvin firmly urged his readers to eschew all forms of dissimulating in worship and in life, calling them to maintain an outward witness consistent with their internal beliefs and consciences. "There is no room," Calvin wrote with characteristic sternness, "for anyone to indulge in crafty dissimulation, or to flatter himself with a false idea of piety, pretending that he cherishes it in his heart, though he completely overturns it by outward behavior. *Genuine piety begets genuine confession*."[6]

Calvin believed that his letters on religious compromise dispensed advice with pastoral sensitivity, but they would be remembered instead for their hardline rhetoric and harsh rebuke of Nicodemite behavior in all its forms. How did Calvin, himself a former religious refuge, gain the reputation of a

---

[4] Kevin Reed, publisher's [anonymous] introduction to John Calvin, *Come Out from Among Them: "Anti-Nicodemite" Writings of John Calvin*, trans. Seth Skolnitsky (Dallas, TX: Protestant Heritage Press, 2001), 8. The sum of Calvin's anti-Nicodemite writings were eventually published as a single collection, entitled *De vitandis superstitionibus, quae cum sincera fidei confessione pugnant, libellus Joannis Calvini. Eiusdem excusatio, ad pseudonicodemos* (Geneva: Jean Girard, 1549), which includes an appendix of compiled responses from some of Calvin's closest colleagues, Philipp Melanchthon, Martin Bucer, and Peter Martyr Vermigli (CO 6:621–24). In these writings, Calvin typically distinguishes between four "archetypes"—to use Carlos Eire's term—of Nicodemite behavior. First, he admonishes Catholic preachers who pretend to preach the gospel, but are primarily concerned with obtaining lucrative positions in the church. Calvin likely has Nicolas Duchemin and Gerard Roussel in view here. The second category of Nicodemite includes high-profile religious advisors who value their prestigious position more than the pure preaching of the gospel. François Richardot, advisor to the duchess of Ferrara, is Calvin's likely referent. A third type mentioned by Calvin includes members of the academy who would halfway transform Christianity into philosophy, lacking the courage to defend the gospel in the face of Catholic error. Finally, Calvin identifies the most common type of Nicodemite: the merchants and commoners who, simply out of convenience and comfort, are unwilling to endanger themselves by voicing objection to Romish superstition and confessing the truth. Calvin distinguishes the main types of Nicodemites in his 1544 treatise, *Excuse a Messieurs les Nicodemites sur la complaincte qu'ilz font de sa trop grand rigueur* (Geneva: Jean Girard), in CO 6:597–601. See also Carlos M. N. Eire, *War against the Idols: The Reformation of Worship from Erasmus to Calvin* (New York: Cambridge University Press, 1986), 244–45.

[5] Calvin, *Petit traicté, monstrant que doit faire un fidele entre les papistes, Avec une epistre du mesme argument. Ensemble l'excuse faicte sur cela aux Nicodemites* (Geneva: Jean Girard, 1545), in CO 6:576.

[6] COR 4/4:10.194–95 (*Epistola Prior*): "Quare non est, quod callida dissimulatione iam hic sibi quisquam placeat, aut falsa pietatis opinione blandiatur eam se fovere in corde fingens, quam externis testificationibus prorsus evertat. *Vera enim pietas veram confessionem parit*" (italics mine). In order to distinguish Calvin's *Epistolae Duae* contained in COR 4/4, I refer to Calvin's letter to Duchemin as *Epistola Prior*, and his letter to Roussel as *Epistola Altera*. ET of *Epistola Prior* available in CTS 3:360–411.

harsh doctrinal enforcer rather than a sympathetic defender of the troubled conscience? A closer examination of the origins of Calvin's anti-Nicodemite polemic reveals that his passionate appeals for genuine piety, pure worship, and the outward confession of faith stemmed from major shifts in Calvin's ecclesiology at a time when his own conscientious objections to Rome were being reinforced by the pangs of personal betrayal.

3.2. Locating the Origins of Calvin's Anti-Nicodemism

Although Calvin would eventually produce a more extensive corpus of anti-Nicodemite writings than any other reformer, it would be incorrect to assume that Calvin's anti-Nicodemite rhetoric was entirely original to himself. The battle against religious compromise was already being waged around Calvin long before the term "Nicodemite" entered his theological vocabulary in 1544.[7] Guillaume Farel had contended as early as 1529 that even the "imitation" of the pagan Mass "is against the commandment of God."[8] Several scholars have attempted to identify the period in time at which the Nicodemite controversy first entered Calvin's purview. Most recently, Frans Pieter Van Stam, Michael Bruening, and Jonathan Reid have argued that there is no evidence of anti-Nicodemism in Calvin's earliest writings, including the first edition of his *Institutio*, which was completed in August 1535 and published in March 1536. According to their analysis, Calvin most likely gained a critical awareness of the temptation for French Protestants to veil their internal commitments through dissimulation no earlier than late 1536, after the publication of his *Institutio* but likely prior to the Disputation in Lausanne (October 1–8).[9]

These authors are certainly correct in detecting no *explicit* reference to Nicodemism in Calvin's first edition of the *Institutio*. Nevertheless,

---

[7] Calvin's first published reference to the term "Nicodemite" is in his 1544 treatise, *Excuse à messieurs les Nicodemites, sur la complaincte qu'ilz font de sa trop grand rigueur* (CO 6:589–614).

[8] Guillaume Farel, *Le sommaire de Guillaume Farel: Réimprimé d'après l'édition de l'an 1534 & précédé d'une introduction*, ed. J. G. Baum (Geneva: Jules-Guillaum Fick, 1867), chap. 19, p. 37. Farel originally published his *Sommaire* in 1529.

[9] Frans Pieter van Stam, "The Group of Meaux as First Target of Farel and Calvin's Anti-Nicodemism," *Bibliotheque d'Humanisme et Renaissance* 68, no. 2 (2006): 254; Michael W. Bruening, "Calvin, Farel, Roussel, and the French 'Nicodemites,'" in *Calvin and the Early Reformation*, ed. Brian C. Brewer and David M. Whitford (Leiden: Brill, 2020), 115; Bruening, *Refusing to Kiss the Slipper: Opposition to Calvinism in the Francophone Reformation* (Oxford: Oxford University Press, 2021), 50–53, 55–57; and Jonathan A. Reid, "The Meaux Group and John Calvin," in *Calvin and the Early Reformation*, 59.

Calvin's dedicatory epistle to the French king, Francis I, dated August 23, 1535, offers some revealing information in terms of the circumstances and motivations undergirding Calvin's purpose in writing the *Institutio*. A brief examination of this letter reveals that Calvin was already aware of some of the peculiar challenges faced by French Protestants, specifically in terms of the temptation to dissimulate and withdraw from making public confession of faith.

3.2.1. "Anti-Nicodemism" in Calvin's Dedicatory Epistle to King Francis I

Calvin begins his epistle to King Francis by identifying his driving motives for composing the *Institutio*. He declares that he undertook this labor especially for "our French countrymen," many of whom were "so overwhelmed by threats and fears" of Catholic persecution that the fledgling French church "dare not even open its mouth."[10] For the majority of the letter, Calvin pleads with the king on behalf of the persecuted evangelicals, attempting to dispel mistaken notions and baseless rumors about the Reformed churches. By the conclusion of his letter, Calvin's attention shifts from the king to his French brothers and sisters. His words are meant to encourage but also admonish the French believers to stand firm in their confession of God's word against the false charges leveled against them. Calvin writes not only to lift their spirits but also to check the "ignorance of others who often happen to be moved by such offenses, and thus troubled, to waver."[11] His specific concern is that French Protestants not cave to the pressures of Catholic persecution and falter in their good confession. To rally his audience, Calvin invokes the example of the apostles' suffering recorded in Scripture, contending that "the apostles in their day experienced the same things that are now happening to us."[12] Having recounted the perils and accusations endured by Christ's earliest followers, Calvin then asks a series of pointed questions: "What were the apostles to do here? Ought they not to have dissembled (*dissimulandum*) for a time, or utterly laid aside that gospel and deserted it because they saw that it was the

---

[10] *Institutes 1536* (CO 1:9, 11; Battles ed., 1–2).
[11] *Institutes 1536* (CO 1:24): "ita rursum aliorum imbecillitati occurrendum est, quos talibus offendiculis commoveri, ac perturbatos vacilare, non raro contigit."
[12] *Institutes 1536* (CO 1:24; Battles ed., 12).

seedbed of so many quarrels, the source of so many dangers, the occasion of so many scandals (*scandolarum*)?"[13] The anticipated answer to Calvin's rhetorical challenge is a resounding, "No!" Like the apostles before them, the persecuted French evangelicals ought not "waver" or "dissemble"—a notable synonym for "dissimulate" frequently found in anti-Nicodemite writings—but rather persist boldly in their profession of the genuine gospel.

It is unlikely that Calvin would have written these things in the abstract, lacking any knowledge of the specific problems associated with Nicodemite behavior. His specific concern for the church, already in the summer of 1535, was that the French Protestants neither "waver" in their confession nor "dissemble" in response to the threat of religious persecution. Moreover, this letter appears to anticipate a common Nicodemite claim that Calvin would reject in several of his later writings, namely, that one could justly veil his or her Protestant beliefs for a time in order to avoid scandalizing one's neighbor or causing quarrels in the church. Calvin also returns to the theme of "scandal" in chapter six of the *Institutio* (1536), which deals with the relationship between Christian freedom and the conscience. Here he appears to anticipate—if not respond to—the Nicodemite claim that engaging in superstitious ceremonies, even in pretense, is a matter of indifference and therefore left to one's freedom. Calvin strongly opposes this idea on the basis that, even though some practices may be "of themselves indifferent," nevertheless, because idolatrous worship practices "gravely wound the consciences" of weak brothers, they "cannot be committed without sin."[14] At very least, then, we may surmise that Calvin's encouragement of suffering Protestants in his dedicatory letter demonstrates that he is already moving toward an anti-Nicodemite polemic prior to—and not merely after—the publication of the *Institutio*. Indeed, Calvin's *Institutio* was *born* of his concern to inculcate genuine Christian piety within his French brothers and sisters, not only with regard to doctrine, but also in terms of the Christian's public life and profession.

---

[13] *Institutes 1536* (CO 1:25; Battles ed., 13).
[14] *Institutes 1536* (CO 1:220; Battles ed., 199). Calvin adds, "Who but a slanderer will say that they thus make a new law, when it is clear that they are only forestalling scandals (*scandalis*) which have been explicitly enough forbidden by the Lord?"

3.2.2. Calvin's Public Anti-Nicodemite Position: Early Letters to Friends (1536–1537)

Although it appears that Calvin was alert to the problem of dissimulation at an earlier point than previously believed, it is nevertheless true that his *explicit* anti-Nicodemite position did not become public until 1537. The young Calvin fired his opening salvo against religious compromise in the form of two public letters, published 1537 in Basel under the title *Epistolae duae*. These letters, written to two erstwhile friends, Nicolas Duchemin and Gérard Roussel, contain an unmistakable emphasis on the relation between confession and conscience that would characterize Calvin's later works on the subject.[15] It is notable that these passionate enjoinders against Nicodemism were in many ways spurred on by Calvin's encounter with religious compromise at a time when he was himself a religious refugee facing the temptation to waver in his own confession. Specifically, Calvin's initial polemics on this matter stemmed from his early travels to Italy while in the company of reform-minded friends. In the aftermath of the *affaire de placards* (October 1534), which posed unique dangers for anyone suspected of belonging to "the cursed Lutheran sect," Calvin and his friend, Louis du Tillet, were forced to flee their native France and seek asylum from Protestant sympathizer Duchess Renata (Renée of France), daughter of King Louis XII of France and sister-in-law of King Francis I.

It was while staying in Ferrara under the duchess's protection during the spring of 1536—having just published his *Institutio*—that Calvin first composed his letters to Duchemin and Roussel. Both men had recently accepted bishoprics in France, ultimately committing to Rome while retaining sympathies for the evangelical reform movement.[16] Roussel, in particular, had been a member of the reformist network connected to King Francis I's sister, Marguerite of Angoulême, who was the wife of Henry of Navarre. During the early 1520s, this gathering of Reformation forerunners in France, known as the Meaux group on account of its town of origin, had also included the later Genevan reformer Guillaume Farel.[17] By the time Calvin

---

[15] Chapter 4 will examine these later works in detail.

[16] Scholars overwhelmingly agree that Duchemin and Roussel are the historical addressees of Calvin's letters, even though they were published as public letters to two anonymous recipients. For a brief overview of the historiography of the *Epistolae duae*, see de Boer and van Stam's introduction in COR 4/4: XX–XXI. Roussel was named bishop of Oléron in 1536.

[17] Reid, "The Meaux Group," 58–59; Van Stam, "The Group of Meaux," 259–60. For a more detailed examination of Roussel's involvement with the Meaux circle, see Bruening, *Refusing to Kiss the Slipper*, 21–34.

composed the letters that would comprise the *Epistolae Duae*, however, his friendly affection for Duchemin and Roussel had grown cold. In his correspondence, Calvin firmly rebukes his former friends for the idolatrous compromise of their former confession, regularly invoking their consciences as testimony against them.

Although these public letters commence with Calvin's usual fraternal salutations, there is no mistaking the urgency with which he lectures Duchemin and Roussel about the "sacrilegious," "abominable," even satanic, character of Romish worship, especially the Mass.[18] Calvin admonishes his French brothers to forsake their compromising position and take bold steps to embrace the evangelical faith without shame or fear.[19] In response to Duchemin's request for counsel on how to live faithfully amidst Romish idolatry, Calvin prompts his friend to subject his "feelings" to the word of God, rather than allow his impulse to escape persecution drive him toward crafty dissimulation. In this context, Calvin excoriates those who feignedly indulge in impious idolatry, foolishly believing they "may devise a defense by which they might arm their consciences before the tribunal of God."[20] They are in fact deceived, for those who claim to belong to God's kingdom and embrace true doctrine and piety "should manifest piety of the heart by outward profession."[21] The worship that God seeks from his people requires the action of the whole person, soul (belief) and body (mouth), making public confession of faith a necessity for the Christian. Although Calvin makes confession a requirement, he purposefully refrains from spelling out "fixed rules" (*certis regulis*) for making such a profession. The believer, guided by godly prudence, will discern "when, with whom, in what place, and to what extent" he or she should give "visible testimony" of their faith.[22]

---

[18] COR 4/4:80.355–61 (*Epistola Altera*). Calvin warns Roussel that the kind of spiritual compromise resulting in pretentious Catholic worship is an "offense (*offensionem*) of Satan." COR 4/4:92.630–40 (*Epistola Altera*).

[19] In both letters, Calvin expresses genuine sympathy and pity for his dear brothers, feeling "extremely troubled" for their sakes on account of their miserable exile in that Egypt and Babylon, "in which so many idols and idol-worship have been heaped up continually before your eyes." COR 4/4:1.1–4 (*Epistola Prior*).

[20] COR 4/4:3.30–43 (*Epistola Prior*): "Interim defensionem quoque meditantur, qua suas conscientias arment coram Dei tribunali." Calvin makes a similar point in his letter to Roussel. See COR 4/4:99.830 (*Epistola Altera*).

[21] COR 4/4:9–10.185–95 (*Epistola Prior*): "Eam ipsam cordis pietatem externa professione declarant.... Vera enim pietas veram confessionem parit." "Finally," Calvin writes, "the Lord calls his own to confession, and those who decline it must seek another master, because he cannot tolerate dissimulation." COR 4/4:10.197–99 (*Epistola Prior*).

[22] COR 4/4:11.226–32 (*Epistola Prior*). Although Calvin refuses to establish fixed rules for the public profession of faith, he does argue from the general progress of redemptive history for the necessity of public confession. See COR 4/4:16.351–56 (*Epistola Prior*).

Calvin insists that genuine confession is necessary not only before God, so that God might receive proper honor, but also for the sake of one's neighbor. Those who "mockingly feign innocence of conscience" in their dissimulation fail to recognize that, by their actions, they are inviting those who witness their conduct to do likewise. The impious worshipper wounds the weak consciences of others by acting with "a doubtful" and "opposing conscience."[23] By their poor example, these idolaters set a poor example for their "weak brothers," who are emboldened to conform due to their own "faltering and vacillating conscience (*nutante vacillanteque conscientia*)."[24] Calvin admonishes Roussel, in particular, for allowing the consciences of his own parishioners to be "disturbed" by performing so much Romish "wickedness."[25] Unlike religious ceremonies that promote the pious confession of faith, Catholic ceremonies—Calvin lists the worship of images, extreme unction, the purchase of indulgences, the sprinkling of water, and exorcisms—are demonstrably wicked for believers to entertain, even in pretense, since they are "openly at war with the word of God" and "bind the consciences of the faithful (*fidelium obligare conscientias*)" to tyrannical human regulations.[26]

In response to the anticipated complaint that Calvin's words misrepresent the character of their piety, Calvin appeals to the consciences of his friends, even going so far as to call their own consciences in witness against them.[27] Their claim that Calvin's evaluation of them is too harsh simply does not hold; their objection is with the Apostolic word, not with him.[28] On this score, Calvin also responds to the oft-cited Nicodemite argument that dissimulation in worship is a matter of adiaphora or indifference. In an attempt to justify feigning Catholicism, Nicodemite apologists frequently turned to the example of the Apostle Paul in Scripture, who desired to make himself "all things to all people" in order to create avenues for the gospel. Calvin retorts that Paul's old covenant vow to shave his head (Acts 21:26) and his willingness to "make himself a Jew to the Jews, that he might win the Jews" (I

---

[23] COR 4/4:20.448–53 (*Epistola Prior*). Calvin excoriates the false prudence of those who believe they may justly feign Catholic allegiances while holding evangelical beliefs, since the poor example they set for "the rude and simple" attending Mass simply emboldens them "to commit the sin which their own conscience condemns."
[24] COR 4/4:49.1127–28 (*Epistola Prior*). Likewise, COR 4/4:46.1037–39 (*Epistola Prior*).
[25] COR 4/4:116.1236 (*Epistola Altera*).
[26] COR 4/4:24.553, 557 (*Epistola Prior*). Such abuses, Calvin writes to Roussel, are characterized by "deceit, theft, robbery, sacrilege, and wicked arts," and do nothing more than unjustly burden the conscience. COR 4/4:67.61–66 (*Epistola Altera*).
[27] COR 4/4:104.945, 955 (*Epistola Altera*).
[28] COR 4/4:29–30.648–55 (*Epistola Prior*).

Cor. 9:20) hardly established precedent for Nicodemite behavior. In no sense were Paul's actions tainted by "impure superstition." Even in its passing Old Covenant usage, Paul's vow was something instituted to render thanks to the Lord. Not so the Mass, which Calvin calls a "sacrilegious rite." Calvin pauses only briefly to contest the adiaphora argument of the Nicodemites, for he is certain that the flagrant sins of these dissemblers lay exposed before the internal tribunal of God, the conscience.[29]

What had transpired in the years leading up to the publication of the *Epistolae Duae* that precipitated Calvin's stern rebuke of Nicodemism? Van Stam, Bruening, and Reid have rightly acknowledged that Calvin's anti-Nicodemism was spurred on by tectonic shifts in his view of the church. At least by 1537, Calvin had come to believe that the traditional Roman Church, its officers, and its worship had become thoroughly wicked, an abomination before God, and injurious to the freedom of conscience. No true believer could justly remain in the Roman Church and participate—either willingly or in pretense—in its "satanic" rites, especially the Mass. Since God requires a genuine profession of faith, in action as well as with the mouth, anyone unwilling to render to God his rightful honor by extracting themselves from false worship was not worthy even to be called a Christian, Calvin would claim.[30]

Calvin's prefatory address to King Francis I indicates, however, that this critical change in his ecclesiology did not occur merely in response to events transpiring *after* the publication of the 1536 *Institutio*. Already at the time Calvin wrote his epistle, he expressed belief that the Church of Rome had become utterly bankrupt spiritually and lacked all evidence of being a true church. His letter specifically denounces the idea that the reformers are teaching a "new" gospel, though Calvin admits that what they teach might *seem new* to their Catholic opponents, "since to them both Christ himself and his gospel are new."[31] Calvin's point, of course, is that the papists lack a fundamental knowledge both of Christ and of the genuine gospel. For Calvin, Rome's ecclesiology amounts to "a deadly butchery of souls, a firebrand, a

---

[29] COR 4/4:57.1356–70 (*Epistola Prior*): "Verum quantum insit in missa flagitii, planum a me factum esse confido; quid animi habeant, ipsi sibi locupletissimi sunt coram Deo testes."

[30] This was the barb with which Calvin concluded his letter to Roussel. By Calvin's estimation, because Roussel was unwilling to extricate himself from Rome, he was "neither a good man, nor a Christian." COR 4/4:118.1296–97 (*Epistola Altera*).

[31] *Institutes 1536* (CO 1:15; Battles ed., 5): "Illis quidem novam esse minime dubito, quibus et Christus novus est, et Evangelium novum."

ruin, and a destruction of the church (*excidium ecclesiae*)."[32] Already in the summer of 1535, then, Calvin's ecclesiology evidenced a clear break from Rome, one that required a full repudiation of the traditional institution without compromise.

To understand Calvin's growing animosity toward Nicodemite behavior as it developed in the mid-1530s, prior to the emergence of his *Institutio*, it is necessary to examine an earlier set of conflicts—especially revolving around Gérard Roussel—that further disclose the nature of the struggle over religious compromise in France, as well as the origins of Calvin's and the reformers' anti-Nicodemite position.

3.2.3. Gérard Roussel and the Problem of Religious Compromise

On September 25, 1525, while the young Calvin was still studying for the priesthood in Paris, Roussel wrote to Farel with alarming news regarding the condition of the Protestant movement in France. Several of the brothers had been confined to prison. Others had withdrawn and denounced the rest, fearful of the Catholic king. Roussel informed Farel that on several occasions, enemies of the church had sought to compromise the Protestants by stirring up accusations from false witnesses. Roussel is candid about the fact that they can no longer confess Christ without exposing their lives to persecution.[33] The next month, Roussel himself faced arrest at the hands of the Parlement of Paris, but fled to Bucer's Strasbourg for safety.[34] Roussel's letters to Farel in the following months reveal the anxiety, threats, and indignities he endured as one suspected of heresy by the Catholic Church. Indeed, Roussel's experience while he remained a religious advisor in the queen's court was decidedly more precarious than that of Farel, who had already fled France in 1524 to take up pastoral care among the diaspora French Protestants in various cities of the Swiss Confederacy.[35]

---

[32] *Institutes 1536* (CO 1:23; Battles ed., 10–11). Part of Calvin's argument, which he defends on the basis of the Old Testament prophets, is that Christ has always and will always preserve his church, even during periods of great darkness when "no form of the true church remained."
[33] Roussel to Farel, September 25, 1525 (Herminjard 1:389–92, #162).
[34] Reid, "The Meaux Group," 62.
[35] For a concise summary of Farel's early reformist efforts, see *Early French Reform: The Theology and Spirituality of Guillaume Farel*, ed. Jason Zuidema and Theodore Van Raalte (London: Routledge, 2016), 7–14.

Despite their cordial relationship during the early 1520s, the tenor of Roussel and Farel's friendship changed quickly beginning in late 1526 when Farel detected a compromising spirit in Roussel. In a letter dated August 27, 1526, Roussel criticized Farel for his hard-line stance against religious compromise. Farel should be more sympathetic about the many perils that surrounded the believers in France, forcing them to "conceal" (*dissimulanda*) many things. Farel should also tone down his style of writing on account of the difficult times, rather than grieve his French brothers and sisters with immoderate demands for reform.[36] Roussel reached out to Farel once again in a letter dated December 7, 1526, proposing that Farel return to France and take up a lucrative position in the household of Robert de la Marck, ruler of the Principality of Sedan (Ardennes). Roussel's offer came with a caveat, however: Farel would have to abstain from voicing dissent against the Catholic Mass and simply "be content to teach Christ and the true benefit of his work."[37] Farel found this proposal to be completely untenable, and maintained that a Reformed understanding of the Lord's Supper, coupled with a total rejection of the Mass, were essential tenets of a Protestant confession of faith. There is no record of any future correspondence between Roussel and Farel after this point, a fact that is emblematic of the kind of complete break Farel believed he, and all faithful believers, ought to make: from the Mass, from the Catholic Church, and, if necessary, from France itself.[38]

It is unclear exactly when Calvin's own antipathy toward Roussel began to develop. In a letter from Calvin to François Daniel, dated October 27, 1533, Calvin still refers to Roussel in more intimate terms as "our Gérard."[39] Throughout that year, the topic of Roussel's dire circumstances in France also comes up in letters exchanged between Calvin and several of his friends, indicating a lingering concern for Roussel's general well-being.[40] It is important to note that Calvin was experiencing a number of "unresolved

---

[36] Roussel to Farel, August 27, 1526 (Herminjard 1:450.24–25, #182): "Scis tempora: hisce, si quid scripseris, attempera tuum stilum."
[37] Roussel to Farel, December 7, 1526 (Herminjard 1:460.14–17, #184): "Sed quid optemus probe nosti, ne scilicet spargatur per quod demum suboriatur dissidium. Quantum mihi displiceat dessentio nuper orta, vix effari possum. Abstine, oro, ab ea, sed contentus esto docere Christum et verum usum operum illius."
[38] Bruening, "Calvin, Farel, Roussel," 115–16.
[39] Calvin to Daniel, October 27, 1533 (Herminjard 3:105.8, #437): "G. nostri."
[40] E.g., Calvin to Daniel, end of October 1533 (Herminjard 3:107, #438). Similar concern for Roussel's safety, as well as hope that the king would not judge Roussel a heretic, is expressed in letters of Marguerite de Navarre during the same period. E.g., Marguerite de Navarre to Anne de Montmorency, end of May 1533 (Herminjard 3:52–53, #417).

ambiguities" in his own life during this time.[41] Having fled Paris following the backlash prompted by Nicolas Cop's controversial inaugural address on All Saints' Day in 1533, Calvin found relative peace and safety in southwest France with the family of his friend, du Tillet, who was then a parish priest in Claix. Records suggest that during these years of critical development, Calvin struggled to discern what implications his growing reformist ideas should have for his own public confession. The account of Catholic jurist Florimond de Raemond, for example, indicates that, while Calvin made some attempts to distance himself from Catholic worship, appearing at the church in Angoulême "as little as possible," he nevertheless preached, taught, and attended Mass on several occasions, doing all according "to the Catholic custom."[42] Had Calvin engaged in some manner of dissimulation by giving outward assent to teachings and practices he had already rejected—at least in part—in his own mind? Absolute certainty eludes us, but we do know that by the spring of 1534, the twenty-five-year-old Calvin officially renounced his benefices, cutting ties with his boyhood church in Noyon around the same time that his "sudden conversion" to an evangelical understanding of Scripture most likely occurred. It may be, as Bruce Gordon has opined, that Calvin's own brief experience with dissimulation fostered enough discomfort of conscience to spark the belief that genuine piety required a complete break with the false Catholic Church—a point Calvin would forcefully emphasize in his letter to Roussel a few years later.[43]

Besides Calvin, Bucer also appears to have taken an especially keen interest in Roussel's case at this time. Several letters exchanged between Bucer

---

[41] Bruce Gordon, *Calvin* (New Haven, CT: Yale University Press), 39.
[42] Florimond de Raemond, *Histoire de la naissance, progrès et décadence de l'hérésie de ce siècle* (Paris, 1605), 889, quoted in Gordon, *Calvin*, 39. Gordon notes that, although de Raemond was not sympathetic toward Calvin, his record of Calvin's time in Angoulême is largely corroborated by the biographical sketches of Theodore Beza and Nicolas Colladon.
[43] Gordon, *Calvin*, 40. Gary W. Jenkins, *Calvin's Tormentors: Understanding the Conflicts That Shaped the Reformer* (Grand Rapids, MI: Baker Academic, 2018), 14, has argued that the young Calvin did in fact live the life of a Nicodemite, however briefly. Settling that issue is not essential to the aims of this chapter, but I do have some reservations about applying the Nicodemite moniker to Calvin, even during his transitional years that were punctuated by a "sudden conversion." Although it is true that Calvin's conversion to Protestantism was gradual—and thus it involved some "dissembling" while Calvin was in the process of shedding familiar Catholic practices and gaining Protestant commitments—it was nevertheless a conversion from one set of fundamental religious beliefs to another. As far as I can tell, at no point did Calvin deliberately express Catholic belief outwardly while holding committed Protestant beliefs internally, merely for the sake of gaining an ecclesial position or escaping persecution. Once converted, Calvin vowed never to return to anything resembling Romish worship. Thus, as Nicodemites generally held committed Protestant beliefs but continued to veil them for the sake of protection or prestige, it is my position that Calvin never truly fit this description.

and his Strasbourg colleague, Jean Sturm, discuss Roussel's case with genuine sympathy, a fact that—as we will later note—is consistent with Bucer's characteristic leniency toward Nicodemite behavior.[44] A letter sent from Nicolas Cop to Bucer on April 5, 1534, informs the Strasbourg reformer that Roussel had been absolved and released from prison by the order of the king.[45] Apparently, by this point Roussel had sufficiently assuaged the king's suspicion that he held Protestant views, confirming for Farel, at least, that Roussel's willingness to compromise the genuine gospel was nearly complete.

3.2.4. The Lausanne Disputation (October 1–8, 1536)

The formal rebuke of Roussel by the anti-Nicodemite reformers finally occurred at the Lausanne Disputation, a gathering of Catholic clergy and Reformed theologians that met October 1–8, 1536, to discuss the formal transition from Catholicism to Protestantism in the Bernese territories. From Van Stam's detailed summary of the proceedings at Lausanne, we know that anti-Nicodemism provided the backdrop against which the reformer's total rejection of the Catholic Church was set. Debates between Catholic and Protestant representatives (if "debate" is quite the right word, given that most of the Catholic participants silently protested the proceedings on grounds that the pope had neither summoned nor authorized the meeting) routinely focused on the question of whether Rome constituted a true church of Christ. In addition to the bold remarks offered by Farel during the meeting, Farel's young assistant, Pierre Viret, took the floor on multiple occasions to emphasize Rome's illegitimacy as a church. He insisted that, because it was the church of the pope, the Catholic Church "is not the true church of Jesus," but rather "a synagogue of Satan," and thus all faithful Christians ought to leave it immediately.[46] Viret's pointed critique of the Roman Church and its

---

[44] Sturm to Bucer, August 23, 1533 (Herminjard 3:72–75, #422). See also a letter from Sturm to Bucer, the middle of October 1533 (Herminjard 3:93–95, #432). The two reformers lament the fact that Queen Marguerite and Roussel, her chaplain, had been mocked in a staged comedy performed at the College of Navarre. The queen appeared to have gotten her revenge, however, as this show of disrespect resulted in the imprisonment of the Grand Master of the college.

[45] Cop to Bucer, April 5, 1534 (Herminjard 3:159, #458).

[46] Arthur Piaget, *Les actes de la Dispute de Lausanne 1536* [Mémoires de l'université de Neuchâtel, 6] (Neuchâtel, 1928), 247, 275: "Et, par tout cecy que a esté dict, s'ensuit que l'eglise papistique et romaine n'est point la vraye eglise de Jesus." Van Stam, "The Group of Meaux," 156, n. 19, reports that Viret spoke even more extensively than Farel at the Disputation. Viret's contention that the Church of Rome did not constitute the church of Christ was already argued by Calvin in his 1536 *Institutio*.

membership anticipated the closing remarks of his mentor. Farel concluded the disputation by excoriating those who were willing to leave their poor brothers and sisters in the darkness and ignorance of Roman idolatry, doing harm to the spiritually weak instead of loving and serving them according to the rule of charity.[47] Farel's anti-Nicodemite diatribe targeted the actions of one man in particular: "One such preacher, who defended himself against the whole Sorbonne, chants the Mass and knows very well what he is doing...." That man was Gérard Roussel, a member of the Meaux circle: a man who, after preaching to a group of up to five thousand in Paris in 1533, had been accused of belonging to the Lutheran sect by theologians of the Sorbonne; a man who, although an erstwhile ally of the reformers, had finally capitulated to Catholic pressure and now regularly served the idolatrous Mass to the "simple" and "impoverished."[48]

It is hard to imagine that Calvin—a modest participant at the Disputation—could have missed Farel's reference to the man "who defended himself against the entire Sorbonne," for he had also been among the crowd of five thousand to hear Roussel's sermons in 1533.[49] We do know for certain that Calvin observed the proceedings in Lausanne with a substantial measure of agreement and satisfaction, as evidenced in Calvin's letter to François Daniel a mere five days after the Disputation concluded.[50] Calvin's favorable assessment of the meeting is likewise reflected in the similarities between his *Epistolae Duae*—the final drafts of which Calvin was completing at the time of the Disputation—and the arguments offered by Farel and Viret

---

[47] Piaget, *Actes*, 396: "Mais, comme dict le sainct apostre, de ceste science ne se fault enfler ne mespriser celuy qui n'a encore entendu ceste libirté, puissance et seigneurie, mais il fault aller et user de ceste science et de ce qu'on sçait et congnoist selon charité (Cor. 8), et, de tout ce que nous est loysible, fault que nous regardions ce que edifie et peult servir a nostre prochain.... En quoy grandement pechent et faillent ceux qui bien sçavent l'abus et l'abomination des choses constituees et ordonnees par les papes et tout son estat ... congnoissans bien que le povre peuple ... est abusé et enchanté par l'eglise papale a suyvre toute idolatrie et superstition ... comme assez a esté dict par avant en la probation de la 4ᵉ conclusion, aucuns n'estimans ces povres gens ... pour freres, et n'ayans aucune pitié d'eux, ne leur disant point qu'ilz font mal."

[48] Piaget, *Actes*, 397: "que ung tel prescheur, qui a mainctenu son dire contre toute la Sorbonne, chante messe, il sçait bien qu'il faict."

[49] Gordon, *Calvin*, 36. Calvin spoke twice at the Lausanne Disputation (on October 5 and 7), and then only briefly, since he was convinced that the responses of Farel and Viret were sufficient and required no elaboration from him. See "First Lausanne Discourse" in COR 4/4:123-36.1-4 (CO 9:877-86). Calvin's remarks mostly demonstrate his ability to defend the reformers based on the authority and testimony of the Church Fathers. In his "First Lausanne Discourse," Calvin also takes time to excoriate the pope for his "intolerable impudence and diabolical pride," and to hold his Catholic opponents to the judgment of their consciences (COR 4/4:125.53-56; 132.213-17).

[50] Calvin writes a glowing report to his friend regarding the success of the meeting. Convinced of the importance of this event, he expects the news has already reached his friend in Orléans, though some 400 kilometers away. See introduction to COR 4/4: XXXIX-XL.

during the course of the meeting. Like his colleagues, Calvin laments the exilic sufferings of his French comrades, comparing their experience to Israel's plight in "Egypt" and "Babylon." With Farel-like boldness, Calvin deems Catholic worship, especially the Mass, to be "of Satan," and excoriates Roussel, in particular, for disturbing the consciences of the weak and doubtful by his own dissimulation. When Calvin thrusts his old friends before the direct condemnation of their consciences, one also hears echoes of Farel's closing comments at the disputation: Roussel "knows very well what he is doing." Although it is impossible to determine which of these elements belonged to Calvin's original drafts—first composed prior to the Lausanne Disputation in the spring of 1536—and which were added later after the Disputation and just prior to publication, it is quite plausible that much of Calvin's critique of religious compromise was solidified in his earliest drafts. Indeed, several of the biblical illusions Calvin employs in his *Epistolae Duae* are already present in his epistle to King Francis (1535), including the "satanic" character of Rome, as well as God's preservation of the church amidst the worship of Baal (I Kings 19) and "the confusion of Babylon."[51]

* * *

Bruening is certainly correct that Calvin "did not create the anti-Nicodemite argument." To conclude that he simply "stole it" from Farel and Viret might be an overstatement, however.[52] So far, this chapter has attempted to demonstrate the plausibility that Calvin's concern for the situation of Protestants in Catholic France developed at an earlier stage than previously assumed. It is likely that Calvin's own thoughts about religious compromise—and about the error of Protestant "dissimulation," in particular—began to develop as early as 1534, when Calvin's own religious convictions were being challenged by life as a refugee while in the company of reform-minded acquaintances. Indeed, Calvin's awareness of his own qausi-dissembling likely factored into the decision to withdraw officially from the Catholic Church around that time. Moreover, although Calvin's *public* solidarity with the anti-Nicodemite position of Farel and Viret should be assigned to the later months of 1536, we may conclude that Calvin's ecclesiastical shift and convictions about public

---

[51] See *Institutes 1536* (CO 1:16, 21; Battles ed., 6, 9–10). While it is certainly true that Calvin's *Epistolae Duae* exhibits close connections with the specific matters raised at the Disputation of Lausanne, the evidence presented above indicates that, already prior to the Disputation, Calvin possessed much of the polemical rhetoric that would characterize his later critiques of Catholic worship and Nicodemite behavior. Cf. COR 4/4: XL–LI.

[52] Bruening, "Calvin, Farel, Roussel," 118.

confession of faith had already begun to develop in his mind several years before the publication of his *Institutio*. From our study of Calvin's dedicatory letter to King Francis I, completed in the summer of 1535, as well as our assessment of the timeline of events that resulted in Calvin's first public anti-Nicodemite work, the *Epistolae Duae*, it seems highly plausible that Calvin's personal views on Nicodemite dissimulation were nearly in place by mid-1535.

3.3. Nicodemism and the Strasbourg Reformers

As simple and straightforward as the issue of Nicodemism may have seemed to Farel, Viret, and Calvin, the Strasbourg reformers saw the matter quite differently. Bucer and Capito believed the Frenchmen had treated their persecuted brothers and sisters too harshly, especially by making their plight a matter of conscience. Echoing the opinion of Roussel, they argued that the admonishments of Farel and the rest should be tempered by prudence, rather than driven by rash zeal and a rigid application of the Scriptures.[53] This did not sit well with Farel, who wrote a rather contentious letter to Capito in May 1537 attempting to warn the Strasbourg reformers about the dangers of their lenient approach to religious compromise. His letter specifically commends Calvin's *Epistolae Duae* for its necessary rebuke of the French Protestants, whose dissimulation, if left unchecked, would certainly bring down God's judgment upon them.[54] Taking aim at Bucer and Capito, Farel denounces all who willingly allow such dissimulation to continue, seeing as it is such an "impiety and stumbling block" to God's "little ones."[55] Moreover, those who would argue that feigning Catholic worship constitutes a form of piety that is indifferent to external things argue against their own consciences; they are no different from those who vainly bowed their knees before Baal.[56] When

---

[53] Bucer, *Consilium Theologicum Privatim Conscriptum* (BOL 4:152–53, ch. 64).
[54] Farel to Capito, May 5, 1537 (COR 4/4:142.99–103, Appendix 2).
[55] Farel to Capito, May 5, 1537 (COR 4/4:142.103–107, Appendix 2): "Qui tantum abest ut se errare fateantur, ut potius suas impietates, etiam post agnitam veritatem, fateantur ultum Dei et observationem mandatorum Dei impietatem et offendiculum pusillorum, et ubi belle collegerunt iuxta propriae voluntatis sensum."
[56] Farel to Capito, May 5, 1537 (COR 4/4:144.140–56, 144–45.165–71, 146.205–13, Appendix 2). Farel's reference to I Kings 19:18 appears to be based on Calvin's exegesis of the same passage in his letter to Duchemin (COR 4/4:13.281–83): "An quorum corda non sunt vanitate ac mendaciis Baal infatuate? Non id modo, sed quorum genua non sunt curvata ante Baal et quorum ora non sunt osculate manum eius."

comparing Calvin's *Epistolae Duae* with Farel's letter to Capito, the similarity of language and biblical illusions is striking, indicating Farel's appeal to Calvin's authority on the matter.

And indeed, the Strasbourgers' apparent leniency did not escape the attention of Calvin, either, who expressed a measure of annoyance at their position. His ire is particularly evidenced by an epistolary exchange with du Tillet, Calvin's former travel companion. Their letters disclose Calvin's growing critique of Nicodemism, including his personal angst over Bucer and Capito's apparent justification of religious compromise. A brief examination of these letters provides a helpful backdrop against which the distinctive views of Bucer and Capito might be assessed.

3.3.1. The Epistolary Exchange of Calvin and du Tillet (1537–1538)

After departing Ferrera together in the spring of 1536, Calvin and du Tillet had parted ways. Calvin journeyed back into France to attend to the affairs of his now-deceased father Gérard. Du Tillet ended up in Geneva, where he assisted Farel in early reform efforts there. The two friends would meet again during Calvin's unplanned stay in Geneva in the summer of 1536. In fact, it was du Tillet who reported Calvin's presence to Farel, who in turn threatened Calvin with God's wrath if he refused to stay in the city and help reform it. Calvin yielded, and for the next eighteen months, Calvin and du Tillet partnered with Farel to consolidate the Reformation in Geneva. Before the spring of 1538, however, not long before Calvin and Farel were expelled from Geneva for over-asserting their disciplinary agenda, the relationship between Calvin and du Tillet took a downturn. Sometime between late 1537 and early 1538—scholars do not agree on the date—du Tillet left Geneva and returned home, notably, via Strasbourg. But he was not merely going home; he was returning to the communion of Rome. The epistolary exchange that commenced between these erstwhile colleagues and fellow religious refugees not only conveys the personal pain caused by broken allegiances; it once again illustrates Calvin's appeal to conscience as his favored means of exposing religious compromise.[57]

---

[57] The six letters passed between Calvin and du Tillet, beginning in January 1538, are contained in Alexandre Crottet, *Correspondance française de Calvin avec Louis du Tillet, chanoine d'Angoulême et curé de Claix: Sur les questions de l'église et du ministère évangélique* (Genève: Cherbuliez, 1850). For

The letters between Calvin and du Tillet are noteworthy in that they contain a vigorous exchange of competing claims to conscience. The two friends are often reduced to disagreeing over whose conscience is in fact sounder and more certain, whether for or against reform. In a letter dated January 31, 1538, Calvin conveys disappointment and grief over his friend's departure. He is thoroughly convinced that du Tillet has abandoned the pure gospel to join a church dominated by ignorance and obstinacy toward God's commands. Moreover, Calvin is quite certain that it is Bucer and Capito who helped du Tillet reach his decision by veiling their consultations in "great piety."[58] Calvin, on the other hand, is certain that he has chosen the right course, stating, "I know that my conscience is quite strong before God [that such compromise is wrong], though against yours, and hope that it will be until the day when I must appear to give an account."[59] Du Tillet, on the other hand, is equally convinced that he was correct to return to the Church of his baptism, since he could discern no divine command to withdraw from Rome. He responds to Calvin's criticism in three rather long letters, dated March 10, September 7, and December 1, 1538. Although du Tillet is saddened by the mischief and hurt his departure has caused Calvin, he confesses, "my conscience has never been appeased by the fact that, without a certain vocation from God, I have withdrawn from the place that I should not leave without God's command."[60] Nothing less than the "affliction of conscience" had

---

concise summaries of Calvin's epistolary exchange with du Tillet, see George H. Tavard, AA, "Calvin and the Nicodemites," 62–69, in *John Calvin and Roman Catholicism: Critique and Engagement, Then and Now*, ed. Randall C. Zachman (Grand Rapids, MI: Baker Academic, 2008), and Jenkins, *Calvin's Tormentors*, 1–15 (Chapter 1, "Louis du Tillet and Calvin the Nicodemite: The Fitful Separation from the Whore of Babylon's Church"). A helpful interpretation of this exchange is also found in Olivia Carpi-Mailly, "Jean Calvin et Louis du Tillet: Entre foi et amitié, un échange révélateur," in *Calvin et Ses Contemporains: Actes du Colloque de Paris 1995*, ed. Olivier Millet (Geneva: Libraire Droz, 1998), 7–19. Although these letters exhibit overtones of common courtesy, there is no mistaking the shared sentiments of personal disappointment and betrayal. An air of secrecy also hangs over these exchanges; Calvin employs a favored pseudonym, Charles d'Espeville, while du Tillet communicates under the guise of the name "de Haulmont."

[58] Calvin to du Tillet, January 31, 1538 (Crottet, 25.15–21): "Je n'ay nullement doubté que les personnages dont vous faites mention n'eussent aucunement aydé, sans y penser, a vous faire prendre une telle conclusion, combine qu'en touchant ce propos par lettres à moi escriptes, il le dissimulent, et certes la grande doctrine et pieté qui est en eulx a grande apparence pour donner authorité a telles consultations."

[59] Calvin to du Tillet, January 31, 1538 (Crottet, 25.8–11): "Je scé bien que ma conscience est assez asseurée devant Dieu du contraire et espere qu'elle sera jusqu'au jour qu'il faudra comparoistre a rendre compte."

[60] Du Tillet to Calvin, March 10, 1538 (Crottet, 29.8–10): "Ma conscience n'a jamais peu s'appaiser de ce que, sans certaine vocation de Dieu, je me estois retiré du lieu que ne devois delaisser sans commandement de Dieu."

driven du Tillet to his decision to rejoin Rome.[61] Thus, he does not believe that Calvin should so brazenly impose the dictates of his own conscience upon others, as if du Tillet should "abandon" and "contravene" his own conscience just to follow the judgment of his friend. No person should be forcibly persuaded to follow a course of action contrary to conscience, simply because of the confident admonitions of another.[62]

Nevertheless, as certain as Calvin is that his friend has gone against conscience by leaving the evangelical faith to return to Romish superstition, du Tillet appears equally convinced that Calvin's sense of calling to Geneva is mistaken. Du Tillet urges Calvin to acknowledge what he presumably knows to be true in his own conscience, that if his baptism in the Catholic Church was valid, then his ministry in that same church must also be from God. "If you have thought about it," du Tillet prompts Calvin, "in my opinion you cannot say otherwise with your conscience."[63] Indeed, du Tillet is convinced that all who deny that elements of the true church reside in Rome "deny it against their conscience."[64] Calvin's ouster from Geneva in 1538 seemed to bolster du Tillet's claim that Calvin's ministry in Geneva was of human origin rather than from God. He thus urges Calvin to let his "conscience be examined in truth before God the judge."[65] For, how could Calvin minister in Geneva "in good conscience," seeing as he was not called there upon God's authority? Calvin answers du Tillet's accusations with detectable annoyance, stating that he could receive his friend's admonitions well, "only if I did not want to contradict my conscience."[66] His letter offers justification for his pastoral calling among the evangelicals, and begs du Tillet to allow him "to follow the reign of [his] conscience," which, Calvin brazenly asserts, "is more certain than yours."[67]

If Calvin's bold claim that he possesses a superior conscience seems offensive according to modern sensibilities, then du Tillet's response is equally patronizing by the same standard. With an air of sarcasm, du Tillet wishes Calvin well in following the rule of his conscience, "as well informed as I wish that mine would be," but ultimately declines to accept Calvin's proposal

---

[61] Du Tillet to Calvin, March 10, 1538 (Crottet, 30.6–7): "L'affliction de conscience."
[62] Du Tillet to Calvin, March 10, 1538 (Crottet, 32).
[63] Du Tillet to Calvin, March 10, 1538 (Crottet, 35.10–11): "Si vous y avez bien pensé, vous ne pouvez a mon advis dire du contraire avec vostre conscience."
[64] Du Tillet to Calvin, March 10, 1538 (Crottet, 37).
[65] Du Tillet to Calvin, December 1, 1538 (Crottet, 71).
[66] Calvin to du Tillet, October 20, 1538 (Crottet, 58).
[67] Calvin to du Tillet, October 20, 1538 (Crottet, 60.20–22): "Mais je vous pry de me permettre suivre la reigle de ma conscience laquelle je scé estre plus certaine que la vostre."

that his conscience is more certain than his. Perhaps only for rhetorical effect, du Tillet concedes that his own view is "very ignorant and imperfect." Nevertheless, he wishes to allow his own conscience, and not Calvin's, to certify that he is within the realm of God's calling.[68] He concludes his final letter by again urging Calvin to "examine himself well according to God."[69]

Calvin's exchanges with du Tillet contain several important details. First, Calvin was not the only one with near-absolute confidence in the ability of his conscience to discern God's will. Du Tillet—although he was not the one to pen the words—could easily have stated that he believed his conscience was sounder than Calvin's, especially given his strong words of admonition regarding the legitimacy of Calvin's ministerial calling in the evangelical churches. Second, we note that Calvin and du Tillet's epistolary exchange ends with this matter totally unresolved; one does not sense that either man has clearly won the debate over religious compromise. Despite all their appeals to conscience as the divine tribunal of the soul, no apparent ground is gained by either man in convincing his friend of the truth. The two men appear to have ended their relationship following du Tillet's last letter, dated December 1, 1538.[70]

The letters passed between Calvin and du Tillet further illustrate that Calvin's own thoughts about Nicodemism were shaped in no small measure by impassioned discourse with friends and colleagues. In these letters, we encounter Calvin in what is perhaps his most vulnerable state: grieving the betrayal of an old friend, casting aspersions upon another's conscience in order to take refuge in his own position, deflecting du Tillet's intimations that *it is Calvin who is going against conscience* by forsaking his genuine call to the Church of his youth and operating instead under the misimpression of a legitimate ministry in Geneva—a ministry that had wholly collapsed around Calvin before his correspondence with du Tillet had even reached the halfway point. That Bucer and Capito would also give safe harbor to du Tillet on his journey back to Catholicism must have been particularly irksome to Calvin. And indeed, this raises another important question: Upon what basis did Bucer and Capito disagree with the dedicated anti-Nicodemite stance of Calvin and his French comrades in Geneva? A brief examination of some of Bucer's and Capito's writings reveals that the answer hinged in no small part

---

[68] Du Tillet to Calvin, December 1, 1538 (Crottet, 76).
[69] Du Tillet to Calvin, December 1, 1538 (Crottet, 78).
[70] Although the epistolary exchange between Calvin and du Tillet appears to have ended in 1538, du Tillet did exchange a few letters with Bucer through the early months of 1539 (Crottet, 21).

upon their perception of the balance between conscience and the communal rule of charity.

3.3.2. Bucer and Capito: Quasi-Nicodemite or Piously Prudent?

The fact of Bucer occupying a mediating position on the matter of Nicodemism is not altogether unexpected. He is often cited as a prime example of sixteenth-century irenicism, even compromise.[71] Nevertheless, when it came to Roman Catholic worship practices, especially the Mass, Bucer was consistently critical. In his 1524 *Grund und Ursach*—an explanation of the ground (*Grund*) and cause or justification (*Ursach*) for the Reformation in Strasbourg—Bucer considered it "the most horrible, most poisonous and most wicked insult and blasphemy of Jesus Christ" to believe the eucharist constitutes a re-sacrificing of his body and blood.[72] He could certainly agree with Farel, Calvin, and Viret that Protestants living in Catholic lands faced an unfortunate dilemma of choosing between the impiety of Romish ceremonies and the call to trust Christ and live holy lives.[73] Bucer also acknowledged that the Bible is replete with examples of God's judgment upon false worshippers who foolishly believed they could hold right and wrong, light and darkness, Christ and Belial in common.[74] Chapter 2 has already shown, moreover, that Bucer was not opposed to the use of external means for regulating personal and communal piety. His plan for expunging Catholic practices and establishing right order in the Strasbourg churches included a citizen's oath and formal confession of faith—so-called externals of religion. Thus, as important as the unity of the church was to Bucer, it was

---

[71] See Brian Lugioyo, *Martin Bucer's Doctrine of Justification: Reformation Theology and Early Modern Irenicism* (Oxford: Oxford University Press, 2010). Despite visions of Bucer as an early-modern "ecumenical," apt to compromise doctrine for the sake of unity—depictions usually drawn from his attempts to find common ground between the Protestant and Catholic camps at the Diet of Regensburg in 1541—Lugioyo nevertheless shows that Bucer was a remarkably consistent theologian, especially on the doctrine of justification. On complaints by other reformers that Bucer was too often the "peacemaker," see Hastings Eells, *Martin Bucer* (New Haven, CT: Yale University Press, 1931), 217.

[72] Bucer, *Grund und Ursach*, sig. C [i]ʳ: ". . . die greülichste vergifftigste unnd allerschedlichste schmach und lesterung Christi Jesu." Likewise, see Bucer's *De Caena Dominica* (BOL 1:1–58). Throughout this treatise on the Lord's Supper, Bucer describes the Catholic Mass—and Catholic worship in general—in such negative terms as "idolatriae," "blasphemiae," "praepostera religio hominum," and "insana figmenta."

[73] Bucer, *Consilium Theologicum* (BOL 4:60, #284).

[74] Bucer, *Epistola Apologetica* (BOL 1:104).

achievable only in accord with the purity of doctrine and life; anything less amounted to a "*pseudoecclesiasticis*" (false church).[75]

Capito was likewise critical of papist worship and had even diagnosed the error of religious compromise in his brief catechism, *De Pueris Instituendis Ecclesiae Argentinensis Isagoge*, published in both Latin and English in 1527.[76] This work, which mimics a dialogue between a father and his obstinate son, commends the instruction of "the pure word of God," warning against the "false dissemblers and hypocrites" whose lives and teachings contradict the pure gospel.[77] Like Bucer, Capito emphasizes that true Christianity is preserved in the simple teachings of the reformers, and stands in stark contrast to the human inventions and unbiblical inventions of the "outward church" that are "vain and of no effect."[78] From these activities "cometh neither goodness nor yet profit to man's neighbor."[79] On the contrary, the father instructs his son that the life of true Christian piety is composed of "a steadfast faith towards God and pure love (*charitate*) without simulation (*simulandi*) towards a man's neighbor."[80]

It is notable that Capito's rebuke of religious compromise anticipates nearly the exact objections that Farel, Viret, and Calvin would voice—publicly and in print—during the 1530s. In his catechism, Capito identifies three primary reasons for why engaging in religious dissimulation is unlawful for the Christian. First, he opposes a radical conception of Christian freedom that "will have a Christian man to be free ... in all outward things." A Christian best serves God by using his or her liberty as an occasion for loving and serving one's neighbor.[81] Capito nevertheless distinguishes, secondly,

---

[75] Bucer, *Epistola Apologetica* (BOL 1:104): ". . . tota anima ad Christum unicum animarum nostrarum pastorem nos convertissemus, et satis superque experti nihil posse iustitiae et iniustitiae, luci et tenebris, Christo et Belial commune esse, istis pseudoecclesiasticis, non autem ecclesiae vale dixissemus, hoc est desiissemus uvas sperare a sentibus, ficus a tribulis." Calvin makes a similar comparison with reference to "Christ and Belial" (2 Cor. 6:15) in his *Institutes 1536* (CO 1:209; Battles ed., 189). Likewise, see Viret's comments during the Disputation in Lausanne, in Piaget, *Actes*, 247.

[76] Capito's *De Pueris* is unique because it is the first Protestant catechism published in English. In the same year that the Latin appeared in print, William Roye, a former assistant of William Tyndale, translated and published Capito's work in Strasbourg under the title *A Lytle treatous or dialoge very necessary for all christen men to learne and to knowe*, also referred to as *A Brefe Dialoge bitwene a Christen Father and his stobborne Sonne*.

[77] Capito, *A Brefe Dialoge bitwene a Christen Father and his stobborne Sonne*, trans. William Roye, ed. Douglas H. Parker and Bruce Krajewski (Toronto: University of Toronto Press, 1999), 103.143, 143.1470–71.

[78] Capito, *A Brefe Dialoge*, 108.331–32. Capito lists "confessions/pardons/pilgrimage/making of difference between days and meats/hearing and reading of masse" as primary examples of man-made Catholic rites (108.328–30).

[79] Capito, *A Brefe Dialoge*, 108.334–35.

[80] Capito, *A Brefe Dialoge*, 103.156–57; Latin text available in Appendix B, 257.

[81] Capito, *A Brefe Dialoge*, 112.483–502.

between worldly and harmful constitutions of the church, which cruelly bind the conscience, and the external demonstration or confession of one's faith, which is required of the believer. True piety demands that Christians worship the only true God "not inwardly in the heart alone but also in every external thing." No one may stand by quietly as God's name is repeatedly blasphemed through the invocation of idols and superstitious rites and expect to avoid "the sharp scourge and cruel judgment of God."[82] All believers "openly should confess Christ. And at all seasons be ready rather to suffer death than willingly to withstand him in one iota."[83] Moreover, Capito calls upon all magistrates to fulfill their duty and observe God's command "to promote his honor [and] to defend the confessors of his name."[84] Finally, Capito denounces religious dissimulation on the basis that it violates the rule of love and charity toward one's neighbor. When a Christian succumbs to "the superstitious inventions of the enemy" by observing perverse Catholic ceremonies, one abuses their Christian liberties, fails to edify one's neighbor, and violates charity.[85]

Given Bucer and Capito's staunch critiques of Catholic worship, including the practice of religious dissimulation, it is all the more surprising to find them at odds with the emerging anti-Nicodemite position of the Reformed camp in the late 1530s. Stranger still is the fact that, by 1550, after many of Calvin's anti-Nicodemite writings had been published under one title, *De vitandis superstitionibus* (with appended opinions rendered by Philipp Melanchthon, Bucer, and Peter Martyr Vermigli), Calvin declares that he detects no substantial difference between his and Bucer's views on the matter.[86] Does the apparent vacillation in Bucer's stance on religious compromise indicate a fundamental lack of conviction, enough to label the Strasbourg reformers themselves as "Nicodemites," or at very least, "Quasi-Nicodemites"?[87] Or, are these apparent discrepancies simply indicative of Bucer's own pastoral prudence, which allowed him to adjust his expectations for those living under the duress of unwonted circumstances?

---

[82] Capito, *A Brefe Dialoge*, 114.520–34.
[83] Capito, *A Brefe Dialoge*, 116.591–94.
[84] Capito, *A Brefe Dialoge*, 116.581–83.
[85] Capito, *A Brefe Dialoge*, 110.399–410. Capito insists, "charity constraineth us to be servants unto all men." See also 113.505–509.
[86] Calvin, *De Vitandis Superstitionibus* [*Ioannis Calvini Consilium et Conclusio*] (CO 6:632). Despite Calvin's complaint that Melanchthon (with whom Bucer and Vermigli agree) failed to respond word for word to his objections, Calvin is content that, "in ipso quaestionis statu, et summa, non puto hoc meum responsum ab aliorum sententia discrepare."
[87] This is Wickersham's claim in *Rituals of Prosecution*, 110–11.

Despite Farel's accusation, Bucer—and to a lesser extent, Capito—do not strictly deserve the Nicodemite moniker.[88] As noted above, their criticism of the traditional church could hardly have been more acute. Moreover, their proposed leniency toward suffering Protestants in France was always intended as a temporary concession.[89] One might argue they held a more positive view of the remnant of the faithful that remained within the Catholic Church.[90] Though overshadowed by the tyranny of the Roman Pontiff, Bucer believed "there are many children of God and true sheep of Christ" remaining in the Old Church.[91] But this was hardly a radical notion, even at the time. Calvin admits at least this much in his letter to King Francis when he acknowledges that God has always preserved his children, "though scattered and hidden in the midst of these errors and darkness."[92] He would later write in his 1559 *Institutes* that there were "traces" (*vestigia*) of the true church that survived, by God's providence, even under the papacy.[93]

Where Bucer and Capito differed from the other reformers was in their perception of the balance, first, between theory and reality, and second, between conscience and the rule of love. The Strasbourg reformers were willing to temper their expectations for how French Protestants should live in Catholic lands to the unique circumstances surrounding their suffering— much like Roussel had urged Farel to do. Although they believed that religious compromise was wrong in principle and should be avoided, they also recognized that desperate situations sometimes required a more measured and patient response, especially toward those who might fall into error

---

[88] Erika Rummel shows that, more so than Bucer, Capito held the reputation of "a systematic defender of Nicodemism" for much of his life (to Luther's great annoyance). Capito's appeals for moderate reform measures that were "piously prudent" in tone was often linked to his love of Erasmian humanism. See Rummel, *The Confessionalization of Humanism in Reformation Germany* (Oxford: Oxford University Press, 2000), 111–20.

[89] Bucer, *Consilium Theologicum* (BOL 4:132, #545). Bucer and Capito do not strictly deserve the Nicodemite brand for another key reason: they would not advocate the misinterpretation of Scripture to legitimize religious dissimulation.

[90] Bucer, *Consilium* [appendix to Calvin's *De Vitandis Superstitionibus*] (CO 6:625): "Quaecunque Dei et Christi supersunt in vulgatis lectionibus, concionibus et aliis ecclesiasticis actionibus, ita vitiari non posse, nec impietate ministrorum, nec irreligiosa humanorum commentorum admixtione, nec superstition abutentium, quin pii homines loquentem et agentem in illis Dominum audire et scutire queant, et ad incrementum pictatis illis uti."

[91] Bucer, *Consilium Theologicum* (BOL 4:49, #234): "Postquam enim mihi dubium non est (nec aliis esse debere credo) quin in hisce ecclesiis omnibus, pontificia tyrannide pressis, sint multi filii Dei [cf. Rm 8, 14] et verae oves Christi." Section five of the *Consilium Theologicum* comprises Bucer's polemical response to Calvin's *Epistolae Duae*.

[92] *Institutes 1536* (CO 1:21; Battles ed., 10): "Interim tamen suos et disperses et delitescentes in mediis erroribus et tenebris servavit."

[93] *Institutes* 4.2.11 (CO 2:775; LCC 21:1051).

unwittingly.[94] An overly aggressive approach, like that taken by Farel and Calvin, could do more harm than good. Thus, Bucer contended that those whose strength had buckled under the weight of persecution should not be scorned or abandoned by the reformers.[95] Rather, they should be loved, counseled, and urged to stand firm in their confession.[96]

Whereas Farel and Calvin believed the plight of French Protestants demanded one of two choices—flee to a place where one could freely confess their faith or die making public confession before one's enemies—Bucer articulated a third option. One could remain in the Catholic Church, keeping certain Protestant views quiet for a time, while actively working toward the reformation of the church and the restoration of its unity based upon God's truth.[97] Bucer saw the Catholic Church as a mission field ripe for the picking. Although he agreed with his colleagues that it was necessary for all Christians to demonstrate their zeal and affection for God by confessing his name by all the ceremonies ordained for that purpose, Bucer believed that French Protestants had a unique and potentially more effective opportunity: they could remain within the Catholic Church and seek to "gain brothers" through their clandestine witness.[98] Farel and Calvin regarded staying in the Old Church and seeking to reform it from within to be an unfruitful, even compromising endeavor. The external Church of Rome was unsalvageable, they believed. Bucer, on the other hand, saw their encouragement to flee as a weakening of the Protestant witness in France.[99] This approach meant abandoning ripe fruit on the vine. Thus, while he agreed that dissimulation was wrong in theory, Bucer denied that all Protestants remaining in Catholic

---

[94] Bucer, *Consilium Theologicum* (BOL 4:152, #668). In his *Grund und Ursach*, sig. E ii^r–sig. E iii^v, Bucer acknowledges that the idolatrous practices of Rome—including the "elevation of the bread and cup of Christ" and all such "external things" (*ausserliche ding*) instituted without any foundation in God's word—are nothing but an "abomination and error." Nevertheless, Bucer allowed such practices to continue in Strasbourg for a time "for the sake of the weak, until they, too, would be more perfectly instructed through the Word." Bucer admits that such "waiting" has earned them the reputation of two-faced "double papists (*dupel papisten*)," but he is willing to absorb insults for the sake of gently guiding weaker members to a fuller understanding of the word. One hears echoes of Luther's 1522 *Invocavit Sermons*, in which Luther advises his followers neither to insist on their own rights nor to turn Christianity into a religion of external regimentation, but rather to deal patiently with papists until they are gradually won over to the true gospel. See especially sermons 1 and 2, in LW 51:70–78.
[95] Bucer, *Consilium Theologicum* (BOL 4:132, #548; 4:150, #651–52).
[96] Bucer, *Consilium Theologicum* (BOL 4:131, #540). See also Bucer's *Consilium* [appendix to Calvin's *De Vitandis Superstitionibus*] (CO 6:626).
[97] Bucer, *Consilium Theologicum* (BOL 4:132, #545).
[98] Bucer, *Consilium* [appendix to Calvin's *De Vitandis Superstitionibus*] (CO 6:626): "lucrifaciendi fratres."
[99] Van Stam, "The Group of Meaux," 274, n. 111, suggests that the weakening of the Protestant witness in France after 1550 was an unintended result of the anti-Nicodemite position.

France were, in reality, concealing or faking their identity. By conveying their true heart and affection for God in both "common and holy things"—albeit with some strategic concealment—they were actually able to teach their brothers and sisters "more conveniently and with greater efficacy."[100] Indeed, it was prudent "to become popish with the papists" (*päpstlich seind worzden mit den päpstliche*) as occasion demanded it if, by engaging in practices of themselves indifferent, they might be able "to proclaim Christ to [the lost] better and ... win them."[101] Bucer's counsel demonstrates that, in terms of the practical aspects of reform, he was more interested in dealing with specific situations than mere theory.[102]

Bucer and Capito also opposed the anti-Nicodemite position of Farel, Viret, and Calvin because they believed that the communal rule of charity was the principal law that should govern one's public life.[103] Peter Matheson and others have noted that Bucer, in particular, was above all "a community person."[104] The individual life must always be guided by the biblical "rule of love" or "charity" that required one to seek the needs of his or her neighbors above all.[105] This emphasis is consistent with the reform measures Bucer promoted in Strasbourg. Despite the complaints of Franck and Schwenkfeld that their consciences should not be bound to human ceremonies, Bucer and Capito insisted, despite pressure from city magistrates, that the Anabaptists were not free to foster disharmony in Strasbourg simply for the sake of assuaging their own consciences. Swearing an oath to the Reformation took precedence over the Anabaptists' consciences, because it was best suited to achieve communal peace and unity, synonymous with charity or Christian love.

Thus, Bucer's primary concern was that the Christian's commitment to sound doctrine should never compromise the communal rule of love. Faith working through love—the essence of true piety, in his mind—required that one be willing to shepherd others and seek their conversion before insisting on one's own rights or safety. Protestants living in Catholic territories could take advantage of the mission field before them in order to restore the

---

[100] Bucer, *Consilium* [appendix to Calvin's *De Vitandis Superstitionibus*] (CO 6:626): "in communibus rebus, tum in sacris ... commodius et efficacious docerent."
[101] Bucer, *Grund und Ursach*, sig. F ii^v–sig. F ii^r.
[102] Eells, *Martin Bucer*, 220, 231, 237.
[103] Bucer, *Grund und Ursach*, sig. F iii^v–sig. F iii^r.
[104] Peter Matheson, "Martin Bucer and the Old Church," in *Martin Bucer: Reforming Church and Community*, ed. David F. Wright (Cambridge: Cambridge University Press, 1994), 12, nn. 70–71.
[105] As Chapter 5 will show, Bucer and Capito's *Tetrapolitan Confession* (1530) heavily reflects this emphasis on the rule of love or charity.

church, even if that meant setting aside personal convictions and enduring some of the superstitious and abominable rites of the Roman Church for a time.[106] Christ's kingdom would certainly prevail over the kingdom of the Antichrist, and since the consciences of true believers were impervious to the external attacks and abuses of Rome, one had to be willing to forgo private impulses in order to promote what was best for the ecclesial community.[107] In this regard, Bucer interpreted Paul's words about "being a Jew to win Jews" rather differently than Calvin, who restricted Paul's instructions to things truly "indifferent," that is, not touching the conscience, such as Old Covenant restrictions clearly abrogated by Christ.[108] The scope of "permitted" things was significantly wider for Bucer than it was for Calvin. Even the external ceremonies of Rome were in themselves harmless and held no real sway over the consciences of believers, Bucer believed. Although superstitious worship in itself was wrong, Protestants committed to godly worship might feign participation in such empty rites for a time, moderating their personal anger and discomfort in order to promote the higher good of gospel missions and social harmony.[109] Whereas Farel and Calvin touted the "heroic alternative" of leaving the Catholic Church as the only option consistent with the freedom and purity of conscience, Bucer insisted there was another way more in keeping with the rule of love and charity. The important question was not what French Protestants should do to "salve their own consciences," but how they could serve the kingdom of Christ, even from within the realm of the Antichrist.[110]

* * *

Our study of the early Nicodemite controversy has revealed that, despite fundamental agreement over the nature of the gospel and the erroneous

---

[106] Bucer, *Consilium Theologicum* (BOL 4:147, ch. 62).

[107] Bucer, *Consilium Theologicum* (BOL 4:155–56, #693–95).

[108] See *Institutes 1536*, §6 (CO 1:195–204; Battles ed., 176–84). Calvin sums up Christian freedom in three points: (1) freedom from the pursuit of law-righteousness (resting in the perfect works of Christ); (2) willing obedience to God's law; and (3) freedom of conscience from observing "outward things of themselves 'indifferent,' " like matters of food or drink. Unlike Bucer, however, Calvin does not include the external elements of Catholic worship in the category of "indifferent" things.

[109] Bucer, *Consilium Theologicum* (BOL 4:152–53, ch. 64). Also, *Grund und Ursach*, sig. E iii^v–sig. E [iv]^r. Capito held a similar aversion to reforming the church at the expense of social order and love of neighbor. See Rummel, *The Confessionalization of Humanism*, 114.

[110] Matheson, "Martin Bucer," 14. Nevertheless, Bucer would later acknowledge that it was becoming increasingly difficult for Protestants to remain in Catholic France and continue to confess their faith, especially among those who would burden their consciences by forcing them to neglect the commands of Christ. See, e.g., Bucer to Marguerite de Navarre, July 5, 1538 (Herminjard 5:40, #721).

character of Romish worship, the reformers nevertheless were not all of one mind in their conception of the essence and scope of genuine piety. Although the Strasbourg reformers agreed in principle that genuine piety was not simply a private matter but should manifest itself publicly—often by means of religious oaths, vows, and professions of faith—they dissented from the French reformers by denying that such outward displays of religious devotion were required to maintain the purity of conscience. Religious externals were of themselves indifferent, and therefore a matter of one's free use or disuse depending on the circumstances. To engage temporarily in the superstitious rites of Catholic worship amounted to nothing, therefore, as long as one maintained godly intention and a personal commitment to pure worship. The rule of love and charity, in particular, superseded the internal conviction of conscience and required that one do what is best for the salvation of one's neighbor, even if this meant enduring Romish "exile" indefinitely until the weak more surely embraced the word of God. Thus, a prudent assessment of times and circumstances, rather than a rigid application of sound doctrine, dictated whether a public confession of faith was necessarily required of believers. As we have seen, this unique brand of spirituality allowed Bucer and Capito to require an oath of subscription from conscientious objectors in Strasbourg (for the sake of communal accord, they argued), while at the same time justifying their patience toward French exiles whose opportunity for a clandestine gospel witness within Rome outweighed in importance the need for strict doctrinal conformity and public confession.

The French reformers were no less committed to the rule of love and charity; Calvin and Farel frequently urged their persecuted brothers and sisters to avoid dissimulation because it set a compromising witness for weaker members. However, their conception of the relationship between conscience and confession resulted in a different application of that very rule. For Calvin, in particular, any form of religious concealment was deemed an act of impiety, since the worship that God requires from his people necessarily includes both the ascent of the soul and the confession of one's mouth. Dissimulation, no matter how well-intentioned, was therefore an adulteration of pure worship. Only those whose consciences were "armed" against God and callous toward other weak sinners could possibly persist in Nicodemite behavior—a reality Calvin's own experiences with erstwhile friends and colleagues seemed to confirm. Thus, Calvin's staunch commitment to the maxim, "genuine piety begets genuine confession," fit hand in glove with his favored means of exposing religious compromise—appealing to the supposedly unequivocal tribunal of the private conscience. As the next chapter will illustrate in further detail, Calvin would continue to oppose Nicodemism for the remainder of his ministry by portraying religious dissimulation as a complete abandonment of the voice of conscience.

4
Confession, Conscience, and Christian Freedom in the Later Anti-Nicodemite Writings of Calvin and the Reformers, 1540–1562

Following the Disputation of Lausanne in October 1536, Calvin could hardly have been more enthusiastic about the reformers' success at convincing leaders of the Bernese territories that Rome constituted a false church, one that all faithful Christians ought to denounce and abandon. Farel and Viret had spoken boldly and decisively at the conference, censuring those, like Roussel, who persisted in wicked dissimulation and vain worship. As the crowning achievement of the disputation, the Council of Bern had decided to remove idolatrous altars and images from its newly conquered lands—a purging that began almost immediately.[1] Moreover, Calvin's *Epistolae Duae*, published in early 1537, seemed to have landed the decisive blow against the pernicious error of Nicodemism.[2] As confident as young Calvin may have been that he and his Reformed allies had sufficiently dispensed with the matter of Nicodemism, however, we might ascribe such assurances to Calvin's youthful optimism, even naivete. Actually, the issue was far from over. Calvin continually found himself obliged to address the Nicodemite error as an unforeseen—and often wearisome—aspect of his later pastoral ministry. And he was not alone. Over the next several decades, Farel and Viret, as well as Italian convert Peter Martyr Vermigli, also felt compelled to

---

[1] Introduction to COR 4/4:XXXIX. In a letter to François Daniel, written shortly after the conclusion of the Disputation on October 13, 1536, Calvin rejoices that "already, in many places, the idols and altars have begun to be removed, and I hope that in a short time, all remaining superstition shall be utterly cleared away." Calvin to Daniel, October 13, 1536 (Herminjard 4:86–91, #573).

[2] See Guillaume Farel's letter to Wolfgang Capito from May 5, 1537; in COR 4/4, Appendix 2, p. 142, ll. 99–103. Farel speaks highly of Calvin's recent publication; in his opinion, Calvin's treatise has sufficiently admonished dissembling Christians to the degree that it ought to correct their impiety.

write pastoral letters of admonition and encouragement for those who were tempted to veil their Protestant commitments out of convenience or fear.

An examination of the treatises and letters of the anti-Nicodemite reformers reveals that Farel, Viret, and Vermigli embraced Calvin's maxim, "genuine piety begets genuine confession," without deviation. All agreed that dissimulating one's internal commitments, both in life and in worship, was a gross perversion of one's duty toward God. While fulfilling his ministry to French-speaking Protestants in Lausanne in 1543, Viret published a consoling treatise for comrades suffering in Catholic lands, admonishing his brothers and sisters to remain faithful in their confession of the truth despite their present exile among the papists. They must not resort to religious dissimulation, for God considers spiritual affection and outward testimony of one's faith to be "inseparable things."[3] Farel, while championing the French Reform movement from Neuchâtel, likewise wrote to French Protestants in 1544, urging them to remember that a godly life joined with a bold confession comprise the fruits of genuine faith.[4] Those who engage in dissimulation and shrink from making public confession "dishonor God," who "requires heartfelt faith, and confession of the mouth."[5] Even Vermigli, who had himself practiced a form of quasi-Nicodemism, preaching Protestant-themed sermons while still wearing his Augustinian habit, would become a staunch critic of Nicodemite behavior.[6] Dissimulation, he came to believe, was a

---

[3] Pierre Viret, *Epistre envoyee aux fideles conversans entre les Chrestiés Papistiques, pour leur remonstrer comment ilz se doyvent garder d'estre souillez et polluz par leurs superstitions et idolatries, et de deshonorer Iesus Christ par icelles* (1543), sig. C iii^r. The most comprehensive—albeit dated—general biography of Viret remains the work of Jean Bernaud, *Pierre Viret: Sa vie et son oeuvre, 1511–1571* (Saint-Amans: G. Carayol, 1911).

[4] Farel, *Epistre exhortatoire à tous ceux qui ont congnoissance de l'Evangile* (Geneva, 1544), sig. A iv^r: "et rendu les vrays fruictz de la Foy." For a brief summary of Farel's life and ministry prior to the 1540s, see *Early French Reform: The Theology and Spirituality of Guillaume Farel*, ed. Jason Zuidema and Theodore Van Raalte (London: Routledge, 2016), 7–14.

[5] Farel, *Epistre exhortatoire*, sig B [i]^v: "Car il demande la Foy au cueur, et la confession de bouche."

[6] For historical background on Vermigli's early life as a quasi-Nicodemite, see Jane K. Wickersham, *Rituals of Prosecution: The Roman Inquisition and the Prosecution of Philo-Protestants in Sixteenth-Century Italy* (Toronto, ON: University of Toronto Press, 2012), 90: "Originally a Florentine, [Vermigli] had joined the Canons Regular of Augustine in 1514. He was active in the reform-minded circle of the *spirituali*; it was most likely in Naples, as a part of Juan de Valdes' circle, that Vermigli first had read Protestant literature. He also had served Pope Paul III at events such as the Colloquy of Worms (1540); and he had undertaken reform programs in Spoleto, Naples, and Lucca. It was in Lucca that Vermigli organized a theological college at which, according to Girolamo Zanchi, another future exile, Vermigli had his students study Bucer, Melanchthon, Bullinger, and Calvin. But in the summer of 1542 Vermigli experienced his crisis of conscience; he was called before the Augustinian chapter in Genoa to account for himself, and his friends warned him that this was a prelude to being called before the newly reconstituted Inquisition. Vermigli therefore fled," eventually ending up in Zurich. Wickersham summarizes, "Vermigli's perspective concerning Nicodemite behavior was therefore one born of his own failed attempt, followed by multiple flights seeking the opportunity to teach, preach, and practice openly" (109).

destructive form of double-mindedness that forsook the command of God to conjoin the faith of one's heart with ritual confession: "The tongue doth confess the thing that lies in the heart by words: so actions do give a confession thereof in deed."[7] Vermigli warns his readers that, when they deny true religion by failing to give a good confession of their faith, even among adversaries of the gospel, they do so "without a doubt against their own conscience."[8] To a person, the reformers therefore claimed that Nicodemism was an inexcusable and condemnable practice, not only on the basis of the authority of God's word, but also according to the testimony of conscience.

What follows is a close reading of select letters and treatises composed by anti-Nicodemite reformers following their initial rebuke of Nicodemism during the 1530s. The overarching purpose of this chapter is to develop some of the themes explored in Chapter 3, which retraced the timeline of events precipitating the Nicodemite controversy. Though accounting for matters of epistolary history and context, the following study primarily aims to show how the anti-Nicodemite views of Calvin and his allies took shape in the aftermath of this controversy and displayed remarkable continuity over the course of several decades. As will be seen, the interwoven themes of ritual confession, conscience, and Christian liberty formed a nexus of concerns that elicited the reformers' ongoing anti-Nicodemite polemic. Their repeated appeals to conscience, particularly as a means of convicting their readers and of vindicating their own position, resulted in the occasional charge that the reformers liked "to philosophize about war while in the shade," arrogantly presuming to rebuke those who were suffering while they themselves enjoyed the protection of Protestant magistrates.[9] Calvin, Farel, Viret, and Vermigli had in fact known what it was like to be religious refugees and face

---

[7] Peter Martyr Vermigli, *A treatise of the cohabitacyon of the faithfull with the unfaithfull* (Strasbourg, 1555), sig. C [vi]ᵛ–sig. C [vii]ᵛ. In his posthumously published *Epistre de M. Pierre Martyr Florentin a Quelques Fideles touchant leur abiuration et renoncement de la verité* (Geneva, 1574), Vermigli also emphasizes the necessity of combining genuine faith with ritual confession. Upon calling people to himself and giving them faith, the Lord wants his children to confess their faith: "Apres vous avoir appelez, vous avoir donné la foy, il voulooit avoir la confession," (sig. A ivᵛ). It is not enough "to have a clean heart and unpolluted soul," as if one could "esteem God to be Lord only of the soul." Vermigli insists that one must also "take care of what is done externally" by way of public confession: "s'excusent qu'il suffit avoir le coeur net et l'ame impollue ... comme s'ils estimoient Dieu n'estre Seigneur que de l'ame suelement ... garde de si pres à ce qui ce fait exterieurement," (sig. B ivᵛ).

[8] Vermigli, *A treatise of the cohabitacyon* [*A Sermon of the true confessing of Christe and the truithe of the gospell* (appended sermon)] (1555), (sig. I iiiᵛ–sig. I iiiʳ).

[9] This accusation was made of Calvin, specifically, but his Reformed colleagues were found to be no less persistent in their rebuke of Nicodemite behavior. In *Epistola Prior* (COR 4/4:63.1546–48), Calvin acknowledges the complaint that his admonitions are too harsh and perhaps even hypocritical: "In alto, inquiries, pinguique ocio viriles istos igniculos iacere facile tibi est, non secus ac de bello in umbra philosophari, at si in rem praesentem ventum fuerit, aliter sentias."

the temptation to compromise their beliefs under threat of persecution. Nevertheless, as the following writings reveal, the reformers insisted that the matter of religious compromise should not be adjudicated on the basis of subjective feelings or experience, but rather on the basis of God's word, the final judge of the conscience.

4.1. Reformed Anti-Nicodemite Treatises and Letters: Themes and Controversies

Guided by the principle that all believers are obligated to exercise their Christian freedom in obedience to God's commands, the reformers composed their polemical but pastoral letters and treatises to make explicit how purity of conscience should be expressed and maintained through the love of God and charity toward one's neighbors.[10] Achieving this goal meant identifying some of the mistaken notions about conscience and Christian piety that Nicodemite sympathizers regularly invoked in their pursuit of validation. As the following texts reveal, Calvin and the reformers pinpointed several important themes and controversies that would shape their critique of Nicodemite behavior. To be examined in turn, these included (1) the necessity of submitting one's conscience to the word of God as well as to the authority of godly ministers, such as the reformers, who had been tasked—they believed—with judging the consciences of others; (2) avoiding the dissimulation of one's faith, not merely for the sake of private conscience, but also out of a charitable concern for protecting the consciences of others; (3) responding to Nicodemite claims that veiling one's faith by dissimulation and participating in Catholic rituals are "indifferent" matters, and therefore justified for believers; and (4) achieving a balance between requiring believers to partake in godly ceremonies, on one hand, while also allowing suffering saints to participate in a simple or accommodated form of confession on account of their trying circumstances.

---

[10] As noted in the previous chapter, a central element of Calvin's understanding of Christian freedom—already in his 1536 *Institutio*—is the idea that believers are free from the condemnation and curse of the Decalogue *so that* they might willingly obey God's will and serve their neighbors in love. See *Institutes* (1536) (CO 1:197–99, Battles ed., 177–79).

4.1.1. Conscience and Pastoral Authority

Although the reformers believed that religious dissimulation constituted a clear violation of God's will, this matter was not as clearly spelled out in Scripture as they might have hoped. Luke 9:26, Romans 10:10, and I Corinthians 10 became standard texts for proving that Nicodemite behavior fell short of genuine Christian piety, but these passages did not necessarily touch on the specific dilemmas Nicodemism posed: Could someone justly veil their commitment to true religion while sleepwalking through the empty rites of false religion? And might sufficiently weighty circumstances exist that could justify such behavior? With only contested biblical support at their disposal, the reformers frequently turned to another source of moral authority to combat the unique problem of Nicodemism: their own consciences as ministers of the word. Calvin and his colleagues assumed that their ministerial offices authorized them to discern in their own consciences what types of practices accorded with the word of God, as well as those that fell under the weight of God's judgment. Calvin, in particular, seemed to think that the consciences of his readers were necessarily mirrors of his own, which meant that other Christians would evaluate Nicodemism as he did, so long as they did not suppress their own consciences. Thus, Calvin routinely appealed to his own tranquility of conscience as proof that his pastoral counsel was biblically sound, and therefore a reliable model his readers could safely emulate.

Several of Calvin's anti-Nicodemite writings illustrate this conviction. While ministering in Strasbourg in 1540, having been exiled from Geneva just a few years earlier, Calvin composed a brief letter offering counsel on how captive Protestants might continue to glorify God and live according to his word, even while surrounded by Romish idolatries.[11] As in his *Epistolae Duae*, Calvin begins this letter somewhat cautiously, vulnerable to the possibility that his admonitions may seem overly strict and lacking in pastoral sensitivity. He remains utterly resolute in his own conscience, however, that his counsel is irrefutably correct—at least if it is received by reasonable persons. "As for the judgment of my conscience," Calvin writes, "I do not see how this [the abominable Mass] can be excused. And my reason, which induces me to judge in this way, seems to me too absolute to be able to refute or reject

---

[11] This letter was written on September 12, 1540, and later appended to Calvin's 1543 *Petit traicté* under the designation, *S'ensuit l'autre Epistre*. The text of this letter is found in CO 6:579–88 and is hereafter cited in abbreviated form as *Epistre*.

it."[12] Utterly confident in the reasonableness of his own assessment, Calvin appeals to his own inner peace of conscience as proof of the validity of his position. Calvin concludes this correspondence by exhorting all his French brothers and sisters to examine their own consciences to see whether his assessment of their predicament is in fact accurate. He admonishes them, "in the name of God, to take stock frequently, by examining their consciences thoroughly, truly recognizing how much is lacking for them to do their duty of serving God as they should do it."[13] Having appealed to the existential surety of his own conscience as evidence of the validity of his critique, Calvin urges his extended flock to do the same, for he is utterly sure that their consciences will—or at least should—accuse them of their hypocrisy and prompt a willing profession of faith.

In the following years, recurring communication with religious dissemblers only entrenched Calvin in his belief that those who disregarded his assessment of religious compromise were acting against their consciences. By 1543, Calvin's interactions with the Nicodemites had left him somewhat exasperated. He began to express personal anguish over the fact that so many people continued seeking his counsel on how to conduct themselves during popish worship, even though their consciences convicted them of their idolatry.[14] Calvin likens such faithless behavior to that of the biblical Balaam, who sought permission for things he knew fell outside of God's will. In his *Petit traicté monstrant que c'est que doit faire un homme fidele congnoissant la verité de l'evangile, quand il est entre les papistes*, Calvin vented his frustration:

---

[12] Calvin, *Epistre* (CO 6:584): "Quant est du iugement de ma conscience, ie ne vois point que cela se puisse excuser. Et ma raison qui m'induit à ainsi iuger, me semble trop peremptoire pour la pouvoir refuter, ou rejecter." The reference to "ma raison" seems to indicate Calvin's belief that his argument is patently logical in nature. Later, in his *Excuse à messieurs les Nicodemites*, Calvin would also contend that his critique of the Nicodemite conscience is "more than reasonable" (CO 6:594): "il appert evidemment que cela est plus que raisonnable." Thus, the phrase, "ma raison," which is absent from *Institutes* (1536), does not appear to be a favored phrase of Calvin denoting surety of conscience specifically, though Calvin certainly believed the reasonableness of his views would be confirmed by the word of God in tandem with his conscience.

[13] Calvin, *Epistre* (CO 6:586): "Ie les admoneste et exhorte au Nom de Dieu, de venir souvent à compte, en examinant droictement leurs consciences, et recongnoissant à la verité combine il s'en faut qu'ilz ne facent leur devoir de servir à Dieu comme ilz devroyent."

[14] Calvin's growing impatience with Nicodemite weakness is rather striking, especially in light of his general instructions for dealing with the weak in *Institutes* (1536). Calvin urged *continued patience* with the weak by tempering "use of our freedom as to allow for the ignorance of our weak brothers" (CO 1:201, Battles ed., 182). Some theologians, like Aquinas, had advised "conditional forbearance" of the weak. By contrast, writes Nelson Deyo Kloosterman, "Calvin nowhere speaks of trying to change the opinion of the weak by seeking to develop his moral insights or his convictions of conscience"; see *Scandalum Infirmorum et Communio Sanctorum: The Relation between Christian Liberty and Neighbor Love in the Church* (Neerlandia, AB: Inheritance Publications, 1991), 64. Clearly, Calvin did not believe that Nicodemites deserved such unconditional forbearance!

I do not understand how it is that most men, after learning that something is displeasing to God, nevertheless take leave to go seeking its defense. Indeed, I have seen a hundred people who asked for my advice on this matter, just like Balaam did of God, wanting to go before King Balak [Num. 22]. For he knew very well that it was against God's will to undertake the journey, yet he nonetheless did not fail to ask permission. Likewise, these people who are fairly convinced in their conscience that it is wrong to bow down before idols, inquire and question about what they should do, not to subdue their affection to God by acquiescing to his word, but so they may have free rein, and having an answer to their liking, may flatter themselves enough to remain in their evil-doing.[15]

Calvin concludes that such requests for advice are not an act of submission to God's will at all, but rather an act of "looking for cushions to put their consciences to sleep."[16] Such individuals are so eager to appease their consciences that they are also willing to twist the Scriptures to obtain favorable, albeit unnatural, meanings of the text.[17]

---

[15] Calvin, *Petit traicté monstrant que c'est que doit faire un homme fidele congnoissant la verité de l'evangile, quand il est entre les papistes* (CO 6:541): "Mais ie ne sçay comment la pluspart des hommes, apres avoir cogneu une chose desplaire à Dieu, se donnent neantmoins congé d'aller à l'encontre de sa defense. Et mesme i'en ay veu cent, sans le premier, qui nous demandoyent conseil sur cest affaire, tout ainsi que Ballam faisoit de Dieu, voulant aller par devers le Roy Balaac. Car il scavoit bien que c'estoit contre la volunté de Dieu, qu'il entreprint le voyage: mais si ne laissoit-il pas d'en demander licence. Pareillement ceux cy estans presque convaincus en leur conscience que c'est mal faict de se prosterner devant les idoles, s'enquierent et interroguent de ce qu'ilz doivent faire, non pas pour assubiectir leur affection à Dieu, en acquiessant à sa parolle: mais affin qu'on leur lasche la bride, et que ayant response selon leur desir, ilz se reposent en leur vice par vaine flaterie."

[16] Calvin, *Petit traicté* (CO 6:541).

[17] Calvin provides examples of Scriptural misuse throughout this treatise (CO 6:617–44). For instance, Nicodemites often sought vindication in the case of Naaman, the Syrian commander who continued to serve his king in the temple of his pagan deities, although he had made a profession of belief in the God of Israel following his miraculous healing. Calvin insists that Naaman is in fact a false example of religious compromise, since he was given special permission by the prophet Elisha to attend to his king's needs while in the temple, thus fulfilling his vocation, yet without compromising his internal commitments to the true God. For Calvin, Naaman's case is exceptional, and thus it provides no biblical justification for Nicodemite behavior. Vermigli and Bucer appear to have diverged from Calvin in their interpretations of Naaman's actions. Bucer considers Naaman to be an inspiring example of courage for suffering Protestants: they might choose to remain among the idolaters, but they should, like Naaman, remain committed to worshipping the true God alone (*De Vitandis Superstitionibus* [*Martini Buceri Consilium*]; CO 6:626). Vermigli, on the other hand, does not regard Naaman as a positive example for believers at all; his only virtue was asking Elisha to plead for forgiveness on his behalf whenever he worshipped at the temple of Rimon. Just as Elisha gave Naaman no reason to think that his behavior was lawful, so dissimulation in Catholic worship falls short of godly behavior, Vermigli argues (*De Vitandis Superstitionibus* [*Petri Martyris Consilium*]; CO 6:628).

The *Petit traicté* represents Calvin's most detailed and nuanced critique of Nicodemism. In particular, Calvin's assessment of the matter has developed to the point that he finds it advantageous to establish a key distinction between dissimulation and "simulation"—the latter being the greater error in his view:

> That is to say that we are not dealing with the difficulty of knowing if it is wrong to dissemble, but to simulate [i.e., imitate] and disguise oneself against the truth. Dissimulation is committed by hiding what one has within the heart. Simulation is more; it is to pretend and fake what is not true. In short, what lying is in words, simulation is in deeds.[18]

In Calvin's mind, the Nicodemites have committed a twofold error: first, perverting spiritual worship by entertaining a "false fantasy,"[19] despite the warning of conscience; and second, transferring God's due worship to another creature, such as an image. By engaging in deceptive worship, Nicodemite behavior fails to render to God the "double honor" he deserves: first, the spiritual service of the heart; then, pious outward worship and public profession of faith.[20]

Throughout this treatise, Calvin refuses to soothe the convicted consciences of his readers. He will not absolve them, but instead appeals to their own consciences as proof of guilt. "I call upon their own conscience, to see if it does not judge them guilty. What do they profit from having a man absolve them, since it is before God that they are convinced of doing evil?"[21] Calvin acknowledges the charge that if he were in their shoes, he would also dissimulate, but he is utterly convinced that he would not. "I answer that I say nothing else, except what my conscience urges me to say, and if I were to speak otherwise I would be wickedly blaspheming the truth."[22] Under similar circumstances, Calvin insists that he would retain his piety while praying

---

[18] Calvin, *Petit traicté* (CO 6:546): "Nous ne sommes pas sur ceste difficulté, assavoir si c'est mal faict de dissimuler: mais de simuler et se contrefaire contre la verité. Dissimulation se commet en cachant ce qu'on a dedans le cueur. Simulation est plus, c'est de faire semblant et feindre ce qui n'est point. En somme, ce qui seroit mentir de bouche, est simuler de faict."

[19] The Latin edition reads, "fantasy *which he has conceived in his heart*"—an apparent reference to a deceived conscience.

[20] Calvin, *Petit traicté* (CO 6:546).

[21] Calvin, *Petit traicté* (CO 6:555): "I'en appelle leur propre conscience, si elle ne les iuge point. Qu'est ce donc qu'ilz profitent de se faire absoudre par un homme, puis que devant Dieu ilz sont convaincus de mal faire?"

[22] Calvin, *Petit traicté* (CO 6:573): "Ie respons que ie ne dis autre chose, sinon ce que ma conscience me presse de dire: et que si ie vouloye autrement parler, ie blasphemeroye meschamment la verité."

for strength and steadfastness under trial, since his conscience is controlled by the truth of God. Still, Calvin's response is not entirely lacking in pastoral sensitivity. Out of his "pity and compassion" for these suffering saints, he admits that he "would gladly find a way to excuse them." Nevertheless, he is bound by his own conscience that will not allow him to dispense empty absolutions: "I say what my conscience urges me to say about them, even for their salvation."[23]

In the same year that Calvin published his *Petit traicté*, Viret also penned a letter to French Protestants languishing in Catholic lands, entitled *Epistre envoyee aux fideles conversans entre les Chrestiés Papistiques, pour leur remonstrer comment ilz se doyvent garder d'estre souillez et polluz par leurs superstitions et idolatries, et de deshonorer Iesus Christ par icelles*. This correspondence, Viret's first major anti-Nicodemite work, dispenses pastoral advice on how Christians should keep themselves from defilement amid the superstitions and idolatries of Rome. With characteristic humility, Viret admits that he is somewhat hesitant to write on the subject, as he suspects that Calvin's little tract might render his letter a general waste of time, paper, and ink.[24] In Viret's opinion, Calvin's treatment of the subject is manifestly biblical and reasonable, even to the point of being unassailable to his opponents. Nevertheless, because Calvin's treatise had not yet been sufficiently disseminated to those desiring to read it—and to follow up on an earlier consolatory letter Viret had written—Viret contributes his own thoughts on the matter.[25] He hopes that, at very least, his letter will "do no harm," and will, at best, "a little better satisfy the crippled conscience[s]" of his readers.[26]

Although his letter exhibits pastoral concern for the consciences of his readership, Viret nevertheless writes with a sense of urgency and conviction born of zeal for the right worship of God. He prompts his readers to submit

---

[23] Calvin, *Petit traicté* (CO 6:575): "Mais que l'en dis ce que ma conscience me presso d'en dire, voire mesme pour leur salut."

[24] Viret, *Epistre envoyee aux fideles* (1543), sig. A ii^r–sig. A iii^v (*l'Epistre au Lecteur*).

[25] In 1541, Viret had composed a general letter to suffering French Protestants, urging them to remain steadfast in their confession of the name of Christ (*Epistre consolatoire envoyée aux fideles qui souffrent persecution pour le Nom de Jesus et Verité evangelique*). The letter mostly employs the examples of faithful saints in the Scriptures to inspire Viret's readers, but it does not specifically deal with the issues of Nicodemism or the conscience.

[26] Viret, *Epistre envoyee aux fideles*, sig. A ii^v–sig. A iii^r (*l'Epistre au Lecteur*). At the conclusion of his epistle, Viret once again indicates that he wrote it at the request of "many troubled consciences" seeking advice in these matters (sig. I iv^r). Unlike in Calvin's case, however, these repeated requests from dissembling persons do not seem to have left Viret annoyed or exasperated. Instead, Viret's letters exhibit great pastoral patience and empathy.

their affections to the admonition of God's word instead of allowing themselves to be deceived by others into worship practices characterized by idolatry, superstition, and all sorts of condemnable evil. The worship of God is a matter of no small importance; no less serious is provoking God to anger by worshipping in a way contrary to his commands.[27] Viret thus singles out those who "dissimulate" in order to avoid the dangers associated with making a Protestant confession of faith, for he is certain that such people demonstrate a sore lack of piety. These dissemblers "have not yet learned to prefer, with Moses, the reproaches, punishments and miseries, the nails and spines of Jesus Christ, to the kings, treasures and temporal delights of Egypt." Though "pressed by their conscience" to condemn their idolatry, they desperately search in God's word for some justification to "clothe and mask" their impiety.[28] Such efforts are vain attempts to conceal the examples of the apostles and martyrs, who preferred the torments of persecution over the false haven of compromise.[29] Viret thus urges his readers to understand that God requires both spiritual affection and outward testimony of one's faith: "the confession of mouth, with the faith of the heart . . . are inseparable things."[30] All faithful believers must resist idolatry and "boldly confess" the truth "in good conscience."[31] Having admonished his readers, partly on the basis of their own consciences, Viret nevertheless concludes his letter on a pastoral note: he has written "not to further disturb and despair the poor, crippled, and afflicted consciences" of his "brothers," but to gently expose their worldliness in order to cultivate godly prudence.[32]

Viret's stated concern that his letter not be received as overly harsh or burdensome to the conscience may indicate that he considered this to be a singular point of weakness in Calvin's *Petit traicté*.[33] Indeed, Calvin's

---

[27] Viret, *Epistre envoyee aux fideles*, sig. A [vii]ᵛ–sig. A [vii]ʳ: "Ce n'est pas peu de cas, de provoquer Dieu à ire."
[28] Viret, *Epistre envoyee aux fideles*, sig. B 4ʳ: "sont presses per leur conscience." Viret lists the kind of biblical figures to which Nicodemites appealed for support: Naaman the Syrian, Nicodemus, and Saint Paul, who sought "to accommodate himself to all" (sig. B [vi]ʳ).
[29] Viret, *Epistre envoyee aux fideles*, sig. C [i]ʳ.
[30] Viret, *Epistre envoyee aux fideles*, sig. C iiiʳ: "Nous voyons, comme il conioinct la confession de bouche, avec la foy du cueuer, à cause que ce sont choses inseparables."
[31] Viret, *Epistre envoyee aux fideles*, sig. E [vii]ʳ.
[32] Viret, *Epistres envoyee aux fideles*, sig. I [iv]v: "mes freres . . . non pas pour troubler et desoler d'avantage les povres consciences infirmes et affligées."
[33] I have not encountered any epistolary evidence suggesting that Viret reprimanded Calvin for treating the Nicodemites too harshly; that task was left to others. It was not uncommon, however, for Viret to gently urge Calvin to give comfort to anxious souls by dealing with them humanely and with Christian modesty. See, for example, Viret to Calvin, September 14, 1543 (Herminjard 9:27–28, #1281). Farel, for his part, had offered a glowing review of Calvin's *Petit traicté*, even prior to its publication. It is highly probable that Farel urged Calvin to publish the work, believing it provided a

anti-Nicodemite harangue had not even tried to mask the irritation he experienced from having to deal repeatedly with a matter he believed was sufficiently settled—in God's word and by the pastoral counsel he had dispensed in his previous writings. Complaints about Calvin's severity did in fact arise, not only from Nicodemites, but also from other reformers who believed that Calvin's letter to the French evangelicals could benefit from Viret's consolatory tone.[34] Thus, Calvin felt personally compelled to devote an entire treatise to answering the common criticism that he had been overly harsh with his French brothers and sisters. He addressed these complaints in his 1544 *Excuse à messieurs les Nicodemites, sur la complaincte qu'ilz font de sa trop grand rigueur*. This was one of the treatises Calvin intended for Martin Luther's eyes—no doubt seeking some validation from the senior reformer—but which Melanchthon chose not to send, fearing it would unduly burden the elder reformer who was at that time occupied with eucharistic controversies.[35]

Though pressed to soften the tone and substance of his admonishments, Calvin's response is decidedly unapologetic. If anything, he uses this treatise as an opportunity to further entrench himself in his position by calling his readers' consciences as witnesses against them. Once again, he excoriates Nicodemite behavior for its blatant hypocrisy and idolatrous witness. Calvin even prefers not to sully the name of Nicodemus by ascribing it to these dissimulators. After all, although he initially came to Jesus under the cloak of night, even Nicodemus later confessed Christ publicly and became his disciple.[36]

---

necessary and biblical corrective of papist behavior among French Protestants. See Farel to Calvin, September 8, 1543 (Herminjard 9:20, #1277).

[34] In the latter months of 1543, Antoine Fumée, a Parisian associate and suspected Nicodemite, wrote to Calvin desiring to confront him about his *Petit traicté*. He found Calvin's work to be rather merciless toward the afflicted, even to the point of hypocrisy. He also expected that Bucer and Melancthon would weigh in on the matter, perhaps to scold Calvin for his immoderation. See Fumée to Calvin, November or December 1543 (Herminjard 9:126–28, #1316). Likewise, in March 1544, Valérand Poullain, an eventual leader of the French refugee community, urged Calvin to continue opposing idolaters but in a more comforting manner patterned after Viret's early letter, *Epistre consolatoire* (1541). Calvin's *Excuse à messieurs les Nicodemites*, released earlier that year, had been neither an apology nor consolatory in tone! See Poullain to Calvin, March 9, 1544 (Herminjard 9:178–81, #1334).

[35] Bruce Gordon, *Calvin* (New Haven, CT: Yale University Press, 2009), 169–70.

[36] Calvin, *Excuse à messieurs les Nicodemites, sur la complaincte qu'ilz font de sa trop grand rigueur* (CO 6:608–609). In his *Epistre envoyee*, Viret also emphasizes the fact that Nicodemus later made public confession of his faith in Jesus. Viret urges his readers to be like the "daytime" Nicodemus, who made public profession despite its danger, and not like the "nighttime" Nicodemus, who only came to Jesus under cloak of darkness (sig. H [vi]ᵛ–sig. H [vii]ᵛ, sig. I [i]ʳ).

As before, Calvin insists that his critique is not only biblical but also manifestly in accord with a reasonable conscience: "when, therefore, I require that the believer take care to keep himself from idolatry designed to please men, and from pretending outwardly to consent to what he believes in his conscience to be wicked and against God, it is obvious that this is more than reasonable."[37] Moreover, his words of admonition are not mere opining, but actual divine instruction: "It is not a question of their opinion or mine. I present what I find about it in the scriptures." In Calvin's mind, the truths he conveys are self-evident, known by all naturally through the aid of conscience. Thus, the complaint that his instructions are too severe simply cannot hold.[38]

Although Calvin's response to his detractors makes no concessions at all, he nevertheless strains to maintain a pastoral tone. He pleads with his readers to accept his instruction as "good and salutary" and for their benefit, "rather than imitating hysterical patients, by striking and insulting the doctor, who is taking pains to help them." Calvin claims that he takes no pleasure in convicting them, but he has been especially blunt with those who have no qualms defiling themselves through idolatry. Yet, Calvin has sufficient pastoral awareness to distinguish such hypocrites from those who suffer in papist lands with a genuine concern for the honor of God: "These [latter] persons recognize with fear and humility the wretched state in which they find themselves, and regret being in the midst of the abominations that they are forced to see there, and with which they sometimes even pollute themselves on account of weakness. I certainly consider them to be in an amazing predicament." Perhaps having learned something from Viret after all, Calvin-the-pastor especially shines through when he admits, "I know that one must deal with timid and troubled consciences in such a way as not to bring them to despair." Calvin wants to stir up their sense of duty to God's word, but he is equally desirous to "comfort those who are faltering, so much that they are not lulled into indifference, or harden themselves against God."[39]

---

[37] Calvin, *Excuse à messieurs les Nicodemites* (CO 6:594): "Quand donc ie requires qu'un homme fidele se garde songneusement d'idolatrer, pour complaire aux hommes: et de faire semblant par dehors de consentir à ce qu'il congnoist en sa conscience estre mauvais et contre Dieu: il appert evidemment que cela est plus que raisonnable."

[38] Calvin, *Excuse à messieurs les Nicodemites* (CO 6:602): "Il n'est pas icy question de leur opinion ou de la miene. Ie monster ce que i'en trouve en l'escriture."

[39] Calvin, *Excuse à messieurs les Nicodemites* (CO 6:610–11): "Ie say qu'il convient tellement traicter les consciences timides et espovantees, qu'on ne les mette point en desespoir."

In 1555, Vermigli published his most direct attack against Nicodemite behavior. Pointed and matter-of-fact in tone, *A treatise of the cohabitacyon of the faithfull with the unfaithfull* passes down judgment on those dissemblers who believe they can safely feign outward conformity to Catholic rites. Such people have deceived consciences, Vermigli declares, because they mistakenly believe that God will be satisfied with the worship of only part of their being: "truly these dissemblers do not give to God this worship of mind and body which is due unto him, but the idolatry of mind and body they do commit, both because they outwardly do join with papists in their idolatry and because in their mind they do persuade themselves that it is lawful for them so to do.... We think (they say) as you think and in our hearts we do retain the truth, and so our mind is pure. But your bodies you do give over to the devil and to idols (I Cor. 6)."[40] Such people place themselves in a dire position, for "their own consciences do miserably torment them."[41] Vermigli's appeal to suffering Protestants—much like Calvin's and Viret's—emphasizes the necessity of not acting against conscience, but rather keeping one's conscience pure in the midst of trial. Those who remain passive bystanders during Catholic worship as God is blasphemed are "dangerously tormented" by fear of judgment brought on by the "stinger left sticking in their conscience."[42] In contrast, those who persevere in their confession of the pure gospel enjoy "the quiet peace of a justified conscience."[43]

4.1.2. Dissimulation, Conscience, and the Rule of Charity

Following the publication of his *Excuse à messieurs les Nicodemites* (1544), Calvin would not publish another formal critique of Nicodemism for

---

[40] Vermigli, *A treatise of the cohabitacyon*, sig. C [vi]ᵛ–sig. C [vii]ᵛ.

[41] Vermigli, *A treatise of the cohabitacyon*, sig. C vʳ. Throughout this treatise Vermigli maintains a strict rule that, if believers have not yet "confessed the gospel in words," they must forsake their dissimulation and follow one of two actions: die confessing the faith, or flee to a region tolerant of the biblical gospel (sig. E vʳ). This obedient course of action is essential, Vermigli takes Paul as saying in 1 Cor. 10, for maintaining "a pure conscience." Moreover, Vermigli believes the Apostle's teaching here is "so plain to the understanding of the most simple that it needs no exposition at all" (sig. B [viii]ᵛ).

[42] Vermigli, *A treatise of the cohabitacyon*, sig. B iiʳ. See also Vermigli's *Epistre ... a Quelques Fideles* (1574), in which he describes the torment of conscience for those who refuse to heed God's call to public confession (sig. C [viii]ʳ–sig. D iʳ).

[43] Vermigli, *A treatise of the cohabitacyon* [*A Sermon*], sig. H ivᵛ. Throughout his *Epistre ... a Quelques Fideles* (1574), Vermigli borrows from the examples of biblical figures who found "faithful rest" in their consciences because of their obedient confession under fire, namely, Peter, Paul, Abraham, Jonah, and Daniel (sig. C iʳ).

nearly a decade.[44] During the interim, however, both Farel and Viret saw fit to address the issue further. In several general letters intended for French Protestants living in Catholic territories, the two reformers identified another important aspect of the relationship between dissimulation and conscience: the scandalizing effects of dissimulation upon the consciences of one's neighbors. In 1544, Farel published his *Epistre exhortatoire à tous ceux qui ont congnoissance de l'Evangile*, admonishing French Protestants to live according to God's will and for his glory, while seeking how best to edify their neighbors both in word and deed. His letter contains a rather Pauline-like appeal to his readers not to forsake their former acceptance of and love for God's word, nor to exchange it for the "perverse doctrine and error of the Antichrist."[45] Farel insists that believers must make a public confession of faith, not only to maintain a pure conscience before God, but also to preserve the integrity of their Christian witness among the lost. "It is not enough for many to be silent where one should cry out for the honor of God, and for the salvation of souls." Indeed, those who stand idly by as God's name is blasphemed come under judgment, because they forsake their obligation

---

[44] Calvin would later allude to the Nicodemite error in four sermons preached in Geneva in 1552. The years leading up to 1552 were especially busy for Calvin, as he maintained a rigorous preaching and teaching regimen. Conflicts with political rivals in the city were also on the rise during this period; see William G. Naphy, *Calvin and the Consolidation of the Genevan Reformation* (Louisville, KY: Westminster John Knox Press, 1994). Calvin's hiatus from writing about the Nicodemite error was not for lack of exposure, however. In the introduction to the *Quatre sermons de M. Iehan Calvin traictans des matières fort utiles pour nostre temps, avec briefve exposition du Pseaume lxxxvii* (Geneva: Robert Estienne), published in September 1552, Calvin explains that, despite the "ample" treatises he had written showing the unlawful character of outwardly consenting to Catholic idolatries while embracing the pure gospel, nevertheless, "every day there are people who ask my advice on this again, as if I never talk about it" (CO 8:373). Hardly masking his irritation, Calvin offers these sermons in an effort to "cut short" the endless inquiries and leave without excuse those who would corrupt the pure worship of God through idolatrous pretensions. Of Calvin's four sermons, two are particularly relevant to our study. In his sermonic exposition of Psalm 16:4, Calvin urges Christians to flee outward idolatry by identifying the characteristics of a sacrilegious or purely human ceremony, such as the Mass: "Let us hold to this rule, that all human inventions that are drawn up to corrupt the simple purity of the word of God overturn the service that he demands and approves, are true sacrileges" (CO 8:383). Those who would contend that the Supper of Jesus Christ and the Mass are compatible celebrations, or that it falls to Christian liberty whether or not to partake of the Mass, know in their consciences (*qu'on en demande a leurs consciences*) that they are simply appeasing the papists in order to avoid persecution (CO 8:388). In another sermon based on Psalm 27:8, Calvin claims that such idolaters are willing to indulge in open sacrilege because of their slumbering consciences: "If their conscience were not fast asleep, it would be impossible for them not to be in continual distress, as if they were being tormented in hell" (CO 8:429). Although the conscience is operational in such people, they refuse to use it properly on account of their blissful self-deception. Despite denouncing his opponents' consciences in his sermons, Calvin nevertheless insists that he is not their judge, "for I only seek to have God heard and obeyed." He declares, "I do not seek to rule consciences according to my own pleasure, nor to impose necessity or law upon them," other than the law of God contained in the Scriptures (CO 8:391).

[45] Farel, *Epistre exhortatoire*, sig. A [vi]ᵛ: "pour la perverse doctrine et pour l'erreur de l'Antechrist."

"against their own consciences."[46] Farel's letter primarily takes aim at those who, by their dissimulation, "ruin their neighbor."[47] Far from being innocuous, the example of "wicked simulation" set by those who are unwilling to confess Christ openly, despite the threat of personal danger, causes "ignorant people [to] perish."[48] Such dissemblers are not even walking as Christians, Farel declares.[49] They violate charity because they pursue self-preservation above all at the expense of "the honor of Jesus" and winning one's neighbor to God; rather than exercising "true charity," their simulation is an act "of great cruelty" toward others.[50] Farel concludes his letter by charging his readers, "Believe with [your] heart and confess with [your] mouth. . . . Do not be afraid to confess [your faith] before men, but above all, beware of denying it either in fact or in words."[51]

In his *Epistre envoyee aux fideles* (1543), Viret had also insisted that Christians combine their internal faith with the external confession of the mouth, which is essential not only for maintaining the glory of God, but also for the edification of one's neighbor.[52] Dissimulation, on the other hand, "scandalizes the faithful, and especially the weak." The mere observance of a brother or sister joining in the "external works" of idolaters causes one's neighbor to be "troubled in their conscience."[53] Even more seriously, the harmful example set by religious compromise "kills and bruises the soul and the conscience of his brother."[54] Willing to distinguish between various types

---

[46] Farel, *Epistre exhortatoire*, sig. B [viii]ᵛ–sig. B [viii]ʳ: "Il ne suffit point à plusieurs de se taire là ou l'on devroit crier pour l'hôneur de Dieu, et pour le salut des poures ames."

[47] Farel, *Epistre exhortatoire*, sig. A iiᵛ.

[48] Farel, *Epistre exhortatoire*, sig. B [viii]ʳ: "faisons contre leurs propres consciences: et ainsi les poures ignorans perissent par la meschante simulation." It is notable that both Farel and Viret began using "simulation" as a preferred term to describe Protestant compromise soon after the publication of Calvin's *Petit traicté*, in which Calvin distinguishes these terms. This observation reveals the strong influence Calvin had on their own thinking about Nicodemite behavior. Like Calvin, they cannot regard religious compromise as anything less than "lying" by one's actions.

[49] Farel, *Epistre exhortatoire*, sig. C 3ʳ.

[50] Farel, *Epistre exhortatoire*, sig. B [vi]ʳ–sig. B [vii]ᵛ: "vraye charité... grande cruauté." Farel laments that Nicodemites are effectively willing to lose their souls in order to gain the whole earth: "pour ne perdre les biens terriens, on perd les biens du ciel." Vermigli, *A treatise of the cohabitacyon* [*A Sermon*], also repeats this twofold rule: "all things which we do are to be referred to the glory of God and to the profit of our neighbor" (sig. I iiiʳ).

[51] Farel, *Epistre exhortatoire*, sig. D [viii]ʳ: "Croyez de cueur, et confessez de bouche . . . et ne craignez de le confesser devant les hommes, mais sur toutvous gardez de le renier ny de fait ny de parolle."

[52] Viret, *Epistre envoyee aux fideles*, sig. C iiiᵛ–sig. C iiiʳ: "mais aussi desire il la confession de bouche, et le tesmoignage exterieur, de ceste foy interieure pour seruir à la gloire de Dieu, et à l'edification du prochain." Viret likens the inseparability of inner faith and outward confession to the relationships between "soul and life, fire [and] its clarity, the sun and its light, the body and its shadow."

[53] Viret, *Epistre envoyee aux fideles*, sig. E ivᵛ–sig. E ivʳ: "il scandalize les fideles, et principalement les infirmes."

[54] Viret, *Epistre envoyee aux fideles*, sig. F [vi]ʳ: "tue et meurtrit l'ame et la conscience de son frere."

of Nicodemites, Viret was decidedly more critical of Protestant dissemblers who held positions of power and influence. In 1547, he composed another treatise mainly aimed at public officials, instructing them how to act in the royal courts.[55] Viret urges them to realize that dissimulation violates charity or neighbor-love, which is a gross transgression of their callings as communal leaders. The "concealment" of their faith constitutes an "impediment" to the spiritually weak and a stumbling block to their acceptance of the gospel. Viret will not excuse their behavior in the least, and issues a stern warning: "The judgment of God will be more grievous on them."[56]

4.1.3. Dissimulation and the Freedom of Conscience in Indifferent Matters

The reformers' insistence that dissimulation violates charity or neighbor love was naturally linked to another controversial question: Did the act of dissimulation itself constitute a violation of the rule of love, or was it a permissible act for those who retained pure intentions even while attending Catholic worship? As we noted in the previous chapter, Nicodemite sympathizers sometimes contended that all so-called externals of religion—public ceremonies and ordinances—are "indifferent," and therefore permitted but never required of a believer. According to this belief, feigning participation in the empty rites of Catholicism amounted to nothing in itself, being neither good nor evil for the believer but simply a matter of adiaphora. Nicodemite defenders regularly sought support for this position from the Scriptures, appealing to the example of the apostles who engaged in acts that were objectionable to some but were of themselves a matter of Christian liberty.[57] The reformers highlighted in this chapter rejected this argument *en bloc* on the basis of two primary claims: First, neither Catholic rites in themselves,

---

[55] The full title of this treatise is, *Remonstrances aux fideles qui conversent entre les papistes: et principalement à ceux qui sont en court, et qui ont offices publiques, touchant les moyens qu'ilz doivent tenir en leur vocation, à l'exemple des anciens serviteurs de Dieu, sans contrevenir à leur devoir, ny envers Dieu, ny envers leur prochain: et sans se mettre temerairement en dangier, et donner par leur temerité et par leur coulpe, juste occasion à leurs adversaires de les mal traitter.* Throughout this treatise, Viret appeals to the examples set by Esther and Mordecai, who fulfilled their vocations amidst pagans in good conscience and in accord with charity and love. E.g., sig. I iv^v; sig. O iv^v.

[56] Viret, *Remonstrances aux fideles*, sig. D [vi]v.

[57] Nicodemite polemicists typically appealed to Paul's decision to circumcise Timothy (Acts 16:1–3) while refraining from circumcising Titus (Gal. 2:3–5) out of concern for his missionary audiences; also, for the same reasons, Paul's willingness to follow some of the purification laws of the Jews, though he did not require the Gentiles to perform them (Acts 21:17–26).

nor even the act of practicing Catholic worship in pretense, are indifferent things, but are in themselves evil. Under no fathomable circumstances could the constitutions of Rome "be used well" by the believer. Second, Nicodemite behavior necessarily scandalizes the consciences of the weak. This is the case not merely because the consciences of the weak are deficient in applying biblical teaching to life, but also because dissimulation itself actively *causes* them offense.[58] As we will see, the reformers defended these claims by attempting to expose the faulty exegesis of their opponents, whose ill-formed consciences—the reformers claimed—prompted them to play fast and loose with God's word rather than submit to its authority. The following medley of Reformed voices, beginning and ending with contributions by Calvin, bear this out.

A year after composing his *Epistre* in 1541, Calvin had sent a letter to the duchess of Ferrara, his former protectress, attempting to warn her about the character and influence of her new religious advisor François Richardot. Under Richardot's influence, the duchess was being persuaded that the Mass was not an abomination after all, but that it was the reformers, "who make this a matter of conscience," who "are the disturbers of the Church, stirring up scandals among the weak."[59] Calvin is acutely aware that Richardot is attempting to influence the duchess by turning the reformers' argument against them; *they* are the ones causing scandal among the weak by treating indifferent things as if they were matters of conscience.

In his letter, Calvin responds to this charge that he and his colleagues, by insisting that dissimulation in worship is a matter of disobedience, rather than indifference, are binding people's consciences to a human standard. Specifically, Calvin marshals biblical support to prove that certain religious externals, such as public confession of faith, are in fact required by Scripture and are not indifferent at all. Based on his reading of Luke 9:26, for example, Calvin insists that the Lord requires not merely belief of the heart, but also

---

[58] There is a long history of Christian reflection on the problem of *scandalum infirmorum* (offending the weak), extending back to Basil the Great (d. 379). Aquinas took up this question in his *Summa Theologica*, positing a distinction between actively or intentionally leading another person into sin (*scandalum activum*) and accidentally causing someone to stumble (*scandalum passivum*). Calvin also addressed this question in his 1550 *De Scandalis* (*Concerning Scandals*), in which he distinguishes various types of scandals or ungodly behavior that might create a stumbling block for the gospel. Though he does not address the issue of Nicodemism in this treatise, it is noteworthy that Calvin and the reformers consistently referred to Nicodemite dissimulation as a "scandal" performed against the weak. For a deeper treatment of this topic, see Kloosterman, *Scandalum Infirmorum et Communio Sanctorum*, chapter 1, "*Scandalum Infirmorum*: Christian Liberty versus Neighbor Love," 13–70.

[59] Calvin to the Duchess of Ferrara, October 1541 (Bonnet, 1:300; CO 11:327).

"the confession of the mouth."[60] No one can justly claim that dissimulation in worship is an indifferent act and therefore irrelevant to the condition of the conscience, since God requires godly practice flowing from genuine faith. Calvin insists that it is Richardot, not the reformers, who has imposed human tradition upon the duchess, proving that he possesses an "ill-informed conscience" that has in turn led him to "overthrow the word of the Lord."[61]

Vermigli would also respond to the specific Nicodemite claim that dissimulation at Mass is allowable because it is not actual idolatry but the mere appearance of idolatry. Like Calvin, Vermigli rejects this notion outright, insisting that any attempt at worshipping God where his word is clouded by false ritual is evidence for a lack of genuine faith: "for where there is no Word of God there is no faith, and where no faith is, there is no worship of God but a filthy hypocrisy and stinking abomination."[62]

Additionally, in his *Petit traicté*, Calvin also reacts to the common Nicodemite argument that dissimulation at Mass is necessary in order to avoid giving offence. Claiming to follow the example of the Apostle Paul's head-shaving and temple purification (Acts 18:18, 21, 26), Nicodemites proposed an alternative application of the rule of love or charity: one *ought to dissimulate* in Catholic worship as an act of loving one's neighbors by shielding them from unnecessary scandal. "For fear of offending," Calvin mimics his opponents, "we are forced to put on a good face, by accommodating ourselves to popish superstitions."[63] Calvin offers a lengthy response here, one that distinguishes legitimate and illegitimate claims to the freedom of conscience. First, Calvin argues that Paul's vows, although pertaining to things that belonged to the passing shadows of the Old Law, were nevertheless freely used for Christian edification and evangelism. The Apostle made himself like a Jew "in order to win them, and observed the law in order to attract them to the gospel" (I Cor. 9:20).[64] Second, Calvin insists that the Mass holds no comparison to the Apostle's actions. The Mass and all related

---

[60] Calvin to the Duchess of Ferrara, October 1541 (Bonnet, 1:302–304; CO 11:328–39).
[61] Calvin to the Duchess of Ferrara, October 1541 (Bonnet, 1:298; CO 11:325).
[62] Vermigli, *A treatise of the cohabitacyon*, sig. C ii[v]. Later in his treatise, Vermigli again states, "for faith has no place where God's Word does not show itself" (sig. D v[r]).
[63] Calvin, *Petit traicté* (CO 6:563): "De paour de scandaliser, disent-ilz, nous sommes contrains de faire bonne mine, en nous accommodant aux superstitions papistiques."
[64] Calvin, *Petit traicté* (CO 6:561). Likewise, in his *Epistre envoyee aux fideles*, Viret argues that Paul occasionally took part in Old Covenant Jewish ceremonies, adapting himself to "indifferent things" (things which of themselves "do not touch the conscience") in order to edify his brothers and create inroads for the gospel (sig. F iii[v]–sig. F iii[r]). The *manner* of caring for his Jewish converts may have been indifferent, but the *necessity of caring* for them was not indifferent or optional for the Apostle.

activities are patently idolatrous and utterly repugnant to the word of God. Those who feign Catholic worship do not share the Apostle's zeal for the salvation of lost idolaters, much less the glory of God; their intention is not to avoid troubling the consciences of their neighbors or to edify the ignorant souls around them. Rather, Calvin opines, "it will be found that they have no concern other than avoiding trouble and danger."[65] Far from avoiding offense, those who mask their Christianity by bowing to idols set a bad example and "grievously harm others" by causing them to stumble.[66] Rather than protect the consciences of one's neighbors, dissimulation harms and burdens the consciences of others, which is a clear violation of Christian liberty. Thus, Calvin sends his opponents "back to the judgment of God and to the testimony of their consciences ... for their own conscience reproves them."[67]

Viret argues similarly in his *Epistre envoyee* (1543), observing that dissimulation constitutes a misuse of Christian freedom that, far from being indifferent or much less an act of charity, violates both tables of the law. By failing to weigh in their consciences the offense of their idolatry before God, Nicodemites sin against the first table. And by abusing their liberty and therefore scandalizing "the simple, ignorant, and infirm" by their poor example, they sin against the second table. Such offenses are necessarily linked, Viret contends, for once someone has violated charity, they act once again "against the first [table of the law], against Jesus Christ, and against God, who wants us to do [everything] to his glory, and to the charity of our neighbor, which is connected with it."[68]

In this letter, Viret explains the important distinction between indifferent things and non-indifferent actions or contexts. He raises the example of Peter, who withdrew from fellowship at the Gentiles' table on account of his fear of the Jews (Gal. 2:12). For Peter, to eat or not to eat the Gentile food was a truly indifferent matter. Peter's error consisted in his act of withdrawing from his Gentile brothers and sisters, which was a decision born not of love but of the fear of man, thus constituting a violation of charity.[69] Likewise,

---

[65] Calvin, *Petit traicté* (CO 6:562).
[66] Calvin, *Petit traicté* (CO 6:564).
[67] Calvin, *Petit traicté* (CO 6:562): "Ie les renvoye au iugement de Dieu et au tesmoignage de leurs consciences ... car leur propre conscience les redargue."
[68] Viret, *Epistre envoyee aux fideles*, sig. E v^r: "Parquoy, quant à eux, et à leur conscience, ne peschoyent point devant Dieu, ny contre la premiere table, quand il n'y euft autre consideration qu'à eux. Mais à cause que leur œuvre redondoit au scandale du prochain, ilz pechoyent contre leur prochain, et contre la seconde table, et par consequent, contre la premiere, contre Iesus Christ, et côtre Dieu, qui veut que nous feruions à sa gloire, et à la charité de nostre prochain, qui est côioincte avec elle.... abusoyent de ceste liberté, en scandale des simples ignorans et infirmes."
[69] Viret, *Epistre envoyee aux fideles*, sig. E [vi]^v.

when Paul decided not to circumcise Titus (to prove that Gentiles were not required to undergo circumcision) but did choose to circumcise Timothy (so that his young assistant would not pose a stumbling block to his synagogue ministry to the Jews), Paul was demonstrating that Christian prudence is needed to determine what the rule of love requires under different circumstances. Whether an indifferent thing ought to be used or required in a non-indifferent manner should be determined by "occasions and circumstances."[70] On this Scriptural basis, then, Viret could not accept the practice of dissimulation as if it were an indifferent act, because although he could possibly concede that a public confession might not always be required of the believer under extraordinary moments of weakness, the deliberate veiling of one's faith while actively joining in Catholic abominations constituted a direct violation of God's law regarding neighbor-love.

The connection between dissimulation and adiaphora remained a foremost concern in the anti-Nicodemite writings of Calvin and the reformers over the following decades. In 1562, just a few years before his death, Calvin produced his final and most severe challenge to Nicodemism. It came as a response to Dirk Volkerts Coornhert, a Dutch polymath who—although he never severed formal ties with Rome—had embraced many doctrinal distinctives of the sixteenth-century spiritualists, especially the ideas of Sebastian Franck, Caspar Schwenkfeld, and Menno Simons. Coornhert would later serve as William of Orange's secretary of state while advocating a nationwide policy of religious tolerance—a stance largely attributed to the influence of Sebastian Castellio, the now-prominent philologist of Basel, whose calls for dogmatic moderation and liberty of conscience often provoked the ire of Calvin and his closer associates following the well-known 1553 execution of Michael Servetus in Geneva.[71] Coornhert vehemently accused Calvin

---

[70] Viret, *Epistre envoyee aux fideles*, sig. F iv^v. Vermigli agrees that the reason why Paul had Timothy circumcised was "to avoid offending the believing Jews" who would otherwise "be alienated and turned away from Christ's gospel, which they had newly received." In the case of circumcision, a ceremony of the Old Law that has truly passed away with Christ's coming, Paul's choice to administer or not to administer the rite counted as nothing, since it was a matter of genuine indifference. "But," Vermigli insists, "we must not compare these ceremonies of the old law with the inventions of men." The Mass and other "popish idolatries," far from being a matter of indifference, "are thrust unto us by the subtlety of the devil and crafty deceiving of men" (*A treatise of the cohabitacyon*, sig. E ii^r).

[71] Coornhert's formal plea for religious toleration is contained in his *Synod on the Freedom of Conscience: A Thorough Examination during the Gathering Held in the Year 1582 in the City of Freetown*, ed. and trans. Gerrit Voogt (Amsterdam: Amsterdam University Press, 2008). Coornhert's primary concern in his treatises and polemic exchanges with Reformed ministers was to protect what he believed were two interchangeable ideas, namely, "freedom of conscience" and "religious toleration," which he saw as the chief issues at stake in the Netherlands' struggle against Hapsburg Spain. For more background, see Gerrit Voogt, *Constraint on Trial: Dirck Volckertsz Coornhert and Religious Freedom*, Sixteenth Century Essays and Studies, Vol. 52 (Kirksville, MO: Truman State University

of violating the freedom of conscience by imposing rigorous rules for worship and personal conduct upon French Protestants. Calvin's reply, *Response à un certain holandais, lequel sons ombre de faire les chrestiens tout spirituels, leur perment de polluer leurs corps en toutes idolatries*, offers both a personal defense and theological counter-argument.

As many times before, Calvin denies that he and his Reformed colleagues have been "cruel" toward their French brothers and sisters simply by upholding particular standards for God's worship. The pure worship of God is never a minor issue. God's honor must be preserved; thus, true affection for him necessarily entails both inward and outward devotion to the kind of worship God desires. Calvin insists that it is *not his instructions* that cruelly vex consciences. Rather, it is because many would "lull themselves to sleep" by their vain dissimulations—deceived into hailing Coornhert as a "prophet"—that they face the reproof of their own consciences.[72]

Calvin takes particular issue with Coornhert's argument for the abrogation of all public religious ceremonies. Like other spiritualists of the day, Coornhert believed that the establishment of Jesus's spiritual kingdom on earth had done away with all external obligations beyond that of loving God and neighbor.[73] By defining the gospel narrowly as "charity," or love for God and neighbor, Coornhert "by this means has destroyed all ceremonies," rendering all external expressions of faith—sacraments, Lord's Day observance, and public confession of faith, including oaths and vows—null and void.[74]

Press, 2000). Coornhert argued that the Reformed had erred by demanding absolute conformity to dogmatic statements of faith instead of emphasizing moral reform through the charitable toleration of religious diversity in the spirit of "The Golden Rule" (Voogt, *Constraint on Trial*, 119–24). Notably, this was also Sebastian Castellio's basic position in *Conseil à la France désolée* (1562) and in his other writings on religious toleration: "J'en prens à tesmoings vos propres consciences, que vous faites à autrui chose que vous ne voudriés qui vous fust faite" (sig. B ii'). Coornhert could therefore muster up some appreciation for Luther's critique of Rome's moral abuses—though not for his emphasis on the teaching of justification by faith—but was entirely critical of Calvin's and Beza's insistence on the doctrine of predestination and their harangue against Castellio's liberalism. See Mirjam van Veen's "Dirck Volckertz Coornhert: Exile and Religious Coexistence," in *Exile and Religious Identity, 1500–1800*, ed. Jesse Spohnholz and Gary K. Waite (2014; New York: Routledge, 2018), 74–75. For more on Castellio's liberal opposition to Calvin and his confessional allies, see Michael W. Bruening, *Refusing to Kiss the Slipper: Opposition to Calvinism in the Francophone Reformation* (Oxford: Oxford University Press, 2021), 139–79 (chap. 5).

[72] Calvin, *Response à un certain holandais, lequel sons ombre de faire les chrestiens tout spirituels, leur perment de polluer leurs corps en toutes idolatries* (CO 9:585).

[73] For more on the so-called spiritualists of the sixteenth century, see Chapter 2, as well as George Huntston Williams's classic study, *The Radical Reformation* (Kirksville, MO: Truman State University Press, 1992).

[74] Calvin, *Response à un certain holandais* (CO 9:587).

Anyone requiring such observances of the faithful were simply trying "to impose a carnal yoke upon their neck."[75]

Calvin finds Coornhert's interpretation of Jesus's summary of the law and prophets to be both innovative and lacking in hermeneutical depth. For, Calvin contends, "when [Jesus] says that the law and the prophets are comprised of these two articles, [he] excludes neither faith, nor prayers, nor any of what is ordered of us in Scripture to strengthen and advance us in the bond of God." Coornhert fails to grasp the heart of Jesus's teaching, that true faith results in pious living according to God's commands. "Therefore, this crackpot mixes up and confuses everything, trying to conclude that our Lord Jesus Christ only left the commandment to love God and our neighbors, when he abolished the ancient ceremonies. For, we must distinguish carefully between the shadows and figures which served the Jews before the coming of Jesus Christ, and that which remains for us forever."[76]

Here, Calvin attempts to make a rather technical point by distinguishing aspects of the Old Law, to which believers have no obligation, from matters of so-called divine adiaphora, that is, matters not strictly required but nevertheless manifestly beneficial for believers to observe. With regard to those ceremonies that were required of the Jews as figures of the Mosaic law, such as sacrificial rites and laws regarding food and personal hygiene, Calvin insists that believers are entirely free; Christ has fulfilled the substance of these ceremonies, thus abrogating their usage. Other types of ceremonies, however, though they are not strictly required of believers, should be prudently observed for their edification and for demonstrating proper reverence toward God. Calvin's underlying principle is that there is "a great difference between the ceremonies which prefigured Jesus Christ in his absence and before his coming and those which have been left to us to help our weakness."[77] Among the ceremonies that are "recommended," though not strictly required by the apostles, Calvin lists ceremonies for prayer, the lifting up of

---

[75] Calvin, *Response à un certain holandais* (CO 9:590).
[76] Calvin, *Response à un certain holandais* (CO 9:587): "Lequel en disant que sous ces deux articles la Loy et les Prophetes sont compris, n'exclud pas ni la foy, ni les prieres, ni tout ce qui nous est ordonné en l'Escriture pour nous exercer et avancer en la fiance de Dieu . . . Parquoy ce brouillon mesle et confond tout, en voulant conclure que nostre Seigneur Iesus Christ n'a laissé que le commandement d'aimer Dieu et nos prochains, quand il a mis bas les ceremonies anciennes. . . . Car il nous faut prudemment distinguer entre les ombres et les figures qui ont servi aux Iuifs devant la venue de Iesus Christ, et ce qui nous est demeure perpetuel."
[77] Calvin, *Response à un certain holandais* (CO 9:588): "Mais, comme l'ay dit, il y a grande diversité entre les ceremonies qui ont figuré Iesus Christ en son absence et devant sa venue, et celles qui nous sont laissees pour aide de nostre infirmité."

hands, bowing knees in prayer, and head coverings. He also appears to be thinking of the public profession of faith by means of oaths, vows, and public subscription. In fact, later in his response, while dismantling Coornhert's argument that the Sabbath Day's rest has also been abrogated, Calvin writes, "Now, the source of such an error is, to restrict the marrow and substance of these commandments to love God, forgetting or forsaking the service which is due him: worship, prayers, *confession of the faith*, and everything that goes with glorifying him as our God."[78] In short, Calvin excoriates Coornhert for his innovative exegesis which, in substance, is no different from that of the libertines and Anabaptists, who refused to make proper use of ceremonies to demonstrate inward service to God (despite Coornhert's preference for distancing himself from these groups).[79] Calvin is convinced that Coornhert is simply a disciple of Sebastian Franck, who falsely accused the reformers of drawing Christians away from spiritual worship toward outward ceremonies. On the contrary, Calvin remarks, "but we say that outward worship derives from spiritual worship, and is accessory to it."[80]

In contrast to Coornhert's innovative exegesis, Calvin persistently maintains that his judgments are not his own. He only speaks "according to Scripture, and even according to common sense."[81] He stands with the pattern set forth in the teachings and example of the apostles, who regularly observed external religious ceremonies for the demonstration and edification of the faith. Calvin again addresses the example of the Apostle Paul,

---

[78] Calvin, *Response à un certain holandais* (CO 9:588): "Or la source de tel erreur est, de restreindre la mouëlle et la substance de ces commandemens à aimer Dieu, oubliant, ou laissant derriere le service qui luy est deu, l'adoration, les prieres, la confession de foy, et tout ce qui appartient à le glorifier comme nostre Dieu." One can find a more detailed explanation of the relationship between head coverings and the freedom of conscience in Calvin's *Institutes* 4.10.31 (LCC: 21:1208–10; CO 2:890). Calvin's basic claim seems to be that, while head coverings and other such "church constitutions" described in Scripture should not be pushed on a believer with excessive force against conscience, the believer should seriously consider following these traditions in order to "nourish mutual love." Although such practices are not strictly necessary for the believer to follow, and thus they are matters of adiaphora, neighbor-love (charity) might compel one to wear head coverings in view of the rules of modesty that are native to one's own culture or customs. In this respect, to wear or not to wear head coverings is an indifferent matter in itself, though circumstances and the divine requirement to love one's neighbor might make an indifferent matter obligatory for the Christian. For a helpful examination of Calvin's heavily nuanced assessment of adiaphora and head coverings, see John L. Thompson, *John Calvin and the Daughters of Sarah: Women in Regular and Exceptional Roles in the Exegesis of Calvin, His Predecessors, and His Contemporaries* (Genève: Libraire Droz, 1992), chapter 6, "Women, Adiaphora, Polity, and Change," 227–68.

[79] Calvin, *Response à un certain holandais* (CO 9:591, 594).

[80] Calvin, *Response à un certain holandais* (CO 9:597): "Mais nous disons que le service exterieur est une dependence et accessoire du service spirituel."

[81] Calvin, *Response à un certain holandais* (CO 9:597): "Veu que ie parle apres l'Escriture, et mesme apres le sens naturel."

who "made these things inseparable: believing with the heart and confessing with the mouth (Rom. 10:10)."[82] Paul set an example of this in purifying himself before offering a vow in the temple in Jerusalem (Acts 21:26). Although Coornhert believes Paul's vow was an act of hypocrisy, Calvin responds, what about singing "Hail, queen (Mary)," when you don't mean it? Paul is exemplary in this: he justly allowed himself "liberty in an indifferent thing," observing a ceremony "which brought neither good nor evil among the Jews," so that he might not create a stumbling block to his ministry among the Jews. Idolatrous pretension, on the other hand, is "something which is in itself evil." The important rule Calvin follows is this: "We must therefore note that as for things which are not wicked in themselves, we are free to use them, or to abstain from them. But where the evil is apparent, we must hold to another rule."[83]

Calvin concludes his response by rebuking Coornhert once again for his deceptive notion of Christian freedom of conscience. "One sees, therefore, how this dimwit upends everything, wanting people to believe that we wrongly bind consciences to things which are permitted them."[84] Coornhert places all external ceremonies in the category of permitted things or adiaphora. But he has thoroughly misunderstood the nature of "indifferent" things, Calvin argues. The Scriptures do not teach, as "this crackpot" contends, "that if we are free at any point, it [our freedom] is entire and universal."[85] On the contrary, just as certain religious acts are manifestly evil in themselves and must not be indulged for the sake of obedience and conscience, others are manifestly good and should be used with great benefit. Such ceremonies are improperly neglected on the basis of "liberty" or "freedom of conscience." There are matters in Scripture that are "permitted" and others that are "prescribed," and when Scripture teaches about matters pertaining to the public worship

---

[82] Calvin, *Response à un certain holandais* (CO 9:599): "Mais il faut noter que sainct Paul met ces choses comme inseparables, Croire de coeur, et confesser de bouche."

[83] Calvin, *Response à un certain holandais* (CO 9:600): "Nous avons donc à noter qu'en choses qui d'elles-mesmes ne sont point vicieuses, nous avons liberté d'en user, ou nous en abstenir. Mais où le mal est tout notoire, il faut bien tenir une autre reigle." Such vain ceremonies, Vermigli concurred, "are things utterly evil and cannot be well used" (*A treatise of the cohabitacyon*, sig. E iii^v). Like Calvin, Vermigli points out that, in contrast to human inventions, the Apostle Paul "used ceremonies instituted of God," such as circumcision and the taking of vows, "for certain and weighty causes (Acts 16, 18, 21)" (*A treatise of the cohabitacyon* [*A Sermon*], sig. L i^r).

[84] Calvin, *Response à un certain holandais* (CO 9:617): "On voit donc comme cest estourdi renverse tout, voulant faire à croire, que nous assubiettisons à tort les consciences à des choses qui leur sont permises."

[85] Calvin, *Response à un certain holandais* (CO 9:617): "Or voici à quoy tend ce brouillon: que si nous avons liberté en quelque endroit, elle est en tout et par tout." ET in Calvin, *Come Out from Among Them*, 290.

of God, it is a matter of the latter category, not the former. Indeed, Calvin concludes, "the ceremonies which are required for the confession of our faith, and to testify to the service which we must render God, must be viewed very differently because of the end with which they are connected," namely, the honor and reverence of God.[86]

4.1.4. Conscience, Confession, and Pastoral Accommodation

We have observed that the anti-Nicodemite reformers felt compelled to identify the standard bevy of wicked Catholic ordinances that Protestants should expressly avoid on account of their "manifest idolatry," which is "contrary to the confession of a Christian."[87] With equal vigor, they also frequently rehearsed believers' duty to make a profession of faith through valid means. Part of the reformers' harangue against religious compromise included an appeal for the proper use of godly ceremonies as elements of right worship and genuine piety. Perhaps surprisingly, however, the reformers often tempered their demands in this regard to the circumstances and concerns of their audiences. Though criticized heavily for their apparent lack of sympathy and unrealistic expectations for their extended flock, the reformers were often willing to be accommodating—or at very least, deliberately unspecific—in their requirements for the public confession of faith.

Despite Calvin's unceasing demands for public confession, even his writings explicitly refuse to impose rigid laws on people for how this should take place. Rather, he asserts his belief that biblical prudence is enough to direct the time and manner of one's confession. Surprisingly, in fact, Calvin emphasizes that his purpose is not to mandate strict requirements—"we have greater need for exhortations than for rules"—but rather to motivate believers on the basis of Christian duty to reject ungodly, superstitious ceremonies and only make use of ceremonies that are beneficial and in accord with God's word. Calvin is confident that the truly pious will not only resist

---

[86] Calvin, *Response à un certain holandais* (CO 9:619–20): "Les ceremonies qui sont requises pour la confession de nostre foy, et pour testifier le service que nous devons rendre à Dieu, doivent bien estre autrement prisees, pour la fin où elles se rapportent." ET in Calvin, *Come Out from Among Them*, 293.

[87] Calvin, *Epistre* (CO 6:585). Calvin specifically lists bowing before images, worshipping relics of saints, pilgrimages, carrying candles before idols, purchasing indulgences, as well as performing services in honor of the dead or the saints.

Romish doctrines as ungodly and thus keep themselves "in purity of conscience," but will also participate in rituals or ceremonies that promote, rather than violate, God's honor.[88] In sum, the witness of God's faithful servants "is constituted in two points, namely in confession of the mouth and in external worship, or in ceremonies."[89] Nevertheless, it falls to each believer to pray for "true prudence" (*vraye prudence*) from the Lord to determine what manner of confession is proper.[90] Calvin's admission here is rather striking: the consciences of his audience, heretofore considered by Calvin with an air of doubt and suspicion, regain prominence—albeit in a guarded sense—as a potent and reliable guide for Christian conduct.

In 1547, Viret published a follow-up letter to his *Epistre envoyee* in which he admonished and consoled those struggling over the decision to leave the Church of Rome and face the dangers and temptations entailed by that choice. Viret's epistle, *Admonition et consolation aux fideles qui deliberant de sortir d'entre les papistes, pour eviter idolatrie, contre les tentations qui leur peuvent advenir et les dangiers ausquelz ils peuvent tomber en leur yssue*, is the most pastoral and accommodating of his anti-Nicodemite writings. He laments how "marvelously difficult, yet nearly impossible" it is to live among the papists without either caving to their idolatries or putting one's life in danger by refusing to comply.[91] Such Christians, who continually battle Satan, the world, and their own flesh, should be treated with great pity and compassion by other believers.[92] Viret is especially generous toward these suffering saints in the matter of their public confession. Those who choose to remain in Catholic lands should do their best to confess Christ "in all the ways that [they] can." Nevertheless, Viret concedes that, "if we do not confess [the faith] as excellently as we should, we must, at the very least, refrain from denying it." Here, Viret likens the experience of these Christians to that of Lot

---

[88] Calvin, *Epistre* (CO 6:581): "En somme nous avons plus grand mestier d'exhortations que de reigles."

[89] Calvin, *Epistre* (CO 6:584): "Ceste testification est constituée en deux poinctz, assavoir en confession de bouche et en adoration exterieure, ou en ceremonies." Although Calvin occasionally demanded specific forms of confession (e.g., a citizen's oath to the Confession of Faith in Geneva; see Chapter 5), in the case of suffering Christians, however, he is willing to accommodate lesser forms of profession for the sake of distinguishing true believers from idolatrous compromisers.

[90] Calvin, *Petit traicté* (CO 6:545).

[91] Viret, *Admonition et consolation aux fideles qui deliberant de sortir d'entre les papistes, pour eviter idolatrie, contre les tentations qui leur peuvent advenir et les dangiers ausquelz ils peuvent tomber en leur yssue*, sig. A ii^r–sig. A v^v: "Il est tout certain, qu'il est merveilleusement difficile, mais presque impossible, de vivre entre les Papistes." Like the other reformers, Viret compares the situation of French Protestants to the struggle of Israel in Egyptian and Babylonian captivity (sig. A iii^v).

[92] Viret, *Admonition et consolation*, sig. A v^r.

in Sodom and Gomorrah.[93] Though opting to remain within the confines of Rome, they must, at the very least, resist its superstitions and blasphemies, even if they do not publicly confess the faith as consistently as they ought. Viret's approach in this letter is decidedly more indulgent than that of the other reformers, who never strayed from requiring at least some form of public confession of faith regardless of circumstance or personal fortitude.[94] In contrast, Viret's pastoral counsel exudes a unique measure of patience and liberality; he urges his readers not to worry too much about their difficult circumstances or the poverty of their witness, but to focus on the promises of Christ that sustain them.[95]

Within his various letters, Viret likewise emphasizes that the Christian's confession should always be offered in "Christian modesty" and with "spiritual prudence."[96] The act of confessing one's faith should not be done haphazardly, but with a regard for God's law and the edification of others. The goal of Christian confession is always to "give glory to God, condemn idolaters, strengthen the faithful, and remove all occasion of scandal and

---

[93] Viret, *Admonition et consolation*, sig. A [vi]^v–sig. A [vi]^r: "Si nous sommes donc entre les idolatres, fachons que nous sommes tenuz, pour le premier de côfesser Iesus Christ, en toutes les manieres que nous pouvons. Si nous ne le confessons pas, si excellemment que nous deussions, nous nous devons, pour le moins, garder de le renyer."

[94] In a recent article, Carlos Eire also notes that Viret, as a frontlines reformer, was especially able to combine a message of active resistance to Nicodemite behavior with a pastoral and patient tone toward those suffering under Catholic persecution. See Carlos M. N. Eire, "Pierre Viret and Nicodemism," in *Pierre Viret (1511–1571) et la diffusion de la Réforme: Pensée, action, contextes religieux*, ed. Karine Crousaz and Daniela Solfaroli Camillocci (Lausanne: Antipodes, 2014), 59–75.

[95] Viret, *Admonition et consolation*, sig. A [viii]^r–sig. B [i]^v. Viret nevertheless distinguishes between those whose weakness of confession is on account of personal danger, and those who willingly compromise their confession simply to retain position or pleasure. Viret notes that there are "many examples" of such people among them who are unwilling to give up the comforts of Babylon for the gospel (sig. C [vii]^v–sig. D [i]^v). Later, in 1559, Viret composed a collection of encouraging letters for persecuted Protestants—his counsel especially intended for those laboring as preachers of the gospel (*Epistres aus fideles pour les instruire et les admonester eet exhorter touchant leur office, et pour les consoler en leurs tribulations*). His instruction hones in on the importance of not violating one's conscience when facing the temptation to dissimulate. He warns his readers, "be careful never to do anything against your conscience ... [to] walk in all fear and reverence ... [and to] have [your] conscience assured ... by [God's] Word" (sig. A [vii]^r; sig. C i^v). Viret's letters, while pastoral in tone, nevertheless exude urgency in requiring all faithful believers to "confess by mouth" what "we believe in heart" (sig. C ii^r). One must "confess and glorify Jesus Christ, as you are required to do," without "simulation and dissimulation" (sig. F iii^v). Those who resist God's commands to confess with the mouth what they believe with their hearts suffer from various maladies of conscience. Dissimulators have an "idle" conscience (sig. F iv^v); those who "defile themselves in all superstition and idolatry" are attempting "to put their conscience to sleep, so that it does not keep them from continuing the evil they are doing" (sig. F v^r–sig. F [vi]^v); such persons who persist in simulation and dissimulation have no excuse when they are "executed," "accused," "tormented," "punched and stung" by their consciences; despite their best efforts, they cannot "numb" their consciences (sig. H ii^v–iii^v).

[96] Viret, *Epistre envoyee aux fideles*, sig. C [vi]^v.

blasphemy from the good, and leave no matter to idolaters to glorify themselves."[97] Like Calvin, Viret requires that one's confession be offered moderately and with regard for times and circumstances. Protestants living among idolaters should confess Jesus Christ as best they can, but it is to be acknowledged that some of them live in countries where there is more freedom to confess the faith and "live according to their conscience." In the case of others, for whom "there is not so much freedom," and whose lives are constantly threatened by many dangers, the expectations for their confession might be less strict.[98] In sum, when accounting for the times, circumstances, and manner of confessing one's faith, Viret advises that the Christian should apply "prudence joined with simplicity."[99]

Vermigli's counsel mirrors that of his predecessors, both in his valuation of pious ceremonies and also in his opinion of the kind of confession that should be required of suffering saints. In contrast to the wickedness of the Mass and related ceremonies, Vermigli acknowledges that certain religious rites still exist that are not only allowable, but also prudent and beneficial to piety. These ceremonies instituted by the magistrates—such as oaths and vows—should be observed and not rejected, because they agree with God's word and can be used well by the believer. In fact, Vermigli argues, God has appointed the magistrates "to enforce [such ceremonies] outwardly to embrace sound and holy rites . . . agreeing with God's word."[100] Like the other reformers, Vermigli also advocates a simple form of confession, rather than a highly regulated procedure. He calls for believers to "freely confess" Christ "in mouth and deeds." The believer's confession should be "simple and plain," such as the Apostles' Creed or some such ecumenical statement of faith.[101]

* * *

Our examination of various anti-Nicodemite letters and treatises penned by Calvin and his closest colleagues reveals several important aspects of the relationship between confession, conscience, and Christian freedom in the reformers' thought. First, all of the reformers highlighted in this chapter

---

[97] Viret, *Epistre envoyee aux fideles*, sig. H iii^r–sig. H iv^v: "Car nostre confession precedente, et tesmoignage de nostre foy, donneroit gloire à Dieu, condamneroit les idolatres, fortifieroit les fideles, et osteroit toute l'occasion de scandale et blaspheme aux bons, et ne laisseroit point de matiere aux idolatres pour se glorifier."

[98] Viret, *Remonstrances aux fideles*, sig. C [viii]^r–sig. D [i]^v.

[99] Viret, *Remonstrances aux fideles*, sig. R iii^r: "prudence, conioincte avec simplicité." Later in this treatise, Viret describes Protestant confession in identical terms; see sig. T iv^v.

[100] Vermigli, *A treatise of the cohabitacyon*, sig. H [viii]r.

[101] Vermigli, *A treatise of the cohabitacyon* [*A Sermon*], sig. I [vii]^v–sig. I [viii]^r.

regarded the public confession of faith as essential to Christian piety. The proper honor and worship of God required that one's internal beliefs be audibly and visibly communicated by the mouth for all to see and hear. Moreover, the substance of the Christian confession—including distinctions about proper worship—is never a minor issue for the church. Nothing less than God's glory is at stake, and so the faithful are required to confess belief in those things which they are compelled to believe by the authority of divine revelation, the Scriptures. Thus, while the reformers (especially Viret) occasionally exhibited pastoral patience by allowing suffering saints to adjudicate the proper time and manner of their confession—something they believed Protestants could (ideally) discern for themselves through the gift of Christian prudence—they could not accept a form of Christianity that entirely lacked the public profession of faith. At the very least, one should be able to affirm his or her faith in a simple way through the ancient creeds of the church.

Second, to a person, the reformers agreed that confession is inextricably bound to the individual conscience. A person does harm to one's own conscience, and to the conscience of his or her neighbor, by failing to confess with the mouth what is believed to be true inwardly. Throughout their anti-Nicodemite writings, the reformers implore their readers to follow the testimony of their consciences, which, they are utterly confident, will not only convict them of their present hypocrisy, but will also prompt them to offer genuine confession. It is assumed, on one hand, that their readers' consciences are operational, albeit in need of special prodding. In principle, their consciences are able to discern what is wicked and against God, as well as what is right and in conformity with his word. Weak consciences may need to be startled awake by the admonition of the reformers, but it is assumed that they are sufficiently intact to discern God's will if adequately motivated. Still, in their writings, the reformers also attribute a variety of serious maladies to the Nicodemite conscience. It can be "deceived," "ill-informed," "idle," or "armed against God." People might "feign innocence" of conscience, allowing themselves to be driven by feelings, rather than by reason and the word of God. Such individuals no doubt experience a "tormented" conscience. Thus, although the reformers ascribe great power and efficacy to the conscience—even calling the consciences of their hearers as witnesses against them—they acknowledge that their consciences are in conflict with their opposing desires and affections, and therefore hindered in some way. The proposed remedy to this problem is that Nicodemites must submit their feelings and experiences to the word of God and make a good confession, so that their consciences might console rather than condemn them.

While the reformers speak freely about the failings of their readers' consciences, they are, on the other hand, supremely confident that their own consciences are sound, reasonable, and even sources of authority in the matters raised by their letters and treatises. Calvin, in particular, routinely cites the assurance and peace of his conscience as evidence of the manifestly biblical and rational position he holds. He appeals to his own conscience not to play the judge, he says, but to prove that a conscience rightly ordered according to God's word serves a believer well. Calvin regards himself as able to call upon his own conscience for support, just as he can invoke the consciences of his opponents to convict them of wrongdoing, because he believes that God through the authority of his word allows him, as a minister, to evaluate the beliefs and actions of others. His conscience confirms that his understanding and application of Scripture is correct and therefore authoritative in dealing with matters of the church. The other reformers were, along with Calvin, apt to invoke conscience as a means of convicting their readers of their blatant hypocrisy.[102]

Finally, the reformers' rebuke of Nicodemism reveals something important about the relationship between Christian freedom and confession of faith in their thought. From their heated exchanges with "adiaphorists," we note that the reformers were abundantly sensitive to the argument that Christian freedom abrogates all forms of external religious ceremony, including oaths, vows of subscription, and corporate professions of faith. Calvin, Farel, Viret, and Vermigli all rejected this notion, first, on the basis that it was a misreading of Scripture. Fundamentally, the rejection of all religious ceremonies, so central to the theology of the Anabaptists, spiritualists, and many Nicodemites, was the result of an erroneous biblical hermeneutic that failed to acknowledge which aspects of the Mosaic administration had been fulfilled and repealed by Christ, and which still remained—not as requirements for salvation, but nevertheless as divinely appointed aids for the continual edification of the church.

Second, while their initial response to the adiaphorist argument was based in hermeneutics—in their understanding of how the New Testament has both preserved and revised the provisions and laws of the Old—the

---

[102] Ironically, Luther had invoked a similar argument in defense of Philip of Hesse's polygamy, though he was widely criticized for this move, even by Calvin. See Chapter 1, section 1.2.3.

reformers were equally concerned about protecting the proper use of oaths and vows as a means of honoring God and loving one's neighbor. As noted, the reformers' anti-Nicodemism included a strong rebuke of those who tried to make dissimulation in worship a matter of Christian freedom or adiaphora on the grounds that all forms of external ceremony had been abolished, with only the "rule of love" remaining in force. The reformers turned this rule back upon their opponents by arguing that love for God and neighbor rather necessitates the proper use of religious ceremonies—not their abandonment. Far from being a free or "permissible" act for the Christian, feigning Catholicism dishonored God and set a destructive example for struggling sinners. Despite what their Nicodemite opponents thought, it is not the proper use of oaths and vows that unduly binds the conscience. To the contrary: it is dissimulation in worship that wounds the conscience and stands as an affront to God. Thus, the reformers argued that the ceremonies required for the confession of faith belong to a category all their own, since they are necessary (in the first place) to render proper service to God, and (then) to protect the consciences of others. In this respect, we might say that the reformers were most concerned about the *public* conscience—that is, the *communal ramifications* of the exercise of one's conscience—since the dictates of private conscience could never justify withholding from God or one's neighbor the devotion and charity that are embodied in the public confession of faith.

Despite their best efforts to inculcate these principles, however, Calvin and his Reformed partners could not shake the persistent accusation that their demands for public confession were burdensome to peoples' consciences. At times, in fact, Calvin's own epistolary responses to Nicodemite inquiries did exhibit great annoyance and harsh rhetoric, even toward seemingly genuine cries for counsel and consolation. The Nicodemite issue pushed at the edges of Calvin's pastoral patience, almost to the point of causing him to transgress his own general instructions on how to deal with the weak. Our study suggests that it was the Nicodemites' continual misapplication of the traditional concept of "indifferent matters" that especially fueled his and the other reformers' opposition. For although they generally agreed with the classical, Thomistic concept of "adiaphora" as things that are in themselves neutral—the "act" or enactment of which may not be indifferent, depending on its circumstances—the reformers generally believed that Nicodemism belonged to an altogether different and unacceptable category of behavior. They refused to concede that veiling one's faith or joining in Catholic rites, regardless of the purity of one's intentions, counted as indifferent or permissible acts. Dissimulation was not something that could be "used well" unto the glory of God or the blessing of one's neighbor. Though the reformers acknowledged that there were various stripes of Nicodemite situations, and though they could exercise pastoral compassion and prudent accommodation toward these saints on occasion, they would not excuse the blatant act of religious dissimulation. Compromising one's confession, whether out of knowing disregard for the spiritual well-being of one's neighbor (active scandal), or even out of ignorance (passive scandal), was not an act of indifference at all, but a wicked perversion of divine worship and a careless violation of charity.

The specific matters of public confession, freedom of conscience, and the obligation of neighbor-love would occupy Calvin's attention throughout his Genevan ministry. In fact, navigating their complex relationship, while still working to gain the upper hand for reform in Geneva, proved to be a full-time job for Calvin, for his Company of Pastors, and for the city magistrates in the years that followed. As my final three chapters go on to illustrate, moreover, none of this would be accomplished without a fair amount of personal and institutional compromise for the sake of troubled consciences.

SECTION III
OATHS, CONFESSIONAL SUBSCRIPTION, AND THE BINDING OF THE CONSCIENCE IN REFORMATION GENEVA

5
Citizen's Oath and Confession of Faith in Reformation Geneva, 1536–1538

Necessary, Indifferent, or a *Tertium Quid*?

When John Calvin and Guillaume Farel began their joint effort to stabilize the newly reformed city of Geneva in 1536, they met with an obstructing complex of social, political, and religious tensions unlike anything the young Calvin, at least, had previously encountered. Political disputes with neighboring powers and persistent internal factionalism, coupled with the Genevans' natural suspicion of foreign ministers and theologians, were a stark contrast to Basel, where Calvin had resided a year earlier.[1] Oswald Myconius, successor to Johann Oecalampadius, had achieved confessional unity by the time Calvin arrived in the city. Its citizens subscribed to the First Confession of Basel under oath a few years after it was published in 1534.[2]

Enacting similar reforms in Geneva would prove more difficult, however. After succumbing to Farel's aggressive recruiting in 1536, Calvin set his mind to organizing and enforcing reform in the city. To that end, he took part in drafting three governing documents—*Articles concernant l'organisation de l'église et du culte a Genève*,[3] the *Confession de la foy*,[4] and his own

---

[1] William G. Naphy, *Calvin and the Consolidation of the Genevan Reformation*, 2nd ed. (Louisville, KY: Westminster John Knox, 2003), 27.

[2] Arthur C. Cochrane, *Reformed Confessions of the Sixteenth Century*, 2nd ed. (Louisville, KY: Westminster John Knox, 2003), 89–90.

[3] Text found in CO 10:1–64; OS 1:369–77.

[4] Text found in CO 9:693–700; OS 1:418–26. Primary authorship of the Genevan Confession remains the subject of scholarly dispute. Whereas early biographies by Theodore Beza (CO 21:126) and Nicolas Colladon (CO 21:59) name Calvin as the primary author, recent studies have generally attributed the Confession to Farel. See, e.g., Jason Zuidema and Theodore Van Raalte, *Early French Reform: The Theology and Spirituality of Guillaume Farel*, St. Andrews Studies in Reformation History (2011; repr., New York: Routledge, 2016), 5–6; and Alisdair Heron, "Calvin and the Confessions of the Reformation: Original Research," *Hervormde Teologiese Studies* 70, no. 1 (2014): 2. Exceptions to this modern opinion include A. D. Pont, "Confession of Faith in Calvin's Geneva," in *Calvin: Erbe und Auftrag: Festschrift für Wilhelm Neuser zu seinem 65. Geburtstag*, ed. Willem van't Spijker (Kampen: Kok Pharos, 1991), 107; and Bruce Gordon, *Calvin* (New Haven, CT: Yale University Press, 2009), 72. At the very least we can agree with Cochrane, *Reformed Confessions*, 119, that, "inasmuch as the order and the thought of the Confession is essentially that of [Calvin's] catechism it

Catechismus, sive christianae religionis institutio, published in 1538.[5] Calvin and Farel soon discovered, however, that the independent-minded Genevans were intolerant of the practice of confessional subscription that the two reformers deemed profitable—even necessary—for organizing the church and city around a united Reformed cause.[6] Internal tensions mounted, especially after they urged the Small Council to order all adult inhabitants in Geneva to swear a public oath to uphold their confession of faith.[7]

Calvin and Farel intended the oath to be a one-time occurrence, required by the pressing need to unite the church around a single confession and to guard the Lord's table from non-professing, unworthy celebrants.[8] Many citizens, however, resented the ministers' request, viewing it more as a threat to Genevan independence than as a means to godly unity. That the "title and prerogatives" of citizenship—spoils of an arduous struggle for independence—should be held captive on condition of signing a document composed by "foreign theologians" seemed an unbearable overreach on the part of the two Frenchmen.[9] And, indeed, it was Calvin and Farel's

---

is highly probable that Calvin was at least involved in compiling and editing it." How to properly date the Confession is also in question among scholars. Cochrane believes it is more likely that that the Confession, along with the *Articles*, was presented to the Genevan authorities on January 16, 1537, when the two reformers asked the Small Council to vote in favor of its observance (118). The *Annales* nevertheless record that the Genevan magistrates received the Confession for consideration on November 10, 1536 (CO 21: 206). Thus, the Confession clearly saw life in 1536, though we may ascribe a later date to its final, partial ratification.

[5] Text found in CO 5:313–62. This is Calvin's Latin edition of his first catechism, *Instruction et Confession de foy*, which was originally composed in French in 1537 (the text may be found in OS 1:378–417).

[6] In addition, the Small Council rejected the ministers' proposals for monthly celebration of the Lord's Supper and the establishment of church discipline independent of civil control. See Alexandre Ganoczy, *The Young Calvin*, trans. David Foxgrover and Wade Provo (Philadelphia: Westminster Press, 1987), 114; and Gordon, *Calvin*, 79. For a helpful account of Farel's reforming labors prior to and during Calvin's stay in Geneva, see Jaques Courvoisier, "Farel and Geneva," *McCormick Quarterly* 21, no. 1 (November 1967): 123–35.

[7] The full title of the Confession reads: "A confession of faith, which all citizens and residents of Geneva and subjects of the region ought to swear to keep and uphold" (*Confession de la foy, laquelle tous bourgeois et habitans de Geneve et subietz du pays doibvent iurer de garder et tenir*, CO 9:693).

[8] In their *Articles*, Calvin and Farel urged the Small Council—by appeals to *necessity*—to set down firm regulations for the worthy celebration of the Lord's Supper, "que ceux qui viennent en ceste communication soyent comme approuuez membres de Iesuchrist" (CO 10:9). In addition to appealing for the church's right to guard the table and excommunicate unrepentant sinners, the two reformers argued that the best way to promote church unity and purity of doctrine in Geneva, given the "trouble and confusion" (CO 10:7) that then plagued the city, was to require its inhabitants "to make confession of and give reason for their faith" (*Le remesde doncq que auons pense a cecy est de vous supplier que tous les habitans de vostre ville ayent a fere confession et rendre rayson de leur foy, pour cognoistre lesquelz accordent a leuangille et lesquelz ayment mieux estre du royaulme du pape que du royaulme de Iesucrist ... et cela seroyt seulement pour ceste foys*, CO 10:11–12).

[9] Amédée Roget, *Histoire du peuple de Genève*, 7 vols. (Geneva: 1870–87), 1:46–48.

persistence in such matters that led to their eventual expulsion from Geneva in 1538.

Although many studies of early Genevan reform have narrated the historical circumstances prompting the ministers' ousting from the city, few have paused to consider the potential incongruity of Calvin and Farel's request that its entire population should make a public vow of submission to a decidedly extra-scriptural document—a demand seemingly contradicting the very purpose of the Reformation. If nothing else, the Reformation was a movement epitomized by Luther's famous declaration that his conscience was captive to the word of God alone. Indeed, the Reformation cornerstone of *sola scriptura* both fostered and lent a voice to the faithful's great distain for Rome's myriad human traditions and external regulations that burdened the conscience. Calvin and Farel vigorously opposed spurious Catholic traditions in their own writings. In his *Summary and Brief Exposition* (1529/34), Farel warned that human laws and ordinances were an "abomination before God"; those who served them "are given over to a disordered conscience."[10] Likewise, Calvin, in his *Institutes of the Christian Religion* (1536), excoriated the pope's exercise of so-called spiritual power in formulating "new teachings," which have "cruelly vexed unhappy consciences."[11]

The two ministers nevertheless believed they had "not without good reason" required the entire Genevan populace to bind itself to uphold their Confession.[12] Commenting on this incident in the preface to his Catechism (1538), Calvin expressed frustration over the great "peevishness of ignorance" he had detected in those who had failed to see the value and necessity of "solemn oath-taking"—in a city that had already *sworn an oath* to the Reformation, no less![13] Though he was quite aware that the taking of oaths

---

[10] Guillaume Farel, "A Summary and Brief Exposition (1529/34)," in Zuidema and Van Raalte, *Early French Reform*, 91. For more on the influence of Farel's *Summary* on early Protestant doctrine and moral reform, see Stephen E. Ozment, *The Reformation in the Cities: The Appeal of Protestantism to Sixteenth-Century Germany and Switzerland* (New Haven, CT: Yale University Press, 1975), 67–74; and Robert White, "An Early Doctrinal Handbook: Farel's *Summaire et briefve declaration*," *Westminster Theological Journal* 69, no. 1 (2007): 21–38.

[11] *Institutes* (1536) (CO 1:221): "spiritualem potestatem . . . novis doctrinis . . . quibus infelices conscientias crudeliter vexarunt."

[12] *Catechismus* (1538), CO 5:319: "Iam vero confessionem, solenni iureiurando ab universe populo editam, non sine ratione adiungendam curavimus."

[13] *Catechismus* (1538), CO 5:319: "imperitiae morositas . . . solenni iureiurando." See the *Annales* entry for May 21, 1536, which records the official adoption of the new evangelical faith by edict. It was certainly not the case that the entire Genevan population embraced the Reformation wholeheartedly—traditional Catholic assumptions ran deep. Nevertheless, a representative portion of the voting citizenry (*bourgeois* and *citoyens*) did, with one voice, offer a sworn pledge to live according to the new faith and renounce papal idolatries: "Surquoy sans point daultre voix que une mesme est esté generalement arreste et par elevation des mains en lair conclud et a Dieu promys

falls under the category of "ceremonies" and "outward things" (that is, not strictly commanded by Scripture), Calvin had no qualms about requiring the practice in Geneva and seemed baffled by the people's resistance.[14] If anything, Calvin and Farel felt constrained by *their own consciences* to insist on public confession in Geneva, admitting, "we were able to obtain peace and quiet with our own consciences on no other condition, than that those who might wish to be counted among his people and be admitted to that spiritual and most holy feast would give deference to Christ by means of solemn profession."[15] But were they justified in requiring others to abide by a practice they felt conscience-bound to enforce? And to what category of human tradition did the practice of swearing an oath to an ecclesiastical document belong, in their minds? Calvin, we noted above, concedes that taking an oath constitutes an external, human ceremony lacking explicit scriptural command. Protestant reformers generally acknowledged, however, that ecclesiastical traditions could range from the wicked and perverse to the prudent and edifying. Remarkably, however, the Geneva Confession claims that some external ordinances are so essential that they should not be regarded as human traditions at all.[16]

This chapter will investigate the category of acceptable traditions to which Calvin and Farel appeal—a category that allows them to *require* vows to the Genevan Confession, yet somehow without burdening consciences. Are such public professions analogous to the performance of civil vows under the authority of the temporal government—vows that are good and even necessary so long as they do not contradict God's word? Does swearing an oath to a confession properly belong in the category of adiaphora, things neither commanded nor forbidden in Scripture, which a person may perform on a voluntary basis in *free* conformity to the "rule of love"? Or does oath-taking in Geneva belong to a kind of *tertium quid*—a tradition justified by a third

---

et iure que trestous unanimement a layde de Dieu volons vivre en ceste saincte loy evangellicque et parolle de Dieu ainsyn quelle nous est annoncee veuillans delaisser toutes messes et aultres ceremonies et abusions papales ymaiges et ydoles et tout ce que cela porroit toucher, vivre en union et obeissance de iustice" (CO 21:202). For a helpful timeline and summary of early Genevan reform efforts, including details surrounding Calvin and Farel's quest for confessional uniformity by means of a sworn oath, see Herman A. Speelman, *Calvin and the Independence of the Church* (Göttingen: Vandenhoeck & Ruprecht, 2014), 57–102.

[14] *Catechismus* (1538), CO 5:322: "caeremoniis . . . rebus externis."
[15] *Catechismus* (1538), CO 5:319: "non alia lege pacem ac quietem obtinere cum nostris ipsorum conscientiis potuimus, quam ut solenni professione nomen Christo darent, qui in eius populo censeri, atque ad spirituale sacrosanctumque illud epulum admitti vellent." Translation mine.
[16] *Confession* (CO 9:697): "nous ne les tenons point pour traditions humaines. . . ."

kind of rule, arising from a distinct, if not always clearly defined, convention of thought? Finally, what do confessions written before 1536 tell us about early Reformation views concerning the intersection of Christian freedom and human traditions?

Over recent decades, scholars of Calvin and the Reformation have scrutinized a number of issues that are relevant to the questions posed by this chapter. Some have sought to decipher Calvin's rather paradoxical stance on the matter of subscription. During his quarrel with Pierre Caroli in 1537, for example, Calvin refused to subscribe publicly to the Athanasian Creed, resisting the idea that classical, conciliar terminology must be the standard for personal orthodoxy. Later, however, when evangelical union was at stake, he chided a fellow pastor for failing to sign the Augsburg Confession unhesitatingly.[17] A few recent essays have also researched the contexts and controversies surrounding citizens' oaths, both in Geneva and in Reformed polemics against the Anabaptist refusal to swear oaths.[18] The related topics of adiaphora, external laws, and individual conscience have also captured the attention of various studies over the years. Notably, several of these works acknowledge a "third category" of sorts among Calvin's (and other reformers') views on "indifferent" matters.[19] It appears, however, that no major study has attempted to trace detectable growth in early Reformed confessions of faith respecting the rule or convention by which wicked and profitable human traditions are distinguished, and by which certain external ceremonies—like

---

[17] See Willem Nijenhuis, "Calvin and the Augsburg Confession," in *Ecclesia Reformata: Studies on the Reformation* (Leiden: Brill, 1972), 113; Nijenhuis, "Calvin's Attitude Towards the Symbols of the Early Church During the Conflict with Caroli," in *Ecclesia Reformata*, 73–96; Gijsbert van den Brink, "Calvin and the Early Christian Doctrine of the Trinity," in *Restoration Through Redemption: John Calvin Revisited*, ed. Henk van den Belt (Leiden: Brill, 2013), 17–19; and David C. Steinmetz, *Calvin in Context*, 2nd ed. (New York: Oxford University Press, 2010), 12.

[18] See Pont, "Confession of Faith," 106–116; and Craig S. Farmer, "Reformation-Era Polemics against Anabaptist Oath Refusal," *Mennonite Quarterly Review* 81, no. 2 (April 2007): 207–26. John L. Thompson's "Confessions, Conscience, and Coercion in the Early Calvin," in *Calvin and the Early Reformation*, ed. Brian C. Brewer and David M. Whitford (Leiden: Brill, 2019), 155–79, well-illustrates how Calvin's conflict with Caroli and the oath-swearing controversy in Geneva together provide early evidence for the reformer's fast-changing and rather paradoxical stance on how appeals to conscience might provide legitimate grounds for private resistance to confessional subscription.

[19] On law and conscience, see John Witte, Jr., *The Reformation of Rights: Law, Religion, and Human Rights in Early Modern Calvinism* (Cambridge: Cambridge University Press, 2007), 39–142; and John L. Thompson, "Second Thoughts about Conscience: Nature, Law, and the Law of Nature in Calvin's Pentateuchal Exegesis," in *Calvinus Pastor Ecclesiae*, ed. Herman J. Selderhuis and Arnold Huijgen (Göttingen: Vandenhoeck & Ruprecht, 2016), 123–46. On the topic of adiaphora, especially see Thompson, *John Calvin and the Daughters of Sarah: Women in Regular and Exceptional Roles in the Exegesis of Calvin, His Predecessors, and His Contemporaries* (Geneva: Droz, 1992), 227–67; and David Anderson Bowen, "John Calvin's Ecclesiological Adiaphorism: Distinguishing the 'Indifferent,' the 'Essential,' and the 'Important,' in His Thought and Practice, 1547–1559" (PhD diss., Vanderbilt University, 1985), accessed December 12, 2016, ProQuest Dissertations & Theses.

swearing an oath—are occasionally granted *divine* status and authority in Reformed polity.

In what follows, then, we will probe the convictions and practices of Farel and Calvin by surveying and analyzing several early Reformed confessions of faith drafted prior to 1536. Of special interest are confessions written by reformers of the German-Swiss regions during the early 1530s—those likely to have had the most influence on Calvin and Farel's own confession. Three confessions from this period are especially worthy of study: the Tetrapolitan Confession of 1530; the First Confession of Basel, published in 1534; and the First Helvetic Confession (i.e., the Second Confession of Basel), adopted in 1536. Our survey and analysis of these confessional documents will focus on three related issues: (1) the definition and purpose of human traditions; (2) freedom of conscience pertaining to indifferent or permitted things, such as vows or oaths; and (3) the importance and meaning of the biblical "rule of love" for determining the nature of Christian duty. A study of these three confessions will enable us to establish a context for understanding how the Geneva Confession of Faith compares to its predecessors on these key related issues, shedding light on Calvin and Farel's struggle for church reform. It will also help us test the possibility that their appeals for confessional uniformity in Geneva reflect the application of a third kind of rule or tradition—a *tertium quid*.

5.1. Human Traditions, Freedom of Conscience, and the Rule of Love in Reformed Confessions Prior to 1536

The Genevan Confession was hardly the first of its kind: the fledgling Reformed movement had already produced several confessions of faith prior to 1536. Notably, these codified statements of faith served both to differentiate and consolidate the evangelical churches. As the documentary fruit of public disputations and local conferences held during the 1530s, these confessions reflect the negotiation of terms between Lutheran and Reformed factions, yet without compromising on certain key doctrinal issues (e.g., the Lord's Supper). In this respect, we may regard confessions of faith as evidentiary traces of the early Reformation's diverse landscape. On the other hand, such declarations of faith were often penned in great haste and under mounting political pressure in an effort to convince civil authorities of the legitimacy and solidarity of the Reformed cause—with mixed results. Consequently, as pragmatic symbols simultaneously aiding evangelical unity and diversity, many early confessions of faith enjoyed only short careers, soon replaced by fresh statements better suited to meet the ever-evolving concerns of the Reformed churches.

Although Reformed confessions written during the early 1530s differ slightly in scope and purpose, they nevertheless share a commitment to the supreme authority of Scripture—including the rejection of errant human traditions—fixed by Ulrich Zwingli in his 1523 *Sixty-seven Articles* or *Conclusions*.[20] The Zurich reformer pledges to submit all the "articles and opinions" of this document to the supreme rule of Scripture, on whose authority they are based (*aus Grund de Schrift*).[21] It is noteworthy that the *Articles* paint the concept of human traditions in entirely negative tones. Zwingli condemns every fraudulent Catholic tradition that burdens believers. Among the human ordinances that Zwingli considers hypocritical and harmful to Christians are the regulations concerning fasting, festivals and pilgrimages, adornment, orders and sects, and clerical marriage laws. As we shall see, his list of perverse ecclesiastical commandments served as a template for later confessions of faith regarding the problem of human traditions.

Of special relevance is the twofold "rule" that Zwingli posits for navigating the relationship between human traditions and Christian freedom. He insists, first (concerning the prohibition of foods), "that no Christian is bound to perform works that God has not commanded" (Art. 24), and second (concerning the ban on clerical marriage), "that everything God permits, or has not forbidden, is lawful" (Art. 28).[22] Zwingli rules that the church should neither require believers to do anything lacking scriptural command, nor prohibit what Scripture does not explicitly forbid.

We find a similar rule contained in the *Theses Bernenses*, articles written for a public disputation between Reformed and Roman representatives in 1527, and ratified in 1528 by important German-Swiss reformers, including Martin Bucer and Wolfgang Capito of Strasbourg. Zwingli also had a

---

[20] Zwingli's *Sixty-seven Articles or Conclusions* were produced amid three public disputations in Zurich between Zwingli and Catholic ministers and theologians (concluding in 1524), and sparked the establishment of the Reformation in Switzerland. See Cochrane, *Reformed Confessions*, 33–34.

[21] Zwingli, *The Sixty-seven Articles or Conclusions*, in Philip Schaff, *Creeds of Christendom*, Vol. 3: *The Evangelical Protestant Creeds* (Grand Rapids, MI: Baker Book House, 1977), 197.

[22] Zwingli, *The Sixty-seven Articles*, Art. 24: "Das ein jeder Christ zu den Werfen, die Gott nicht geboten hat, unverbunden ist" (Schaff, *Creeds*, 3:201). Art. 28: "Das Alles, was Gott erlaubt, oder nicht verboten hat, recht ist" (Schaff, *Creeds*, 3:202).

significant hand in the revision and publication of these articles.[23] Article 2 of the *Theses* declares, "The Church of Christ makes no laws or commandments without God's Word. Therefore, all those human traditions that are called ecclesiastical commandments bind us only to the extent that they are grounded and commanded in God's Word."[24] This article substantially echoes Zwingli's rule: ecclesiastical commands must not bind a Christian to any practice that is not commanded by and "grounded in" Scripture. One nevertheless detects some development or expansion of the rule. The *Theses* concede that the category of "human traditions" may not be altogether wicked and perverse; indeed, they may entail certain practices having a degree of scriptural precedent and authority, and are therefore incumbent on the believer. But no comment is offered on what such an ecclesiastical commandment based on God's word might be, or what positive function they serve. The Tetrapolitan Confession, to which we now turn, was the first confession to address such matters in a deliberate manner.

5.1.1. The Tetrapolitan Confession, 1530 (*Confessio Tetrapolitana*)

Martin Bucer, aided by Wolfgang Capito, drafted and presented the Tetrapolitan Confession, also known as the *Vierstädtebekenntnis* (the Confession of the Four Cities), to Emperor Charles V at the Diet of Augsburg in 1530.[25] The document was hastily written following the announcement that the Strasbourg delegation to the Diet would not be permitted to sign the Augsburg Confession due to their disagreement with its article on Christ's bodily presence in the Eucharist.[26] This Bucerian statement of faith plainly mirrors the Augsburg Confession in its structure and content and has been called "the first attempt at an evangelical union symbol" because it pursues middle ground between Zwingli and Luther on the question of the Lord's

---

[23] Cochrane, *Reformed Confessions*, 45–48.
[24] *Theses Bernenses*, Art. 2: "Die Kirche Christi macht nicht Gesetze und Gebote ohne Gottes Wort; deshalb alle Menschensassungen, die man Kirchengebote nennt, uns nicht weiter binden, als sie in Gottes Wort gegründet und geboten sind" (Schaff, *Creeds*, 3:208).
[25] The confession reflects Bucer's characteristic lack of brevity.
[26] James M. Kittelson, "Tetrapolitan Confession," in *Oxford Encyclopedia of the Reformation*, ed. Hans Hillerbrand (New York: Oxford University Press, 1996), 4:148.

Supper.[27] Nonetheless, Arthur Cochrane notes that "in spite of, or perhaps just because of, Bucer's intense efforts to reconcile the differences between the Zwinglians and Lutherans, the Tetrapolitan Confession was soon superseded. The representatives of the four cities later subscribed to the Schmalkald Articles in February, 1531."[28] Thus, the *Tetrapolitana*—the oldest German *Reformed* confession—played an important but short-lived role in shaping the confessional voice of the German-Swiss Reformed churches.

Consonant with Zwingli's *Articles*, the *Tetrapolitana* is characterized by its deliberate emphasis on the centrality and sufficiency of Scripture for defining the doctrine of the church. Chapter 1 exhorts Reformed pastors to teach from the pulpit "nothing else than is either contained in the Holy Scriptures or hath sure ground therein."[29] Importantly, in the chapters that follow, the Confession settles on a key scriptural—and distinctly Augustinian—rule for human conduct that is summative of the moral law, namely, the command of love encompassing both tables of the Decalogue. For Augustine, the command of love comprises a rule for exegesis that has far-reaching ethical implications for Christians. Because Scripture's literal or clear sense always teaches what ought to be believed, obeyed, or hoped for, proper biblical interpretation should naturally engender the twofold love of God and neighbor.[30] Thus, even when exegetes encounter passages that are not obviously instructive, they should interpret such texts figuratively in order draw out their latent edification in accord with the rule of love.[31] Reflecting this Augustinian rule in its statement on justification and good works, for example, the Tetrapolitan Confession (chap. 4) rejects the idea of a so-called

---

[27] Schaff, *Creeds*, Vol. 1: *The History of Creeds*, 529. See also Michael W. Bruening, *Calvinism's First Battleground: Conflict and Reform in the Pays de Vaud, 1528–1559*, Studies in Early Modern Religious Reforms (Dordrecht: Springer, 2010), 73.

[28] Cochrane, *Reformed Confessions*, 53.

[29] Cochrane, *Reformed Confessions*, 56. *Confessio Tetrapolitana*, Cap. I: "ut nihil aliud quam quae sacris literis aut continentur, aut certe nituntur, e suggestu docerent," in H. A. Niemeyer, *Collectio confessionum in ecclesiis reformatis publicatarum* (Lipsiae: Klinkhardt, 1840), 745. Where I use Cochrane's English translations of these confessions, I have compared his translation to the original, occasionally inserting the text itself either from Schaff's *Creeds* or Niemeyer's *Collectio confessionum*.

[30] Augustine, *De doctrina christiana libri 4*, ed. Joseph Martin, *Corpus Christianorum* Series Latina XXXII (Turnhout: Brepols, 1962), I.36.40: "Quisquis igitur scripturas diuinas uel quamlibet earum partem intellexisse sibi uidetur, ita ut eo intellectu non aedificet istam geminam caritatem dei et proximi, nondum intellexit."

[31] Augustine, *De doctrina christiana*, III.10.14. James Samuel Preus, *From Shadow to Promise: Old Testament Interpretation from Augustine to the Young Luther* (Cambridge, MA: Belknap Press, 1969), 13, calls this Augustine's "two-value literal sense" of Scripture: "For the passage that in its literal meaning does not edify must (according to Augustine's understanding of the divine intention) be a *figura* of something that does edify—a *signum* of some spiritual or theological *res* whose true meaning must be revealed as *credenda, diligenda*, or *speranda*, that is, as *doctrina, lex*, or *promissio*."

formless faith devoid of godly works, citing Scripture's teaching that genuine faith "is efficacious through love." Justified believers are by necessity those who follow the commandment of "mutual love" (*dilectione mutua*) for God and neighbor—the essence of the entire Law *and* the proper goal of all of Scripture.[32]

Before addressing the topic of human traditions proper, the Confession enumerates the specific *duties* of a Christian that ought to be governed by this rule of mutual love (chap. 6). Believers should devote their energies principally to those things that profit their neighbors in keeping with the second table of the Law. Among these duties are the management of the government, submission to civil authorities, devotion to one's family and its particular needs, and the encouragement of the arts and other "honorable branches of learning." The standard for deciding which activities properly belong among the Christian's duties, and which do not, is as follows: "nothing at all is to be counted from among the duties of a Christian person that is not driven by some motivation to take account of one's neighbor."[33] Christians are duty-bound to perform activities that distinctly profit their neighbors, but anything outside this realm is not justly required of them.

In light of this standard for distinguishing which activities a Christian is obligated to perform, the Confession also re-evaluates the purpose and value of such "holy functions" as prayer and fasting in view of the rule of love (chaps. 7–8). We should recall that Zwingli's *Articles* listed regulations for fasting under the category of wicked and perverse Catholic traditions; he considered them harmful to Christian liberty. The *Tetrapolitana* adopts a more moderate approach, allowing that such ordinances may in fact be deemed "holy" and "especially proper for Christians" in some circumstances, and in those circumstances, church leaders should encourage them for promoting personal godliness. Strictly speaking, however, such holy functions as prayer and fasting do not belong to the highest order of Christian duty; they are not to be preferred over "other duties whereby our neighbor at once receives profit."[34] Consequently, they should not be so strictly regulated as those matters pertaining to the rule of love. Although exhortations to fast may profit the

---

[32] Cochrane, *Reformed Confessions*, 58–59; Niemeyer, *Collectio confessionum*, 748. Chapter 4 adds: "seeing that we are sure that no man can be justified or saved except he supremely love and most earnestly imitate God."

[33] *Confessio Tetrapolitana*, Cap. VI, in Niemeyer, *Collectio confessionum*, 749: "Unde inter Christiani hominis munera, nihil omnino numerandum est, quod non momentum aliquod, rationibus proximi adferat." Translation mine.

[34] Cochrane, *Reformed Confessions*, 62.

individual who freely receives them, such regulations should not be forced upon believers so as to oppress and bind their consciences as if their salvation depended on such practices, which would transform these regulations into extra-scriptural, human demands. Indeed, "experience itself more than proves that such commandments concerning fasts have been a great hindrance to godliness." The Confession insists that Christians have "liberty in external things," and should never have their consciences bound "to such laws as are the inventions of men," which lack explicit divine command.[35] In sum, the Confession teaches that Christians are conscience-bound to do only what is clearly profitable to their neighbors. In matters of conscience, however, such as private habits of piety, the faithful should never be forced to comply with an external, human law—however profitable it may seem.

Finally, and most relevant to our study, *Tetrapolitana's* Chapter 14 addresses the topic of human traditions proper:

> [We] reckon no traditions among human traditions (such, namely, as are condemned in the Scriptures) except those that conflict with the law of God, such as bind the conscience concerning meat, drink, times and other external things, such as forbid marriage to those to whom it is necessary for an honorable life, and other things of that stamp. For such as agree with the Scripture, and were instituted for good morals and the profit of men, even though not expressed in Scripture in words, nevertheless, since they flow from the command of love, which orders all things most becomingly, are justly regarded divine rather than human.[36]

In this chapter, the *Tetrapolitana* revisits matters of Christian duty and freedom of conscience first considered in Chapter 6. Specifically, it proposes a rule for distinguishing human traditions from a separate species of external ordinance that has value for the Christian. Similar to Zwingli, the Confession acknowledges that the category of "human traditions" denotes the wicked imposition of human laws that have no scriptural warrant, and therefore unjustly "bind the conscience." Human traditions, by this definition, are those "condemned in the Scriptures." But the Confession does allow for

---

[35] Cochrane, *Reformed Confessions*, 63–64; *Confessio Tetrapolitana*, Cap. VIII, in Niemeyer, *Collectio confessionum*, 751: "libertatem rerum externarum." Likewise, Calvin acknowledged that practices like swearing an oath to a confession of faith, though extremely profitable, still amounted to "rebus externis." See Calvin, *Catechismus* (1538), CO 5:322.

[36] Cochrane, *Reformed Confessions*, 71–72.

an alternative type of tradition that agrees with Scripture and serves "good morals and the profit of men." Traditions of this alternative kind, though they have no *explicit* scriptural command, are not reckoned among human traditions at all, "since they flow from the command of love" (*praecepto dilectionis*).[37] Traditions belonging to this latter category are deemed not only profitable but also *necessary* to the right order of the church, and "justly regarded divine rather than human."

Included among such profitable human traditions are those commanded by Paul in 1 Corinthians 11–14, where the Apostle sets forth rules for head coverings, orderly celebration of the Lord's Supper, speaking in tongues with an interpreter, as well as prophecy—practices that ought to follow the rule of love. The writers of the Confession concede that these traditions were unique to Paul's day. Nevertheless, many traditions passed on in Scripture, like those of Paul and the apostles, "the church today rightly observes, and on occasion also establishes new ones, [and] whoever should reject them disdains not the authority of men, but of God, *for whom tradition is whatever is profitable*."[38] Here we can note several characteristics of this alternative category of tradition. First, these traditions are implemented when occasion demands them; they have a circumstantial validity or necessity. Second, divine rather than human authority is ascribed to such ordinances. And third, the Confession offers an implicit definition of such a *divine* tradition; it is *whatever is profitable*. Hence, the Confession attributes divine authority to external ordinances that have proved, through scriptural example or from necessity arising from circumstance, to profit the right order of the church and fulfill the command of love. These traditions, by virtue of the pious function they perform, are more "justly regarded divine rather than human."

The Confession concedes, in the end, that no easy answer exists to the question of what specific ordinances qualify as beneficial traditions: "But oftentimes there is disputing about this as to what tradition is profitable, what not—i.e., *what promotes and what retards godliness*." It then adds, perhaps ironically: "But he who shall seek nothing of his own, and consecrates

---

[37] *Confessio Tetrapolitana*, Cap. XIV, in Niemeyer, *Collectio confessionum*, 757. The confession thus distinguishes between "traditiones . . . quae in scripturis damnantur. . . . Nam quae cum scriptura consonant."

[38] *Confessio Tetrapolitana*, Cap. XIV, in Niemeyer, *Collectio confessionum*, 758: "ecclesia hodie iure observat, et pro occasione quoque condit novas, quas qui reiecerit, is non hominum, sed Dei, cuius traditio est, quaecunque utilis est, authoritatem contemnit," emphasis added.

himself entirely to the public profit, shall easily [!] see what things correspond to God's law and what do not."³⁹

The principle expressed here coincides with the rule affirmed in Chapter 6 for distinguishing Christian duties from mere human commands. The Christian's true duty is to do whatever serves "public profit" more than one's own needs or interests. Likewise, traditions justly termed "divine" clearly promote, rather than impede, godliness. Thus, the idea expressed here is that believers whose minds are especially committed to fulfilling the command of love (the truly pious) will receive divine wisdom to discern which traditions or commands truly reflect God's law and profit his people—something that, ideally, the truly prudent will not have difficulty perceiving. In short, the *Tetrapolitana* holds that if a human ordinance or tradition promotes godliness—especially with respect to one's duty to his neighbor—then it ought to be obeyed. External ordinances belonging to this alternative *divine tradition* effectively hold the same measure of authority as an explicit scriptural command.

5.1.2. The First Confession of Basel, 1534 (*Confessio Fidei Basileensis prior*)

Oecolampadius composed the first draft of the Basel Confession in 1531, just shy of a month before his death. Oswald Myconius, his successor, finalized the Confession and saw to its eventual publication. The Confession is a simple statement of faith, spanning only twelve brief articles, and opposes errors on two fronts: the teachings of Roman Catholicism and the Anabaptists.⁴⁰ A few years after its publication, the citizens of Basel swore an oath to uphold the Confession, and Cochrane notes that "until 1826 it was read each year from the pulpits in Basel on the Wednesday of Holy Week, and until 1872 all ministers were required to subscribe to it"—practices Calvin would have witnessed during his brief stay in the city from 1535 to 1536.⁴¹

In true evangelical form, the Confession humbly submits its claims "to the judgment of the sacred Biblical Scriptures."⁴² And like the *Tetrapolitana*, the

---

[39] Cochrane, *Reformed Confessions*, 71–72.
[40] Schaff, *Creeds*, 1:387.
[41] Cochrane, *Reformed Confessions*, 89–90.
[42] *Basileensis prior*, Art. XII, in Niemeyer, *Collectio Confessionum*, 104: "hanc nostrum Confessionem Iudicio Sacrae Biblicae Scripturae subiicimus."

Basel Confession describes the Christian church as a "spiritual assembly" of saints who confirm their faith "by works of love."[43] The church is above all a confessing body whose citizens affirm the substance of their confession through acts of godliness and neighborly service.

The Basel Confession addresses the topic of human traditions explicitly under Article 11, which bears the heading, "Concerning Things Commanded and Not Commanded (*Von gebot und nit gebot*)." This heading, as well as what follows, reflects the rule established in Zwingli's *Articles* and repeated in the *Theses Bernenses*:

> We confess that just as no one may require things which Christ has not commanded [e.g., the confessional, Lenten fasting, holy days, and "other such things introduced by men"], so in the same way no one may forbid what He has not forbidden [e.g., clerical marriage]. ... Still less may anyone permit what God has forbidden [e.g., the veneration and invocation of dead saints, setting up images, etc.]. Moreover, no one may forbid what God has permitted [e.g., enjoying food with thanksgiving].[44]

The general rule outlined here is that no human authority—ecclesiastical or otherwise—may require a Christian to perform what is not commanded, permit what is explicitly forbidden, or forbid what is not forbidden but permitted in God's word. In contrast to the lengthy, detailed *Tetrapolitana*, the more concise Basel Confession does not explicitly acknowledge that a different species of tradition exists beyond the Roman Church's bevy of abusive human commands. Nor does Article 11 admit to any difficulty in determining which kinds of human tradition Scripture actually permits or even requires—or whether such things properly belong in the category of human tradition at all. Indeed, we are left wondering whether, on the basis of this Confession, a church or civil authority *may require or command things that are merely permitted.*

A partial answer to this question comes in Article 12, where the Confession affirms that at least one human practice—swearing an oath—may in fact be *required* under certain circumstances and for particular reasons. This article specifically responds to the errors of the Anabaptists, who are deemed "tumultuous spirits," and whose "false doctrines" are especially abominable

---

[43] Cochrane, *Reformed Confessions*, 92–93.
[44] Cochrane, *Reformed Confessions*, 95–96; *Basileensis prior*, Art. XI, in Niemeyer, *Collectio confessionum*, 83–84.

because of their divisive effect on the church—namely, by compromising its proper order and godliness.[45] One critical problem with the Anabaptist sect, according to this Confession, is its prohibition of oaths in all cases, "even though the honor of God, and love of neighbor, require it."[46] Notice that the Confession does not regard the practice of oath swearing (presumably in a variety of appropriate situations) to be *permissible* only. Rather, the tradition of swearing an oath is indeed *required* when circumstances are such that God's honor and the love of neighbor depend on it—that is, when the rule of love and godliness demands that an oath be sworn.

Importantly, there is a brief marginal note appended to Article 12 (*Disputatio XXXIII*). It reads: "It is lawful to make use of an oath on occasion; for God ordered it in the Old Testament; and Christ did not prohibit it in the New; finally, Christ and his apostles themselves swore (oaths)."[47] This appended apology for swearing oaths makes several acknowledgments: (1) oaths have a circumstantial validity, that is, when occasion demands them; (2) they are *allowed* because Christ *has not forbidden them*—they belong in the category of things "permitted"; and (3) there is scriptural precedent for swearing oaths in the Old and New Testaments.

The above analysis further suggests, however, that the Basel Confession is not overtly consistent—or is at least unclear—in communicating just where the human tradition of swearing oaths falls within the spectrum of matters commanded and not commanded. It appears to assign oaths simultaneously to the category of things permitted but not commanded, *and* to the category of things required by application of the scriptural command to love God and one's neighbor. Moreover, the question of whether a civil or church authority can require something that is permitted does not receive an explicit answer. The implicit answer nevertheless seems to be yes, if only *when circumstances require swearing an oath in order to properly fulfill the Christian duty to honor God and love one's neighbor*. In other words, the Confession implies that there is a distinction between an indifferent *letter* and non-indifferent *contexts*—such as occasions of religious controversy, in which indifferent things may cease to be indifferent. Thus, swearing an oath may be required when piety

---

[45] *Basileensis prior*, Art. XII, in Niemeyer, *Collectio confessionum*, 103: "erroneas doctrinas... turbarum Spiritus."

[46] *Basileensis prior*, Art. XII, in Niemeyer, *Collectio confessionum*, 103: "etsi gloria Dei, et charitas Proximi, id requirant."

[47] *Basileensis prior*, Art. XII, in Niemeyer, *Collectio confessionum*, 104: "Suo tempore Iuramento uti licet. Deus enim ius hoc in Veteri Testamento; et in Novo Christus non prohibuit; imo Christus et Apostoli ipsi iurarunt."

or godliness, described in Article 5 as faith confirmed by works of love, depends on it.

5.1.3. The First Helvetic Confession, 1536 (*Confessio Helvetica prior*)

Directly following Pope Paul III's promise to convene a general council that next year in Mantua (1537), Strasbourg reformers Bucer and Capito anxiously sought ways to unite the Lutherans and the Swiss.[48] They chose Heinrich Bullinger, Simon Grynaeus, Myconius, Leo Jud, and Kaspar Megander to draft a confession to that end, over which they also had great influence. The Confession "was examined and signed by all the clerical and lay delegates [to a conference in Basel], February, 1536, and first published in Latin."[49] The *Helvetica* did not actually prove successful at uniting the Swiss and German churches, but "it did serve to unite the Reformed Churches in German-speaking Switzerland, and formed the basis upon which the [more comprehensive] Second Helvetic Confession of 1566 was built."[50] As with the Basel Confession, Anabaptist polemics loom large in this document.

The *Helvetica* follows suit with the Reformed confessions surveyed above by pledging its absolute commitment to the rule of Scripture. It calls the inspired word of God the "most perfect and loftiest teaching" and the only rule for human doctrine that "deals with everything that serves the true knowledge, love and honor of God, as well as true piety and the making of a godly, honest and blessed life" (Art. 1). Scripture itself should be interpreted according to this express purpose; it is to be moderated "by the rule of faith and love" (*charitatis fideique regula*) (Art. 2).[51] Moreover, Scripture must be received by an active faith that "is manifested and demonstrated by love for our neighbor" (Art. 5).[52] In sum, the Holy Scriptures are the only truly sufficient standard for the life of true piety and godliness, and are themselves to

---

[48] Timothy George, "Helvetic Confessions," in *Oxford Encyclopedia of the Reformation*, ed. Hans Hillerbrand (New York: Oxford University Press, 1996), 2:220.

[49] Schaff, *Creeds*, 1:388.

[50] Cochrane, *Reformed Confessions*, 97–98. Also see Bruening, *Calvinism's First Battleground*, 75–76.

[51] Here the Confession collapses two technical terms, namely, the "rule of faith" (*regula fidei*)—a patristic term denoting orthodox doctrine, and one used by the reformers to distinguish Scripture as the sole foundation of true religion—and the "rule of love." See section 5.1.1.

[52] Cochrane, *Reformed Confessions*, 100–1; *Helvetica*, Art. I–II, in Niemeyer, *Collectio confessionum*, 115–16.

be interpreted and enforced by the rule of faith and love—the essence of the divine moral law.

On the topic of human ordinances, however, the *Helvetica* deviates slightly from its predecessors. Absent is the topic of human traditions as such; the Confession does not contain the generic list of errant Catholic traditions that bind the believer's conscience to extra-biblical commands. Nor does the Confession treat external ordinances on a spectrum of things *either* commanded *or* not commanded, as does the Basel Confession. Instead, the *Helvetica* is the first Reformed confession to address the topic of adiaphora proper. Article 24 contains the heading, "Concerning Things Which Are Neither Commanded Nor Forbidden, but Are Adiaphora and Voluntary," and reads:

> All things that are called, and properly speaking, are adiaphora, may be freely used by devout, believing Christians at all times and in all places, provided he does so judiciously and with love. For a believer is to use all things in such a way that God's honor is promoted and the Church and his neighbor are not offended.[53]

The substance of Article 24 reflects the Apostle Paul's directives in I Corinthians 8 and Romans 14 for dealing kindly with "weaker" brothers and sisters. The force of Paul's directives is that, while a believer is free from all dietary laws and human ceremonies, "stronger" members of the church ought to avoid any practice that might cause other Christians undue distress. The godly Christian may be free to partake of or abstain from such external things, at least in theory, but should prudently consider and do "what leads to peace and to mutual edification" (Rom. 14:19). The *Helvetica* closely parallels Paul's directives concerning "indifferent" things. While it allows that things properly deemed adiaphora "may be freely used by devout, believing Christians at all times and in all places," nevertheless, a rule exists to curb the potentially immoderate use of such freedoms. Believers are free with respect to indifferent matters, but only to the extent that they exercise their freedom "judiciously and with love." A person is not conscience-bound to any external command *as long as* one's decisions also fulfill the biblical rule

---

[53] Cochrane, *Reformed Confessions*, 109–10. The Latin texts of the *Helvetica* in Schaff, *Creeds*, 3:228 and Niemeyer, *Collectio confessiorum*, 121–22, number this article differently. Cochrane's translation, which I use, retains the German ordering.

of faith and love, in that "God's honor is promoted and the Church and his neighbor are not offended."[54]

This principle carries over into Article 26, which concerns the temporal government. The article begins with a concessive statement: "Although we are free in Christ," believers should nevertheless be prepared to obey the "supreme authority" with everything they have, demonstrating their subjection to civil authorities with "sincere love and from faith," even performing vows and oaths on the condition that these civil commandments "are manifestly not opposed to Him for Whose sake we honor and obey [the temporal government]."[55] The somewhat guarded language here ("not manifestly opposed") invokes several questions: With regard to the Christian's duty to civil authorities, how does the category of adiaphora function? Are Christians duty-bound to obey all civil commands? The Confession clearly concedes that, no, Christians are not obligated to comply with practices that "manifestly" oppose God's word. Stated differently, this means that many other human ordinances, although they are not explicitly commanded or forbidden in Scripture, ought to be obeyed because they promote godliness, maintain God's honor, and serve one's neighbor. The scriptural rule of love regulates human freedom, but individual conscience and genuine piety will guide the way toward deciding which permissible practices or traditions (neither commanded nor forbidden) are deemed necessary under different circumstances.

* * *

Our survey of Reformed confessions drafted prior to 1536 has yielded several key observations. We notice, first, that articles and statements of faith emerging out of the German-Swiss Reformation do not speak uniformly about the legitimacy of human traditions or ecclesiastical commands. They encompass a diverse spectrum of views, ranging from complete rejection to a more circumscribed and balanced assessment of the validity and profit of human ordinances. The earliest Reformed estimation of human traditions, like that contained in Zwingli's *Articles*, tended to reject all extra-biblical commandments mandated by ecclesiastical authorities. It considers the category of human traditions to encompass an entirely reprehensible set of injurious rules that burden the faithful, imperiling Christian freedom. Polemics

---

[54] Cochrane, *Reformed Confessions*, 109–10.
[55] Cochrane, *Reformed Confessions*, 111.

against Catholic efforts to regulate piety—by rules for prayer and fasting, for example—loom large in Zwingli's document.

Confessions of faith written during the early 1530s, however, saw fit to offer a more circumscribed account of what actually constitutes a human tradition. They also model general rules or principles by which someone might distinguish harmful human traditions from useful—even necessary—external ordinances serving the proper order and function of the church. The standard convention for determining what practices a Christian is duty-bound to perform has several elements. First, every believer's actions should conform to the scriptural command of love, which these confessions identify variously as "the rule of mutual love" (*Tetrapolitana*), faith confirmed "by works of love" (Basel Confession), and "the rule of faith and love" (*Helvetica*). This rule exists to moderate Christian freedom so that it is exercised "judiciously and with love" toward the public good. Second, the command of love guides Christian practice under changing circumstances. Occasion often establishes anew the proper use of human traditions. When it can be determined that such ordinances genuinely serve God's honor, profit one's neighbor, and rightly order the church, then such traditions are "justly regarded divine rather than human." And finally, the *conscience* of a pious individual should direct his or her course in deciding which permissible ordinances are deemed necessary by occasion, circumstances, and the rule of love. Indeed, believers will *easily* discern (it is claimed) which traditions they ought to heed, as long as they genuinely desire to follow God's will.

5.2. The Geneva Confession of Faith (1536)

Not surprisingly, the Genevan Confession—presented by Calvin and Farel to the Small Council for final ratification on January 16, 1537—mirrors its predecessors by treating the doctrine of Scripture first in the order of sound doctrine. Article 1 affirms that Holy Scripture—the church's "spiritual government"—holds ultimate authority in all matters of faith and life. It likewise calls God's word the "rule of our faith and religion" (*la reigle de nostre foy et religion*).[56] Moreover, the scriptural command of love—so prominent in the confessions we surveyed—comes to the fore in Article 3 concerning the divine moral law. There the Confession states that the faithful are bound to

---

[56] CO 9:693.

obey only the principles of justice codified in God's law, for his will alone "has dominion over our consciences."[57] Indeed, believers "ought to have no other rule of good and just living, nor invent other good works to supplement it than those which are contained" and summarized in the Decalogue.[58]

The Genevan Confession is uniquely concerned about the protection of Christian freedom; specifically, it insists that the church must not introduce anything beyond God's explicit will in Scripture that might harmfully bind a believer's conscience. God's will alone has exclusive dominion over the conscience, implying that the faithful have freedom regarding things that are external to God's word.[59]

The Confession nevertheless states that Christian freedom does not permit immoderate or self-indulgent living. Articles 7–8 convey that the remission of sins and regeneration necessarily result in newness of life and zealous good works—a central theme in the Basel Confession, which states that a godly life characterized by works of love gives substance to one's confession of faith. Articles 9–10 make clear that such works are not meritorious. Believers should put no faith in their works, since their godly actions are themselves only the result of God's daily grace.[60] Although Christians experience "rest of conscience" only by apprehending God's saving benefits, good works done in faith are nevertheless "pleasing and agreeable" to God and the believer.[61] Calvin's *Institutes* (1536) likewise argues that a key part of Christian freedom

---

[57] CO 9:693. Likewise, in *Institutes* (1536) (CO 1:50–51; Battles ed., 36), Calvin argues that the law primarily functions as an exhortation to obedience: "This is not something to bind their consciences with a curse, but to shake off their sluggishness, by repeatedly urging them, and to pinch them awake to their imperfection." Thus, the law has been abrogated for believers only in the sense that "it may no longer condemn and destroy their consciences by confounding and frightening them with the message of death."

[58] *Confession of Faith* (LCC 22:27; CO 9:694). Importantly, this article on the divine law proved most controversial during the oath-taking affair in Geneva. Many people saw it as a demand and pledge for perfect obedience, which was an impossible feat. Calvin, for his part, deemed their complaint groundless, since he and Farel had made it clear that the law did not exist to prompt vain thoughts about works-righteousness, but to encourage complete dependence on God's grace—a point he would argue even more strongly in his later polemics against the Anabaptist radicals. See Calvin's "Brief Instruction for Arming All the Good and Faithful against the Errors of the Common Sect of the Anabaptists," in *Treatises against the Anabaptists and against the Libertines*, trans. and ed. Benjamin W. Farley (Grand Rapids, MI: Baker Academic, 1982), 98–99. Indeed, a primary aspect of Christian freedom, according to Calvin's *Institutes* (1536), is that the consciences of believers "rise above and advance beyond the law, forgetting all law-righteousness" (Battles ed., 176; CO 1:196).

[59] See also *Institutes* (1536) (CO 1:209; Battles ed., 189).

[60] *Confession of Faith* (LCC 22:27–29; CO 9:695–96).

[61] *Confession of Faith* (LCC 22:28–29; CO 9:696). The notion that the good works of believers, although non-meritorious, are acceptable and "pleasing" to God, is a central theme in Calvin's *Institutes* (1536) (CO 1:53; Battles ed., 39).

is "that consciences observe the law, not as if constrained by the necessity of the law, but that freed from the law's yoke willingly obey God's will."[62]

The Genevan Confession's emphasis on liberty of conscience, in accord with the moral law and profitable good works, sets the stage for addressing human traditions, which is the subject of Article 17. There we read:

> The ordinances that are necessary for the internal discipline of the Church, and belong solely to the maintenance of peace, honesty and good order in the assembly of Christians, we do not hold to be human traditions at all, in as much as they are comprised under the general command of Paul, where he desires that all be done among them decently and in order. But all laws and regulations made binding on conscience which oblige the faithful to things not commanded by God, or establish another service of God than that which he demands, thus tending to destroy Christian liberty, we condemn as perverse doctrines of Satan.[63]

Several observations based on this passage are noteworthy. To begin with, the similarities between the Genevan Confession and the Bucerian *Tetrapolitana* are striking. Both confessions deliberately try to distinguish profitable ordinances from perverse human traditions. They purposefully concede that external ordinances akin, but not identical, to human traditions serve a profitable role in the government of the church. Indeed, these two confessions deny most emphatically that practices deemed necessary for the order and discipline of the church are properly called "human traditions" at all. The Genevan Confession closely parallels the *Tetrapolitana* in other ways by emphasizing the sacred liberty of conscience, and by appealing to St. Paul's directives to the Corinthians as partial justification for maintaining profitable church traditions.

Even more interesting is how Calvin and Farel appear to furnish this document with a defense of the kind of tradition most conducive to implementing their own Confession in Geneva. The opening claim in Article 17 fairly anticipates the complaint that all human ordinances lacking scriptural command unjustly bind the conscience, and need not be obeyed. Remarkably, the Confession responds to this implicit claim by answering that ordinances required for "the maintenance of peace, honesty and good order" in the church

---

[62] *Institutes* (1536) (Battles ed., 177; CO 1:197).
[63] *Confession of Faith* (LCC 22:30–31; CO 9:697–98).

simply *are not* human traditions at all; thus, arguments employed against wicked Catholic traditions do not apply to these profitable ordinances.

Indeed, if one follows the logic of the second half of Article 17, it becomes clear that such ordinances serve the direct opposite function of human traditions, which claim to bind the conscience. Human traditions, according to the Confession, involve laws and regulations that force believers to do things "not commanded by God, or establish another service of God than that which he demands." Such traditions, which lack explicit scriptural command, effectively "destroy Christian liberty." Reversing the logic, then, we may conclude that the unspecified human ordinances endorsed by the Confession neither represent a service alien to God's demands, nor do they destroy the liberty of conscience. The Genevan Confession closely parallels the *Tetrapolitana*'s claim that such ordinances are "more divine than human," in that they fall into the category of whatsoever promotes, rather than hinders, godliness.

This allowance for godly but human ordinances brings us back to the original question framed by this chapter: To what category do Calvin and Farel ascribe the practice of swearing an oath when the oath is sworn to an extrabiblical confession of faith? And what is their justification for requiring this practice in Geneva? The analysis in this section of the chapter suggests that the reformers tried to vindicate their demands by appealing to a third type of rule for judging human traditions—a rule distinguishable from those governing civil obedience and matters of adiaphora. Although somewhat obscure, this *tertium quid* appears to have some precedent in earlier Reformed confessions. Practices belonging to this third type of ordinance are derived from the scriptural rule of faith and love, born of circumstantial necessity, and confirmed by pious intention.

This rule or category is reflected in the Genevan Confession itself, as well as in Calvin and Farel's struggle for early reform in Geneva, and is distinguishable from related categories having to do with Christian freedom and duty. We notice, for example, that the reformers do not justify demanding a sworn oath to the Confession simply by employing arguments used to legitimate civil obedience, including civil oaths. The reformers acknowledge that temporal power serves its appointed end to promote order and peace in society, and that believers should obey civil authorities when they do what is "expedient for public welfare."[64] Exceptions to civil obedience nevertheless exist. God alone has dominion over a person's conscience. The Confession states

---

[64] *Institutes* (1536) (CO 1:242; Battles ed., 220). Commenting on the third commandment, especially the legitimacy of pledges and oaths, Calvin writes in *Institutes* (1536) (Battles ed., 22; CO

that believers are therefore only obligated "to obey statutes and ordinances which do not contravene the commandments of God."[65] Likewise, Calvin's 1538 Catechism declares that obedience to God's earthly magistrates should "never lead us away from obedience to him, to whose decrees the commands of all kings ought to yield."[66] Believers may—indeed must—resist civil authorities when they demand compliance to commands that contradict God's word or lack clear evidence of public edification. Strictly speaking, however, Calvin and Farel's demand for public, personal adherence to their Confession of Faith was not a civil ordinance, but a mandate that served the spiritual function of regulating individual conformity to sound doctrine.[67] The reformers sought to establish this practice—as part of the administration of their pastoral office—for the express disciplinary purpose of guarding the "spiritual and most holy feast" of the Lord's Supper.[68] It would have been inappropriate, therefore, to validate the spiritual function intended for the Genevan oath on the same basis for allowing civil vows, since the souls of the faithful were free from all civil jurisdiction.[69]

Nor does the practice of swearing an oath to a confession strictly belong to the category of adiaphora proper. Calvin's *Institutes* (1536) are especially illustrative of this fact. In discussing key aspects of Christian freedom, Calvin interprets adiaphora to mean "that we are bound before God by no religious obligation to outward things of themselves 'indifferent;' but are permitted sometimes to use them, sometimes to leave them, indifferently."[70] Plainly stated, no regulations known as "spiritual laws"—that is, human

---

1:35): "In short, we are not to use even a true oath rashly, unless God's glory or the need of the brethren demands it as necessary." Considering the example of Paul, Calvin points out that, "oath-taking was permitted not for the sake of lust or desire, but because of necessity." Oaths taken and required by the magistrates are not opposed to the third commandment when they promote God's "honor and glory" and serve "the public good."

[65] *Confession of Faith* (LCC 22:33; CO 9:700).

[66] Calvin, *Calvin's First Catechism: A Commentary. Featuring Ford Lewis Battles' Translation of the 1538 Catechism*, ed. I. John Hesselink (Louisville, KY: Westminster John Knox Press, 1997), 38 (CO 5:354). On this point, the Catechism repeats—almost verbatim—Calvin's teaching in the *Institutes* (1536) (CO 1:248; Battles ed., 225), where he writes that obedience to God's earthly authorities "is never to lead us away from obedience to him, to whose will the desires of all kings ought to be subject."

[67] In the preface to his Catechism, Calvin shows awareness that there are many in Geneva "who openly grumble that we have simply forced people to promise fulfillment of the law by oath" (*1538 Catechism*, 5).

[68] *Catechismus* (1538), CO 5:319.

[69] In keeping with Calvin's doctrine of the "twofold government." See *Institutes* (1536) (CO 1:228–29; Battles ed., 207).

[70] *Institutes* (1536) (CO 1:198–99; Battles ed., 179).

laws declared to be necessary for eternal life—may bind the believer's conscience.[71] Nevertheless, Christian liberty ought always to be moderated by the rule of love; that is, "we must use our freedom if it results in the upbuilding of our neighbor, but if it does not help our neighbor, then we must forego it."[72] Pausing here, Calvin explains that his instructions about avoiding offenses and "yielding to weakness" pertain *only* to "things intermediate and indifferent" (adiaphora proper).[73] He intimates, moreover, that other kinds of things exist "that have to be done," and these are things that "must not be omitted for fear of some offense." Indeed, such actions are necessarily taken—despite potential objections from one's neighbor—so that "we may not offend God."[74]

This alternate category of things "that have to be done" fulfills the agenda guiding Calvin and Farel's quest for confessional uniformity in Geneva. For indeed, they did not believe that public oath-swearing was simply a matter of indifference—an optional activity that its inhabitants were permitted, but not required, to observe. Rather, the "trouble and confusion" that then plagued Geneva and seriously called into question the people's acceptance of the pure gospel made it appropriate, even necessary, for those living in the city to "make confession of and give reason for their faith."[75] In the *Articles*, Calvin and Farel therefore urged the Genevan Council to adjudge their directives as more divine than human—a fact they believed "prudent and sagacious men" would easily discern:[76]

> [I]f you regard these intimations and exhortations *as being truly from the Word of God, and take them not at all as from us, but as from him from whom they do proceed*, that you similarly consider of what importance and consequence they are for the maintenance of the honour of God in this State and the conservation of the Church in its integrity.[77]

One cannot help but notice—with some sense of irony—how similar this claim sounds to the Catholic Church's argument from apostolic tradition,

---

[71] Calvin distinguishes between the proper and improper exercise of "ecclesiastical power" in his treatment of Christian freedom in the *Institutes* (1536) (CO 1:204–29; Battles ed., 184–207).
[72] *Institutes* (1536) (CO 1:203; Battles ed., 183).
[73] *Institutes* (1536) (CO 1:202; Battles ed., 182).
[74] *Institutes* (1536) (CO 1:203; Battles ed., 183).
[75] *Articles* (CO 10:7, 11–12).
[76] *1538 Catechism*, 3.
[77] *Articles*, LCC 22:55, emphasis mine.

which Calvin mentions (and rejects) in his *Institutes*, writing, "I hear the answer they make for themselves—that their traditions are not from themselves but from God."[78] Of course, the traditions Calvin has in mind are those supposedly "perverse rites, which are performed ... according to the willfulness of human nature," such as those listed in Zwingli's *Articles* and repeated in several Reformed confessions before 1536.[79] It is nevertheless uncertain that the naturally cautious Genevans would have detected the difference, at least at first blush. Indeed, Calvin's opinion, that the whole oath-swearing affair resulted from poor understanding and "circulating rumors" about the reformers as "innovator[s]" seems a telling detail.[80] It may very well be that Calvin and Farel's demands smacked of *Reformed papism* more than the two Frenchmen were ready to admit.[81] What remains clear is that, although the reformers believed the practice of swearing an oath to the Confession was both profitable and necessary, most of the population found the request highly burdensome.

* * *

William Naphy's claim, that we should not attribute the crisis surrounding the swearing of public oaths *mainly* to doctrinal or moral issues in Geneva, seems fair.[82] Given what we know about the city's political struggles and prevalent factionalism even prior to Calvin's arrival, it is more accurate to see this crisis "as a *continuation* of the divisions arising from the disputes in Geneva over authority and who was to exercise it."[83] We should not fail to

---

[78] *Institutes* (1536) (CO 1:210; Battles ed., 190): "Audio, quid ipsi pro se respondeant: suas traditiones non a se, sed a Deo esse." See also *Institutes* (1536) (CO 1:221; Battles ed., 200), on Rome's abuse of "spiritual power."

[79] *Institutes* (1536) (CO 1:224; Battles ed., 202).

[80] *Catechism* (1538), 3.

[81] The term *reformed papism* is a modified reference to Ozment's section, "From Pamphlet to Catechism and Church Ordinance: The Reformers as New Papists," in *The Reformation in the Cities*, 151–64.

[82] Naphy, *Calvin and the Consolidation*, 27. We might be tempted to conclude that public resistance to discipline and instruction indicates an anemic moral condition in Geneva during its early years of reform. Naphy argues quite convincingly, however, that this conclusion should be resisted. In his study of Geneva's early factionalism and political unrest, he shows that the magistrates' concern for moral purity in Geneva was in fact very high (29–32). Likewise, Robert M. Kingdon, "The Control of Morals in Calvin's Geneva," in *The Social History of the Reformation*, ed. Lawrence P. Buck and Jonathan W. Zophy (Columbus: Ohio State University Press, 1972), reveals that laws regulating morals in Geneva (especially clerical laws concerning prostitution, concubinage, etc.) "were enacted by the lay members of the city council entirely on their own authority ... before Farel had been named to any position of authority, and before John Calvin had even arrived in Geneva" (5).

[83] Naphy, *Calvin and the Consolidation*, 32–33, emphasis added. It is very likely that the Genevans largely opposed the enforcement of this Confession on account of the fact that Bern, its protectorate, opposed making discipline an exercise of the church. Indeed, "since the very existence of the

discern the extent to which doctrinal matters contributed to this struggle for authority, however. For Calvin and Farel, at least, Genevan oath-refusal signaled a crisis of identity. The people had, after all, sworn an oath to follow the Reformation, pledging to be governed by the *authority of God's word*. The two Frenchmen thus felt duty-bound to ensure that Genevan reform would be guided by the principle of *sola scriptura*.[84]

Nevertheless, Brad Gregory has noted that, in many Protestant regions, this "would-be solution for reforming the late medieval church immediately became an unintended, enormous problem of its own, one different in kind from the problem of how to close the gap between the Roman Church's prescriptions and the practices of late medieval Christians."[85] Reformers living in cities that had severed ties with Rome still faced the difficult task of applying the rule of Scripture to differing needs and circumstances. The Reformation required *"hermeneutic authorities"* to interpret Scripture's meaning, just as reformers also needed their interpretations to be *"backed by political authorities"* in order to enforce them.[86] Indeed, it was this complex, and sometimes conflicting triad of biblical, ecclesiastical, and political authorities—more than a basic adherence to *sola scriptura*—that most often determined which ordinances and traditions were deemed to be based on God's word and thus conducive to achieving a united, godly society.[87]

In Geneva's case, it was Calvin and Farel's hermeneutic jurisdiction and sense of pastoral duty that led them to choose an oath as the necessary procedure for uniting the faction-prone church and city around a single confession of faith. Calvin, for his part, freely conceded that this public profession

---

Republic depended upon Bernese military might it is not surprising to find that many Genevans would strive to avoid anything which could cause offense to their benefactors" (28).

[84] As they insisted at the outset of their Confession (CO 9:693) and Catechism (1538): "Moreover, the doctrine with which we are instructing the people entrusted to us by the Lord we believe to be so in accord with holy truth, that there will be no one of the godly who does not recognize in it what awareness of religion he has, seeing that we have endeavored not to pour forth our own views but to dispense things taken soberly and faithfully from God's pure Word" (*Catechism* [1538], 2; CO 5:318).
[85] Brad Gregory, "Reforming the Reformation: God's Truth and the Exercise of Power," in *Reforming Reformation*, ed. Thomas F. Mayer (2012; New York: Routledge, 2016), 29.
[86] Gregory, "Reforming the Reformation," 31. Italics original.
[87] Ozment, *The Reformation in the Cities*, 151–52, also describes the conflict between freedom and the need for discipline that sometimes troubled early reform efforts: "What began in the heady name of freedom soon came face to face with the sober demand for discipline, not only from magistrates but also from Protestant reformers. Whether they had misunderstood the high expectations of the reformers or were just not up to them, Protestant congregations in the late 1520s and 1530s were to encounter the end of a leash. Protestant leaders now undertook the extremely awkward task of making religious discipline and enforced orthodoxy prominent in a religion that had succeeded primarily in the name of freedom from religious tyranny."

amounted to an external ceremony—a human ordinance lacking explicit scriptural command, yet binding a person to a specific action. It was, however, the only means by which the reformers could avoid a *personal* crisis of conscience, and make sure only worthy individuals partook of the Holy Supper. Peace of conscience, above all, prompted them to require a human ordinance for testing whether the Genevan populace was genuinely and unanimously committed to the gospel.[88]

Moreover, the reformers' Confession, by delineating an alternative type of "tradition" having no explicit scriptural command, yet being justly required of the faithful in some cases, clearly reflects the more circumstantiated assessment of human traditions found in Reformed confessions of faith drafted in the early 1530s.[89] This chapter has traced out the rule commonly stated, or at least implied, in these early confessions for determining which kind of human ordinances believers are justly bound to obey—those best regarded divine rather than human. These include any established practice that clearly serves God's honor, edifies one's neighbors, and contributes to the right order of the church. Such traditions will be promptly received and practiced by the most "wise and sagacious" Christians, whose minds are especially attuned to God's will.

Nevertheless, Calvin and Farel were ultimately unsuccessful at convincing the Genevan populace that swearing an oath to their new Confession was indeed an act of prudence. What they believed to be a necessary tradition, critical to Genevan reform, was chiefly the product of their own unique interpretation—of Scripture as well as of local circumstances—and most of the population simply disagreed with it. In the end, the reformers' chosen means for acquiring confessional uniformity in the city—by appealing to a rather obscure third type of tradition—further stoked the Genevans' ire and stiffened their distrust of foreign figures of power.

---

[88] Cf. Heron, "Calvin and the Confessions of the Reformation," 2.

[89] To the extent that this alternative type of tradition belongs neither to the category of adiaphora proper nor to the category of essential ordinances (necessary for salvation), Bowen's analysis of Calvin's "third category" is relevant and insightful: "For Calvin, the general rules of Scripture began to regulate ecclesiastical conduct where the specific Scriptural instructions ceased. It was therefore the case, in his opinion, that most controversies within and among churches were not over 'indifferent' matters but rather over 'important' ones." See Bowen, "John Calvin's Ecclesiological Adiaphorism," 59–60.

6
"Make Them Afraid of Bearing False Witness"

Oaths, Conscience, and Discipline in the Registers of the Genevan Consistory, 1541–1564

Calvin's first stay in Geneva was a public failure. Expelled from the city along with Farel for over-asserting their disciplinary agenda, Calvin eventually retreated to Strasbourg—wearied, angry, and not a little discouraged.[1] Freed from his troubled charge in Geneva, Calvin again took consolation in the hope that he would find a quiet corner somewhere where he could finally devote himself to literary pursuits. Upon his arrival in Strasbourg, however, Bucer quickly dashed this hope, invoking God's judgment—like that upon a reluctant Jonah—if he refused to hold a teaching post in the city.[2] Calvin consented and thus began some of his most fulfilling and peaceful years in the service of Christ's church.

Back in Geneva, the city rulers were already beginning to regret their decision to banish the two French reformers from their midst. Although Calvin and Farel's zealous efforts to regulate reform in Geneva through sacramental administration, polemical preaching, and mandatory citizens' oaths had proven to be immensely unpopular among the native Genevans, the vacuum left by the two reformers' absence proved to be an even greater burden on the republic. Shortly after their expulsion in April 1538, factionalism took root in the city and threatened to destroy the independence its residents had so long pursued. Even in his absence, Calvin would prove his worth to the people of Geneva, advising the city leaders and warding off Catholic infiltration through his skillful epistolary defense of reform against Cardinal Sadoleto in 1539. It did not take the Genevan rulers long to realize that their best chances

---

[1] For events surrounding the expulsion of Calvin and Farel from Geneva, and its immediate aftermath, see Bruce Gordon, *Calvin* (New Haven, CT: Yale University Press, 2009), 82–85.

[2] John Calvin, "Author's Preface," in *Commentary on the Book of Psalms* (CTSOT 1:xliii; CO 31: 25–28).

of overcoming the city's factionalism and restoring moral reform was to recall the young Frenchman. When the pro-Farel group (*Guilluermins*) regained power in Geneva in 1541, Viret, who had been invited back to fill pulpits temporarily, took charge over efforts to recall Calvin back to the city.[3]

The prospect of returning to Geneva filled Calvin with palpable dread. On March 29, 1540, Calvin confessed to Farel that he would rather "submit to death a hundred times than to submit to that cross, on which I had to perish daily a thousand times over."[4] Viret's efforts to recall him were largely resented, at least at first. Calvin warned his friend in a letter dated May 19, 1540, that if he truly wished him well, he would "make no mention of such a proposal" to return "to that place of torture" ever again.[5] Calvin later wrote to Farel on October 21 of the same year, admitting that even though he regarded the Christian life as one of trial and suffering, the thought of being recalled to Geneva severely vexed his conscience:

> Whenever I call to mind the state of wretchedness in which I spent my life there [in Geneva], how can it not be but that my very soul must shudder when any proposal is made for my return? . . . When I call to mind by what torture my conscience was racked at that time, and with how much anxiety it was continually boiling over, pardon me if I dread that place as having about it something of a fatality in my case.[6]

Later, writing again to Farel from the Diet of Ratisbon (Regensburg) on May 4, 1541, Calvin nevertheless declared that he had an undeniable love for the Genevan flock. Despite his best efforts to suppress a sense of calling, his conscience would not allow him rest if he abandoned his duty to Christ's church.[7] Calvin had made the decision to return.

---

[3] This narrative is well-known; see, e.g., T. H. L. Parker, *John Calvin: A Biography* (Louisville, KY: Westminster John Knox Press, 2007), 103–7.

[4] Calvin to Farel, March 29, 1540 (Herminjard 6:199.5–6, #857): "Sed centum potius aliae mortes quam illa crux: in qua millies quotidie pereundum esset."

[5] Calvin to Viret, May 19, 1540 (Herminjard 6:228–29, #865): "Eam vero epistolae partem non sine risu legi, ubi tam bene valetudini meoe prospicis. Genevamne, ut Melius habeum? Cur non potius recta ad crucem? Satius enim fuerit semel perire quam in illa carnificina torqueri. Ergo, mi Virete, si salvum me esse cupis, consilium istud omittas."

[6] Calvin to Farel, October 21, 1540 (Herminjard 6:325–26, #898): "Quoties memoria repeto quam misere illic habuerim, fieri non potest quin toto pectore exhorrescam, ubi agitur de me revocando. . . . dum cogito quibus tormentis excruciata tum fuerit conscientia mea, et quibus curis aestuarit, ignosce si locum illum velut mihi fatalem reformido."

[7] Calvin to Farel, May 4, 1541 (Herminjard 7:103–7, #971).

When Calvin set foot back in Geneva in September 1541, he was not entirely the same reformer. Although he held the same standards for implementing moral reform in Geneva, his methods for attaining this goal were noticeably different. In place of subscription oaths, Calvin insisted upon the creation of a Consistory that would serve the disciplinary purposes he had earlier sought by insisting on the right of excommunication. The Consistory, a body of pastors and elders in which Calvin held a prominent role, would not have direct authority to excommunicate or to exact punishment on criminal offenders according to the new Ecclesiastical Ordinances (1541); it would serve the important role, however, of examining the residents of Geneva with respect to their doctrine and morality. Calvin thus envisioned a "two-track system of morality" that reflected his understanding of the proper division of labor between church and state. The Consistory would regulate the spiritual condition of Geneva's residents by reminding them of their Christian duties and threatening spiritual discipline for various offenses. Those who resisted the Consistory's moral admonition, however, would be handed off to the Small Council—Geneva's board of twenty-five members in which political power was centralized—to receive civil and criminal penalties.[8]

Scholars of Reformation Geneva have described the Consistory in various ways: as a "morals court" or "quasi-tribunal" with the power to summon—but not convict—those suspected of violating biblical morality;[9] as a "mandatory counseling service" that attempted to reconcile those embroiled in personal disputes;[10] and as an "educational institution" that sought to inculcate in each Genevan an understanding of the Christian religion through a Reformed lens.[11] Each of these descriptors reflects some aspect of the Consistory's vital impact upon Genevan life—an impact that was invariably wide-reaching. Residents of the city were summoned before the Consistory to answer for sins of all kinds and degrees, the most common being blasphemy, illicit

---

[8] John Witte, Jr., *The Reformation of Rights: Law, Religion, and Human Rights in Early Modern Calvinism* (Cambridge: Cambridge University Press, 2007), 78; and Witte, "Calvinist Contributions to Freedom in Early Modern Europe," in *Christianity and Freedom*, Vol 1: *Historical Perspectives*, ed. Timothy Samuel Shah and Allen D. Hertzke (Cambridge: Cambridge University Press, 2016), 215.

[9] Jeffrey Watt's depictions of the Consistory in *The Consistory and Social Discipline in Calvin's Geneva* (Rochester, NY: University of Rochester Press, 2020), and in "Reconciliation and the Confession of Sins: The Evidence from the Consistory in Calvin's Geneva," in *Calvin and Luther: The Continuing Relationship*, ed. R. Ward Holder (Göttingen: Vandehoeck & Ruprecht, 2013), 105–20.

[10] Robert M. Kingdon's description of the Consistory in "Calvin and the Family: The Work of the Consistory of Geneva," *Pacific Theological Review* 17 (1984): 5–18.

[11] A characterization also coined by Kingdon in "The Geneva Consistory in the Time of Calvin," in *Calvinism in Europe, 1540–1620*, ed. Andrew Pettegree, Alastair Duke, and Gillian Lewis (Cambridge: Cambridge University Press, 1994), 21–34.

sexuality (*paillardise*), quarreling, frivolity, and perjury.[12] The Ecclesiastical Ordinances identified these sins, among others, as "scandals," which, if not immediately addressed or punished, posed a great threat to the spiritual health of the entire Genevan community. Thus, upon his return to the city, Calvin and his pastoral colleagues quickly asserted their right both to define and discipline scandalous behavior in Reformation Geneva.[13]

But the Consistory was also "a school for consciences," in that it regularly admonished individuals for holding beliefs or committing acts that conflicted with their Protestant confession of faith.[14] The pastors and elders of Geneva routinely urged those suspected of moral impropriety to examine their consciences before God's word, hoping to impress the seriousness of sin's consequences upon those who were prone to regard their transgression casually. Indeed, if Calvin could subject his troubled conscience to God's righteous calling, so could the Genevans! And the Consistory's most effective method for educating laypersons regarding the importance of a good conscience was the use of oaths and vows. Geneva's Consistory vastly preferred an oath-administered form of justice and discipline—one that placed people before the direct tribunal of the private conscience. In fact, the *Registers of the Consistory of Geneva* indicate that something of a reciprocal relationship existed between oaths and the conscience in the moral oversight of Geneva. On one hand, litigants were required to examine their consciences to ensure they only swore oaths with proper seriousness and with no intention to dissimulate. Equally important, as well, was the realization that once someone had sworn an oath before the Consistory or Small Council, their consciences were bound to whatever consequences might result from their testimony—tranquility of soul for those who spoke the full truth in detail,

---

[12] Watt, *The Consistory and Social Discipline in Calvin's Geneva*, 105. Though not always recognized as a common reason for being summoned by the Consistory, the sin of perjuring oneself before the Consistory occurs with impressive regularity in the Genevan archival records explored in this chapter. By 1555, after the anti-Perrinists (Calvin supporters) regained power in Geneva, the Consistory gained significant authority to exercise church discipline over those who lied to its members. And thus, Scott Manetsch, *Calvin's Company of Pastors: Pastoral Care and the Emerging Reformed Church, 1536–1609* (Oxford: Oxford University Press, 2013), 187, notes that, by 1556, "lying to the Consistory constituted the civil crime of perjury."

[13] For a deeper study of the concept of *scandale* as it is found in the civil and ecclesiastical records of Geneva, including its pervasive application to Genevan communal life, see Karen Spierling, "'Il faut éviter le scandale': Debating Community Standards in Reformation Geneva," *Reformation & Renaissance Review* 20, no. 1 (2018): 51–69.

[14] This apt depiction is from John L. Thompson, "Reforming the Conscience: Magisterial Reformers on the Theory and Practice of Conscience," in *Christianity and the Laws of Conscience: An Introduction*, ed. Jeffrey B. Hammond and Helen M. Alvaré (Cambridge: Cambridge University Press, 2021), 142.

but guilt and condemnation for those who chose to skew reality for any reason whatsoever.[15] The prevalence of personal appeals to conscience before the Consistory—by members of the Consistory but also by defendants themselves—indicates that the relationship between oaths and the conscience had a practical and pervasive influence upon the moral constitution of Genevan society.

The purpose of this chapter is to enhance our understanding of Reformation-era developments in the perceived relationship between oaths and the conscience by examining discipline cases in the local context of Calvin's Geneva. This chapter will explore specific concerns about conscience that appear among the anecdotal evidence contained in the Consistory records, especially where these conscientious complaints intersect with the Consistory and Council's requirement for residents to testify under oath. The following pages examine a selection of well-known cases as well as more obscure entries in the registers, all of which illustrate how the residents of Geneva either assimilated the conscience- and oath-driven reform measures of the Consistory, or turned the accusation of conscience against their fellow residents, or appealed to the conscience in order to oppose the disciplinary tactics of the Consistory members themselves. Our assessment of the relationship between oaths and the conscience uncovers the variety of ways that Calvin and his pastoral colleagues sought to navigate the challenging relationships between theory and practice, between law and accommodation, and between obedience and charity, in order to protect the sacred dictates of the individual conscience while also removing scandal from the Christian community in Geneva.

6.1. Oath-Administered Justice and the Binding of the Conscience

During Calvin's second ministerial tenure in Geneva, the Consistory actively sought to regulate morals in the city by establishing a strong link between the swearing of oaths and the binding of the conscience. By requiring those accused of moral transgression to swear oaths, the pastors and elders of Geneva believed they could better assure that sinners' consciences would feel the

---

[15] As I note in the pages that follow, the Consistory itself did not hold the right to administer oaths until 1556. Nevertheless, even prior to this, the Consistory availed itself of the Council to administer formal oaths to witnesses on very regular occasion.

weight of their testimony and its consequences—before God, first, and then before the civil and ecclesiastical authorities. Such oath-driven disciplinary measures are especially striking because, until July 1556, the Consistory did not even hold the right to swear witnesses in and interrogate them under oath.[16] For most of Calvin's ministry, in fact, the authority to administer oaths and pass down sentence remained the sole prerogative of Geneva's Small Council. What the Consistory lacked in authority it made up for in persistence, however. It referred accused parties and their witnesses to the Council with impressive regularity, demanding they be placed under oath before testifying. Members of the Consistory—Calvin chief among them—insisted that a truthful statement could only be obtained in most cases by issuing an oath, which had the effect of either convicting or cleansing the conscience of the one swearing. Indeed, examples abound within the Consistory records of calls for individuals to be *interrogué par serment* ("examined by oath") or *purger par serment* ("purged or exonerated by oath").

Especially after 1556—when the Consistory had become quite proficient at swearing in its witnesses—the relationship between oaths and the conscience becomes more explicit in the Consistory registers. Individuals are sent back to their homes, for example, "to think in [their] conscience" before returning to testify under oath before the Consistory or Council at a later date.[17] On November 13, 1561, Claude Mestral, from the village of Landecy, and Pernette, daughter of Antione Guignet of Feigères in Savoy, were summoned before the Consistory to determine whether they had promised marriage to each other and had engaged in *paillardé* (illicit sex). The Consistory advised Mestral to "examine his conscience first" prior to taking an oath.[18] A week later, the two lovers returned to Geneva's moral court where Mestral attempted to "purge himself" by oath, claiming that he had not promised marriage to Pernette. He nevertheless admitted they had had sexual relations—a fact he could not deny, since Pernette was now with child. The Consistory admonished him again to "enter into his conscience before

---

[16] The Consistory was granted permission by the Council to administer the oath on July 30, 1556. The register notes that "this was the result of a complaint made to Messieurs that some persons did not scruple to lie before the Consistory, indulging in various kinds of falsification and dissimulation, and a proposal that the administration of the oath to them would have the effect of making them afraid of bearing false witness." RCP 2:68 (Hughes ed., 317): "le serment leur estant donné ilz auroient plus grande craincte."

[17] E.g., having reprimanded one Claude Bernod on several occasions for *paillardise*, the Consistory registers indicate that "est ranvoyé en sa maison pour penser en sa conscience." AEG, R.Consist. 15:173ʳ (September 7, 1559).

[18] AEG, R.Consist. 18:156ʳ–156ᵛ (November 13, 1561).

taking such an oath."[19] Having been warned to protect the security of his conscience, Mestral ultimately declined to take an oath before the Council, though he again insisted he had not proposed marriage. The following week, on November 27, Mestral confessed that he was open to marrying Pernette if her parents consented—making clear that he indeed had intentions for matrimony—but the case was later referred to the Council, since his father (not Pernette's) refused to approve the union.[20]

The abundance of oaths required of Geneva's residents also tells us something about the Consistory's evaluation of its constituents, namely, that they had serious doubts about the people's capacity for truth-telling. Individuals called before the Consistory were apt to claim ignorance, withhold information, make excuses, or even downright lie. Calvin and his ministerial colleagues employed the oath, therefore, as a means of getting at the truth more quickly and efficiently than mere questioning could. On April 19, 1548, the wife of Pierre Biolley, a barber living in La Fusterye, was called before the Consistory to be questioned about some insulting words she had allegedly uttered about their pastor. In a recent sermon, the minister had apparently chastised members who never came for the preaching unless the Lord's Supper was being offered. Assuming this remark had been directed at her—for she had indeed made herself scarce at preaching the previous five months—Biolley's wife retorted, "On il preschent de belles merdes" ("They preach some beautiful shit"). When asked to explain her offensive comment, Pierre's wife refused to confess and denied (twice) that such things had been said, prompting the Consistory to delay rendering advice until further witnesses could be called.[21] The following month, on May 3, the Consistory questioned the chambermaid of Nicollas Droet—a *bourgeoisie* member of the Council of Two Hundred (*Deux Cents*)—who had been with Pierre's wife on the day in question. The maid revealed that she had reported to Biolley the preacher's words from that morning, that such people who attended the preaching only to receive the Supper would do better "to eat a toad," which elicited the crass remark about the ministers' preaching. Seeming to be more concerned about these disparaging comments against one of their ministers than about the wife's lax attendance at preaching, the Consistory received

---

[19] AEG, R.Consist. 18:158ᵛ (November 20, 1561).

[20] AEG, R.Consist. 18:164ʳ–164ᵛ (November 27, 1561). For a more detailed examination of this case, see Watt, *The Consistory and Social Discipline in Calvin's Geneva*, 118–19.

[21] R.Consist. 4:50 (April 19, 1548). A week later, on April 26, Pierre's wife was summoned back to the Consistory to repeat her alleged words, but she again refused. See R.Consist. 4:53 (April 26, 1548).

additional witnesses but found the others unable—or possibly unwilling—to corroborate the servant girl's testimony. Determining that they would not hear the truth, precisely "because no oath is [yet] given," the Consistory ordered that the case be brought to the Council, and that the witnesses be made to "swear and repeat the aforementioned testimonies in order to be able to get the truth."[22] Similar examples are found throughout the registers of the Consistory sending obstinate, tight-lipped individuals before the Council to be sworn in; it is assumed that, in the case of such people, they will not get at the truth by any other way.[23]

Residents of Geneva responded to the Consistory's oath-dominated form of questioning in different ways. Some, on occasion, strongly objected to the Consistory's demand that they make confession under oath, as the case of Michel Conte illustrates. On June 5, 1550, Conte was reproached by the Consistory for blaspheming God's name. He made a partial confession of his guilt, admitting he had spoken in anger, but expressed some hesitancy to own his fault completely. The Consistory responded by urging Conte to confess his sin fully, or else they would seek his testimony by oath to extract an honest confession. He responded that, if the Consistory required him to swear an oath to confirm his own denial of misconduct, he would refuse to do so. Yet, because there were witnesses able to prove he had blasphemed, Conte reluctantly confessed his crime.[24] In this case, it does not appear that Conte's oath-refusal was due to a lack of respect for the swearing of oaths per se; on the contrary, the thought of invoking God's judgment by admitting his false testimony on a guilty conscience gave him reason for serious pause. Despite angering Conte, the Consistory's demand for an oath—made weightier by the threat of consulting witnesses—proved successful at bringing out the truth.

Still other residents of Geneva recoiled at the Consistory's specific request that the accused should evaluate their consciences before giving testimony under oath. Matthieu Tartonne, a furbisher of weapons and armor, was sent to the Consistory on March 23, 1559, to answer for charges of usury leveled against him by several fellow craftsmen, including Jehan Jaquemard,

---

[22] R.Consist. 4:58–59 (May 3, 1548). This matter never came to much, apparently, as the Council records from the following week contain no mention of the case. See R.Consist. 4:59, n. 319.

[23] See, e.g., the case of Steph Du Molard, in R.Consist. 3:125–26 (June 2, 1547). Although offered several chances to confess his adultery and to abusing his wife, he was warned by the Consistory that if he continued to refuse, he would be sworn in before by the Council to tell the truth.

[24] R.Consist. 5:118 (June 5, 1550). At the end of this account, Conte denies having told his accusers to "bugger off" and then kisses the ground (*a baysé terre*)—the typical requirement for someone who had blasphemed.

a potter.²⁵ Tartonne denied extending loans at excessive interest but was immediately contradicted by witnesses. The investigation spilled over into the next week, and on March 30 Tartonne was soundly rebuked by the Consistory for having lied about his unjust business practices. His excuse was that the Consistory's questions had taken him by surprise, so that he had not thought of responding with the truth.²⁶ This answer held no credibility with the Consistory, however, since they had admonished him soundly to testify only in truth. Tartonne was also advised by his accuser, Jaquemard, to "enter into his conscience" so that he might answer honestly. Tartonne responded that he would not examine his conscience, nor would he take the name of God as an oath. For this reason, seeing that Tartonne had "added fault to fault" by lying and by refusing to take an oath in good conscience, the Consistory barred him from the Lord's Supper and delivered him to the Council for punishment.²⁷

Despite some resistance, the Consistory remained committed to promoting the binding character of oaths, even if those swearing seemed apathetic about their oath's significance. In October 1556, Jean Goula, a member of the *bourgeoisie* who had held various city functions in the 1530s and 1540s, was summoned by the Consistory to confess that he had fathered an illegitimate child. During the proceedings, Goula claimed that he was living in the local tavern as a "stranger" to Geneva. Upon investigating, however, the Consistory discovered that he was in fact a citizen who had attempted to renounce his *bourgeoisie* status and become a subject of Berne. Later, when Goula attempted to flee Geneva, he was caught, imprisoned, and required to "take the oath of bourgeois again in Geneva."²⁸ Modern readers

---

²⁵ AEG, R.Consist. 15:48ᵛ (March 23, 1559). For a detailed assessment of the Consistory's concern for the relationship between economic fairness and social reform in Geneva, particularly with regard to the crime of usury, see Mark Valeri, "Religion, Discipline, and the Economy in Calvin's Geneva," *SCJ* 28, no. 1 (Spring 1997): 123–42. Also see André Biéler's classic study examining Calvin's exegetical and practical thoughts on usury, *Calvin's Economic and Social Thought*, ed. Edward Dommen, trans. James Greig (Geneva: World Alliance of Reformed Churches/World Council of Churches, 2005), 400–22.

²⁶ On an interpretive level, it seems unlikely that Tartonne could have been altogether surprised by the Consistory's questions, since he was answering for charges leveled against him by several of his fellow guildsmen—suggesting this was not an unexpected or isolated incident. In any case, the Consistory was not satisfied with his answer, which they, and Jaquemard, linked to the condition of Tartonne's conscience.

²⁷ AEG, R.Consist. 15:56r (March 30, 1559). Frequently, the ministers and elders of Geneva seemed more troubled by a person's willingness to lie to the authorities than by the actual sin for which they had been summoned. See, e.g., the case of Mermet Mut of Silligny, who was barred from the Supper by the Consistory, not for the crime of striking his neighbor's horse with the point of his lance, but for perjuring himself before the *châtelain* (rural magistrate) when confronted. AEG, R.Consist. 18:174v (December 18, 1561).

²⁸ R.Consist. 11:229–30 (October 1, 1556). See n. 1284.

might struggle to grasp how the Council could force Goula to renew a vow he clearly had no intention of keeping, but the registers do not indicate that the Genevan leadership agonized over this decision. The important thing was that they had restored the conditions necessary to uphold Goula's former citizen's oath, thus avoiding public scandal. At least in this case, the question of whether Goula had a conflicted conscience seemed to be a matter of secondary importance compared to preserving the inviolable character of a properly sworn oath.[29]

Although some residents of Geneva objected strongly to the swearing of oaths—or at least showed little regard for its importance—others seemed thoroughly willing to assimilate the Consistory's demands for binding one's conscience by oath. Indeed, some individuals were remarkably eager to bind their conscience—and even the consciences of others—to an oath. When Jehan Benez, a farm laborer from Cranves, was called before the Consistory on July 13, 1542, to testify whether he had promised marriage to and had impregnated Jana, daughter of Aymoz Grenier, he responded by denying both charges. Repentant of the fact that they had made love to one another in a local meadow on one occasion, Benez nevertheless repeated that the child was not his and that another man would be in a better position to care for her child than he. He was willing to make one concession, however: if Jana gave him the child "on her conscience, he will take it, but only if she swears to it." The child was not his and he had not promised marriage, Benez repeated again, but he might still be compelled by the oath and conscience of his lover to care for the child.[30] Although the registers do not record the Consistory's decision in this matter, Benez's conscientious concession might suggest that he knew the child was in fact his responsibility.[31]

Not all personal appeals to conscience met with the Consistory's approval, however. Some Genevans were severely chided for looking to their own consciences above the needs of others in the community. One example of this took place on August 9, 1548, when Jacques Duval and Guillaume

---

[29] For similar cases of individual conscience being either privileged or disregarded by legal courts, see Richard H. Helmholz, "'Conscience' and the English Courts between 1500 and 1800," in *Das Gewissen in den Rechtslehren der protestantischen und katholischen Reformationen*, ed. Michael Germann and Wim Decock (Leipzig: Evangelische Verlagsanstalt, 2017), 209–11.

[30] R.Consist. 1:87 (July 13, 1542).

[31] Although the registers do not record the Consistory's decision in this matter, the case was passed on to the Council that very day. Benez continued to swear that the child was not his, and so, on March 5, 1543, the Council finally released him from the obligation to marry Jana, though not without requiring him to pay for her delivery costs and some basic necessities. See RC 1:362 (March 5, 1543), n. 87.

Rougement were called before the Consistory to answer whether they had made slanderous statements about several ministers of the Lord, including Calvin. Duval had apparently called Calvin *ung vindicatifz* ("a vindictive man")—likely betraying anti-French sentiments that were common among the native-born citizens of Geneva—but then lied about his "calumnious" statements before the Consistory.[32] Rougement, for his part, also denied having said such things about the ministers, but nevertheless shared his deep-seeded frustration that "there were so many foreigners [Frenchmen] who came here who were miserable hypocrites." The Consistory dismissed Rougement in peace, but not before admonishing him to relinquish his judgmental scorn of others and instead tend to his own conscience. He ought to curb his prejudice against foreigners in Geneva and subject his conscience to the rule of love and charity for the sake of his neighbors.[33]

In certain cases, the obligations of neighbor-love trumped the dictates of one's own conscience, even when someone acted out of concern for sound doctrine. On May 24, 1548, the Consistory chastised Jeronime Patron because, although he had come to Geneva and professed to be a Christian, he had allowed his wife "to remain in papacy" and participate in "idolatries and superstitions." Patron answered that it was true that he had moved his wife back to a Catholic place to live, but that she dared not abandon her father until he had passed on and she had received her inheritance. Since his wife had no desire to resolve the situation, Patron claimed that he had no other recourse but to leave her in her present state. The Consistory demonstrated little sympathy for Patron's claim, insisting that he must have a "miserable conscience" to stay in Geneva while his wife languished in that "abyss of hell." After being handed over to the Council, Patron was ordered to return quickly to gather his wife and bring her to Geneva where they could "live

---

[32] R.Consist. 4:109–10 (August 9, 1548). For a detailed study of the anti-French bias of many natural-born citizens of Geneva, see William G. Naphy, *Calvin and the Consolidation of the Genevan Reformation* (Louisville, KY: Westminster John Knox Press, 2003), chapter 4, "Geneva: Hospitality and Xenophobia," 121–43.

[33] R.Consist. 4:110 (August 9, 1548): "A esté renvoyé en paix avec admonition de ne regarder tant aux aultres, que il n'advise specialement à sa propre conscience." Although Calvin had come to Rougement's defense in an earlier case, he later opposed Calvin by aligning himself with Jerome Bolsec in the 1551 predestination controversy. See n. 575. It is rather striking that the Consistory treated Rougement's anti-French sentiments as a matter of conscience. This might suggest that the pastors and elders of Geneva also considered "the right of private judgment"—even in the form of nationalistic bias—to be part of the individual conscience. For a related study, see chapter 9, "Individualist Conscience and Nationalist Prejudice," in Edward G. Andrew, *Conscience and Its Critics: Protestant Conscience, Enlightenment Reason, and Modern Subjectivity* (Toronto, ON: University of Toronto Press, 2001), 154.

under the Christian religion" together.³⁴ The Consistory's rather harsh response to Patron's case is somewhat surprising, since it appears that he had come to Geneva out of a valid concern for the practice of true religion. The Consistory apparently believed, however, that the husbandly duty to protect his wife from false religion was more important than his desire to take residence in a Protestant city. Indeed, Patron's conscience could only remain "miserable" until the situation was properly resolved.

Even more surprising is the fact that, in 1559, Calvin and the Consistory seemed to take an altogether different approach to spousal abandonment for the sake of religion, as illustrated by the case of Galeazzo Caracciolo. The details of Caracciolo's situation are well known due to Robert Kingdon's thorough examination of the case in his *Adultery and Divorce in Calvin's Geneva*.³⁵ Caracciolo, an Italian nobleman and heir to the marquis of Vico, settled in Geneva in the summer of 1551 after being converted to Protestantism—mainly through the influence of Peter Martyr Vermigli. Well-received in the city on account of his noble heritage and palpable zeal for reform, Caracciolo became a fast friend and advocate of Calvin and the Consistory. The people of Geneva soon regarded the affluent foreigner as a paragon of religious courage, for he had given up wealth, prestige, comfort, and family, all for the sake of the pure gospel. Caracciolo's presence in Geneva nevertheless posed a challenging dilemma for the Consistory: Was he justified in abandoning his family for the sake of the gospel? Despite multiple attempts at bringing his wife and children to Geneva—even suggesting they could live in the Swiss Grisons, a religiously neutral area, where his wife "could live as a papist and he could live as an evangelical"—it soon became clear that his wife and her aristocratic family would never acquiesce to this "heretical" compromise.³⁶ Extremely saddened by these developments, but nevertheless staunchly committed to Geneva and the tenets of pure religion, Caracciolo determined his only recourse was to seek the right to divorce and remarry. His formal appeal for a divorce began on April 6, 1559, and ended on November 7 of the same year. Throughout the proceedings, Caracciolo was able to produce

---

[34] R.Consist. 4:69 (May 24, 1548). See n. 390.

[35] The following summary of this case is drawn from chapter 6, "The Galeazzo Caracciolo Case: Divorce for Religious Desertion," in Robert M. Kingdon, *Adultery and Divorce in Calvin's Geneva* (Cambridge, MA: Harvard University Press, 1995), 143–65.

[36] This proposal was not acceptable to the Genevan Council, either. Caracciolo's offer and its rejection is found in AEG, Jur. Pen. A2, f. 42 (August 14, 1559), quoted in Kingdon, *Adultery and Divorce*, 153. Caracciolo's own family would have been scandalized by his Reformed convictions; in fact, his great-uncle, Gian-Pietro Carafa, would later rise to the position of Pope Paul IV in 1555 as a staunch repressor of Protestantism. See Kingdon, *Adultery and Divorce*, 145–46.

witnesses to prove that he had done everything in his power to reconcile with his wife and family. Calvin and the Consistory also approached the Zurich theologians for advice in this matter; they argued that even the Apostle Paul had allowed a Christian to abandon his or her unfaithful spouse who refused to move to a new region that practiced the only true faith. Despite some hesitancy on Calvin's part, the Council finally granted Caracciolo a divorce and allowed him to remarry—which he did a scant two months later, on January 15, 1560. That same year, Caracciolo was also elected to the Consistory as Geneva's first foreign-born elder.

The cases of Patron and Caracciolo raise a perplexing question: Why was Caracciolo allowed to satisfy his conscience and desert his wife and family on account of his religious convictions, whereas Patron was excoriated for entertaining a bad conscience in allowing his wife to remain under the papacy while he sought to practice true Christianity in Geneva? The two cases share obvious similarities but perhaps subtler differences. The Consistory may have detected a measure of apathy in Patron; perhaps, unlike Caracciolo, he had not exhausted all effort to extricate his family from the realm of false religion. More likely, the leaders of Geneva were simply enamored with Caracciolo's aristocratic prestige and were thus more inclined to treat his case sympathetically.[37] At very least, these two situations reveal that the Consistory and Council were apt to deal with such matters on a case-by-case basis, rather than applying an impersonal standard with no regard for circumstances.

On rare occasion, instead of referring sinners to the Counsel for testimony and punishment, the Consistory decided to forgo the swearing of an oath and simply leave obstinate sinners to the affliction of their own consciences. This act of quasi-sentencing presumed that sending moral transgressors to their consciences seemed as good as placing them before the judgment of God himself. On March 22, 1548, the wife of Lord Bertin, known as the hostess of l'Anonciade, appeared before the Consistory with Jean Achillier to testify about some heated dispute between the two men. The Consistory admonished Bertin and Achillier to live "peacefully and faithfully without scandal." However, since they would not admit to any particular grudge, they were left to consult their own consciences regarding the matter.[38]

[37] Watt, *The Consistory and Social Discipline in Calvin's Geneva*, 133–34.
[38] R.Consist. 4:23 (March 22, 1548). Just a few months later, these two men were summoned together before the Consistory because Bertin had been spreading false rumors about Archillier. At the Consistory's prompting, however, Bertin apologized for his defamatory remarks and the men were sent on their way in peace. See R.Consist. 4:70 (May 24, 1548). Similar cases of discipline and reconciliation are found in Jeffrey R. Watt, "Settling Quarrels and Nurturing Repentance: The Consistory

On other occasions, members of the Consistory seemed to think that the punishments meted out based on a person's testimony before the Council were inadequate until the judgment of the conscience had also been added. On September 2, 1550, Thomas Coysenent, a shoemaker and citizen of Geneva, was questioned by the Consistory about his alleged marriage promises to Jenon Basseta, a woman with whom he had reportedly fathered an illegitimate child. Coysenent stubbornly denied having pledged marriage (though he admitted to giving Jenon two rings) and contended that he was not the child's father. Unable to get the truth from him, the Consistory handed Coysenent over to the Council, which chose to overlook his purported engagement vow and obstinate behavior before the Consistory but imprisoned him for *paillardise* and required him to provide childcare.[39] The Consistory was not yet finished with Coysenent, however. When he was recalled on September 25, having just been released from prison, the elders and pastors chided him for the fornication he had previously denied committing while being questioned in their presence. The Consistory did not appreciate being lied to, and, although Coysenent had already paid the civil penalty for his crime, the Consistory determined that one final rebuke was in order: he ought to evaluate himself and act "in a better conscience," since God would judge him for the things he had done in secret.[40]

The Consistory's commitment to placing moral transgressors before the direct tribunal of their consciences was not lost on the citizens of Geneva. As was noted earlier, some received such counsel positively, showing themselves willing to submit their consciences to God's law, to the will of the Consistory, and even to the desires of others. Some, however, thoroughly resented the Consistory's conscience-driven form of questioning and discipline. On March 25, 1557, spouses Anthoine and Gabrielle Munier were summoned to the Consistory for spreading false rumors about François Châteauneuf, a member of the Consistory. Gabrielle claimed that Châteauneuf had made "indecent proposals" to Françoise, widow of Hudriod Du Molard, though no witnesses came forward to corroborate this claim; Françoise herself denied

---

in Calvin's Geneva," in *Revisiting Geneva: Robert Kingdon and the Coming of the French Wars of Religion*, ed. S. K. Barker (St. Andrews: The Centre for French History and Culture of the University of St. Andrews, 2012), 71–84.

[39] R.Consist. 5:195, 206 (September 2 and 11, 1550); see also 194, n. 1338. Coysenent's case was familiar to the Consistory; he had already been punished by the Council in 1548 for fornicating with the same woman. See R.Consist. 4:21–22 (March 22, 1548), n. 103–4.

[40] R.Consist. 5:216–17 (September 25, 1550).

that anything of the sort had taken place.[41] The following month, the Muniers were recalled before the Consistory where Gabrielle obstinately repeated her claims. As a result, the Consistory declared that the Muniers—especially Gabrielle—had defamed one of their company and should be sent to the Council for examination under oath and punishment.[42] The Council Records indicate that Gabrielle was imprisoned for three days for defamation.[43] The matter was not over, however. On May 13, minister François Bourgoin (listed in the registers as Monsieur d'Agnon), reported to the Consistory that Anthoine had approached him on the public street, insisting that his wife had not lied under oath and that she had been unjustly convicted.[44] At this point, Châteauneuf also recounted some words Gabrielle had apparently uttered following her brief stint in prison. Upon being released, she had publicly shouted, "Conscience, conscience, I have been in prison on account of the convenience of my neighbors, but nevertheless, I have spoken the truth, and I have not at all recanted."[45] The Consistory reprimanded the Muniers soundly, recalling them to the Council, where it was determined that Gabrielle's insolent outburst had earned her an additional three days in prison.[46] It is difficult to discern the intended meaning of Gabrielle's insolent remarks. Her emphatic mention of "conscience" seems—at very least—to reflect a deep-rooted resentment of the inquisitorial methods of Geneva's Consistory. If part of the standard for determining innocence was individual surety of conscience, then Gabrielle was willing to play along—so long as the Consistory would finally rest its case against her.

The residents of Geneva were not the only ones to fall under the judgment of the Consistory when acting contrary to the city and ecclesiastical ordinances. On rare occasion, Consistory members themselves were reprimanded for contravening the terms of their official oath—a clear violation of conscience.[47] On Wednesday, November 1, 1553—mere days after Michael Servetus had been burned alive for heresy—Guillaume Farel visited

---

[41] R.Consist. 12:85–86 (March 25, 1557).
[42] R.Consist. 12:97, 104 (April 1 and 8, 1557).
[43] See R.Consist. 12:85 (March 25, 1557), n. 340.
[44] R.Consist. 12:161 (May 13, 1557).
[45] R.Consist. 12:168 (May 20, 1557): "Conscience, conscience, j'ay esté en prison à l'appoint de mes voysins, mais neantmoings j'ay dict la verité, et ne m'en suys point desdicte."
[46] See R.Consist. 12:85 (March 25, 1557), n. 340.
[47] For an examination of later cases of clerical indiscretion in Geneva, see Scott M. Manetsch, "Ministers Misbehaving: The Discipline of Pastors in Calvinist Geneva, 1559–1596," in *Agir pour l'église: Ministères et charges ecclésiastiques dans les églises réformées*, ed. Didier Poton and Raymond Mentzer (Paris: Indes Savantes, 2014), 31–42.

Geneva and preached a sermon that strongly criticized the behavior of the city's youths. As a result, some of these adolescents—even those who had not heard the sermon themselves—protested that Farel had been too harsh with them, purportedly having called them all "atheists." Determining that the matter warranted an investigation, the Council (Messieurs) summoned Farel back to Geneva and requested that he not preach "until the matter had been resolved."[48] On the following Monday, November 13, Calvin, along with several ministers, including Viret, as well as a sizable number of citizens, appeared before the Council to oppose the accusations leveled against Farel. They testified that he had offered nothing but "paternal correction and remonstrances," and that the youths' ire was unfounded.[49] Despite overwhelming support for Farel, not all of Geneva's ecclesiastical leaders had received his message positively, however. At least one Consistory member, Jaques-Nycollas Vulliet, had in fact joined in the youths' protest of Farel's sermon. This was a direct violation of the Ecclesiastical Ordinances (1541), which listed "schism" and "rebellion against ecclesiastical order" among those vices which are "intolerable in a pastor"—or, for that matter, in an elder.[50] Believing, like Calvin, that this revolt would cause "scandal and disgrace" in the church, the Consistory rebuked Vulliet on November 16, 1553, for his impious actions toward Christ's minister. Moreover, the body made sure to point out that Vulliet's Consistorial oath disqualified him from participating in such protests. Soon after, the Council sent word to the Messieurs in Neuchâtel informing them that Farel could preach in Geneva again "whenever he pleases."[51]

In the spring of 1555, Pastor Michel Cop (father of Nicolas Cop) was also admonished by the Consistory for acting contrary to his ministerial oath of office. This case originated on March 21, when the Consistory began an investigation into the proposed marriage of Claude de Rohault (Lord of Granval), a French refugee, to Claude Videl, the niece of Pastor Cop. Claude had accepted the marriage proposal of Rohault, but on the condition that her parents consented to the union, which they did not. Lacking parental

---

[48] RCP 2:53 (Hughes ed., 292).
[49] R.Consist. 8:201, n. 1244. RCP 2:53 (Hughes ed., 292) also records this initial hearing, during which many citizens testified that they "esteemed Farel as a true servant of God and his preaching as good and godly, and had received profit and edification from his exhortations."
[50] CO 10:19.
[51] R.Consist. 8:200–201 (November 16, 1553). RCP 2:53 (Hughes ed., 293), November 1, 1553, records that Farel was told he could return to Geneva "when he wished, accompanied by a herald, and that his expenses would be paid by this city." The register adds, "all of this was a great consolation to the children of God and a cause of confusion to the wicked."

support, the Consistory forbade Rohault to visit or even speak with Claude.[52] Although Rohault initially obeyed the Consistory's order, he apparently was not willing to let go of the matter, causing turmoil in the family. The situation became so heated that, on June 27, Rohault visited the Consistory with the complaint that Cop had verbally abused both him and Claude, casting aspersions upon them with insults like "whore" and "fornicator." When called before the Consistory later that day, Cop gave a rather lengthy account of himself, confessing that the whole matter of the contested marriage came very close to home, and was thus "related to his conscience." When his wife came to testify, she likewise stated that Cop had brought the matter to his conscience, but that he was not convinced he had done wrong. Determining that Cop's insulting language was contrary to his ministerial office, the Consistory admonished him repeatedly to examine his conscience, confess his faults, and ask both God and Rohault for forgiveness.[53] Cop, however, refused to admit any guilt, stating that it would be hypocritical to ask for forgiveness and admit error if in his conscience he was not convinced he had done anything wrong. The conflict ended when the Consistory ordered Rohault to stop irritating Cop regarding the matter, nor to bring it before the body again.[54] In this case, the Consistory was more inclined to accommodate the conscience of a trusted fellow minister than to entertain the angry claims of a jilted suitor.[55]

Conflicts often arose between the civil and ecclesiastical leaders of Geneva that posed serious crises of conscience for the Company of Pastors. Geneva's ministers took particular interest in cases that involved the critical intersection between their pastoral oaths and the tranquility of their consciences. Indeed, the *Register of the Company of Pastors*, though "spasmodically" written and frequently lacking in detail, is uncharacteristically thorough when recording conflicts between the Council and Consistory that involved a dispute over a minister's oath and conscience.[56] Two related cases, both contained in the registers, suffice to illustrate this phenomenon.

---

[52] R.Consist. 10:46–47 (March 21, 1555). See also n. 257.

[53] The Ecclesiastical Ordinances (1541) distinguished "intolerable vices" in a pastor from "vices which can be endured provided they are rebuked." In the Consistory's view, Cop's insulting outburst would have fallen under this latter category, alongside "dissolute language," "rashness," and "uncontrolled anger" (CO 10:19–20).

[54] R.Consist. 10:136–37 (June 27, 1555).

[55] Despite Cop's protest, on July 11, 1557, Rohault was eventually able to provide witnesses to confirm his and Claude's engagement. Claude's mother finally approved of the union, so the Consistory determined that the marriage must take place. See R.Consist. 10:148 (July 11, 1557).

[56] See "Introduction" in RCP, Hughes ed., 3.

In March 1552, a dispute erupted between the magistrates and ministers over the allocation of pastors to new churches. Jean de Saint-André, minister in the Bernese village of Foncenex, near Jussy, had recently been imprisoned and then banished from that territory after preaching against members who considered the Lord's Supper to be especially sacred on Christmas Day. With a rural vacancy to fill, the Messieurs determined that Saint-André should be reassigned to the city while another minister took his place in Jussy. The Company of Pastors held an election and determined that Philippe de Ecclesia should fill the vacancy at Jussy, while Jean Fabri would take de Ecclesia's place in Vandoueuvres. Objecting to this arrangement, de Ecclesia stated that he would not go to Jussy unless it was the will of the Council.

When Calvin and the ministers appeared before the Messieurs the following week to announce the Company's decision, the Council, upon hearing de Ecclesia's complaint, decided that he and Fabri would do better to stay where they were, and that the ministers should hold a new election. This troubled the ministers greatly, who promptly "objected that they could not have acted better and more conscientiously than they had done, and could not choose others than those they had already chosen." The Council refused to budge; if the ministers would not hold a new election, the Messieurs would take that prerogative for themselves. The ministers refused to concede but quickly learned that the Council was not bluffing. Soon after the encounter, the Council sent word to Minister François Bourgoin that he should go to Jussy to live and serve as preacher there. Bourgoin quickly expressed his anxiety about this decision to his fellow ministers, who, "after calling on the name of God," determined to return before the Council and object to its overreach of power. In fact, the Ecclesiastical Ordinances were not explicit about the specific matter of ministerial transfers, though it had more generally entrusted the evaluation and election of pastors to the Consistory.[57] By taking the job of appointing and moving ministers upon itself, the Company of Pastors firmly believed the Messieurs had violated "ecclesiastical order and policy." Their objection once again met with obstinacy, however, as the Council defended its previous decision.

Bourgoin thus faced a crisis of conscience. He complained to the Company once again that he had no legitimate calling to Jussy, since the demands of the Council were not valid or binding. Bourgoin pleaded with his fellow ministers to be allowed to stay in his current charge, since "the assurance

---

[57] See CO 10:17-18.

which he had had hitherto in the exercise of his office was entirely the result of his legitimate calling in accordance with ecclesiastical order; if this was lacking, he could not continue to exercise his ministerial office with a good conscience." So troubled by his conscience was Bourgoin that, if forced to go to Jussy without having a legitimate call through the brothers, he threatened to resign from the ministry altogether. This proposal added serious weight to the Company's assessment of the situation. On April 22, ministers from various regions contended that it would be better to acquiesce to the will of the Council than for Bourgoin to renounce his divine calling as a minister—a proposal that gained little traction, however, as the entire body could not agree. The next Monday, two city ministers and two rural ministers again ventured before the Council, reporting that Geneva's ministers could not give consent "to so violent an infraction of ecclesiastical order, since such an example could only be prejudicial to the future." The Messieurs, true to form, held to their former decree. Finally, despite protest from Calvin and others, but so as to avoid any appearance that the Council had won the day, Fabri stepped in and agreed to take the Jussy charge—albeit, only with the Company's rightful approval.[58]

Later that March, de Ecclesia—whose initial refusal to accept the ministry at Jussy had generated this fiasco—was accused of colluding with Jerome Bolsec to commit usury. Bolsec, an apparent friend of de Ecclesia, had spouted aberrant ideas concerning the doctrine of predestination and would be a constant thorn in the side of Calvin and the Consistory in the months that followed.[59] Following this initial accusation, on November 14, the Council summoned de Ecclesia, requiring him to answer these charges and also confess whether he was sympathetic to Bolsec's doctrine of predestination. Scandalously, de Ecclesia "had no answer to offer by way of defence or excuse," which earned the censure and condemnation of the Messieurs. Nevertheless, the Council urged leniency in de Ecclesia's case, requesting that the Company "pardon him once again and to keep him in our Company in the position which he had been occupying, on condition that he requested forgiveness and acknowledged his fault." The Company, having witnessed de Ecclesia's obstinacy for some time already, protested that they held out

---

[58] RCP 1:133 (Hughes ed., 188–89): "il ne pourroit demourer ministre ne exercer ceste charge en bonne conscience."

[59] RCP 1:34 (Hughes ed., 189–90). For a brief summary of the Bolsec affair, consult Naphy, *Calvin and the Consolidation of the Genevan Reformation*, 171–72.

little hope that he would reform but would nevertheless follow the Council's advice.[60]

Over the course of the next month, the Company questioned de Ecclesia in greater depth about his involvement with Bolsec and his associates. With each question, however, de Ecclesia became increasingly unwilling to divulge the nature of his relationship with them. Frustrated by his lack of participation, and discerning no repentance or change of heart, the Company declared to de Ecclesia "that they could no longer accept him in their Company, and he was admonished to consider whether he could conscientiously retain the office of a minister in the church." De Ecclesia did not take this news well and immediately presented himself to the Messieurs to complain that his brothers in the ministry were vindictive and unwilling to retain him as one of their company. Preying on the Council's protected sense of authority, de Ecclesia claimed that the Consistory had tried to concoct new evidence against him, even establishing a quasi-tribunal by which to judge him—a clear usurpation of the Council's power, he made sure to point out. The Council took this charge seriously, such that Calvin himself was summoned to explain the Company's actions. Calvin denied de Ecclesia's calumnious accusations, and pointed out the fact that the Company had "instituted no form of legal procedure and had required no oath, but that [they] had acted as before God, in whose presence it was necessary to proceed in truth."[61] De Ecclesia's fate would have been quite different, Calvin pointed out, if he had acknowledged his sin as the Messieurs had requested.

Despite Calvin's argument, the Council summoned the ministers on December 23 and demanded they be reconciled with de Ecclesia. Uproar ensued. All the ministers of the city replied that they "could not acknowledge de Ecclesia as a brother and could not consent to be ministers with him without wounding [their] conscience."[62] This time, the conscience-driven persistence of the ministers met with success. After several more failed attempts at getting de Ecclesia to show signs of repentance, the Messieurs agreed that the ministers were justified in bringing action against their

---

[60] This case drew great interest; ministers from the city and country, as well Farel and Viret, were present at de Ecclesia's arraignment. See RCP 1:144 (Hughes ed., 201–2).

[61] Calvin also notes that the Company had followed the "simplest possible procedure" in trying de Ecclesia's case; unlike the ministers of Berne, they had not administered an oath while questioning de Ecclesia. See RCP 1:146 (Hughes ed., 203–4).

[62] RCP 1:146: "que nous ne pouvions tenir led. de Ecclesia pour frere et ne pouvions estre ministres avec luy de nostre consentement sans blesser nostre conscience."

former brother. On Monday, January 27, the Council determined that de Ecclesia should be deposed, setting Easter as his last day in office.[63]

The cases considered in this section reveal that the ministers of Geneva were extremely conscientious about fulfilling their office with all the rights and privileges appended to it; they would not allow themselves to be coerced into performing any action that went against their ministerial oath or conflicted with their consciences. The Company of Pastors were also rather strategic in finding persuasive ways to retain their ministerial rights, while also pushing back against the Council's occasional attempts at transgressing the boundaries of its own authority. Appealing to their ministerial oath to uphold the Ecclesiastical Ordinances and threatening resignation if their consciences were not assuaged—these were just two of the means by which the ministers believed they could successfully attain their vision of a rightly ordered church and society.

6.2. Improper Marriage Oaths and the Conscience

Preserving the essential link between oaths and the conscience consisted, in large part, of distinguishing properly made oaths from those that violated city standards and the rule of charity. For the Consistory—though not always for the Small Council—the important thing was not simply that an oath had been sworn but that a *valid* oath had been made in a *proper form* under conditions regulated by the civil and ecclesiastical ordinances of Geneva. As a general rule, only oaths sworn in a proper manner by someone with genuine intentions counted as binding. Thus, the Consistory generally frowned upon oaths that were made rashly or in an irreverent or frivolous manner. These included empty marriage promises, superstitious vows to Catholic saints, and even the oaths of guildsmen or professional corporations, whose "unofficial" or "private" oaths were considered by the reformers to be empty and cultish.[64]

Most often, Consistory cases involving improperly sworn—and therefore illegitimate—oaths pertained to some violation of the city's marriage

---

[63] The whole de Ecclesia affair is recorded in RCP 1:144–48 (Hughes ed., 201–6), November 14, 1552–January 27, 1553.

[64] For a helpful summary of Calvin and the Consistory's aversion to secretive guild oaths, see "Introduction" to R. Consist. 9: xxxv–xxvi. The Consistory did admonish anyone who made vows to Catholic saints, though it could be very lenient in cases where the offender expressed genuine regret. See, e.g., R. Consist. 1:277–78 (November 29, 1543).

ordinances, which Calvin originally drafted in November 1545.[65] These ordinances ruled on a variety of practical issues, including: those who could marry with or without permission; types of marriage vows and wedding celebrations that were appropriate; length of engagement; as well as legitimate reasons for rescinding a marriage promise. Although an engagement was more than a simple contract between two people, the Consistory recognized that the exchange of marriage vows did signal that a contractual agreement had taken place. It was essential to ensure, then, that both parties had given their free consent to marry.[66]

Geneva's marriage ordinances outlined four general conditions needing to be met before marriage vows would be recognized as contractual and binding. Young couples desiring matrimonial union must demonstrate they had (1) exchanged proper engagement oaths in the presence of witnesses (clandestine marriage vows were forbidden); (2) received parental consent (if under twenty years of age for a man, and eighteen for a woman); (3) agreed to publish the banns (engagement announcements) for at least three weeks leading up to the wedding; and (4) made plans to marry in the church building.[67] Even those who were old enough to pledge marriage without the consent of a parent were nevertheless urged to swear in a proper form and with godly reverence, rather than empty frivolity. The ordinances ruled that "all promises of marriage should be made honorably and in the fear of God and in no way dissolutely or frivolously, as when merely touching glasses when drinking together without first having made a sober proposal, and those who do otherwise shall be punished; but at the request of one of the parties, claiming to have been taken by surprise, the marriage shall be rescinded."[68] Calvin's marriage ordinances were clearly written with an awareness of this common practice among the youth, for in so ruling, it anticipated a violation of proper marriage oaths that would dominate the Consistory's attention for the majority of Calvin's ministry. Indeed, the Consistory records are replete with cases of individuals who came before

---

[65] Calvin's Marriage Ordinances are found in CO 10:33-44. A later version is contained in RCP 1:30-38.

[66] On the importance of contractual consent in engagement or marriage in Geneva, see chapter 4, "Love Thyself as Thy Neighbor: Individual Consent to Engagement and Marriage," in John Witte, Jr., and Robert M. Kingdon, *Sex, Marriage, and the Family in John Calvin's Geneva*, Vol. 1: *Courtship, Engagement, and Marriage* (Grand Rapids, MI: Eerdmans, 2005), 119-63.

[67] RCP 1:30-33. For a recent and thorough treatment of disciplinary cases related to marriage and sexuality, see chapter 4, "Controlling Lust and Regulating Marriage," in Watt, *The Consistory and Social Discipline in Calvin's Geneva*, 100-37.

[68] RCP 1:31 (Hughes ed., 73).

the Consistory having "drunk in the name of marriage," or having given gifts in the name of marriage. This almost inevitably led to one party expressing next-morning regrets, claiming they had not intended to drink in marriage after all—if they even remembered the event! In most of these cases, when no witnesses came forward to confirm that marriage was clearly intended by both parties, or if relatives objected to the union, the Consistory declared the engagement null and void.[69]

Although the Consistory frowned upon the practice of frivolous and unplanned marriage vows and did not consider them inherently binding but rather discipline-worthy, the Council applied the marriage ordinances of Geneva with noticeably greater leniency. On August 10, 1542, Pernette Aubrier came before the Consistory to declare that Pierre Mamburier of Bons had "swore faith" to her by drinking with her in marriage, and that "she understood that it was in the name of marriage." Despite Pernette's claims, Mamburier, who had apparently promised himself to another woman, vehemently denied even being in the company of Pernette, much less having promised marriage to her. When confronted with one another, Pernette insisted that she could prove they had drunk together in marriage, and that she came before the Consistory of her own accord with only God advising her. After bringing her witnesses to the Council at the Consistory's recommendation, the Council determined they had in fact drunk in the name of marriage, and because Pernette had sworn to these things under oath before witnesses, "the said marriage should go into effect." In the view of the Council, the superficial form of oath they had taken was of little consequence compared to the evidence that proved their promises were consentual, and therefore binding.[70]

As noted, the Consistory required that certain conditions needed to be met before it would consider a couple lawfully engaged. Genevans sometimes took advantage of this precedent by adding conditions of their own to a marriage promise in hopes of obtaining collateral benefits. The registers contain examples of individuals who made the acquisition of goods or favors dependent on a pledge of marriage, and vice versa.[71] John Witte and Robert Kingdon note that, in most of these cases, "such conditional

---

[69] As in the case of Pierre Cristin and Pernette Du Crest. See R.Consist. 1:331–32, 336–39 (March 20, 1544).

[70] R.Consist. 1:96–97 (August 10, 1542). See n. 451. RC 36:95, 99 (August 15 and 21, 1542).

[71] For examples beyond the one explored in my chapter, see Witte and Kingdon, *Sex, Marriage, and the Family*, 132–37.

engagement contracts were enforced [by the Consistory and Council] regardless of whether the ancillary condition had been breached—and regardless of whether this breach now put the couple at such odds that they both wanted out. The mutual consent of the parties was essential to form the engagement contract; but, once properly formed, the engagement contract could not be dissolved even by mutual consent."[72] When Mychie, daughter of Gallatin, from Peney, came before the Consistory on December 14, 1542, she stated that she no longer desired her promised husband Jehan Jallio, because he was a squanderer and had lost the assets he once held when she had promised marriage to him. The Consistory determined that, although Jallio's financial situation had changed since their pledged matrimony, their oaths were valid and should be upheld. The couple agreed to be married the next week.[73]

In cases of deception or intimidation, however, the Consistory would often look past the bare utterance of an oath between two consenting parties.[74] If someone's conscience had been violated by another's extortive use of marriage vows, the Consistory quickly came to the defense of the injured party. On March 24, 1552, Anne de Beaumont, a former nun, contested her engagement to Jaques Charvier, a carpenter, on the grounds that he had deceived her into promising marriage if he rescued her from a prison in Vienne.[75] A week later, on March 31, the two appeared before the Consistory, where Anne conceded that she had promised marriage to Charvier "on compulsion, wanting to leave the prison," but that it was nothing but a *frivolle promesse* ("frivolous promise") of which her family and friends did not approve. She added that, when she had made the promise to Charvier, she was "greatly troubled and disturbed in spirit," and that he had taken advantage of her pitiful estate and "persuaded her to her dishonor." Taking her claims seriously, the Consistory admonished Anne to consider *en vray conscience* ("in true conscience)" the promises she had made under such circumstances, and whether she was willing to marry Charvier. To this, she insisted that she was "badly informed" and deceived by Charvier into promising marriage, so she would not marry him.[76] Later, on April 7, Master Jean Budé—son of

---

[72] Witte and Kingdon, *Sex, Marriage, and the Family*, 119.
[73] R.Consist. 1:147 (December 14, 1542).
[74] Witte and Kingdon, *Sex, Marriage, and the Family*, 125.
[75] R.Consist. 7:29 (March 24, 1552). This case is also found in Witte and Kingdon, *Sex, Marriage, and the Family*, 146–47. Jaques had likely arranged Anne's release from prison through his father who was a warden there.
[76] R.Consist. 7:31 (March 31, 1552).

renowned philologist Guillaume Budé—testified as a witness to the marriage announcement of Anne and Charvier. Anne had told Budé—in Calvin's presence—that she hoped to marry Charvier "on the condition that the church of this city consented." Now, she was attempting to change her story. The case was apparently sent to the Council, which ordered that the marriage should be annulled because, regardless of the couple's initial intentions to be wedded, the bond had been improperly formed through coercive tactics. The case was ultimately settled when Anne produced proof that her parents objected to the marriage.[77] Although Anne could hardly have been praised for maintaining a sound conscience in the whole matter, the Consistory and Council determined that the deceptive circumstances surrounding their initial marriage promises were sufficient to nullify their mutual vows.

Occasionally, scrupulous residents of Geneva observed Calvin's marriage ordinances with an acute awareness of what was expected of them, revealing that the Consistory was fairly successful at instructing peoples' consciences regarding proper marriage vows. On December 8, 1552, Jaques d'Orléans, along with a bookseller named Nicolas and his daughter, were summoned by the Consistory to testify about a reported marriage agreement between d'Orléans and the girl. Nicolas, the father, admitted that the marriage had been discussed a year prior but nothing had been made final. When the Consistory questioned d'Orléans about the proposal, he admitted that he had given the girl some rings and a serge apron with the hopes of marrying her, but she had returned the gifts and they had "put off the solemn swearing" until witnesses could be present. The girl confirmed this was true. Although the Consistory initially urged Nicolas to go and finalize the marriage "in good conscience," the pastors and elders changed their minds and decided to leave the matter to the consciences of all involved, since no oaths or testimony had been offered. If that arrangement proved insufficient, the three of them would be sent to the Council "to put them on oath about the case, and if they swear to what they have said let them be set at liberty."[78] In this case, because all parties had demonstrated a sufficient awareness of the seriousness of marriage vows and of the proper procedure for a lawful engagement, they could be left to their own consciences to resolve the case.

The Consistory and Council were fairly consistent at annulling proposals of marriage that did not abide by the requirements set forth in Geneva's

---

[77] R.Consist. 7:35–36 (April 7, 1552). See n. 35.
[78] R.Consist. 7:190 (December 8, 1552). This case is also listed in Witte and Kingdon, *Sex, Marriage, and the Family*, 189–90.

marriage ordinances. If pledges of marriage were made in an improper form, or if lovers were not honest with one another about conditions that could threaten the legitimacy of their engagement, then the leaders of Geneva generally ruled that those in question were no longer obliged to each other. Extenuating circumstances did exist, however, that could alter the Consistory's judgment of such cases, even if someone involved was troubled by the conviction of his or her own conscience. The case of Pierre Boucheron and Marguerite des Bordes—reported in the *Registers of the Company of Pastors*—is anecdotal of such accommodation. On November 1, 1547, Boucheron, a former French monk of the Jacobin habit, confessed to having contracted marriage with Marguerite, a French Protestant. The engagement and marriage were properly conducted in France with the approval of Marguerite's father. It was not until several days later, however, on the way to Geneva, that Boucheron shared with his new wife that he had previously been a Jacobin. Marguerite immediately "felt some scruples about this in her conscience," since Boucheron had clearly violated his monastic vow by marrying her. Sensitive to her dilemma, Boucheron came to the *Company of Pastors* desiring that they would console Marguerite and assure her of the legitimacy of their marriage. He expressed a pious concern, moreover, that "there should remain no scandal to the Church of our Lord." Upon being summoned before the *Company*, Marguerite repeated again that "she had been troubled in her conscience" to learn of her husband's former life. The brothers assured her that Boucheron's vows had been monastic vows and were no longer binding, and that it was right for him to seek marriage if he could not contain himself and remain celibate. They urged Marguerite, however, to assess for herself whether she was able to live with Boucheron as her husband "with a clear conscience." Having been consoled, Marguerite stated that she could remain married. Finally, after conferring as a body, the ministers admonished Boucheron and Marguerite about that fact that their marriage had not begun well, "since what is not done in faith is not done with a clear conscience and is contrary to God." Nevertheless, although their marriage had been solemnized under deceptive circumstances—grounds for an annulment in other cases—because they intended to live together in harmony, their marriage would be recognized as legal, provided they could attest to its legality by providing testimonies from witnesses in France. Boucheron and Marguerite were sent away with the injunction that, since they "had been united they should agree to [live together] in good conscience and . . . in seemly union."[79] Thus, although the Consistory and Council were fairly consistent in their decision to annul vows that did not meet the requirements set forth in Geneva's marriage ordinances, they could make exceptions in cases where the genuine desire for a godly marriage outweighed the dubious origins of the union.

6.3. Discipline, Conscience, and the Supper

Although the Consistory lacked the authority to pass physical sentence upon guilty members of Genevan society, it did exercise a public form of spiritual censuring by placing limits on transgressors' participation in the Lord's Supper. To partake of the Supper meant that a person was, by all appearances, in good standing with Christ and his church. Only those who had properly examined their consciences before God's law, confessed their sins publicly and privately, and pledged to lead a godly life in harmony with others, were to be admitted to this holy feast. Thus, the celebration of the Lord's Supper in Geneva had both a spiritual and social dynamic: anyone with a purified conscience was at liberty to enjoy the state of belongingness expressed through the mutual partaking of the body and blood of Christ at the communion table; conversely, those mired in unconfessed and unrepentant sin would be ostracized from this public ceremony and made to feel the scandal of their transgression.[80] The Consistory's eagerness to wield the Supper as a disciplinary tool demonstrates its belief that sin was never simply a private matter, but had real and serious implications for the peace and harmony of Genevan public life. The Consistory frequently recommended to the Council that certain individuals be barred from the Lord's Supper, not only to promote the purity and unity of the church, but also to protect the consciences of those convicted—or even reasonably accused—of sin. Geneva's "morals court" ruled that anyone who could not partake of the Supper of "good will" or with a "good conscience" should remain absent until they could give evidence of genuine repentance; God's judgment would surely befall those who presumed to partake of the holy elements while living in iniquity.[81]

---

[79] RCP 1:27 (Hughes ed., 68–70): "Car ce qui n'est faict en foy n'est en saine conscience et est contre Dieu."

[80] See Valeri, "Religion, Discipline, and the Economy," 141; and Watt, *The Consistory and Social Discipline in Calvin's Geneva*, 195–200.

[81] E.g., R.Consist. 8:190 (June 30, 1558); R.Consist. 6:223 (December 24, 1551).

The seriousness of participating in the Supper with a clear conscience was impressed upon transgressors of all stripes: from the adulterous to the idolatrous, from the lecherous to the liar—all would have to "think in their conscience" and acknowledge their sins before being readmitted to the Supper.[82] Geneva's pastors and elders also believed that individuals embroiled in a grudge match should abstain from Communion, not only to avoid public scandal, but also for the sake of conscience. Such cases, in particular, reveal that many Genevans internalized the rule that forbade them to partake of the Supper if they were troubled in conscience or felt animosity toward a neighbor. On February 19, 1551, for example, Henri Bully and his cousin, Paquillon the Younger, were summoned before the Consistory, where Henri confessed to having skipped the Lord's Supper five times in a row due to "some grudge he had with his cousin over some proceedings."[83] Although Henri had previously abstained from the Supper, not being in a right mind to receive it on account of the ongoing conflict, he now expressed the desire to be reconciled with his cousin. Paquillon agreed, and the two shook hands "as a sign of good friendship."[84] On March 27, 1551, Paule Anblet and Jaques Duval also came before the Lieutenant following a dispute. Anblet had apparently struck Duval for blaspheming God's name. In order to determine whether the two men had made peace, the Consistory inquired whether they were now "in a disposition to receive the Lord's Supper." Both men responded that they did not mean to harm each other, and intended to receive Communion again if it pleased the Council. Seeing that the two men were repentant of their sin, the Consistory advised them "to make whole reconciliation of their hearts" before returning to the Supper. To this, Duval responded that, "his conscience was not [yet] in a position to receive the Supper." Although the Consistory encouraged him to reconsider, Duval

---

[82] As in the case of papist idolater, Aymé Pillisson, AEG, R.Consist. 15:34r (March 16, 1559). For additional cases of discipline meted out by the Consistory for illicit sexual behavior, see Watt, *The Consistory and Social Discipline in Calvin's Geneva*, 100–6. The Consistory often barred moral miscreants from the Supper for the specific sin of lying under oath (perjury). See, e.g., AEG, R.Consist. 17:181v (November 21, 1560). Cases of the Consistory barring individuals from the Lord's Table abound following the year 1556, a phenomenon likely related to the Consistory's newly acquired authority to examine people under oath.

[83] R.Consist. 5:326 (February 5, 1551), records that Bully had appeared before the Consistory two weeks earlier to answer for why he had missed the Lord's Supper five consecutive times. At that time, Henri apologized for his absence, but explained that he had chosen to refrain from Communion due to the ongoing dispute with his cousin.

[84] R.Consist. 6:8 (February 19, 1551).

repeated that he was not in a right mind or conscience to partake.[85] He was apparently allowed to abstain until the state of his conscience had improved.

Not all residents of Geneva were willing to accept their suspension from the Supper as a legitimate disciplinary measure of the Consistory, however. Some obstinately refused to be denied this right, finding clandestine ways to take Communion against the Consistory's wishes—and against conscience. On September 29, 1558, Pastor Mathias Grandjean, minister of Russin and Marval, reported to the Consistory that he had refused to serve the Supper to Jehan Truffa, partly on account of some apparent blasphemy he had uttered the previous week.[86] Not to be denied, Truffa journeyed to Sattigny instead and "received the Supper in bad conscience" from Minister Jaques Bernard, who had not been informed about the suspension. Truffa's obstinacy concerning the Supper was not an isolated incident. Several years earlier, on January 23, 1556, he had been remanded by the Consistory for failing to attend sermons, mocking public officials, and despising the Supper by claiming to have received it elsewhere—also in Sattigny—while under prohibition.[87] After hearing testimony from both ministers, Calvin confirmed that Truffa had taken Communion in bad conscience, not least because he had deceived ministers of the gospel into serving him the sacred meal unworthily! The Consistory sent Truffa back to the Council for punishment, suspending him from the Supper until December 1559, when he was finally forgiven and reinstated.[88]

Truffa's case was not the only instance of a resentful Genevan making light of the Consistory's disciplinary measures through the Supper. On September 14, 1559, four witnesses came before the Consistory to testify against Noël Bagnol, a sailor, who was accused of abusing his wife. Placed under oath, the witnesses detailed Bagnol's cruel behavior: when calling for his wife, he "whistles at her like a dog"; upon entering a room with his wife behind him, he closes the door in her face, and if she tries opening the door to come in, he threatens to "give her a hundred kicks to her stomach." Bagnol was overheard boasting to his children that he had received the Supper "in a better conscience than she [his wife] had." Witnesses also accused him of making light of the Holy Supper by responding with a pun to his wife when she reminded him that he should prepare himself for the coming celebration, effectively

---

[85] R.Consist. 6:51 (March 27, 1551).
[86] R.Consist. 13/14:288–89, 298 (September 22 and 29, 1558).
[87] R.Consist. 10:290 (January 23, 1556).
[88] AEG, R. Consist. 16:240^v (December 21, 1559).

mocking both his wife and the Supper in one breath.[89] After spending three days in prison at the wishes of the Council, Bagnol was deprived of the Supper he had treated so lightly before being sent back to the Consistory to beg for forgiveness on hands and knees.[90]

While some residents of Geneva made improper appeals to conscience in order to partake of the Supper unworthily, others took advantage of the Consistory's emphasis on conscience by using it as an excuse to stay away from the Supper, which greatly irked the Consistory as well. One such case involved a member of the large and influential Favre family, which was linked to the anti-French group, the Children of Geneva (*Enfants de Genève*), led by Captain Ami Perrin. This political faction, also known as the Perrinists, opposed the influx of French refugees into Geneva and was extremely critical of the ministers' perceived attempts to gain rights traditionally belonging only to the magistrates. As early as 1545, members from many of these powerful, native-born families also came before the Consistory to answer for their scandalous behavior, where they frequently sought to defend their actions by arguing that the Consistory had no genuine moral authority in Geneva.[91] On March 17, 1552, Gaspard Favre, son of the merchant François Favre, was summoned before the Consistory because he had fornicated with a maid, resulting in the birth of a daughter. The Consistory especially reprimanded Favre because it had also been a long time since he had taken the Lord's Supper. Gaspard informed the body that he was deliberately abstaining out of a concern for the "damnation of his soul," since he did not find himself "disposed of his conscience" to receive the Supper. Favre's claims seem pious—at least at first glance—but the Consistory records reveal that Gaspard had been embroiled in a long-standing conflict with the Consistory over the new edicts that prohibited parents from ascribing "superstitious" names to their children.[92] "Gaspard" had not made the list of acceptable names, which prompted Favre—who apparently took the matter quite personally—to

---

[89] AEG, R.Consist. 15:177ʳ (September 14, 1559); see also Bagnol's denial in AEG, R.Consist. 15:180ᵛ–181ʳ (September 28, 1559). Concerning the Supper, Bagnol mockingly stated, "Je te ceneray." N. 1261 suggests that Bangol's pun "probably plays on the similar sounds of the words *ceneray* and *segnerai*, of the verb *segner*: to sign; to make a sign; make the sign of the cross, bless" (Godefroy 7:357). When Bagnol's wife was called to testify, she confirmed that her husband had beaten her, even to the point of breaking her wrist.

[90] AEG, R.Consist. 16:189r (October 5, 1559); AEG, Jur. Pen. A2, f. 50v (October 2, 1559).

[91] For more on the *Enfants de Genève*, see Naphy, *Calvin and the Consolidation*, 12–25.

[92] On Favre's obstinate behavior concerning baptismal names—including his disruption of other baptism ceremonies—also see Karen E. Spierling, *Infant Baptism in Reformation Geneva: The Shaping of a Community, 1536–1564* (Louisville, KY: Westminster John Knox Press, 2005), 97–98, 149–50; and Naphy, *Calvin and the Consolidation*, 151.

insist that he would therefore not present any of his children for baptism in the church! Favre's absence from the Supper was therefore an act of protest against the Consistory's authority, and much less (if at all) a decision born of genuine concern for the soundness of his conscience. Indeed, Gaspard's claim that he was deliberately abstaining from the table for the sake of conscience likely indicates that he was attempting to subvert the Consistory's use of the Supper as a disciplinary tool in his case. It is telling that, at least on this visit, the Consistory seemed more concerned about Favre's neglect of the Supper—a sign of a bad conscience—than for the illegitimate child he had fathered.[93]

If exclusion from the Supper meant that someone had been temporarily cut off from the full rights of the Christian community on account of a particular sin, then being readmitted to the holy feast signaled true repentance, freedom of conscience, and restored harmony with Christ and his church. The Consistory and Council did not always see eye to eye when it came to reinstating individuals to the Supper, however. Such disagreements could generate a crisis of conscience for those involved, though in decidedly different ways. One representative case involved Philibert Berthelier, an infamous citizen of Geneva who was another close ally of the *Enfants de Genève*. Berthelier had made life particularly hard for Calvin and the Consistory in the early 1550s when he and his faction incited several revolts against the Genevan authorities over the matter of excommunication.[94] Calvin and his Company of Pastors had long argued for the Consistory's right to excommunicate the unrepentant without having to appeal to the civil magistrates. Berthelier and his political allies, having a deep distrust of foreign figures of power, vehemently opposed the proposal of Calvin and the other pastors, insisting that excommunication should remain the sole prerogative of the Genevan Council. Because of Berthelier's insolence and rebellion against the Consistory, he was excommunicated in 1553.

In late August 1553, however, after being suspended from the Supper for over a year, Berthelier, along with an accomplice, Jehan-Phillibert Bonna, came before the Consistory to declare that he was *en bonne volunté* ("of a good will") to receive the Supper again. The very next day, on September 1,

---

[93] R.Consist. 7:19 (March 17, 1552). See n. 107.
[94] Berthelier and his brother François-Daniel had terrorized the Genevan authorities for many years. In 1546, they incited an anti-French riot in response to one of Calvin's sermons; see Naphy, *Calvin and the Consolidation*, 105. During Philibert's run-in with the Consistory in 1553, François hastened to lambast the Consistory for its treatment of his brother, "asserting that they wished to tyrannize and dominate and were disobedient to the Seigneurie." See RCP 2:54 (Hughes ed., 293).

the Council heard Berthelier's case for readmission and decided to grant him absolution and readmit him to the Supper if he felt his conscience was ready to receive it.[95] This decision was made, however, without any concurring advice from the Consistory. Calvin and the other ministers protested immediately, unanimously declaring that they could not admit Berthelier to the Supper until they could verify that he was truly repentant. From the perspective of the Consistory, Geneva's Small Council had committed a twofold error: not only had they declared an unrepentant sinner worthy of receiving the holy feast, but the ministers also objected that "the order of the Church laid down that authority to forbid or admit to the Lord's supper belonged to the Consistory, and not to Messieurs." That Sunday, before the Supper would be served, Calvin himself took to the pulpit to denounce the Council's decision, stating that "under no circumstances would he receive such a rebel at the supper, and that it was not for men to compel him to do what was scandalous."[96] Still, the Council would not budge.

Employing a different tactic, the ministers of the city appeared before the Council a week later to repeat their complaints, this time arguing "that it was not lawful for them to break the oath they had sworn to maintain the order constituted in this church in accordance with the Word of God, and as laid down also in Messieurs' own ordinances." The ministers' argument must have seemed convincing, at least to them, since it was unlikely that the magistrates of Geneva would allow their ministers to violate city ordinances *they* had passed. But the Council would not take the bait. The Messieurs replied that they had not "introduced any innovation into their ordinances" at all; on the contrary, they had preserved the intended purposes of the law. The ministers were once again sent on their way, but not before being presented with a copy of the ordinances so they could refresh their memory of the relevant articles.[97]

The ministers would not admit defeat, however. Returning to the Council the next day, they argued that the ordinances did not in fact support the

---

[95] R.Consist. 8:155 (August 31, 1553).

[96] RCP 2:48 (Hughes ed., 286). Back in March 1551, Bertellier came before the Consistory under suspicion of *paillardise*—charges he denied. On this visit, Bertellier once again voiced his opposition to the Consistory's disciplinary authority, even taking jabs at Calvin: "With great arrogance, [Bertellier] told Monsieur Calvin that he was as good a man as he was, and that he was as certain in his conscience as Calvin was in his." R.Consist. 6:40 (March 24, 1551): "Avec grosse arrogance, disant à monsieur Calvin qu'i estoit aussi homme de bien que luy et qu'i se falloit aussi bien fier en sa conscience que en cela de monsieur Calvin."

[97] AEG, RC 47:147ᵛ. To further entrench themselves in their position, the ministers also proclaimed that they would rather die or be exiled from Geneva than allow Berthelier to receive the sacrament.

ruling that the Council was trying to force upon them against their oath and consciences, and if the ministers proceeded to follow the ruling, "the very authority which these same articles conferred would be removed from the Consistory." The ministers promptly returned the book of ordinances to the Messieurs, and with it submitted a letter composed by the Consistory. The letter stated in no uncertain terms that, while the minsters of Geneva remained committed to submitting to the God-given authority of the civil magistrates, even that obedience met its limit when conflicting with the ministers' consciences. A portion of the ministers' epistolary plea reads:

> But if there are times when our conscience forbids us to comply with your injunctions, we pray you, in the name of God, to receive our excuses indulgently and to give heed to pleas that are backed by good and just reasons, so that we may be able to fulfill the duties of our office faithfully, both towards God and towards you. For we shall never serve you with a loyal and free spirit if we do not uprightly and openly follow God's commands without turning to the right hand or the left.[98]

The Consistory's letter repeated once again that, although the Ecclesiastical Ordinances declared that the Council retained "the power of the sword" to punish evildoers, this should only be performed with the corresponding advice of the Consistory, "after having ordered what is in accordance with its office, namely, the banning from the supper of those who show themselves unworthy."[99] Moreover, the ministers argued there was no cause whatsoever to readmit someone to the Supper who remained obstinately opposed to the Consistory's authority and correction.[100]

On November 7, this matter came before the Council of Two Hundred, where the Messieurs repeated their intention "to reserve to themselves the power of absolving those who had been banned from the Supper." Calvin

---

[98] RCP 2:49 (Hughes ed., 287).

[99] RCP 2:49 (Hughes ed., 287): "Mais si nostre conscience nous empesche de vous complaire en tout et par tout, nous vous prions, au nom de Dieu, de recevoir humainement nos excuses, et pourvoir tellement à ce qui vous sera remonstré par bonnes et justes raisons, que nous puissions fidelement nous acquicter du devoir de nostre office, tant envers Dieu que envers vous. Car jamais nous ne vous servirons loialement et d'ung franc courage, si nous ne suivons en integrité et rondeur ce que Dieu nous commande sans fleschir çà ne là."

[100] RCP 2:51: "Sur tout, il n'y auroit nul propoz qu'ung homme qui(l) monstrera ung mespris manifeste du Consistoire, y fut receu: car c'est autant comme s'il vouloit faire son triumphe en despitant ceux qui sont commis de par vous pour representer le corps de vostre Eglise et avoir la charge du regime spirituel que Dieu veult estre precieusement gardé et maintenu."

and the ministers offered a thorough rebuttal, again emphasizing that they could not "acquiesce in the pretensions of Messieurs" without going against conscience. Despite this, the *Deux Cents* ruled in favor of the Small Council. Not to be denied, the ministers returned to the Small Council the following Thursday, unanimously declaring that "they were unable to consent to this ruling, and that to compel obedience would drive them from their charge, for they would choose this or death rather than consent to the abandonment of so holy and sacred an order, which had for so long been observed in this church."[101] The ministers, especially Calvin—who appealed to the promises made to him upon his return to Geneva in 1541—demanded that they be heard again before the Council of Two Hundred and the General Council. The Messieurs would not grant the request, but nevertheless promised they would resolve the matter.

Finally, on December 21, 1553, the Small Council arrived at a practical and judicious decision. To appease the consciences of Calvin and the members of Consistory, it ruled that Berthelier should first be reconciled to the Consistory before receiving the Supper. To maintain the status quo of authority in Geneva, however, the Council made sure to uphold its previous decision regarding Berthelier's absolution. Privately, they asked Berthlier to abstain one more time from the Supper before being readmitted.[102]

* * *

The foregoing examination of anecdotal evidence in the Consistory registers makes abundantly clear that Calvin and his company of pastors and elders were staunchly committed to an oath-dominated form of discipline. The swearing of oaths was the crucible in which Geneva's ecclesiastical leaders believed they could best elicit genuine confessions of guilt or innocence, thus separating truth from lies, good consciences from bad. Placing residents before the direct tribunal of their consciences under oath was also a means by which the Genevan authorities—including the Small Council—sought to shield the community from scandals that threatened to unravel the social and moral fabric of Genevan life. Although it is true that, in most disciplinary cases, the Consistory's immediate concern was for an individual to regain a sound conscience in order to be restored to the Holy Supper, it also believed that the status of a person's conscience would have a direct effect upon the

---

[101] RCP 2:52 (Hughes ed., 291).
[102] RCP 2:54 (Hughes ed., 293).

larger community. Only those who had confessed their guilt under oath and had repented before the elders could be expected to return to normal life and serve their neighbors peaceably in good conscience.

The Consistory registers indicate, moreover, that these oath-driven disciplinary measures were relatively successful at instilling in Geneva's residents a heightened awareness of the conscience and its importance for everyday life. In many cases, the habitants of Geneva demonstrated that they had internalized the Consistory's emphasis on having a good conscience by manifesting a genuine concern for the peace and security of their own consciences—and those of others—when called to testify under oath. Some explicitly acknowledged the threat of divine judgment that awaited them if they failed to speak truthfully or if they refused to accept responsibility for sins they had committed when confronted by their accusers. Others felt compelled to make life-altering choices simply because of the surety of another's conscience while testifying under oath before the Consistory. Even those who severely opposed the Consistory's disciplinary methods proved they were well-informed about the intrinsic link between their testimony under oath and the security of their consciences. Although they resented the Consistory's oversight as being too invasive, such individuals were still prone to appeal to the conscience as a source of moral authority, even if they did so obstinately and with little regard for the Consistory members themselves.

Despite criticisms that the Consistory was all about implementing a draconian form of discipline in Geneva, the cases examined in this chapter indicate that the Consistory could, in fact, be rather patient with those who refused to swear oaths on account of a troubled conscience. Residents embroiled in some conflict with a neighbor, for example, were granted leave from the Lord's Supper until they could demonstrate they were once again in a right mind or conscience to rejoin the holy feast. Geneva's pastors and elders were also willing to judge discipline cases with an eye toward extenuating circumstances. If someone faced a bad conscience due to an oath made under deceptive conditions, the Consistory almost always came to the defense of the injured party and nullified the oath. Thus, although the ministers and elders of Geneva took oaths seriously, wanting to preserve the inviolability of a properly rendered vow, the Consistory could also be rather accommodating when the security of a person's conscience would be threatened by a rigid and impersonal application of the city ordinances.

Members of Consistory proved to be less accommodating, however, when their own consciences were being threatened by the perceived moral overreach of Geneva's civil officials. The pastors and elders of Geneva held the Consistory to be the chief disciplinary agency in Geneva; the Council often acted, however, as if the Consistory exercised this function only with its permission and approval, having no real authority of its own. This greatly vexed Calvin and his colleagues in the ministry, who argued that the Council's encroachment upon their spiritual jurisdiction severely hampered Consistory members' ability to enforce godly discipline in accord with their oath of office. By appealing to this binding oath—a vow to uphold *the magistrates' own laws* as stipulated in the Ecclesiastical Ordinances—the ministers and elders of Geneva found a strategic means of defining and defending their own tasks and authority by invoking conscience to reinforce their cause. Thus, the connection between oaths and the conscience often stood at the heart of tense conflicts between the Consistory and Small Council during Calvin's ministry. Indeed, very few aspects of Genevan life remained untouched by this relationship between oaths and the conscience, including the city's academic institution—the subject of my final chapter.

7
After Calvin

Oaths, Subscription, Conscience, and Compromise in the Genevan Academy, 1559–1612

On November 26, 1559, Calvin penned a letter to his friend and colleague François Daniel, concerning the future of his son, who had matriculated at the Academy of Geneva. Destined for the study of civil law by his father's will, young Daniel had confided in Calvin that he had no great love for that science, enumerating the often-corrupt practices adopted by those of the legal profession. Although he found the boy's reasons convincing, Calvin nevertheless urged him to obey his father's wishes and press on dutifully with his studies. Responding to his friend, Calvin informed François that he would also encourage the young man to study theology, for the most important thing was that, in whatever career he pursued, "he should be carefully imbued with sentiments of piety."[1]

As a matter of fact, the inculcation of personal piety through the knowledge of true religion was the founding cornerstone of Calvin's Academy. Dedicated earlier that year, Geneva's new school had grown out of the emerging confessional impulse that characterized many Protestant regions in early modern Europe. Beginning by the late 1550s, following the initial wave of the Reformation, whole societies began to formally embrace distinct and comprehensive statements of faith, which "developed into internally coherent and externally exclusive communities distinct in institutions, membership, and belief."[2] Part of this historical paradigm of confessionalization involved the creation of Protestant academies to accommodate the

---

[1] Calvin to François Daniel, November 26, 1559 (CO 17:680–81, Bonnet 4:77): "Certe apprime necessarium est, ad quodcunque vitae genus eum destines, ut se probe exerceat in pietate."
[2] Heinz Schilling, "Confessional Europe," in *Handbook of European History, 1400–1600: Late Middle Ages, Renaissance, and Reformation*, Vol. 2 ed. Thomas A. Brady Jr., Heiko A. Oberman, and James D. Tracy (Grand Rapids, MI: Eerdmans, 1995), 641. Though the process of "confessionalization" has officially been linked to the latter decades of the sixteenth century, it is clearly observable in earlier conflicts arising from Luther's initial protest. Chapter 2, for example, has illustrated that the Strasbourg reformers were seeking the cooperation of the civil magistrates to support the Reformation of the city already in the 1530s—notably, by means of formal confession of faith.

consciences of those who could no longer attend Catholic schools or swear Catholic oaths. The formation of Protestant schools not only provided viable alternatives to Catholic universities; they also offered students a rich learning environment where good order and moral discipline could thrive under the authority of magistrates and clerics bound to the standards of the Reformed confessions.[3] Nevertheless, Michael Bruening indicates that little confessional unity actually existed in French-speaking Switzerland when the Genevan Academy was founded in 1559. Not all of the cities in the Pays de Vaud had embraced the same narrow confessional commitment to the doctrines and practices of the Reformed faith as Calvin's Geneva had done.[4]

One recurring matter that illustrates the confessional tensions between Geneva's Academy and several other schools in the Pays de Vaud involved the common practice of swearing academic oaths. In Geneva, city authorities required that an oath of matriculation be sworn by all incoming students. In addition, students and faculty members were obligated to sign their names to a form of subscription, promising to obey the civil magistrates and hold beliefs in accord with Geneva's *Confession of Faith*. The rigor of this practice distinguished the Genevan Academy from its neighboring educational centers, including the prominent Lausanne Academy, whose leaders believed that the survival of their schools depended upon finding the most qualified professors and willing-minded students, regardless of their confessional stance.[5] Nevertheless, not long after Calvin's death in 1564, the new leaders of the Genevan Academy would also respond to internal and external pressures by broadening the confessional vision and ordinances of the school, significantly altering its oath and subscription policies.

The aim of this chapter is to explain the place and purpose of academic oaths and formal subscription during a critical period of institutional development for the Genevan Academy. This will be done, on one level, by simply offering a fresh narrative of these events based on my reading of available primary and secondary sources. Most of the standard works on the founding and expansion of the Genevan Academy have been written by French historians.[6] Karin Maag's 1995 comparative study of the Academy remains

---

[3] Karin Maag, *Seminary or University? The Genevan Academy and Reformed Higher Education, 1560–1620*, St. Andrews Studies in Reformation History (Aldershot, UK: Scolar Press, 1995), 1.

[4] Michael W. Bruening, *Calvinism's First Battleground: Conflict and Reform in the Pays de Vaud, 1528–1559* (Dordrecht: Springer, 2005), 211–55.

[5] Maag, *Seminary or University?*, 2.

[6] Standard French works include: Charles Borgeaud, *Histoire de l'Université de Genève: L'Académie de Calvin, 1559–1789* (Genève, 1900); Louis J. Thévenaz, "L'Ancien Collège de sa fondation à la fin du XVIIIe siècle, précédée d'une introduction sur l'instruction publique à Genève au Moyen-Age,"

the most complete and updated account among English-speaking scholars.[7] No recent work appears to have been produced, however, that examines the conflicts surrounding oaths and subscription as an important window into the debates over the confessional character of the Academy. In what follows, then, I set out to mine the official records of Geneva's civic and ecclesiastical authorities in order to construct an analytic narrative of these events, in hopes of offering some plausible answers to the following questions: How did the Academy's requirements for the matriculation oath and confessional subscription change between the years 1559 and 1612, and what do these changes reveal about the importance of these measures for attaining the pastors' and civic leaders' respective visions for reform? In what ways did the pragmatic concern for institutional viability eventually eclipse the need for hard confessional boundaries, including oath and subscription requirements established by the Academy's founders? Relatedly, what do the following cases reveal about the significance of sworn oaths as binding agents upon the individual conscience?

7.1. Oaths, Subscription, and the Founding of the Genevan Academy

On June 5, 1559, a large gathering of prominent citizens and nearly six hundred schoolchildren filled the nave of St. Peter's Cathedral to commemorate the founding of the Genevan Academy. An impressive list of dignitaries attended the event, including Senate members, advisors, pastors, professors, and regents of the fledgling institution. First to ascend the church pulpit that morning, tasked to officially announce the institution of the Academy and lead the assembly in prayer, was John Calvin, the school's primary conceptual architect. By the recounting of Robert Estienne and Theodore Beza, inaugural rector of the Academy, this was a joyful event for "all men of science and faith" and for all who received the new school as the fruit of God's blessing upon the city for seeking to educate its youths in the "science of true religion."[8]

in *Histoire du Collège de Genève*, ed. Thévenaz et al. (Geneva, 1896); and J. E. Cellérier, *L'Académie de Genève: Esquisse d'une histoire abregée de l'Académie fondée par Calvin en 1559* (Geneva: A. Cherbuliez, 1872).

[7] Maag, *Seminary or University?*
[8] Borgeaud, *Histoire*, 48–49.

In emphasizing the Academy's existence as a bastion of "true religion," the inaugural ceremony clearly reflected the vision of its founder. For as much as it was a joint project supported by Geneva's civic and spiritual leaders, the Academy was primarily the brainchild and crowning achievement of Calvin. His intention for the school—a vision he had conveyed to the magistrates upon his recall to the city in 1541—was to establish an educational model with the goal of instilling piety through the knowledge of true religion in everyone who matriculated there. As this seemed to require pervasive ministerial control over the order and enrollment of the school, the *Ecclesiastical Ordinances* of 1541, anticipating the creation of the Academy, declared that no one would be received at the *escole* unless approved by the ministers.[9] Although political opposition and a dearth of financial backing had delayed the implementation of Calvin's vision for nearly twenty years, the required cooperation and resources fell into place shortly before 1558.[10] At long last, Calvin's desire to transform the city's educational system was realized in the creation of an elite theological and pedagogical "seminary" whose teachers would train Geneva's youths for ministerial and civic duty.[11]

The Academy took institutional shape as the creation of two distinct yet complementary schools: the lower-level Latin school (*schola privata*), also called the "gymnasium," which comprised seven classes with strictly assigned programs; and the upper-level "seminary" or "university" (*schola publica*), established to prepare young students for Christian ministry, and

---

[9] *Ordonnances Ecclesiatiques* (1541): "Que nul ne soit recue sil nest approve par les ministres avec leur tesmonage de peur des inconveniens." Text in OS 2:339; CO 10:22; LCC 22:63.

[10] Maag, *Seminary or University?*, 8. For more on Calvin's defeat of his political opponents, which resulted in a period of relative peace beginning in 1555, see William G. Naphy, *Calvin and the Consolidation of the Genevan Reformation* (Louisville, KY: Westminster John Knox Press, 1994), 208–32.

[11] *Ordonnances Ecclesiatiques* (1541): "[I]l fauldra dresser college pour instruire les enfans, affin de les preparer tant au ministere que gouvernement civil." Text in OS 2:338; CO 10:21; ET in LCC 22:63. Borgeaud, *Histoire*, 51, and Scott Manetsch, *Calvin's Company of Pastors: Pastoral Care and the Emerging Reformed Church, 1536–1609* (Oxford: Oxford University Press, 2013), 49, both note that, in the early years of the Academy, the school most resembled a theological seminary, existing for the primary purpose of training ministerial candidates. As Manetsch points out, the founding of the *escole* certainly reflected Calvin's controlling desire to increase the theological competence of ministers of the Reformation: "Well over half—forty-seven out of eighty-three—the pastoral candidates admitted to the Company of Pastors between 1560 and 1609 are known to have received theological training at the Academy" (49). Of course, it was not the case that all students were expected to pursue ministerial service, as many would go on to serve in government or business. Nevertheless, Calvin's founding vision was one that required all students to receive theological training under ecclesiastical oversight as the best way to achieve harmony between Geneva's ecclesiastical and civic realms. Cf. Gillian Lewis, "The Geneva Academy," in *Calvinism in Europe, 1540–1620*, ed. Andrew Pettegree, Alastair Duke, and Gillian Lewis (Cambridge: Cambridge University Press, 1994), 47–48, who argues that the Academy was neither a seminary nor a university at its inception.

later for law and medicine.[12] As evidenced by the *Ordinances*, it was Calvin's intention for the school to have a ministerial focus in nearly all respects. Not only was it to be a training ground for potential candidates for the ministry, but its teaching staff and students would also be subject (like ministers) to ecclesiastical approval and even discipline—a standard approved by the Little Council, the Council of Two Hundred, as well as the General Council of Citizens.[13] Although it was not Calvin's intention that the Company of Pastors would have sole authority over the school, he believed that Geneva's ministers should retain primary influence upon the character and order of the Academy. When it came to the matter of determining appropriate compensation for its instructors, for example, Calvin decided that the Academy's professors should not receive the high salaries customary in the German schools, but would have to be content with the modest support that was also given to Calvin's Company of Pastors.[14] The lifestyle and vocational aims of the professors would not differ greatly from those of the Genevan ministeriat.

A critical element of Calvin's founding vision for the Academy was its distinct confessional impulse. As a training ground for ministers and magistrates, the *escole* was to operate in accord with the doctrines and principles set forth in Calvin's rather lengthy *Confession of Faith*, presented by Calvin and Farel to the Small Council in 1536.[15] In order to assure personal adherence to these governing tenets of faith, the school's founding ordinances (*L'Ordre du Collège de Genève*) stipulated that regents, professors, and students alike must pronounce or formally subscribe to the formula of the *Confession* as a requirement both for employment and matriculation.[16] Students of the Academy had to declare before the rector that they would adhere to the doctrines contained in Calvin's *Catechism*, that they would be subject to the discipline of the church, and that they would not disrupt the unity of church and city by embracing the error of sects. Gillian Lewis

---

[12] Manetsch, *Calvin's Company of Pastors*, 28; Borgeaud, *Histoire*, 43–44. See *RCP* 2, 1559, p. 86, for a report on the initial appointment of professors in Hebrew, Greek, and Math, as well as the primary regent for the Academy. Maag, *Seminary or University?*, 9, notes that the registers of Geneva's Small Council refer to the whole institution as the *escole*, the *collège*, and sometimes as the *académie*. In this chapter, I explore the place and purpose of oaths and formal subscription in the *schola publica*, or the Academy proper.

[13] *Ordonnances Ecclesiatiques* (1541): "Que touz ceulx qui seront la soient subiectz a la discipline ecclesiastique comme les ministres." Text in OS 2:339; CO 10:22; ET in LCC 22:63.

[14] Borgeaud, *Histoire*, 37.

[15] Text available in OS 1:418–26; ET in LCC 22:26–33.

[16] Thévenaz, "L'Ancien Collège," 58. These ordinances, which also bear the Latin title, *Leges Academiae Genevensis*, are found in CO 10:65–90.

describes the weighty demands required of all who came forward to make formal subscription:

> [The *Confession*] demands assent to sola-fideism, the practice of infant baptism, and to the doctrine of predestination. It demands rejection of the errors of the Manicheans, the Nestorians, the Anabaptists and the Papists, expressly condemning the "alleged" five sacraments and the "abominations" of the mass. It has a powerful rhetorical rhythm, using repetition of the formula "Je confesse .... ainsi je déteste. ..." It is categorical, almost ceremonial. Anyone made to read this document out loud in the presence of the Rector and to put his hand to it when he signed the Rector's book could have been in no doubt of the seriousness of the engagement he had made.[17]

By requiring personal subscription to this distinctive and thorough confessional standard in the early years of the Academy, Calvin and the Genevan ministers revealed their desire to attain doctrinal unanimity among its students, "demonstrating again how close the *schola publica* was to a seminary model."[18]

Likewise, all professors and regents of the *collège*, in addition to signing their name to the form of subscription, were required to take a solemn oath before entering their charge. Professors and regents took the following oath before the rector:

> I promise and swear to carry out loyally the charge that has been appointed to me, namely, to work for the instruction of children and auditors, to give the lectures that are ordered by the statutes of our lords and superiors. And in general, to go to great pains to ensure that the school is conducted in good order. And to make sure, as far as I can (as I hope God will grant me) that the students live peacefully, in all modesty and honesty, to the honor of God, and to the profit and repose of the city.[19]

---

[17] Lewis, "The Geneva Academy," 47–48.

[18] Maag, *Seminary or University?*, 17.

[19] CO 10:89: "Serment Pour les Professeurs et Regens. Ie promets et iure de m'acquiter loyaument de la charge qui m'est commise, à scavoir de travailler pour l'instruction des enfans et auditeurs, de faire les lectures qui me sont ordonnees par les statuts de nos seigneurs et superieurs. Et en general de mettre peine que l'eschole soit conduicte en bon ordre. Et de procurer, selon qu'il me sera possible (comme l'espere que Dieu m'en fera la grace), que les escholiers vivent paisiblement, en toute modestie et honnesteté, à l'honneur de Dieu et au profit et repos de la ville." For more on the accoutrements of this oath, see Thévenaz, "L'Ancien Collège," 66.

In so swearing, professors and regents bound themselves solemnly to the sacred duty of promoting true religion and good order, both in the school and city, to the glory of God.

Although the Academy's ordinances required formal submission by oath to the doctrinal standards of Geneva, and although the original edition of the academic confession in *L'Ordre du Collège de Genève* was lengthy, spanning some eight small quarto pages, it is nevertheless important to note that some articles in this confession were simpler and less developed on certain points of doctrine than one might assume. This is evident from the rather short and bare-bones paragraph on the doctrine of the Trinity, whose brevity gained Calvin's express approval: "I content myself with this simplicity, that in the unique essence of God there is the Father who engendered from eternity his Word and also always had his Spirit, and that each person has so much of his property that the divinity always remains in its entirety."[20] Calvin's satisfaction with a relatively simple form of confession illustrates his measured—albeit no less dedicated—approach to securing doctrinal conformity for those entering the Academy. Even Calvin realized that not all would become ministers or be called to make complex doctrinal arguments. All those who entered the *escole* should, nevertheless, affirm the necessary tenets of Reformed orthodoxy as the *Confession* defined it and submit to its truth in all areas of life.

Even so, it appears that not everyone who attended courses at the *schola publica*, totally free of charge at the beginning, actually signed the *Confession of Faith* prior to matriculation. Borgeaud identifies several distinguished students of Calvin—people like Thomas Bodley, Lambert Daneau, and François du Jon—whose names are missing from the rector's book of subscribers, but who nevertheless studied in Geneva with great benefit. The register was maintained for the primary purpose of receiving "formal adhesions to the statutes of the school and, especially, to the confession of faith of the Geneva Church," yet some students were admitted who had not signed it, even in the earliest years.[21] Despite Calvin's ardent commitment to requiring the practice, administrative shortfalls and unforeseen factors resulted in some registrants falling through the cracks. As this chapter will

---

[20] "Me contentant de ceste simplicité, qu'en l'essence unique de Dieu il y a le Pere qui a engender de toute eternite sa Parolle et aussi tousiours eu son Esprit, et que chacune personne ha tellement sa propriété que la divinité demeure toujours en son entier." Text in Cellérier, *L'Académie de Genève*, 149–50.

[21] Borgeaud, *Histoire*, 55–57.

go on to illustrate, imposing subscription upon the students of the Academy would become even harder to maintain as time went on.

7.1.1. The Lausanne Academy

It is notable that the Genevan Academy's oath and subscription requirement broke with the example set by the Lausanne Academy. Founded in 1537 under the teaching leadership of such famous persons as Pierre Viret, Mathurin Cordier, François Hotman, Conrad Gesner, and Theodore Beza, the Lausanne Academy was the original Protestant academy of the Francophone world until the creation of the Genevan Academy some twenty-two years later.[22] It was in the intellectual center of Lausanne, not Geneva, that Protestant "high studies" were originally developed.[23] In fact, dividing the Genevan Academy into the *schola privata* and *schola publica* was a decision adopted after the pattern set by the Lausanne Academy, which comprised "a higher education division and a secondary school division."[24] Despite this similarity, the Lausanne school was decidedly more liberal in its matriculation policies than Geneva, especially toward foreign students. Although Swiss students were required to pass an entrance exam before being admitted to public lessons or attaining entrance to the college, foreigners were exempt from this policy. Made aware of the order of the lessons, they could freely choose the courses they desired to take without following a strict path. Nor, interestingly enough, were students obliged to subscribe to a standard profession of faith. Only a promise of civic obedience, scholarly diligence, and respect for their masters had to be made before the rector of the school.[25] Even professors were allowed to swear an oath of

---

[22] Calvin's letters reveal his repeated attempts to secure many of these men to teach in Geneva prior to the organization of the Academy; e.g., Calvin tried to draw Viret and Cordier to Geneva to serve as professor and president of regents, respectively, but both remained in Lausanne until the Academy took shape in 1559. See Calvin to Viret, October 24, 1545 (CO 12:193–94).

[23] Michael W. Bruening, "Un nouvel eclairage sur l'academie de Lausanne, a partir de la correspondence inedite de Pierre Viret," in *La Naissance Des Académies Protestantes (Lausanne, 1537–Strasbourg, 1538) et la Diffusion du Modèle*, ed. Monique Vénaut and Ruxandra Vulcan (Clermont-Ferrand: Presses Universitaires Blaise Pascal, 2017), 37.

[24] Borgeaud, *Histoire*, 38–42. Borgeaud notes that the Lausanne school was itself organized according to the system promulgated by the Catholic humanist Andre de Gouveia.

[25] Henri Meylan, *La Haute École de Lausanne, 1537–1937* (Lausanne: Université de Lausanne, 1986), 21. Students admitted to the Lausanne Academy were merely called to promise that they would be "pious to the Lord, faithful to the magnificent Republic of Berne and to the very lofty magistrate, obedient to the just commandments, diligent in their studies, devoted to the school, respectful in regard to their masters."

service that was totally devoid of religious content. In 1559, before being appointed principal of the Lausanne school, Blaise Marcuard simply swore that he would offer his full loyalty and zeal to train the young people entrusted to his charge.[26]

This broad confessional standard spelled trouble for Lausanne's Academy in the years that preceded the founding of the Genevan college. Beginning in the 1540s, ministers in the city, led by Viret, began to embrace Calvin's vision for church government. As a result, they faced growing opposition and pressure from their Bernese protectors who were unwilling to hand over the right of excommunication to Lausanne's ministers.[27] Heated debates over the nature of the Lord's Supper, Calvin's doctrine of predestination, and the need for effective church discipline reached a boiling point around 1558–1559. Unwilling to challenge Bern's authority, Lausanne's council refused to comply with the wishes of Viret and his pastoral colleagues to change the city's ecclesiastical ordinances. After several failed attempts at reaching an agreement with the city council, Viret was banished from Bernese territory, leaving the Lausanne church and school in a state of confusion. In the aftermath of this schism, at least four professors from the Academy and fourteen pastors left Lausanne to join Viret in Geneva, taking with them a large number of students.[28] The coincidence of the Lausanne crisis and the founding of the Genevan Academy led some to believe that it was the result of a Genevan coup.[29] One such person, Jean Haller, a Reformed pastor in Bern, was so incensed by the recent events that he wrote to Heinrich Bullinger on October 8, 1559, gleefully predicting the swift downfall of the new school.[30]

It is plausible that the practice of requiring a matriculation oath and confessional subscription at the Genevan Academy was a policy embraced in response to the lack of confessional harmony that plagued and eventually decapitated the Lausanne school. Regardless, Lausanne's loss proved to be Geneva's gain. Even with Calvin's lengthy profession of faith being imposed

---

[26] Karine Crousaz, L'Académie de Lausanne entre Humanisme et Réforme (ca. 1537–1560) (Leiden: Brill, 2012), 231. Crousaz's book is the most comprehensive and recent study on the Lausanne Academy.

[27] Bern reformer Jean Haller was particularly critical of the Lausanne ministers who claimed that their consciences would no longer permit them to stay and minister in the city. "Singular consciences," scoffed Haller, "who cannot remain in churches where Christ is purely taught and the sacraments administered according to the rule! But that's what they dispute, because they are denied the right to excommunication." See Meylan, La Haute École de Lausanne, 26.

[28] Bruening, Calvinism's First Battleground, 254. For Bruening's detailed account of the crises of 1558–1559 in Lausanne, consult pp. 237–55.

[29] Borgeaud, Histoire, 41.

[30] Borgeaud, Histoire, 51.

upon the students, enrollment did not suffer. The Genevan Academy flourished from the start, discrediting Haller's spiteful prediction.

7.2. Broadening the Confessional Character of the Academy (1564-1584)

Although Calvin's original intentions for the Genevan Academy are well documented, it is also evident that very early on, the civil magistrates and several prominent pastors envisioned a grander purpose for the fledgling institution. Many city leaders, as well as Calvin's "junior partner and colleague" Theodore Beza, believed "the foundation of the Academy offered the opportunity to develop a prestige institution of higher education, on a par with Europe's long-established universities."[31] After Calvin's death in the spring of 1564, Beza naturally took over the reins of the *collège*. His professorial background at Lausanne and five years as rector in Geneva certainly qualified him to find adequate teachers for the *schola publica*. Beza also succeeded Calvin as the leader of the Company of Pastors, which afforded him the opportunity to sway the opinion of Geneva's ministers with regard to the shape and direction of the Academy.[32]

Recent scholarship on Calvin and his theological heirs has marshaled convincing evidence to show that Beza and his Company of Pastors, in their ministerial, teaching, and apologetic labors, maintained substantial continuity with the doctrinal emphases of Calvin. It is nevertheless the case, as these studies have also shown, that, despite the accusations of their Roman Catholic antagonists, Beza and his colleagues were not "Calvin creatures."[33] In fact, between 1564 and 1568, the *Compagnie* introduced several important

---

[31] Maag, *Seminary or University?*, 3.

[32] Maag, *Seminary or University?*, 23. On Beza's talent as a churchman and scholar, hand-picked by Calvin himself, see Manetch's discussion in *Calvin's Company of Pastors*, 38–39.

[33] Manetsch, *Calvin's Company of Pastors*, 245. See n. 131. A number of recent studies have convincingly disproved the "Calvin against the Calvinists" theory (I am referring to Basil Hall's famous article). These scholars have shown that, while Calvin's heirs took his ideas and occasionally applied them in unique ways, they remained substantially in line with Calvin's central commitments. See, e.g., Heiko A. Oberman, *The Dawn of the Reformation: Essays in Late Medieval and Early Reformation Thought* (Edinburgh: T&T Clark, 1986); David Steinmetz, *Calvin in Context*, 2nd ed. (Oxford: Oxford University Press, 2010); Richard A. Muller, *The Unaccommodated Calvin: Studies in the Foundation of a Theological Tradition* (Oxford: Oxford University Press, 2000); R. Scott Clark and Carl R. Trueman, eds., *Protestant Scholasticism: Essays in Reassessment* (Carlisle, UK: Paternoster, 1999); and Willem J. van Asselt and Eef Dekker, *Reformation and Scholasticism: An Ecumenical Enterprise* (Grand Rapids, MI: Baker Academic, 2001).

changes in the *schola publica* with the aid of the Genevan magistracy. These changes, brought on in no small part by the shifting atmosphere of church and state in France in the years following 1564, would begin to transform the *schola publica* from a training ground for ministers, primarily, to something resembling the medieval university. The gradual abandonment of the seminary model largely resulted from the shifting religious situation in France. During the first five years of its existence, the *collège* primarily served as a training ground for missionary pastors to France.[34] However, Calvinism's growth and expansion in France reached its zenith after the first war of religion ended with the Peace of Amboise in 1563.[35] As the number of French Reformed churches plateaued, the need for missionary pastors trained at Calvin's Academy rapidly declined. Partly for this reason, the focus of the *schola publica* shifted away from ministerial training to embrace a wider spectrum of subjects, including law and medicine.

Early intimations of this broader vision for the *escole* had been published in the Latin version of *L'Ordre du Collège*, which concluded with this brief statement: "If God in his goodness will allow us, as we hope that he will, we intend to complete that which is unfinished, by adding professors in jurisprudence and in medicine."[36] It is highly unlikely that these words reflect Calvin's hopes for the school. His original sketch of the Academy, presented to the Council in 1558, included no proposal for the hiring of professors in law or medicine, and Calvin's somewhat negative impression of the role of jurists and civic powers is also well recorded. Nevertheless, it appears that Calvin—certainly aware of this broader vision for the Academy—was not willing to protest his colleagues' sense of purpose for the school. Thus, it was Beza's support for adding chairs in law and medicine to the existing chairs of Hebrew, Greek, arts, and theology that resulted in their creation soon after

---

[34] Indeed, the rapid growth of the Reformation in France made Geneva highly sought after as the principal ministerial training grounds of the Francophone world. Geneva received so many requests for ministerial help that they were often turned down simply by necessity. See, for example, the request of a French church in Strasbourg, whose request for a short-term minister to be sent was rejected due to the already depleted Company ranks. RCP 2:95 (1561). For more information on the growth of French Calvinism amidst the context of rising political hostilities between Catholics and Protestants during the latter half of the sixteenth century, see Robert M. Kingdon's seminal work, *Geneva and the Coming of the Wars of Religion in France, 1555–1563* (Genève: Librarie Droz, 1956).

[35] Maag, *Seminary or University?*, 23.

[36] ET in Lewis, "The Geneva Academy," 49 (CO 10:70). "Quod si, ut speramus dei bonitate freti, idem Deus istorum consiliorum autor ea promoverit, tum de istis perficiendis quae sunt inchoata, tum etiam de reliquis adiiciendis, puta iuris prudentiae ac medicinae professione, cogitatio suscipietur."

he assumed leadership. Law courses were approved by the small council and instituted as early as 1565. A chair of medicine was added in 1567.[37]

Although the addition of these two chairs would not immediately alter registration rates at the Academy, other internal and external influences from this period did encourage the adoption of measures discontinuous with Calvin's founding vision—measures that would directly affect matriculation oaths and confessional subscription, which Calvin had deemed necessary institutional policies. Between 1565 and 1572, as Beza and the city leaders sought to expand academic offerings at the *collège*, a five-year-long plague surged through the city and school, taking the lives of at least two regents and greatly reducing the number of schoolchildren able to attend classes.[38] As the plague gradually thinned out the student body and made quality faculty members progressively difficult to acquire and retain, Beza and his colleagues were forced to reorganize the classes.[39] This, in turn, sparked differences of opinion among the Company and Genevan magistrates regarding the structure and policies of the *schola publica*. During this period, under the rectorship of Jean Trembley (1566–1568), students were admitted to the academy who had not signed the *Confession of Faith*. Additionally, the register of rectors frequently included registrations on the basis of a simple declaration of acquiescence to the "pure evangelical doctrine" taught in Geneva—a declaration deemed satisfactory, despite being only a faint reflection of Calvin's original form of subscription.[40]

Then, on August 30, 1572, the Company received harrowing news of the St. Bartholomew's Massacre, some six days after it began in Paris. Reports of these events shocked the Genevan populace as residents flocked to the churches for pastoral exhortation and prayer.[41] Soon French refugees, including French Reformed ministers, began to flood the cities of the Pays du Vaud seeking asylum. Like its neighboring towns, Geneva opened its gates to receive a large influx of refugees. Company registers from the months following the massacre report on a collection taken for the French ministers who had escaped the massacre. It was determined that these funds should

---

[37] Lewis, "The Geneva Academy," 49.
[38] RCP 3:22–23 (1569).
[39] RCP 3:92 (1572).
[40] Borgeaud, *Histoire*, 140. E.g., the declaration of one Robert Mornet: "Je soussigné proteste devant Dieu qui m'a appellé au nombre de ses enfans de sa pure bonté et grace, vouloir vivre et mourir selon la pure doctrine evangelique qui est annoncée en ceste cité de Genève, tesmoing mon seing manuel ci mis."
[41] RCP 3:86 (August 30, 1572).

be distributed by the refugee pastors among their own parishioners, in a private manner and according to need.[42] This generous act, however, placed an immediate financial burden on the entire city, precipitating down to the Academy as well, which was already struggling with vacant chairs since 1567 due to the plague. New professors, selected by the Company, were called and hired, but several departed soon after due to lack of funds. This debilitating combination of factors brought the *schola publica* to a "virtual standstill" by 1572.[43]

During this period of instability in terms of the overall viability of the school, the Academy's shifting identity became more obvious. For reasons of necessity, and in an attempt to re-establish the school's reputation and financial stability, the city magistrates obtained greater control over the internal affairs of the *collège*. With the support of a few prominent Company members—most notably Beza and Charles Perrot—Geneva's magistracy assumed more prerogative in the appointment of professors and in the creation of a funded school of law to attract more students to the Academy. The new vision for the school was now firmly in place: the Academy would grow to resemble a medieval university, one that would create students to be "citizen[s] of the world," and not simply clerics.[44] This broader academic vision did not sit well with the Company of Pastors on the whole, many of whom believed that adding a funded chair of law would not only prove to be a financial burden but would disrupt order and discipline within the *escole*.[45] Nevertheless, at the recommendation of Beza and Perrot, the Company relinquished a good measure of its ecclesiastical oversight over the *collège* by agreeing to let the magistrates "take the best decision" in these matters.[46] Twelve years after its founding, the Geneven Academy was officially loosening its grip on its exclusive confessional identity.

To achieve their newly revised intentions for the school, it seemed to the magistrates that certain concessions needed to be made. In particular, it was decided that the broadening identity of the Academy called for less stringent

---

[42] RCP 3:88 (September 1572). The registers report that at least twenty French ministers were present at the meeting for this collection.
[43] Maag, *Seminary or University?*, 32.
[44] Borgeaud, *Histoire*, 137. Borgeaud describes the university students as envisioned by the Genevan authorities in this way: They would be students with a grasp of Latin, knowledge of Aristotle and Lombard, and the ability to build a syllogism. In other words, the university student would have the world as his classroom.
[45] Borgeaud, *Histoire*, 126–27. Beza and Perrot appeared in person before the magistrates to outline the ministers' concerns over the creation of the school of law.
[46] Borgeaud, *Histoire*, 127. See also Maag, *Seminary or University?*, 48.

matriculation rules for students, while calling for an accommodating spirit in dealing with new professors' demands. One example of this took place beginning in the winter of 1574, just a few years after the creation of the chair of law at the Academy. On February 10, 1574, famed French jurist Ennemond de Bonnefoy died, having filled a law chair at the Academy for the brief span of only nine months. While the magistrates sought his replacement, former Lausanne professor François Hotman agreed to add Bonnefoy's courses to his own until a suitable replacement was acquired. After a few months of jockeying for an acceptable work-to-pay ratio, the magistrates, desperate to retain Hotman's services, yet without compromising their own frugality in running the school, agreed to pay Hotman a third of Bonnefoy's salary, in addition to his own, while also lowering his lecture load from five to three a week.

Later that summer, however, the magistrates' commitment to maintaining the school of law was tested once again, resulting in further compromise. In June 1574, as another plague besieged the populace, Hotman requested permission of the magistrates to leave the city and continue his lectures for students who were willing to join him in the safer regions of the Genevan countryside. Hotman's request was extremely problematic in light of the fact that his professorial oath prohibited him from the leaving the city during periods of civic danger, but rather required him "to procure as far as I can ... the profit and repose of the city."[47] Nevertheless, Hotman suggested to the magistrates that, if they would release him from the terms of his oath, he would not hold them to the conditions of his three-year contract. Remarkably, after considering Hotman's proposal, the magistrates replied in purely pragmatic fashion and without any mention of the inviolable nature of Hotman's oath:

> Considering on the one hand the minimal progress which the teaching [of law] has made in this city and the expense of it, and other factors, but on the other hand the reputation of this city, which could be affected if we let him go before the agreed-upon time, and that God might pour greater blessings on the teaching of law in the future than in the past, it is agreed that we will let him choose to go or stay in our service, so long as he makes a rapid decision.[48]

---

[47] CO 10:89.
[48] Borgeaud, *Histoire*, 278. ET in Maag, *Seminary or University?*, 50.

Because the school of law was floundering—which, the magistrates feared, meant that the Academy as a whole would also flounder—Hotman's proposal to remain as law professor, albeit from a distance, seemed the only acceptable option. No doubt this decision would have severely vexed the Genevan pastors, whose own oath prohibited them from abandoning their flocks in times of crisis.[49] Nevertheless, this case does not appear in the *Registres*, although mention of the plague and its negative impact on the number of students attending the college *is* noted there.[50] In any case, the situation with Hotman clearly illustrates how desperately the magistrates desired to sustain the school and its chair of law, even at the expense of preserving the sacredness of the professors' oath and of respecting the will of Geneva's ministers concerning the order and discipline of the school.

Several years later, matriculation oaths and formal subscription to Calvin's *Confession of Faith*—requirements for attending the *schola publica*—encountered the next wave of compromise by the Genevan leadership. From May 5 to 6, 1576, the Company met under Beza's leadership to assess and re-order various elements of the *Ecclesiastical Ordinances*.[51] The following month, on Sunday, June 3, the General Council approved and published the altered version presented by the ministers. One modification, among other minor changes, stands out: in approving the new *Ordinances*, the Council specifically chose to remove the previous oath requirement, which had stated "that everyone has had to take an oath to observe both civil and ecclesiastical ordinances."[52]

On the heels of this decision, a proposal originating from within the Company also sought to change the matriculation policy stated in *L'Ordre du Collège* regarding student subscription. On June 29, 1576, Charles Perrot assumed the task of reviewing the school statutes to assess whether anything should be rectified or added before being printed as an appendix to the new *Ordinances*.[53] After a brief period of deliberation, Perrot presented his revision to the Council on July 2, 1576, suggesting one principal amendment: to abolish student subscription to the *Confession of Faith*.[54] At the organization

---

[49] Although the company of pastors routinely discussed whether some of the more prominent ministers in Geneva, such as Beza, should be allowed to abstain from ministering to the afflicted during times of plague. See RCP, Hughes ed., 367–70.

[50] RCP 3:136 (June 22, 1574).

[51] RCP 4:50 (May 1576). Plans for changing the Ecclesiastical Ordinances are recorded as early as April 16, 1576.

[52] RCP 4:53 (May 31, 1576), n. 62.

[53] RCP 4:54 (June 29, 1576).

[54] RCP 4:54 (June 29, 1576), n. 68. The revised *Leges Academiae* were printed with the new Ecclesiastical Ordinances in 1577.

of the college, it had been established that not only professors and regents, but also students, should subscribe to Calvin's *Confession* as part of the general regulations of the school.[55] But on July 2, 1576, Perrot officially announced the Company's proposal that students of all ages should no longer be bound to subscribe to the *Confession* in the presence of the rector. "It does not seem reasonable," Perrot argued, "to thereby press a conscience that is resolved not to sign what it does not understand." Matriculating students would now only be required to record their name with the rector and receive a brief exhortation to study and live modestly in the fear of God, "according to the ordinances of the Church."[56] From this point on, a new title also prefaced Calvin's *Confession*, which read, "A Summary of Christian doctrine, which is taught in the School of Geneva"—merely signaling the official transition to a practice that had already been permitted some years earlier! Calvin's document would never again serve to bind the Academy's students to the confessional standards of Geneva and its church. Indeed, Calvin's original oath to the confession was so seriously modified in 1576 that it was practically "annulled by the change of the title."[57] From this date onward, only teachers and regents were required to subscribe to the confession to guarantee the orthodoxy of their teachings.[58]

Although confessional subscription no longer seemed to be a tenable option for promoting general order and submission in the *escole*, Geneva's civic and ecclesiastical leaders were not ready to abolish the matriculation oath altogether. Nevertheless, in following years, this oath, too, was altered to reflect the broadening confessional identity of the Academy. In 1584, at the request of the Counsel, the Company of Pastors established a new academic oath, which new students were to swear at the time of registration. This oath bore very little resemblance to Calvin's former profession of faith. The student oath of 1584 was not a confessional formula at all, but rather a declaration of obedience to the magistrates and laws of Geneva. In fact, doctrinal matters appear only in the final paragraph of this oath, by which students promised merely to live according to the word of God, abjure all papal superstitions, and oppose all manifest and condemned heresies.[59]

---

[55] Cellérier, *L'Académie de Genève*, 149–52.
[56] RCP 4:58 (July 2, 1576): "et qu'il ne semble raisonnable de presser ainsy une conscience qui n'est resolue de signer ce qu'elle n'entend pas ancores... selon les ordonnences de l'Eglise."
[57] Cellérier, *L'Académie de Genève*, 150.
[58] Borgeaud, *Histoire*, 141.
[59] Borgeaud, *Histoire*, 148–50. See text of the oath on pp. 149–50.

Thus, the years of 1564 to 1584 brought about major changes to the structure and culture of the Genevan Academy. "By emphasizing the role of lay powers in the running of the Academy, and by revising the matriculation and attestation procedures of the *schola publica* to bring them more in line with the practice in other centres of learning, the magistrates were attempting to transform the *schola publica*'s outlook ... and develop their own alternative vision of a more conventional institution of higher education that would bring prestige to the city and with it additional income."[60] As we will see, use of matriculation oaths would continue to decline in importance, eventually caving to conscientious objections and practical concerns for institutional viability.

7.3. Diversification, Growth, and Problems with the Oath

The Genevan magistrates' adoption of new measures in the 1570s and 1580s was significantly motivated by their desire to increase the prestige and financial stability of the Academy by attracting foreign students to its doors. The addition of courses in law and medicine proved very successful in the attainment of this goal. Over this decade, a noticeable influx of students arrived from the German states, the Netherlands, and Scandinavia to matriculate at the college. Their number frequently surpassed that of Swiss and French students. The burgeoning size and diversity of the student body fostered new kinds of problems, however. After 1572, the registers of the small council and of the Company of Pastors record a growing number of complaints about the unruly behavior of foreign students, especially those originating from the German states.[61] The ministers reported various sorts of unacceptable behavior to the Council between 1577 and 1606. In March 1577, a group of German students were reported to the magistrates for hosting lavish dinners and drinking parties, a matter that was referred to the Consistory.[62] On May 11, 1579, several ministers and elders informed the Council that young people had been playing cards for money, which was prohibited in the city. The magistrates opened an inquiry into the matter.[63] Later, in the spring of

---

[60] Maag, *Seminary or University?*, 52.
[61] Maag, *Seminary or University?*, 55–58.
[62] RC 72:32 (March 5, 1577); Cited in Maag, *Seminary or University?*, 59.
[63] RCP 4:145 (May 11, 1579). Laws against card-playing in Geneva were passed in 1536, pre-dating Calvin's arrival in the city. See Naphy, *Calvin and the Consolidation of the Genevan Reformation*, 30.

1585, the Company of Pastors chastised three students from the *schola publica* for neglecting their lessons; instead of attending classes, they had been loitering around a bridge by the Arve River eating capons.[64]

Occasionally, the moral transgressions of Geneva's students were more serious in nature. On January 27, 1578, the Company of Pastors addressed a scandal that had taken place in the home of a certain Monsieur Nicolas, a bookseller in the city, whose maid had engaged in indecent acts with a student currently living under his roof. The ministers admonished Nicolas, and all those housing students, to keep careful watch over the chastity of their maidservants, whether young or mature. Also, any students given to insolent behavior or drunkenness at the expense of their studies must be warned by their hosts to live according to the laws of God and the city, or be sent to the rector for discipline.[65] Likewise, the ministerial records from June 11, 1585, report a similar event involving a German student named Albrecht, who, after violating a local man's wife, was forcefully reproached by all the Company for his immodest behavior and handed over to the authority of the Council.[66]

The primary goal of attracting German students to the Academy had been motivated by practical, monetary concerns. German students, unlike the French and Genevan students, were known to come from affluent, even noble households, and their matriculation fees—now imposed on foreign students—proved beneficial both to the school and to Geneva's economy. This practical commitment, however, quickly led to concerns that the German students would be more likely to dishonor and resist the governing authorities, given their prestigious parentage. One way in which the Genevan authorities sought to control the German students' behavior was through the official process of matriculation, which required that students swear an oath to abide by all civic ordinances. In fact, however, "the oath did not appear to restrain the students greatly," as reports of disobedience persist in the official records.[67]

From Maag's analysis of the overall discipline problem in the Academy, it appears that the German students' impious behavior partially stemmed from their unfamiliarity with Geneva's ordinances, which, despite having undergone

---

[64] RCP 5:60 (March 1585).
[65] RCP 4:104–105 (January 27, 1578).
[66] RCP 5:78–79 (June 11, 1585). See also n. 166 for a reference to the Company's earlier request that such issues be handled by the Council.
[67] Maag, *Seminary or University?*, 58–59.

several changes, remained relatively strict. The Council records make note of students' failure to follow standard matriculation procedure. On February 27, 1578, the ministers reported to the Council that the German students had failed to come and swear the confession of faith, the school's matriculation oath, and "seemed puzzled at its existence." But as in years prior, the Genevan authorities were again willing to compromise. To accommodate these valuable foreign students, and to avoid the appearance of trying to bind their consciences to swear to what they did not understand, "the small council decided not to force them to take any oath except one of obedience to the civil authorities."[68] Apparently, the Genevan authorities even had trouble getting students to take this civic oath with any regularity. The registers of the Company of Pastors contains a note from January 24, 1606, which records a stern warning conveyed to Gaspard Laurent, current rector of the Academy, reminding him that all foreign students arriving at the *escole* were not only to be enrolled in the rector's book but should also swear an oath to the Genevan Lordship—a practice Laurent had apparently allowed to fall into disuse.[69] By removing the student oath to the Confession of Faith in 1584, the Academy had officially opened its doors to a confessional diversity that, in years following, would prove impossible to reverse.

7.4. Pastors or Professors? A Tenuous Relationship and an Accommodated Oath

The steady influx of foreign students into the Academy, while garnering substantial profit, generated another set of problems for the Genevan authorities. On one hand, the Academy needed to maintain a strong faculty to support its growing number of foreign and domestic students. Occasionally, this required the Company of Pastors to search within their own ranks for suitable teachers when chairs at the school became vacant. Although Calvin had carefully distinguished the work of pastors and doctors, he had also "believed that on occasion doctors might also be called by God to exercise the pastoral functions of preaching and administrating the sacraments." Following Calvin's death, an impressive lineup of Geneva's religious leaders accepted—sometimes reluctantly—the role of pastor-doctor, including Theodore Beza, Lambert Daneau, Bonaventure Bertram, Antoine de La Faye, Jean Diodati,

---

[68] Maag, *Seminary or University?*, 59–60.
[69] RCP 9:177–78 (January 24, 1606).

and Theodore Tronchin.[70] On the other hand, those called upon to hold double office frequently struggled to balance the pastoral and teaching labors they had sworn to fulfill, creating all sorts of problems.

Those holding the offices of pastor and doctor in Geneva faced a unique set of challenges following Charles Emmanuel I's succession as the duke of Savoy in 1580. An aggressive Catholic leader, Charles I set out to reclaim Geneva and its surrounding territories for the Catholic faith. During the 1580s and 1590s, rural pastors from the parishes surrounding Geneva were almost constantly harassed by Savoyard officials and soldiers, and when the Savoyard War commenced in 1589, most of these countryside pastors were forced to retreat from their parishes and take shelter in the city, often leaving their congregations behind to be pillaged and killed.[71] During the Savoyard blockade of Geneva in 1586, the Academy also struggled to obtain reputable professors for its classes, forcing the Genevan authorities to turn to their own parish pastors to fill vacant chairs. In some cases, ministers willing to teach were required to continue their own pastoral labors in addition to fulfilling the tasks outlined in the professors' oath, which occasionally proved burdensome.[72] This period also saw a progressive weakening of leadership, both within the Company of Pastors and in the Academy, with the result that "magisterial interventions in the affairs of the Academy and the church were on the increase."[73]

Troubles relating to the oath of office became especially acute when the Genevan magistrates decided that certain professors should also be willing to fill pastoral vacancies in the city parishes. Although several prominent individuals—most notably Calvin and Beza—had successfully executed the hybrid office of pastor-doctor, by the turn of the century most of the professors at the *collège* were strict academicians. The Genevan magistrates occasionally tried to reverse this trend, however.[74] In September 1606, Jean Pinault, minister of the city church of La Madeleine, died. The Company of Pastors proposed filling the vacancy by temporarily appointing one of

---

[70] Manetsch, *Calvin's Company of Pastors*, 29.

[71] Manetsch, *Calvin's Company of Pastors*, 139–40. The truce between Geneva and Savoy, signed in 1594, accomplished little to no peace for the countryside pastors and their parishes. Catholic defenders continued to make headway in reclaiming Protestant lands and souls. By December 1598, thousands of people "on the southern shore of Lac Léman adjacent to Geneva . . . had renounced the Protestant religion and embraced the Catholic faith" (p. 140).

[72] See several illustrative cases in Maag, *Seminary or University?*, 65–73.

[73] Maag, *Seminary or University?*, 88.

[74] Much of the following is recounted in Maag, *Seminary or University?*, 88–93, but I have consulted the registers in order to include additional details about these events that are especially pertinent to the ministerial oath.

Geneva's rural ministers to the post, at least until the more permanent replacement, Jean Chauve, was allowed to leave his current charge in France.[75] The magistrates, on the other hand, thought it more convenient to mine the *schola publica*'s faculty for a substitute. On September 15, they determined that Jean Diodati, professor of theology, and Gaspard Laurent, professor of Greek, "whose profession is very much in accord with the holy ministry," could easily fill the vacancy in La Madeleine while also continuing to manage their academic responsibilities.[76]

This proposal encountered stiff opposition both from the Company of Pastors and the two professors. Geneva's ministers could agree with the city magistrates—to a point—that Academy professors served the holy ministry by instructing pastoral candidates. Nevertheless, they strongly believed that investing these two professors with the dignity of the pastoral office itself was out of step with the *Ecclesiastical Ordinances*, which, in their eyes, clearly distinguished the official tasks of pastors and doctors.[77] Moreover, when asked by the Company of Pastors about their intention and desire to be ordained as ministers, Diodati and Laurent declared that they could not even consider such a burdensome task, "especially since it is a question, not only of preaching God's Word, but also of making [pastoral] visits."[78] The magistrates reluctantly conceded this initial skirmish to the Company of Pastors, which refused to appoint Diodati minister "in accordance with the ecclesiastical ordinances."[79] Rural ministers were assigned to the vacant parish for the interim.[80]

---

[75] RCP 9:204 (September 12, 1606). It appears that Monsieur Chauve was delayed for a span of years before coming to Geneva. Despite complaining to the synod of Saint-Maixent that he felt conscience-bound to take up his vocation in Geneva, the body refused to give him leave out of the conviction that he should exercise his ministry in his homeland of France. This put Geneva's Small Council in a position of protracted waiting. RCP 10:86, 90 (1608), n. 171.

[76] RCP 9:206 (September 15, 1606). Jean (Giovanni) Diodati is most remembered for his 1607 translation of the Bible into Italian, and for his *Annotationes in Biblia*, an exposition of difficult passages in Scripture.

[77] RCP 9:206 (September 15, 1606), n. 177.

[78] RCP 9:210 (September 19, 1606).

[79] RCP 9:211 (September 22, 1606), n. 198. On October 6, 1606, the magistrates chided the pastors for continuing to "stubbornly thwart their will" about Jean Diodati, and also rejected their request to call Daniel Chamier to fill the empty parish. See RCP 9:213, n. 204. Although the magistrates had surrendered to the Company of Pastors by accepting the appointment of a rural pastor to serve in La Madeleine, the Council proved equally "stubborn" in their insistence that a *citoyen*, instead of a *bourgeois* minister, should be elected to the position. The ministers' first choice to fill the pastoral post was Samuel Perrot, a foreign-born minister serving the rural church in Satigny. Although the Company of Pastors contended that Perrot, a *bourgeois*, was the most capable candidate, the Council refused to concede this issue and required the ministers to appoint their least popular choice, a Genevan citizen named Matthieu Scarron. See RCP 10:4–5 (January 23, 1607), and nn. 4, 5, 11.

[80] RCP 9:213 (October 13, 1606).

In 1608, however, the Council again tried to appoint Diodati to a vacant parish while also urging Theodore Tronchin, professor of Hebrew, to join him in the effort.[81] Although by this point the Company of Pastors had warmed to the idea of ordaining professors for ministerial service, they were no less firm in making all involved aware of the weighty nature of the pastoral office. At a meeting of the Company on June 24, 1608, it was considered that "it was neither fitting nor reasonable to establish a free or simply honorary ministry, as that would not only denigrate the charge, but also could not bring relief" to the problem of vacant parishes. The sacred ministry was a full-time job that required swearing an oath, supervising the morals of Genevan society, and attending Consistory meetings; in sum, seeing to *all* of the aspects of ministry, not merely some. When asked again about their willingness to be ordained to the ministry, the two professors responded in much the same way as they had several years earlier. Tronchin begged to be excused from accepting the ministry, as he could not at the moment accept the duties of its charge.[82] Diodati, however, admitted to the Company of Pastors that he had always desired ordination, as it was his parents' wish for him. He declared that he would come forward after some time to accept the office as long he would be elected by the other ministers and not solely by the magistrates.[83] This greatly pleased the Company of Pastors.[84]

Despite unresolved concerns about the type and amount of pastoral work they would have to perform, Diodati and Tronchin finally agreed to become ministers by November 1608. They were received as regular ministers of the Genevan church on December 2, 1608—not, however, without exceptions.[85] Tronchin, for his part, remained very cautious about taking on full pastoral responsibilities in addition to his professorial work at the Academy. He "protested that he did not wish, and had not promised to tie himself to the ministry, nor to fulfill all the duties attached to it, nor to bind himself to the ministry by oath." In response, the Company of Pastors decided that the only way to retain Tronchin's services, while also protecting the weightiness of the ministerial oath, was to alter the oath in order to accommodate the situation. The ministers conceded, "As for the oath, our brother can detail to

---

[81] RCP 10:87 (June 17, 1608).
[82] Tronchin did, nevertheless, agree to teach catechism classes at the ministers' request. See RCP 10:96 (July 15, 1608), n. 201; and RCP 10:99 (July 22, 1608).
[83] RCP 10:91 (June 24, 1608). See also RCP 10:93 (July 1, 1608), n. 187.
[84] RCP 10:93 (July 1, 1608).
[85] RCP 10:124 (December 2, 1608).

Messieurs the exceptions that he wants put in, so that his conscience may be less burdened. As well, as regards the duties of ministry, our brother will not be forced nor constrained to fulfill them against his will."[86]

It appeared that the Genevan ministers had found a convenient way to fill the city's vacant pulpits, yet without binding the professors' consciences by oath to a set of unrealistic duties. Nevertheless, the Council records seem to indicate that Diodati and Tronchin never swore an amended ministerial oath in 1608, nor did they fulfill their ministerial office beyond preaching the occasional sermon and teaching catechism. On November 7, 1611, Geneva's pastors again lamented the lack of ministerial help, noting that Diodati and Tronchin were unavailable to serve "because they are busy teaching theology."[87]

Thus, as time went on, the Company of Pastors became more convinced of their original stance that requiring professors to hold ministerial office was turning out to be an unfruitful solution to filling vacant parishes. The duties of pastors and doctors were, in the end, too distinct to allow any one man to fulfill the responsibilities outlined in his oath of office with any measure of success. The ministers' opinion did not persuade the magistrates, however, who ruled in November 1612 that Diodati and Tronchin should in fact swear the ministerial oath and fulfill the tasks of the office. In complaint, the two professors insisted that their professors' oath of obedience to the civil magistrates was sufficient, and that they did not need to take the additional oath prescribed of ministers. The council records of November 28, 1612, report on their complaint: "they do not want to undertake everything which the ministers' oath entails, such as visiting the sick, inspecting the *dizaines* and attending consistory meetings." Although willing to fill pulpits on occasion, Diodati and Tronchin expressed an unwillingness to fulfill any other ministerial tasks, for "they declared that they feel tied to their prior obligation [teaching] as the principal one, and that they cannot take on two full work-loads."

As they had done so many times in the past, the Genevan Council found a way to compromise while still maintaining its will and authority over the situation. The magistrates commanded the two professors to swear the ministers' oath, but, as in Hotman's case, the Council announced they would not expect Diodati and Tronchin to actually fulfill everything included in the

---

[86] RCP 10:124 (December 2, 1608). ET in Maag, *Seminary or University?*, 91.
[87] RC 108:282 (November 7, 1611); cited in Maag, *Seminary or University?*, 91.

oath. They would not be required to make pastoral visits, inspect the *dizaines*, or be present at consistory meetings.[88] By manipulating the conditions of the ministerial oath, and yet still requiring it of the two men, the magistrates succeeded at retaining the professors' assistance in the churches while further entrenching their own authority over Geneva's ecclesiastical and academic realms.

* * *

The account of the founding and expansion of the Genevan Academy is a story of continuity, cooperation, and compromise. From its inception, the *collège* existed as a beacon of Calvinist confessional orthodoxy, attracting large numbers of Swiss and French Reformed students to its doors. Its rigorous matriculation oath and subscription policies supported Calvin's firm resolve to train churchmen and statesmen in the science of true religion. In one respect at least, this overarching vision for the *escole* remained intact following his death in 1564. Per Calvin's intentions, the Academy was subject to dual governance by Geneva's magistrates and Company of Pastors who, for their own part, remained committed to the doctrinal tenets of the original *Confession of Faith* as they oversaw the diverse vocational aims of its students. Nevertheless, in the decades following Calvin's death, an unprecedented spirit of cooperation among the magistrates and pastors of Geneva fostered hopes of a broader and more illustrious purpose for the Academy, resembling that of an elite medieval university. As much as the Genevan authorities might have intended, at least at first, to retain a firm hold on the practices Calvin had deemed necessary for preserving the school's distinct confessional identity, their controlling desire for the Academy to develop and grow gradually outweighed this commitment. Over time, a variety of internal and external factors—recurring plagues, political upheaval, and personnel and financial shortages—established conditions that would severely complicate efforts to enforce academic and ministerial oaths and formal subscription, forcing Geneva's magistrates and pastors to compromise these measures in various and inventive ways.

The historical account presented in this chapter yields several important observations regarding the place and purpose of sworn oaths and confessional subscription in the Genevan Academy. From the years following Calvin's death, the use of oaths and subscription signaled less of a

---

[88] RC 110:65 (November 28, 1612); cited in Maag, *Seminary or University?*, 92.

commitment to maintaining strict doctrinal unanimity in the *escole*, and more of the general desire to distinguish the Academy from its Roman Catholic counterparts. Not only was student subscription to Calvin's *Confession* eventually abolished altogether, but the academic oath itself became less about binding individual consciences to uniquely Calvinistic—as opposed to Lutheran, Zwinglian, or Anabaptist—tenets, and more about preparing the Academy to accommodate foreign Protestant students. This is evident from the stark difference between the matriculation oath of 1559, which required full adherence to Calvin's lengthy and detailed *Confession*, and the poorly regulated oath in use after 1584, by which students merely promised to abide by Geneva's civil ordinances. These changing measures indicate, in other words, that the confessional impulse of the city and its *collège* had shifted from distinctly Calvinistic to broadly non-Catholic.

This study has also shown that the Genevan authorities found different ways to accommodate oaths to the changing situations and pressing problems in the city, church, and school. The Company of Pastors, for its part, would occasionally change the terms of an academic or ministerial oath in an attempt to protect its inviolable nature. In so doing, they expressed a commitment to protecting the consciences of those who came to swear by the tenets of their respective oaths. Because the individual conscience should never be forced to bind itself to unrealistic or unfavorable demands, the terms of the oath could therefore be altered to accommodate the will and intentions of the one who swore. The inviolable power of an oath, therefore, did not reside in its substance—which could, in fact, be changed as circumstances dictated—but in the intention and ability of the one swearing to actually perform the obligations stipulated by their oath.

The city magistrates, on the other hand, appeared to be far less concerned about the individual conscience or about the inviolable nature of the oaths they frequently required of Geneva's residents. The Council's apprehension of the function of oaths in the church and school was far more pragmatic than that of the pastors. Oaths were a useful tool for promoting civic obedience and public order, a sort of "social glue" to enhance the magistrate's will and authority. As we noted, during periods of pastoral vacancy in Geneva, the magistrates did not hesitate in requiring Academy professors to swear the oath of ordination, despite their unwillingness to fulfill the tasks outlined in that oath. Eager to compromise so as to preserve the status quo, the Council assured these doctors that they would not actually be expected to perform everything they had sworn to do. Protecting the inviolability of the oath concerned the magistrates very little. The important thing *was that an oath had been sworn*, thereby adding ceremonial weight to a person's pledge of obedience to the governing authorities. Thus, the academic and ministerial oath proved to be a rather malleable force in the hands of the Genevan authorities in the decades following the formation of Calvin's Academy.

Conclusion

Recent scholarship on the relationship between law and individual liberty during the Reformation has emphasized the shifting nature of Calvin's ecclesiology over time. The French reformer is portrayed as having an initial, Luther-like zeal for the freedom of conscience against all human traditions, but whose early commitment to individual liberty gradually surrendered to an over-valuation of the laws and authority of the institutional church in his later ministry. John Witte has argued, for example, that Calvin's "radical expansion of the law and authority of the visible church in his later writings and actions served at once to contract and to expand the province of religious liberty." Calvin maintained, of course, that believers' consciences were free from the condemnation of the moral law under its Old Covenant administrations, and that Christians were no longer bound to observe "popish" superstitions or blasphemous Catholic ceremonies. Witte suggests, however, that "what Calvin gave with one hand" in terms of spiritual freedom, "he [later] took with the other." In Calvin's view, believers' spiritual liberty did not leave them much "freedom of exercise as members of the church," especially with respect to the control of doctrine and morals in Geneva. Calvin's version of Christian freedom required Geneva's residents to " 'freely' bind themselves to obey the church's 'well-ordered constitution' and comprehensive code of spiritual discipline, . . . to 'gladly' submit to the mandated forms and habits of worship, ritual, and liturgy . . . [and to] 'voluntarily' restrict their spiritual freedom even in discretionary matters of spiritual living so that weaker members of the church will not be offended and misled" (*scandalum infirmorum*). Thus, Witte concludes, Calvin's reform measures gradually resulted in the contraction of personal liberty of conscience within the church, even while he granted an expanded role to "corporate religious order and organization"—the authoritative domain of Calvin and his fellow ministers.[1] One gathers that, if

---

[1] John Witte, Jr., *The Reformation of Rights: Law, Religion, and Human Rights in Early Modern Calvinism* (Cambridge: Cambridge University Press, 2007), 74.

we accept a "radical" distinction between Calvin's earlier and later ecclesiology, we are left with a Calvin of the bait-and-switch variety—promising the liberation of believers' consciences from the burdens of Catholicism, but then imposing a Protestant yoke through the surprise implementation of oath-dominated discipline and conscience-binding confessionalism.

Doubtless, there is some truth in this portrayal: during his two pastoral stints in Geneva, Calvin gained the reputation of a staunch disciplinarian; he could be fiercely protective of Geneva's Consistory and of his own rights and privileges as a minister of the word; and the reformers were relentless in pointing out the dividing line between ecclesiastical and civil authority. Nonetheless, the specific texts and controversies explored in this book reveal that Calvin and the reformers conceived of the relationship between the authority of the private conscience and the power of "ecclesiastical constitutions" or religious observances with greater nuance than some general portrayals of their ecclesiology might suggest.[2] By examining Calvin's thoughts and actions surrounding the relationship between oaths, confession, conscience, and discipline within the local context of the reformers' conflicts with religious dissidents and obstinate laypersons, this study has suggested three important revisions to the generally received impressions of Calvin and the Reformation. First, this study has reassessed and challenged the notion that Calvin's mature ecclesiology represents a radical enlargement of church law and authority that effectively undercut his earlier commitment to the freedom of conscience. Indeed, one could say that Calvin's so-called mature ecclesiology is on display far earlier than many have conceded. Second, it has demonstrated how Calvin and the reformers defended a modified form of individual liberty on the basis of a highly nuanced conception of the relationship between conscience and tradition—an alternative type of tradition so manifestly beneficial to piety that it remained impervious to all conscientious objections—a sort of "divine adiaphora." And finally, this study has enhanced our view of Calvin as a pastoral theologian, in that it further illustrates Calvin's ability to accommodate law—and even conscience—to the causes that ranked, for him, even higher: namely, to the causes of individual and communal reform.

---

[2] In his *Institutes* 4.10.27 (1559), Calvin uses the phrase "ecclesiasticas constitutiones" to refer to the laws and ceremonies "by which the order of the church is shaped" (LCC 21:1205; CO 2:887).

C.1. Calvin's Ecclesiology: Shifting or Stable?

It is true that Calvin's ecclesiology passed through stages of development. This was certainly the case during the 1530s, as he was coming to terms with the far-reaching implications of his conversion to Protestantism. Calvin gradually found his own Reformed voice through early involvement at various colloquies and disputations, as well as by defending the cause of the Protestant churches in his *Institutio* (1536). When initially called to Geneva, Calvin's conception of the offices and order of the church began to develop and expand quite rapidly on account of the simple necessity of consolidating reform in a city that still lacked a clear vision for how Christian piety should manifest itself in the church and in society. Especially during his second charge in Geneva, Calvin's growing conception of the proper structure of the church—codified in the Ecclesiastical Ordinances of 1541 and embodied in the founding of the Consistory—resulted in the establishment of new measures for enforcing law, promoting discipline, and preventing scandal.

Nevertheless, even as some of the formal aspects of Calvin's ecclesiology evolved over time, his vision for how genuine piety and the liberty of conscience should coexist within the Christian life was remarkably consistent. Even before he set foot in Geneva, and not long after his own "sudden conversion," Calvin was thoroughly convinced in his own mind that genuine piety required a willing and public confession of faith by means of "external ordinances" (*rebus externis*). True Christians, he and his Reformed colleagues believed, were never free to invoke their consciences as an excuse for failing to worship God properly by means of duly established church constitutions. Indeed, all believers, regardless of their circumstances, were obligated to align themselves publicly with the catholic creeds and Reformed confessions—and to do so, remarkably, even despite Calvin's admission that such standards are, in some sense, "*human* constitutions."[3] As much as Calvin emphasized the freedom of the Christian by developing this topic in later editions of the *Institutes*, he never contemplated a form of individual liberty of conscience that could circumvent the corporate religious order or confessional character of the Reformed faith.[4]

---

[3] *Institutes* 4.10.30 (LCC 21:1207; CO 2:889): "humanas constitutiones." Emphasis mine.

[4] The matter of the liberty of conscience never waned in importance in Calvin's thought. Instead, Calvin's understanding of the relationship between conscience and the authority of the church was constantly developing up until the final edition of the *Institutes*. François Wendel notes that when Calvin published his new Latin edition in 1543 (followed by a French translation in 1545), he added four new chapters: "Two of these chapters dealt with vows and with human traditions." Moreover,

Calvin also remained rather consistent in implementing oath-driven methods for obtaining ecclesiastical order and unity, despite their critical reception by parishioners, civil magistrates, and even fellow ministers. Although Calvin and the other reformers shared Luther's general animosity toward the canon law tradition—particularly in terms of its theology and its myriad spiritual regulations perceived as burdening the conscience—they often reappropriated certain aspects of the medieval civil law in the service of reform. They largely shared the assumption of the common law tradition they had inherited, that oaths were the most preferred and persuasive means for advancing the virtues of justice and truthfulness in the courts, in the church, and in public life. Indeed, requiring public oaths and vows—as a pledge of adherence to Protestant ideals, as a means of securing valid testimony in "good conscience," or as part of the formal subscription to Reformation creeds and confessions—largely served the same purpose as the oaths mandated by medieval common law. Oaths, public profession, and confessional subscription enforced the strategic link between thought and practice. By taking an oath or making public confession, individuals clothed their oral promise with an added guarantee that they would act upon their pledge for the glory of God and for the good of the whole community. Swearing an oath or pledging adherence to sound doctrine required agents to measure carefully the penalties for swearing or promising falsely prior to taking an oath before God, the prime witness and judge of the conscience. From early on, then, Calvin judged these oath-driven measures to be consistent with his calling to enforce the dictates of God's word in a Reformed church and society.

The stability of Calvin's ecclesiology over time is also evidenced by regular appeals to his own authority and conscience as an ordained minister of the word. Even before taking up full-time pastoral labor in Geneva—with the genuineness of his call in that city still questionable—Calvin was apt to appeal to the security of his own conscience as a means of staving off the accusations of his opponents. Later, Calvin and other members of the Consistory made sure to emphasize that God had ordained them to their respective offices, instilling them with direct authority to instruct and admonish—if not judge—human behavior in accord with their own "official" consciences.

---

the 1550 edition (followed by the translation of 1551) also contained several noteworthy additions, including "an original exposition on the human conscience." See François Wendel, *Calvin: Origins and Development of His Religious Thought*, trans. Philip Mairet (reprint; Grand Rapids, MI: Baker, 1997), 117.

Evoking peace of conscience in connection with the authority of their pastoral office was just one means by which the Genevan Consistory urged its parishioners to submit their own consciences to the word of God *that the ministers had preached*. Practically, the Consistory members' appeals to ministerial office and conscience also enabled them to maintain the balance of power in Geneva, guarding against the Council's impulse to transgress the boundaries of its own authority over the church and city.

Thus, although Calvin's ecclesiology underwent obvious developments over the course of his ministry, several of his fundamental commitments regarding church authority and individual liberty remained quite stable: the compatibility of individual freedom of conscience and church discipline; the value—even necessity—of oaths, confession, and subscription as tools for discerning genuine Christian piety; and a strong sense of divine authority invested in the offices of the church, and even in the consciences of its office-bearers. These long-standing commitments suggest that Calvin's mature ecclesiology did not constitute so great an expansion of church law and authority that it undermined his earlier dedication to the freedom of conscience—at least in his own mind.

C.2. Calvin, Human Traditions, and "Divine Adiaphora"

Such commitments do indicate, however, that Calvin's understanding of the relationship between the liberty of conscience and church constitutions was heavily nuanced. Although Calvin and the reformers denied that their oath- and conscience-driven measures for reform and discipline constituted a violation of individual liberty, they were often troubled by the persistent accusation that their standards were in fact inconsistent with a biblical understanding of the freedom of conscience. In order to win people over to their visions for reform, they realized they had to offer a plausible defense for requiring church constitutions that had the appearance of binding consciences to human or quasi-human ordinances. Each chapter of this study has examined ways in which Calvin and the reformers sought to answer their critics and resolve this dilemma by appealing—whether explicitly or implicitly—to an alternative type of "tradition" having no specific command in Scripture, yet nevertheless being required of the faithful under certain circumstances.[5]

---

[5] What I refer to in Chapter 4 as "divine adiaphora," or as a "*tertium quid*" in Chapter 5.

Basically, Calvin and his colleagues justified their reform measures by distinguishing a special category of church constitution: one distinct from mere human traditions, which frequently bind peoples' consciences to impious behavior (as they alleged to be the case in Catholicism); but also distinct from an explicit command of God's word, since such observances are not necessary for salvation, nor "place the conscience under religious obligations."[6] Nevertheless, Calvin insisted that such observances—including oaths, confessional subscription, and public confession—are not ancillary but rather essential to authentic piety. Such "legitimate church observances," he writes in his *Institutes* (1559), are required practically so that "in the sacred assembly of believers all things be done decently and with becoming dignity; and that the human community itself be kept in order with certain bonds of humanity and moderation."[7] Such human constitutions, though not explicitly commanded in Scripture, are nevertheless "founded upon God's authority" (mediated through the offices of minister, elder, and magistrate), "drawn from Scripture" (derived from the reformers' interpretation of various texts), and "therefore, *wholly divine.*"[8] Calvin even denied that ordinances necessary for the confession of faith are to be considered "human traditions" at all, because they do not belong to the kind of ceremony that may be refused for the sake of private conscience (adiaphora proper). Instead, insofar as they edify one's neighbor and serve the order and unity of Christ's church in keeping with God's will, such observances are best regarded as divine rather than human, and therefore are not open to the charge that they *harmfully* bind the conscience.[9] These ordinances, as a kind of bond, are not injurious to the conscience precisely "because the whole necessity of observing them respects their general end [of glorifying God and serving one's neighbor charitably], and does not consist in the things commanded."[10] Such ceremonies—not

---

[6] *Institutes* 4.10.27 (CO 2:887; LCC 21:1205–1206): "Id tantum semper in istis observationibus excipiendum est, ne aut ad salute credantur necessariae, atque ita conscientias religione obstringant." In 4.10.4, Calvin states that, while human religious obligations unlawfully burden the conscience, the holy law of God, "binding only outward works, leaves the conscience free" (LCC 21:1183; CO 2:870).
[7] *Institutes* 4.10.28 (CO 2:887–88; LCC 21:1206): "legitimas ecclesiae observationes."
[8] *Institutes* 4.10.30 (LCC 21:1207; CO 2:889). Emphasis mine.
[9] *Institutes* 4.10.27 (LCC 21:1205; CO 2:887). Unlike the corrupting influence of Nicodemite dissimulation, which, according to Calvin, "disturbs" the consciences of the weak. See Chapter 3, section 3.2.2.
[10] *Institutes* 4.10.5 (CO 2:871): "[L]eges humanas, sive a magistratu, sive ab ecclesia ferantur, tametsi sint observatu necessariae (de probis et iustis loquor), ideo tamen non ligare per se conscientiam, quia tota observandi necessitas ad generalem finem respicit, non autem consistit in rebus praeceptis."

strictly required by Scripture but nevertheless critical to genuine piety under certain circumstances—might be called "divine adiaphora."

The previous chapters illustrate how Calvin and others struggled to define and defend this type of ordinance in various contexts. In Strasbourg, where Bucer and Capito faced conscience-driven opposition from Anabaptists and Spiritualists, the reformers determined that, while it was wrong to compel someone to believe something against his or her will, an important distinction had to be made between the coercion of the conscience and the necessary regulation of doctrine and piety in a Reformed community (Chapter 2). The Strasbourg preachers thus posited a fundamental difference between pushing faith on someone and regulating doctrine for the public good by means of citizens' oaths and a common confession of faith. For Bucer and Capito, the communal rule of charity took precedence over the internal conviction of conscience in guiding one's public confession, a rule that later led them to embrace a more accommodating and pragmatic approach to the treatment of Nicodemite dissimulators than that taken by Calvin, Farel, Viret, and Vermigli (Chapters 3–4). Indeed, for the French reformers and Vermigli, the rule of charity obligated Nicodemites to forsake their compromise precisely because it set a destructive example for weaker members of the church. The ceremonies required for the confession of faith were not optional or "indifferent" at all, but rather necessary to render genuine praise to God and to protect the consciences of weaker members who might be scandalized by the witness of Nicodemite dissimulation. In a similar manner, while attempting to establish confessional uniformity in Geneva between 1536 and 1538, Calvin and Farel insisted that their oath-driven reform measures were not burdensome for the populace, since any ordinance that served God's honor, edified one's neighbor, and unified the church ought to be received by prudent individuals with a sound conscience (Chapter 5). Similarly, while establishing moral reform in Geneva through the strict oversight of the Consistory, Calvin and his colleagues insisted on the use of oaths and public confession, along with direct appeals to the conscience, to ensure that the impulse of charity, rather than self-interest, would govern the behavior of Geneva's residents (Chapter 6). Despite complaints from some of the city's more obstinate inhabitants, Calvin and his Company of Pastors strained to emphasize that their oath- and conscience-driven disciplinary measures were not a violation of personal freedom at all, but manifestly Scriptural, edificatory, and in keeping with the love of neighbor. These same commitments guided Calvin's requirement of confessional subscription for professors and students of the Genevan Academy following its founding in 1559 (Chapter 7). Such ordinances provided the necessary bond to create a school that was committed to the doctrinal standards set forth by the Reformation. Revealingly, the gradual breakdown of these confessional moorings brought trouble to the school after Calvin's death.

In Book Four of his *Institutes* (1559), after devoting several sections to the topic of the right ordering of the church and its relationship to the liberty of conscience, Calvin censures those who mistakenly confuse human traditions with the laws and regulations that are necessary for the order and unity of the church. Following his defense of necessary church constitutions, Calvin poses a revealing question: "What sort of freedom of conscience could there be in such excessive attentiveness and caution?"[11] Critics of Calvin's invasive measures for church reform and spiritual discipline must have thought that very little freedom remained for them! Indeed, Calvin's rhetorical inquiry—nestled as it is amid his defense of practices deemed necessary to reform, in contrast to mere human traditions—indicates that Calvin remained eversensitive to the charge that the church constitutions over which he frequently presided represented violations of the freedom of conscience. One does not sense that even Calvin believed he had justified this alternative form of "tradition" to his own satisfaction—much less the satisfaction of others. His treatment of this subject in the *Institutes* reflects an ongoing struggle over this matter: although Calvin wants to affirm that all "human constitutions" *based on* God's word are "wholly divine," he must admit that such ordinances remain essentially human, in that they are "suggested rather than explicitly stated" in Scripture. At very least, he wishes to maintain they are *more* divine than human.[12]

C.3. Calvin as Defender and Critic of the Conscience

The cases examined in this volume also present Calvin as both a defender and critic of the conscience. Calvin genuinely believed that the conscience—as the tribunal of the soul, instinctually guided by God's natural law written on the heart—is, in theory, a reliable moral standard that serves either to condemn or to justify human behavior. As a defender of the conscience, Calvin warned

---

[11] *Institutes* 4.10.31 (LCC 21:1209; CO 2:890).
[12] *Institutes* 4.10.30 (LCC 21:1207–8; CO 2:889).

friends and foes alike that if they ignored or contravened their consciences, they would do so only to their own peril. In Geneva, Calvin and his Consistory routinely urged lay members to examine their consciences closely before binding themselves under oath and facing the consequences of their testimony—whether good or bad. Calvin's special concern for protecting the security of the conscience sometimes placed him and his pastoral colleagues at odds with the civil rulers of Geneva. For while the magistrates sought to regulate outward conformity to city ordinances in order to promote social unity and preserve the status quo of authority in the city, the Consistory was more concerned about the assimilation—even interiorization—of Reformed piety among Geneva's residents. In the minds of Calvin and his fellow ministers, it was essential that those who misbehaved or ran afoul of Geneva's laws and morals should not only pay the civil penalty for committing an offense, but also examine their own conscience and repent of their sin in order to be reconciled to God, to their fellow inhabitants, and to the pastors and elders of Geneva. The goal of Calvin's conscience-driven instruction was always the restoration of authentic piety in the hearts and lives of the Genevan people. Indeed, it was the reformers' desire to reform and defend the conscience that partially accounts for why the disruption caused by sectarian and lay appeals to conscience—in Strasbourg and in Geneva—gradually polarized the civil and ecclesiastical leaders in these cities, often frustrating their cooperation by pushing them toward their disparate visions for reform.

As much as Calvin and his fellow reformers sought to defend vulnerable consciences, then, they also considered it their divine duty to admonish and correct erring consciences. In theory, the conscience remained a powerful and reliable guide for Christian conduct in every person. But in practice, the reformers had significant doubts and suspicions about the lay consciences under their charge. Believers often acted in bad conscience and with little regard for God's word, for charity, or for the instruction of the Consistory. Although still seeking to protect such erring consciences from burdensome rules and regulations, the reformers insisted that no one could justly appeal to the freedom of conscience in order to thwart the authority of God's word, to violate neighbor-love, or to subvert the divine authority invested in the offices of the church. Thus, when it came to matters concerning the order and purity of the church, the unity of Genevan society, or the conscientious defense of the ministers' own office and authority, Calvin regularly considered these matters to be of greater importance than the supposed freedom of the individual's conscience. The Christian life was indeed a call to spiritual freedom, to be sure, but such freedom required that one's conscience be subject to God and his word, as well as to the ongoing rule of God through the official preaching of the moral law and by various church ordinances regulated by ordained clerics. Thus, Calvin and his Reformed colleagues could both defend and criticize the consciences of their parishioners as they attempted to navigate the difficult relationship between the freedom of conscience, in theory, and the practical necessity to inculcate Christian piety while disciplining frequent cases of impiety in Geneva.

In all of this, even in the tension between his theory and practice, Calvin appears before us as a pastoral theologian—one who learned to accommodate even his own preferences for reform to the complicated and often-messy reality of life in a Christian community. The evidence presented in this study suggests that Calvin and the reformers were, on one hand, guardedly successful at inculcating in people an elevated awareness of the need for a sound conscience—before God and before others. Quite frequently, however, their oath- and conscience-driven methods for reform did not work, despite their best intentions and efforts. Indeed, both in medieval common law and in Reformation-era conflicts surrounding oaths and the conscience, the ideal that oaths and vows were inherently binding and should be strictly upheld was regularly challenged by human dissoluteness or by the necessity to determine the best possible outcome of a complex and compromised moral situation. It was sometimes the case that oaths and confessions of faith—both in their content and in terms of their enforcement by civil and ecclesiastical leaders—needed to be altered or at least mitigated for various reasons: to protect the consciences of oath-takers, who might otherwise be disenfranchised by the literal application of the law; to accommodate complaints that it was burdensome to swear to uphold impossible or obscure standards; or out of the reformers' practical need for the civil authorities to back their reading of Scripture—indeed, to back their consciences—in order for necessary reforms to take place. Thus, the effectiveness of Calvin and his Reformed colleagues often resided in their ability to navigate these ever-fluid circumstances, accommodating their standards to better serve the overarching cause of reforming societies and transforming consciences according to the word of God.

Bibliography

Archival Sources

Archives d'État de Genève, Geneva, Switzerland
Juridictions Pénales A$_2$: "Livre des Criminelz," i.e., sentences du Conseil, 1559–1561
Registres du Conseil
Registres du Consistoire de Genève

Primary Sources

Abelard, Peter. *Ethica seu Liber Dictus Scito te Ipsum*. In J.-P. Migne. ProQuest Information and Learning Company, ProQuest (Firm), and Chadwyck-Healy, Inc. *Patrologia Latina Database*. Vol. 178. 1885. Accessed April 23, 2021. http://pld.chadwyck.com/.

Aquinas, Thomas. *Summa Theologica*. Vols. 2–3. In *Doctoris angelici divi Thomae Aquinatis opera omnia*, edited by Stanislai Eduardi Fretté and Pauli Maré. 34 vols. Paris: Ludovicum Vivés, 1871.

Augustine, Aurelius. *De doctrina christiana libri 4*. In *Corpus Christianorum Series Latina* 32, edited by Joseph Martin. Turnhout: Brepols, 1962.

Bonaventure. *Commentarius in secundum librum sententarium*. 1255. Latin text in S. Bonaventurae. *Opera Omnia*. Vol. 2. ET of q.39 (abridged) by Timothy C. Potts, in *Conscience in Medieval Philosophy*, 110–21. Cambridge: Cambridge University Press, 1980.

Brenz, Johannes. *Ob eine Obrigkeit wenn sie falsche Lehre ausrottet, darum uber die Gewissen herrsche, und ob von der Obrigkeit die Irrigen wider ihr Gewissen tönnen zu anderen Glauben gezwungen werden*. In F. Bidenbach, *Consiliorum Theologorum Decas 3, Consilium 9*, 196–202. Frankfurt, 1611.

Bucer, Martin. *Concerning the True Care of Souls*. ET by Peter Beale. East Peoria, IL: The Banner of Truth Trust, 2009.

Bucer, Martin. *Consilium Theologicum Privatim Conscriptum*. Latin text in BOL 4. 1982.

Bucer, Martin. *De Caena Dominica*. Latin text in BOL 1:1–58. 1982.

Bucer, Martin. *Epistola Apologetica*. Latin text in BOL 1:59–225. 1982.

Bucer, Martin. *Grund und Ursach*. Köpfel, 1525. Retrieved from https://books.google.com.

Calvin, John. *Articles concernant l'organisation de l'église et du culte a Genève*. 1536/7. Latin text in CO 10:1–64; OS 1:369–77.

Calvin, John. *Calvin's Commentaries*. Calvin Translation Society. 23 vols. Edited by Henry Beveridge. Reprint. Grand Rapids, MI: Baker Books, 2009.

Calvin, John. *Calvini Opera Selecta*. Edited by Peter Barth and Wilhelm Niesel. 5 vols. München: Kaiser, 1926–1952.

Calvin, John. *Catechismus, sive christianae religionis institution.* 1538. Latin text in CO 5:313–62. ET by Ford Lewis Battles. *Calvin's First Catechism: A Commentary.* Edited by I. John Hesselink. Louisville, KY: Westminster John Knox Press, 1997.

Calvin, John. *Confession de la foy, laquelle tous bourgeois et habitans de Geneve et subietz du pays doibvent iurer de garder et tenir.* 1537. Latin text in CO 9:693–700.

Calvin, John. *De vitandis superstitionibus, quae cum sincera fidei confessione pugnant, libellus Joannis Calvini. Eiusdem excusatio, ad pseudonicodemos.* Geneva: Jean Girard, 1549. doi: 10.3931/e-rara-2461.

Calvin, John. *Excuse a messieurs les Nicodemites sur la complaincte qu'ilz font de sa trop grand rigueur.* Geneva: Jean Girard, 1544. Latin text in CO 6:589–614. ET by Seth Skolnitsky, in *Come Out from Among Them: "Anti-Nicodemite" Writings of John Calvin*, 99–125. Dallas: Protestant Heritage Press, 2001.

Calvin, John. *Ioannis Calvini Opera Omnia.* Series 4: *Scripta Didactica et Polemica.* Volume 4: *Epistolae Duae (1537), Deux Discours (Oct. 1536).* Edited by Erik Alexander de Boer and Frans Pieter van Stam. Geneva: Droz, 2009.

Calvin, John. *Institutes of the Christian Religion* (1536 edition). Translated by Ford Lewis Battles. Grand Rapids, MI: H. H. Meeter Center for Calvin Studies/Eerdmans, 1986.

Calvin, John. *Institutes of the Christian Religion* (1559). Edited by John T. McNeill. Translated by Ford Lewis Battles. The Library of Christian Classics 20–21, 1960; Louisville, KY: Westminster John Knox Press, 2006.

Calvin, John. *Joannis Calvini Opera Quae Supersunt Omnia.* Edited by G. Baum, E. Cunitz, E. Reuss. 59 vols. Brunswick, 1863–1900.

Calvin, John. *Petit traicté monstrant que c'est que doit faire un homme fidele congnoissant la verité de l'evangile, quand il est entre les papistes.* 1543. Latin text in CO 6:541–78. ET by Seth Skolnitsky, in *Come Out from among Them: "Anti-Nicodemite" Writings of John Calvin*, 47–95. Dallas, TX: Protestant Heritage Press, 2001.

Calvin, John. *Petit traicté, monstrant que doit faire un fidele entre les papistes, avec une epistre du mesme argument. Ensemble l'excuse faicte sur cela aux Nicodemites.* Geneva: Jean Girard, 1545. doi: 10.3931/e-rara-2501.

Calvin, John. *Quatre sermons de M. Iehan Calvin traictans des matières fort utiles pour nostre temps, avec briefve exposition du Pseaume lxxxvii.* Geneva: Robert Estienne, 1552. doi: 10.3931/e-rara-2487. ET by Seth Skolnitsky, in *Come Out from among Them: "Anti-Nicodemite" Writings of John Calvin*, 129–237. Dallas, TX: Protestant Heritage Press, 2001.

Calvin, John. *Response à un certain holandais, lequel sons ombre de faire les chrestiens tout spirituels, leur perment de polluer leurs corps en toutes idolatries.* Latin text in CO 9:585–628. ET by Seth Skolnitsky, in *Come Out from among Them: "Anti-Nicodemite" Writings of John Calvin*, 241–306. Dallas, TX: Protestant Heritage Press, 2001.

Calvin, John. *S'ensuit l'autre Epistre.* 1540. Latin text in CO 6:579–88.

Calvin, John. *Theological Treatises.* Edited by J. K. S. Reid. Library of Christian Classics 22. Philadelphia, PA: Westminster Press, 1954.

Calvin, John. *Tracts and Treatises.* Calvin Translation Society. 3 vols. Edited by Henry Beveridge. 1851; Grand Rapids, MI: Eerdmans, 1958.

Calvin, John. *Treatises against the Anabaptists and against the Libertines.* Translated and edited by Benjamin W. Farley. Grand Rapids, MI: Baker Academic, 1982.

Capito, Wolfgang. *A Brefe Dialoge bitwene a Christen Father and his stobborne Sonne.* Translated by William Roye. Edited by Douglas H. Parker and Bruce Krajewski. Toronto, ON: University of Toronto Press, 1999.

Castellio, Sebastian. *Concerning Heretics: Whether they are to be persecuted and how they are to be treated. A collection of the opinions of learned men both ancient and modern. An anonymous work attributed to Sebastian Castellio.* Translated by Roland H. Bainton. 1935; New York: Octagon Books, 1965.

Castellio, Sebastian. *Conseil à la France désolée*, Geneva: Droz, 1967. Retrieved from https://books.google.com.

Chrysostom, John. *Discourses against Judaizing Christians*. In *Fathers of the Church*, Vol. 68. Translated by Paul W. Harkins. Reprint. Washington, DC: Catholic University of America Press, 1988.

Cochrane, Arthur C. *Reformed Confessions of the Sixteenth Century.* 2nd edition. Louisville, KY: Westminster John Knox, 2003.

Compostellanus antiquus, Bernardus. *Compilatio Romana (1208).* In *Die Dekretalensammlung des Bernardus Compostellanus antiquus*, edited by Heinrich Singer. Vienna: Alfred Holder, 1914. https://web.colby.edu/canonlaw/category/decretal/.

Coornhert, Dirk Volkerts. *Synod on the Freedom of Conscience: A Thorough Examination during the Gathering Held in the Year 1582 in the City of Freetown.* Edited and translated by Gerrit Voogt. Amsterdam: Amsterdam University Press, 2008.

Crottet, Alexandre. *Correspondance française de Calvin avec Louis du Tillet, chanoine d'Angoulême et curé de Claix: Sur les questions de l'église et du ministère évangélique.* Geneve: Cherbuliez, 1850.

Erasmus, Desiderius. *Life and Letters of Erasmus.* Edited by James Anthony Froude. London: Longmans, Green, 1894.

Erasmus, Desiderius. *Paraphrasis in Evangelium Marci.* Köln, 1524. Retrieved from https://daten.digitale-sammlungen.de/bsb00029940/image_1. ET by Erika Rummel, in *Collected Works of Erasmus*, Vol. 49: *Paraphrase on Mark.* Edited by Robert D. Sider. Toronto, ON: University of Toronto Press, 1988.

Erasmus, Desiderius. *Paraphrasis in Evangelium Matthaei.* Nürnberg, 1525. Retrieved from https://daten.digitale-sammlungen.de/bsb00037136/image_1. ET by Dean Simpson, in *Collected Works of Erasmus: Paraphrase on Matthew*, Vol. 45, edited by Robert D. Sider. Toronto, ON: University of Toronto Press, 2008.

Farel, Guillaume. *Epistre exhortatoire à tous ceux qui ont congnoissance de l'Evangile.* Geneva: Jean Girard, 1544. doi: 10.3931/e-rara-35865.

Farel, Guillaume. *Le sommaire de Guillaume Farel: Réimprimé d'après l'édition de l'an 1534 & précédé d'une introduction.* Edited by J. G. Baum. Geneva: Jules-Guillaum Fick, 1867. Retrieved from https://books.google.com.

Franck, Sebastian. *Chronica und Beschreibung der Türkei.* Nürnberg, 1530. Retrieved from https://www.digitale-sammlungen.de/en/view/bsb11071945?page=,1.

Franck, Sebastian. *Letter to John Campanus (1531).* In *Spiritual and Anabaptist Writers*, edited by George H. Williams and Angel M. Mergal, 147–60. Library of Christian Classics 25. Philadelphia, PA: Westminster Press, 1958.

Franck, Sebastian. *Paradoxa ducenta octoginta.* Ulm, 1534. Retrieved from https://daten.digitale-sammlungen.de/bsb00020890/image_1.

Herminjard, A. L. ed. *Correspondance des réformateurs dans les pays de langue française.* 9 vols. Geneva/Paris: 1866–1897.

Ivo of Chartres, *Decretum* (Prologue). ET in Eugene R. Fairweather, ed. *A Scholastic Miscellany: Anselm to Ockham*, 238–42. Library of Christian Classics 10. Reprint. Louisville, KY: Westminster John Knox Press, 2006.

Kingdon, Robert M., and Jean-François Bergier, eds. *Registres de la Compagnie des Pasteurs au Temps de Calvin*. 2 vols. Geneva, 1962–1964. ET by Philip C. Hughes. *The Register of the Company of Pastors of Geneva in the Time of Calvin*. Grand Rapids, MI: Eerdmans, 1966.

Krebs, Manfred and Hans Georg Rott, eds. *Quellen zur Geschichte der Täufer. Elsaß* I–II. Teil: Stadt Straßburg, 1522–1535. Vols. 7–8. Heidelberg: Gütersloher Verlagshaus Gerd Mohn, 1959–1960.

Luther, Martin. *In Epistolam Pauli ad Galatas M. Lutheri Commentarius*. 1519. Latin text in *Martin Luthers Werke: Kritische Gesamtausgabe*, 2:436–618. Weimar: H. Boehlaus Nachfolger, 1883–.

Luther, Martin. *Invocavit Sermons*. 1522. ET in *Luther's Works* ("American Edition"). Vol. 51. *Sermons I*. Edited by Jaroslav Pelikan, Helmut T. Lehmann, and John W. Doberstein, 70–100. 5 vols. St. Louis, MO: Concordia; Philadelphia, PA: Fortress Press, 1955–1986.

Luther, Martin. *Ein Sermon von dem Sakrament der Buße*. 1519. German text in WA 2:709–23.

Luther, Martin. *Ermahnung zum Frieden auf die zwölf Artikel der Bauerschaft in Schwaben* (1525). German text in WA 18:279–334.

Luther, Martin. *On Secular Authority: To What Extent It Should Be Obeyed*. 1523. German text in WA 11:229–80. ET in *The Annotated Luther*, Vol. 5: *Christian Life in the World*, edited by Hans J. Hillerbrand, 79–130. Minneapolis, MN: Fortress Press, 2016.

Luther, Martin. *The Freedom of a Christian*. 1520. Latin text in WA 7:49–73. ET in *The Annotated Luther Study Edition*, Vol 1: *The Roots of Reform*, edited by Timothy J. Wengert, 467–538. Minneapolis, MN: Fortress Press, 2016.

Luther, Martin. *Widder die stürmenden bawren*. 1525. German text in WA 18:357–61.

Niemeyer, H. A. *Collectio confessionum in ecclesiis reformatis publicatarum*. Lipsiae: Klinkhardt, 1840.

Pegis, Anton C. ed. *Basic Writings of Saint Thomas Aquinas*. 2 vols. New York: Random House, 1945.

Piaget, Arthur. *Les actes de la Dispute de Lausanne 1536* (Mémoires de l'université de Neuchâtel, 6). Neuchâtel, 1928.

Schaff, Philip. *Creeds of Christendom*, Vol. 3: *The Evangelical Protestant Creeds*. Grand Rapids, MI: Baker Book House, 1977.

Schwenckfeld, Caspar. *Corpus Schwenckfeldianorum*. 19 vols. Edited by Chester David Hartranft. Leipzig: Breitkopf & Härtel, 1913.

Schwenckfeld, Caspar. *De Cursu Verbi Dei*. Basel: Thomas Wolff, 1527. Retrieved from https://books.google.com.

Scott, Samuel Parsons, ed. *The Civil Law*. 17 vols. Cincinnati, OH: Central Trust, 1931.

Vermigli, Peter Martyr. *A treatise of the cohabitacyon of the faithfull with the unfaithfull*. Strasbourg: W. Rihel, 1555. Retrieved from http://hdl.handle.net/20.500.12024/A14354.

Vermigli, Peter Martyr. *Epistre de M. Pierre Martyr Florentin a Quelques Fideles touchant leur abiuration et renoncement de la verité*. Geneva, 1574. doi: 10.3931/e-rara-12726.

Virck, Hans, ed. *Politische Correspondenz der Stadt Strassburg im Zeitalter der Reformation*, Vol. 1: *1517–1530*. Urkunden und Akten der Stadt Strassburg, 2. Abt. Strasbourg, 1882.

Viret, Pierre. *Admonition et consolation aux fideles qui deliberant de sortir d'entre les papistes, pour eviter idolatrie, contre les tentations qui leur peuvent advenir et les dangiers ausquelz ils peuvent tomber en leur yssue*. Geneva: Jean Girard, 1547. Retrieved from https://www.digitale-sammlungen.de/en/view/bsb10173496?page=,1.

Viret, Pierre. *Epistre envoyee aux fideles conversans entre les Chrestiés Papistiques, pour leur remonstrer comment ilz se doyvent garder d'estre souillez et polluz par leurs superstitions et idolatries, et de deshonorer Iesus Christ par icelles.* 1543. Retrieved from https://books.google.com.

Viret, Pierre. *Epistres aus fideles pour les instruire et les admonester eet exhorter touchant leur office, et pour les consoler en leurs tribulations.* Geneva: Jean Rivery, 1559. doi: 10.3931/e-rara-6053.

Viret, Pierre. *Remonstrances aux fideles qui conversent entre les papistes: Et principalement à ceux qui sont en court, et qui ont offices publiques, touchant les moyens qu'ilz doivent tenir en leur vocation, à l'exemple des anciens serviteurs de Dieu, sans contrevenir à leur devoir, ny envers Dieu, ny envers leur prochain:et sans se mettre temerairement en dangier, et donner par leur temerité et par leur coulpe, juste occasion à leurs adversaires de les mal traitter.* Geneva: Jean Girard, 1547. doi: 10.3931/e-rara-5938.

Watt, Isabella M., Thomas A. Lambert (vols. 1–5), Jeffrey R. Watt (vols. 6–14), and M. Wallace McDonald (vols. 2, 9), eds. *Registres du Consistoire de Genève au temps de Calvin, 1542–1557.* With the collaboration of Jeffrey R. Watt (vol. 1), M. Wallace McDonald (vols. 3–8), and James S. Coons (vol. 9). Under the supervision of Robert M. Kingdon (vols. 1–6) and Lee Palmer Wandel (vols. 8–9). 14 vols. Geneva: Droz, 1996–2020.

Secondary Sources

Abray, Lorna Jane. *The People's Reformation: Magistrates, Clergy, and Commons in Strasbourg, 1500–1598.* Ithaca, NY: Cornell University Press, 1985.

Agamben, Giorgio. *The Sacrament of Language: An Archeology of the Oath.* Translated by Adam Kotsko. Stanford, CA: Stanford University Press, 2011.

Althaus, Paul. *The Theology of Martin Luther.* Philadelphia, PA: Fortress Press, 1970.

Andrew, Edward G. *Conscience and Its Critics: Protestant Conscience, Enlightenment Reason, and Modern Subjectivity.* Toronto, ON: University of Toronto Press, 2001.

Ballor, Jordan J. "Discipline, Excommunication, and the Limits of Conscience: Magisterial Protestant Perspectives on Church and Civil Authority in the Era of the Reformation." In *Das Gewissen in den Rechtslehren der protestantischen und katholischen Reformationen*, edited by Michael Germann and Wim Decock, 111–25. Leipzig: Evangelische Verlagsanstalt, 2017.

Balke, Willem. *Calvin and the Anabaptist Radicals.* Translated by William J. Heynen. Grand Rapids, MI: Eerdmans, 1981.

Baylor, Michael G. *Action and Person: Conscience in Late Scholasticism and the Young Luther.* Leiden: Brill, 1977.

Benedict, Philip. *Christ's Churches Purely Reformed: A Social History of Calvinism.* New Haven, CT, and London: Yale University Press, 2002.

Benedict, Philip. "*Un roi, une loi, deux fois*: Parameters for the history of Catholic-Reformed co-existence in France, 1555–1685." In *Tolerance and Intolerance in the European Reformation*, edited by Ole Peter Grell and Bob Scribner, 65–93. Cambridge: Cambridge University Press, 1996.

Bernaud, Jean. *Pierre Viret: Sa vie et son oeuvre, 1511–1571.* Saint-Amans: G. Carayol, 1911.

Biéler, André. *Calvin's Economic and Social Thought*. Edited by Edward Dommen. Translated by James Greig. Geneva: World Alliance of Reformed Churches/World Council of Churches, 2005.

Bietenholz, Peter G. *Encounters with a Radical Erasmus: Erasmus' Work as a Source of Radical Thought in Early Modern Europe*. Toronto, ON: University of Toronto Press, 2009.

Bohatec, Josef. *Budé und Calvin*. Graz: Herman Böhlaus, 1950.

Bohatec, Josef. *Calvins Lehre von Staat und Kirche*. Breslau, 1937.

Bohatec, Josef. *Calvin und das Recht*. Aalen: Scientia Verlag, 1991.

Borgeaud, Charles. *Histoire de l'Université de Genève: L'Académie de Calvin, 1559–1789*. Genève, 1900.

Bowen, David Anderson. "John Calvin's Ecclesiological Adiaphorism: Distinguishing the 'Indifferent,' the 'Essential,' and the 'Important,' in His Thought and Practice, 1547–1559." PhD dissertation, Vanderbilt University, 1985, accessed December 12, 2016. ProQuest Dissertations & Theses.

Bradley, James E., and Richard A. Muller. *Church History: An Introduction to Research Methods and Resources*. 1995; Grand Rapids, MI: Eerdmans, 2016.

Brady, Thomas A., Jr. *Ruling Class, Regime and Reformation at Strasbourg, 1520–1555*. Leiden: Brill, 1978.

Breen, Quirinus. *John Calvin: A Study in French Humanism*. Hamden: Archon Books, 1968.

Bruening, Michael W. "Calvin, Farel, Roussel, and the French 'Nicodemites.'" In *Calvin and the Early Reformation*, edited by Brian C. Brewer and David M. Whitford, 113–24. Leiden: Brill, 2020.

Bruening, Michael W. *Calvinism's First Battleground: Conflict and Reform in the Pays de Vaud, 1528–1559*. Studies in Early Modern Religious Reforms. Dordrecht: Springer, 2010.

Bruening, Michael W. *Refusing to Kiss the Slipper: Opposition to Calvinism in the Francophone Reformation*. Oxford: Oxford University Press, 2021.

Bruening, Michael W. "Un nouvel eclairage sur L'academie de Lausanne, a partir de la correspondence inedite de Pierre Viret." In *La naissance des Académies Protestantes (Lausanne, 1537–Strasbourg, 1538) et la diffusion du modèle*, edited by Monique Vénaut and Ruxandra Vulcan, 37–47. Clermont-Ferrand: Presses Universitaires Blaise Pascal, 2017.

Brundage, James A. *Medieval Canon Law*. Reprint. New York: Routledge, 2013.

Burnett, Amy. "Church Discipline and Moral Reformation in the Thought of Martin Bucer." *Sixteenth Century Journal* 22, no. 3 (1991): 438–56.

Carpi-Mailly, Olivia. "Jean Calvin et Louis du Tillet: Entre foi et amitié, un échange révélateur." In *Calvin et ses contemporains: Actes du Colloque de Paris 1995*, edited by Olivier Millet, 7–19. Geneva: Libraire Droz, 1998.

Cellérier, J. E. *L'Académie de Genève: Esquisse d'une histoire abregée de l'Académie fondée par Calvin en 1559*. Geneva: A. Cherbuliez, 1872.

Chrisman, Miriam Usher. *Strasbourg and the Reform: A Study in the Process of Change*. New Haven, CT: Yale University Press, 1967.

Clark, R. Scott, and Carl R. Trueman, eds. *Protestant Scholasticism: Essays in Reassessment*. Carlisle, UK: Paternoster, 1999.

Corran, Emily. *Lying and Perjury in Medieval Practical Thought: A Study in the History of Casuistry*. Oxford: Oxford University Press, 2018.

Courvoisier, Jaques. "Farel and Geneva." *McCormick Quarterly* 21, no. 1 (November 1967): 123–35.
Crousaz, Karine. *L'Académie de Lausanne entre humanisme et réforme (ca. 1537–1560)*. Leiden: Brill, 2012.
De Kroon, Marijn. "Martin Bucer and the Problem of Tolerance." *Sixteenth Century Journal* 19, no. 2 (1988): 157–68.
De Raemond, Florimond. *Histoire de la naissance, progress et décadence de l'héresie de ce siècle*. Paris, 1605.
Diop, Ganoune. "The Sixteenth Century Reformation's Context and Content: Highlighting the Pivotal Role of Freedom of Conscience." *Scientia Moralitas: International Journal of Multidisciplinary Research* 2, no. 1 (2017): 1–16.
Dougherty, M. V. *Moral Dilemmas in Medieval Thought: From Gratian to Aquinas*. Cambridge: Cambridge University Press, 2011.
Eells, Hastings. *Martin Bucer*. New Haven, CT: Yale University Press, 1931.
Eire, Carlos M. N. "Pierre Viret and Nicodemism." In *Pierre Viret (1511–1571) et la diffusion de la Réforme: Pensée, action, contextes religieux*, edited by Karine Crousaz and Daniela Solfaroli Camillocci, 59–75. Lausanne: Antipodes, 2014.
Eire, Carlos M. N. *War against the Idols: The Reformation of Worship from Erasmus to Calvin*. New York: Cambridge University Press, 1986.
Fossier, Robert. *The Axe and the Oath: Ordinary Life in the Middle Ages*. Princeton, NJ: Princeton University Press, 2010.
Ganoczy, Alexandre. *The Young Calvin*. Translated by David Foxgrover and Wade Provo. Philadelphia, PA: Westminster Press, 1987.
George, Timothy. "Helvetic Confessions." In *Oxford Encyclopedia of the Reformation*, edited by Hans Hillerbrand, 2:219–22. New York: Oxford University Press, 1996.
Gordon, Bruce. *Calvin*. New Haven, CT: Yale University Press, 2009.
Gray, Jonathan Michael. *Oaths and the English Reformation*. Cambridge: Cambridge University Press, 2013.
Gregory, Brad. "Reforming the Reformation: God's Truth and the Exercise of Power." In *Reforming Reformation*, edited by Thomas F. Mayer, 17–42. 2012; New York: Routledge, 2016.
Grell, Ole Peter. "Introduction." In *Tolerance and Intolerance in the European Reformation*, edited by Ole Peter Grell and Bob Scribner, 1–12. Cambridge: Cambridge University Press, 1996.
Hemholz, Richard H. "'Conscience' and the English Courts between 1500 and 1800." In *Das Gewissen in den Rechtslehren der protestantischen und katholischen Reformationen*, edited by Michael Germann and Wim Decock, 200–211. Leipzig: Evangelische Verlagsanstalt, 2017.
Hemholz, Richard H. *The Spirit of Classical Canon Law*. Athens: University of Georgia Press, 2010.
Heron, Alisdair. "Calvin and the Confessions of the Reformation: Original Research." *Hervormde Teologiese Studies* 70, no. 1 (2014): 1–5.
Jenkins, Gary. W. *Calvin's Tormentors: Understanding the Conflicts That Shaped the Reformer*. Grand Rapids, MI: Baker Academic, 2018.
Kingdon, Robert M. *Adultery and Divorce in Calvin's Geneva*. Cambridge, MA: Harvard University Press, 1995.
Kingdon, Robert M. "Calvin and the Family: The Work of the Consistory of Geneva." *Pacific Theological Review* 17 (1984): 5–18.

Kingdon, Robert M. "Confessionalism in Calvin's Geneva." *Archiv für Reformationsgeschichte* 96 (2005): 109–16.

Kingdon, Robert M. *Geneva and the Coming of the Wars of Religion in France, 1555–1563.* Geneva: Librarie Droz, 1956.

Kingdon, Robert M. "The Control of Morals in Calvin's Geneva." In *The Social History of the Reformation*, edited by Lawrence P. Buck and Jonathan W. Zophy, 3–16. Columbus: Ohio State University Press, 1972.

Kingdon, Robert M. "The Geneva Consistory in the Time of Calvin." In *Calvinism in Europe, 1540–1620*, edited by Andrew Pettegree, Alastair Duke, and Gillian Lewis, 21–34. Cambridge: Cambridge University Press, 1994.

Kittelson, James. "Tetrapolitan Confession." In *Oxford Encyclopedia of the Reformation*, edited by Hans Hillerbrand, 4:148–49. New York: Oxford University Press, 1996.

Kittelson, James. *Toward an Established Church: Strasbourg from 1500 to the Dawn of the Seventeenth Century.* Mainz: Philipp Von Zabern, 2000.

Kloosterman, Nelson Deyo. *Scandalum Infirmorum et Communio Sanctorum: The Relation between Christian Liberty and Neighbor Love in the Church.* Neerlandia, AB: Inheritance Publications, 1991.

Langston, Douglas C. *Conscience and Other Virtues: From Bonaventure to MacIntyre.* University Park: Pennsylvania State University Press, 2001.

Lecler, Joseph A. *Toleration and the Reformation.* 2 vols. Translated by T. L. Westow. New York: Association Press, 1960.

Levy, Ian Christopher. "Liberty of Conscience and Freedom of Religion in the Medieval Canonists and Theologians." In *Christianity and Freedom*, Vol. 1: *Historical Perspectives*, edited by Timothy Samuel Shah and Allen D. Hertzke, 149–75. Cambridge: Cambridge University Press, 2016.

Lewis, Gillian. "The Geneva Academy." In *Calvinism in Europe, 1540–1620*, edited by Andrew Pettegree, Alastair Duke, and Gillian Lewis, 35–63. Cambridge: Cambridge University Press, 1994.

Loewen, Harry. *Luther and the Radicals.* Waterloo, ON: Wilfrid Laurier University Press, 1974.

Lugioyo, Brian. *Martin Bucer's Doctrine of Justification: Reformation Theology and Early Modern Irenicism.* Oxford: Oxford University Press, 2010.

Luria, Keith P. *Sacred Boundaries: Religious Coexistence and Conflict in Early-Modern France.* Washington, DC: Catholic University of America Press, 2005.

Maag, Karin. *Seminary or University? The Genevan Academy and Reformed Higher Education, 1560–1620.* St. Andrews Studies in Reformation History. Aldershot, UK: Scolar Press, 1995.

Manetsch, Scott M. *Calvin's Company of Pastors: Pastoral Care and the Emerging Reformed Church, 1536–1609.* Oxford: Oxford University Press, 2013.

Manetsch, Scott M. "Ministers Misbehaving: The Discipline of Pastors in Calvinist Geneva, 1559–1596." In *Agir pour l'église: Ministères et charges ecclésiastiques dans les églises réformées*, edited by Didier Poton and Raymond Mentzer, 31–42. Paris: Indes Savantes, 2014.

Matheson, Peter. "Martin Bucer and the Old Church." In *Martin Bucer: Reforming Church and Community*, edited by David F. Wright, 5–44. Cambridge: Cambridge University Press, 1994.

McLaughlin, Emmet. "Spiritualism: Schwenckfeld and Franck and the Early Modern Resonances." In *A Companion to Anabaptism and Spiritualism, 1521–1700*, edited by John D. Roth and James M. Stayer, 119–62. Leiden: Brill, 2007.

Ménager, Daniel. "Erasmus, the Intellectuals, and the Reuchlin Affair." In *Biblical Humanism and Scholasticism in the Age of Erasmus*, edited by Erika Rummel, 39–54. Leiden: Brill, 2008.

Meylan, Henri. *La haute école de Lausanne, 1537–1937*. Lausanne: Université de Lausanne, 1986.

Muller, Richard A. "Biblical Interpretation in the Era of the Reformation: The View from the Middle Ages." In *Biblical Interpretation in the Era of the Reformation*, edited by Richard A. Muller and John L. Thompson, 3–22. Grand Rapids, MI: Eerdmans, 1996.

Muller, Richard A. *The Unaccommodated Calvin: Studies in the Foundation of a Theological Tradition*. Oxford: Oxford University Press, 2000.

Murray, Alexander. *Conscience and Authority in the Medieval Church*. Oxford: Oxford University Press, 2015.

Naphy, William G. *Calvin and the Consolidation of the Genevan Reformation*. Reprint. Louisville, KY: Westminster John Knox Press, 2003.

Nijenhuis, Willem. *Ecclesia Reformata: Studies on the Reformation*. Leiden: Brill, 1972.

Oberman, Heiko. *The Dawn of the Reformation: Essays in Late Medieval and Early Reformation Thought*. Edinburgh: T&T Clark, 1986.

Oberman, Heiko. *The Harvest of Medieval Theology: Gabriel Biel and Late Medieval Nominalism*. Durham, NC: Labyrinth Press, 1983.

Oberman, Heiko. "The Travail of Tolerance: Containing Chaos in Early Modern Europe." In *Tolerance and Intolerance in the European Reformation*, edited by Ole Peter Grell and Bob Scribner, 13–31. Cambridge: Cambridge University Press, 1996.

Olson, Roger. *The Story of Christian Theology: Twenty Centuries of Tradition and Reform*. Downers Grove, IL: Intervarsity Press, 1999.

Overell, M. Anne. *Nicodemites: Faith and Concealment between Italy and Tudor England*. Leiden: Brill, 2019.

Oyer, John S. *Lutheran Reformers against Anabaptists: Luther, Melanchthon and Menius and the Anabaptists of Central Germany*. The Hague, Netherlands: Martinus Nijhoff, 1964.

Ozment, Steven. *The Reformation in the Cities: The Appeal of Protestantism to Sixteenth-Century Germany and Switzerland*. New Haven, CT: Yale University Press, 1975.

Parker, T. H. L. *John Calvin: A Biography*. Louisville, KY: Westminster John Knox Press, 2007.

Peachey, Paul P. "The Radical Reformation, Political Pluralism, and the Corpus Christianorum." In *The Origins and Characteristics of Anabaptism: Proceedings of the Colloquium Organized by the Faculty of Protestant Theology of Strassburg*, edited by Marc Lienhard, 10–26. The Hague, Netherlands: Martinus Nijhoff, 1977.

Pont, A. D. "Confession of Faith in Calvin's Geneva." In *Calvin: Erbe und Auftrag: Festschrift für Wilhelm Neuser zu seinem 65. Geburtstag*, edited by Willem van't Spijker, 106–16. Kampen: Kok Pharòs, 1991.

Potts, Timothy C. *Conscience in Medieval Philosophy*. Cambridge: Cambridge University Press, 1980.

Preus, James Samuel. *From Shadow to Promise: Old Testament Interpretation from Augustine to the Young Luther*. Cambridge, MA: Belknap Press, 1969.

Pries, Edmund. "Anabaptist Oath Refusal: Basel, Bern and Strasbourg, 1525–1538." PhD dissertation, University of Waterloo, 1995, accessed February 23, 2018. ProQuest Dissertations & Theses.

Prodi, Paolo. *Il sacramento del potere: Il giuramento politico nella storia constituzionale dell'Occidente*. Bologna: Società editrice il Mulino, 1992.

Reid, Jonathan A. "The Meaux Group and John Calvin." In *Calvin and the Early Reformation*, edited by Brian C. Brewer and David M. Whitford, 58–95. Leiden: Brill, 2019.

Remer, Gary. *Humanism and the Rhetoric of Toleration*. University Park: Pennsylvania State University Press, 1996.

Roget, Amédée. *Histoire du Peuple de Genève*. 7 vols. Geneva: 1870–1887.

Ross, Richard J. "Binding in Conscience: Early Modern English Protestants and Spanish Thomists on Law and the Fate of the Soul." *Law and History Review* 33, no. 4 (November 2015): 803–37.

Rummel, Erika. *The Confessionalization of Humanism in Reformation Germany*. Oxford: Oxford University Press, 2000.

Scheussler, Rudolf. "Conscience, Renaissance Understanding of." In *Encyclopedia of Renaissance Philosophy*, edited by Marco Sgarbi, 1–7. New York: Springer, 2018, https://doi.org/10.1007/978-3-319-02848-4_602-1. Accessed April 15, 2021.

Schilling, Heinz. "Confessional Europe." In *Handbook of European History, 1400–1600: Late Middle Ages, Renaissance, and Reformation*, Vol. 2, edited by Thomas A. Brady, Jr., Heiko A. Oberman, and James D. Tracy, 641–81. Grand Rapids, MI: Eerdmans, 1995.

Scribner, Bob. "Preconditions of Tolerance and Intolerance in Sixteenth-Century Germany." In *Tolerance and Intolerance in the European Reformation*, edited by Ole Peter Grell and Bob Scribner, 32–47. Cambridge: Cambridge University Press, 1996.

Selderhuis, Herman J. "Calvin's Views on Conscience and Law." In *Das Gewissen in den Rechtslehren der protestantischen und katholischen Reformationen*, edited by Michael Germann and Wim Decock, 33–50. Leipzig: Evangelische Verlagsanstalt, 2017.

Shogimen, Takashi. *Ockham and Political Discourse in the Late Middle Ages*. Cambridge: Cambridge University Press, 2007.

Speelman, Herman A. *Calvin and the Independence of the Church*. Göttingen: Vandenhoeck & Ruprecht, 2014.

Spierling, Karen. "'Il faut éviter le scandale': Debating Community Standards in Reformation Geneva." *Reformation & Renaissance Review* 20, no. 1 (2018): 51–69.

Spierling, Karen. *Infant Baptism in Reformation Geneva: The Shaping of a Community, 1536–1564*. Louisville, KY: Westminster John Knox Press, 2005.

Steinmetz, David C. *Calvin in Context*. Reprint. New York: Oxford University Press, 2010.

Strauss, Gerald. *Manifestations of Discontent in Germany on the Eve of the Reformation*. Bloomington: Indiana University Press, 1971.

Strauss, Gerald. "Success and Failure in the German Reformation." *Past & Present* 67 (1975): 30–63.

Tavard, AA, George H. "Calvin and the Nicodemites." In *John Calvin and Roman Catholicism: Critique and Engagement, Then and Now*, edited by Randall C. Zachman, 59–78. Grand Rapids, MI: Baker Academic, 2008.

Thévenaz, Louis J. "L'Ancien Collège de sa fondation à la fin du XVIIIe siècle, précédée d'une introduction sur l'instruction publique à Genève au Moyen-Age." In *Histoire du Collège de Genève*, edited by Thévenaz, et al., 1–221. Geneva, 1896.

Thompson, John L. "Calvin's Exegetical Legacy: His Reception and Transmission of Text and Tradition." In *The Legacy of John Calvin*, edited by David Foxgrover, 31–56. Calvin Studies Society Papers, 1999. Grand Rapids, MI: Calvin Studies Society, 2000.

Thompson, John L. "Confessions, Conscience, and Coercion in the Early Calvin." In *Calvin and the Early Reformation*, edited by Brian C. Brewer and David M. Whitford, 155–79. Leiden: Brill, 2019.

Thompson, John L. *John Calvin and the Daughters of Sarah: Women in Regular and Exceptional Roles in the Exegesis of Calvin, His Predecessors, and His Contemporaries*. Geneva: Libraire Droz, 1992.

Thompson, John L. "Reforming the Conscience: Magisterial Reformers on the Theory and Practice of Conscience." In *Christianity and the Laws of Conscience: An Introduction*, edited by Jeffrey B. Hammond and Helen M. Alvaré, 132–51. Cambridge: Cambridge University Press, 2021.

Thompson, John L. "Second Thoughts about Conscience: Nature, the Law, and the Law of Nature in Calvin's Pentateuchal Exegesis." In *Calvinus Pastor Ecclesiae*, edited by Herman J. Selderhuis and Arnold Huijgen, 123–47. Göttingen: Vandenhoeck & Ruprecht, 2016.

Thompson, John L. *Writing the Wrongs: Women of the Old Testament among Biblical Commentators from Philo through the Reformation*. Oxford: Oxford University Press, 2001.

Tierney, Brian. *Liberty and Law: The Idea of Permissive Natural Law, 1100–1800*. Washington, DC: Catholic University of America Press, 2014.

Tuininga, Matthew J. *Calvin's Political Theology and the Public Engagement of the Church: Christ's Two Kingdoms*. Cambridge: Cambridge University Press, 2017.

Tutino, Stefania. *Shadows of Doubt: Language and Truth in Post-Reformation Catholic Culture*. Oxford: Oxford University Press, 2014.

Tyler, James Endell. *Oaths: Their Origin, Nature, and History*. London: John W. Parker, 1834.

Uhalde, Kevin. *Expectations of Justice in the Age of Augustine*. Philadelphia: University of Pennsylvania Press, 2007.

Valeri, Mark. "Religion, Discipline, and the Economy in Calvin's Geneva." *Sixteenth Century Journal* 28, no. 1 (Spring 1997): 123–42.

Van Asselt, Willem J., and Eef Dekker, eds. *Reformation and Scholasticism: An Ecumenical Enterprise*. Grand Rapids, MI: Baker Academic, 2001.

Van den Brink, Gijsbert. "Calvin and the Early Christian Doctrine of the Trinity." In *Restoration through Redemption: John Calvin Revisited*, edited by Henk van den Belt, 15–30. Leiden: Brill, 2013.

Van Stam, Frans Pieter. "The Group of Meaux as First Target of Farel and Calvin's Anti-Nicodemism." *Bibliotheque d'Humanisme et Renaissance* 68, no. 2 (2006): 253–75.

Van Veen, Mirjam. "Dirck Volckertz Coornhert: Exile and Religious Coexistence." In *Exile and Religious Identity, 1500–1800*, edited by Jesse Spohnholz and Gary K. Waite, 67–80. 2014; New York: Routledge, 2018.

Verkamp, Bernard J. "The Limits Upon Adiaphoristic Freedom: Luther and Melanchthon." *Journal of Theological Studies* 36, no. 1 (1975): 52–76.

Voogt, Gerrit. *Constraint on Trial: Dirck Volckertsz Coornhert and Religious Freedom*. Sixteenth Century Essays and Studies, Vol. 52. Kirksville, MO: Truman State University Press, 2000.

Watt, Jeffrey R. "Reconciliation and the Confession of Sins: The Evidence from the Consistory in Calvin's Geneva." In *Calvin and Luther: The Continuing Relationship*, edited by R. Ward Holder, 105–20. Göttingen: Vandehoeck & Ruprecht, 2013.

Watt, Jeffrey R. "Settling Quarrels and Nurturing Repentance: The Consistory in Calvin's Geneva." In *Revisiting Geneva: Robert Kingdon and the Coming of the French Wars of Religion*, edited by S. K. Barker, 71–84. St. Andrews: The Centre for French History and Culture of the University of St. Andrews, 2012.

Watt, Jeffrey R. *The Consistory and Social Discipline in Calvin's Geneva*. Rochester, NY: University of Rochester Press, 2020.

Wendel, François. *Calvin: Origins and Development of His Religious Thought*. Translated by Philip Mairet. Reprint. Grand Rapids, MI: Baker, 1997.

Wendel, François. *L'Église de Strasbourg: Sa constitution et son organisation, 1532–1535*. Paris: Presses Universitaires de France, 1942.

White, Robert. "An Early Doctrinal Handbook: Farel's *Summaire et briefve declaration*." *Westminster Theological Journal* 69, no. 1 (2007): 21–38.

Wickersham, Jane K. *Rituals of Prosecution: The Roman Inquisition and the Prosecution of Philo-Protestants in Sixteenth-Century Italy*. Toronto, ON: University of Toronto Press, 2012.

Williams, George Huntston. *The Radical Reformation*. Kirksville, MO: Truman State University Press, 1992.

Witte, John, Jr. "Calvinist Contributions to Freedom in Early Modern Europe." In *Christianity and Freedom*, Vol 1: *Historical Perspectives*, edited by Timothy Samuel Shah and Allen D. Hertzke, 210–34. Cambridge: Cambridge University Press, 2016.

Witte, John, Jr. *Law and Protestantism: The Legal Teachings of the Protestant Reformation*. Cambridge: Cambridge University Press, 2002.

Witte, John, Jr. *The Reformation of Rights: Law, Religion, and Human Rights in Early Modern Calvinism*. Cambridge: Cambridge University Press, 2007.

Witte, John, Jr., and Robert M. Kingdon, eds. *Sex, Marriage, and the Family in John Calvin's Geneva*, Vol. 1: *Courtship, Engagement, and Marriage*. Grand Rapids, MI: Eerdmans, 2005.

Woo, Kenneth J. *Nicodemism and the English Calvin, 1544–1584*. Leiden: Brill, 2019.

Worthen, Molly. "Who Would Jesus Smack Down?" *New York Times Magazine*, January 6, 2009. https://www.nytimes.com/2009/01/11/magazine/11punk-t.html.

Wright, David F. "Why Was Calvin So Severe a Critic of Nicodemism?" In *Calvinus Evangelii Propugnator: Calvin Champion of the Gospel; Papers Presented at the International Congress on Calvin Research, Seoul, 1998*, edited by Wright, A.N.S. Lane, and Jon Balserak, 66–90. Grand Rapids, MI: CRC, 2006.

Wright, William J. *Martin Luther's Understanding of God's Two Kingdoms: A Response to the Challenge of Skepticism*. Grand Rapids, MI: Baker Academic, 2010.

Zuidema, Jason, and Theodore Van Raalte, eds. *Early French Reform: The Theology and Spirituality of Guillaume Farel*. London: Routledge, 2016.

Index

For the benefit of digital users, indexed terms that span two pages (e.g., 52–53) may, on occasion, appear on only one of those pages.

Abelard, Peter, 30–31, 33, 67n.64
adiaphora (indifferent things), 7–8, 29–30, 31–32, 34–35, 38–39, 44–46, 73–74, 75, 79, 82–83, 90–91, 99–102, 107, 119–21, 122–24, 125–28, 133, 134–35, 142–44, 153–54, 155–56, 160, 161–62, 233–35
Affaire de placards (1534), 80
Agamben, Giorgio, 5–6
Albert the Great, 30–31
Alexander of Hales, 29–30
All Saints' Day, 85–86
Anabaptists, 4–5, 11, 37–38, 49–50, 54–57, 61–62, 64–65, 66, 68–69, 70, 73, 100, 125–26, 133, 143–44, 151, 152–53, 154, 207, 225–26, 234–35
Apostles' Creed, 131
Aquinas, Thomas, 28, 30–35, 42n.81
  Summa Theologica, 30–32, 34–35
Athanasian Creed, 143–44
Augsburg Confession, 143–44, 146–47
Augsburg, Diet of, 146–47. *See also* Augsburg Confession
Augustine, Saint, 4n.10, 18–19, 28, 29–30, 67n.64, 147–48, 147n.31

Balaam, 109, 110
Balak, King. *See* Balaam
Basel (Switzerland), 123–24, 139, 151
  First Helvetic Confession (1536), 144, 154–56, 157
Bern (Switzerland), 174–75, 210
  Theses Bernenses (1528), 145–46, 152
Bernard of Compostella (the elder), 18n.7, 32
Berthelier, Philibert, 196–97, 197n.96, 199. *See also* Geneva: Children of Geneva

Bertram, Bonaventure, 220–21
Beza, Theodore, 204, 209–10, 211–13, 214, 216, 220–22
Biel, Gabriel, 39–40
Bieler, Andre, 6
Bodley, Thomas, 208–9
Bohatec, Josef, 6
Bonaventure, Saint, 29–30
Borgeaud, Charles, 208–9
Brenz, Johannes, 66–68
Bruening, Michael W., 3n.8, 77, 83, 89–90, 202–3
Bucer, Martin, 42n.81, 53, 57–60, 61–62, 64–65, 66–68, 70, 73, 74–75, 84, 86–87, 90–91, 92–93, 94–96, 97–102, 99n.94, 145–47, 154, 166, 234–35
  Articles of Faith (1533), 59–60, 68–69
  Grund und Ursach (1524), 95–96
  One Should Not Live for Oneself Alone but for Others, and How to Go About It (1523), 66
  Tetrapolitan Confession (1530), 68–69, 144, 145–52, 157, 159, 160
Bullinger, Heinrich, 62, 64–65, 154, 210

Calvin, John, 1–2, 3–7, 9–10, 11–12, 15–16, 27, 42n.81, 44, 46, 73–74, 84, 95–97, 98–101, 102–3, 130–31, 135, 139–44, 151, 157–58, 159–65, 166–71, 172–73, 175–76, 177–78, 180–81, 183–86, 187–88, 189–90, 194, 196–97, 198–201, 202–3, 204–7, 208–9, 210, 211–13, 216, 220–22, 225–27
and his anti-Nicodemite colleagues, 74–75, 88–90, 104–8, 131–32, 133, 134–35

Calvin, John (*cont.*)
  and his anti-Nicodemite polemic, 75–79, 76n.4, 89–90, 97, 108–12, 113–15, 117n.44, 121, 123–28
  Catechism (1538), 139–40, 141–42, 160–61
  ecclesiology of, 9–10, 76–77, 83–84, 89–90, 228–35
  Epistolae duae, 80–81, 83, 88–91, 104–5, 108–9
  Excuse à messieurs les Nicodemites (1544), 113–14, 116–18
  exegesis of, 8–9, 15–16, 15n.2
  and Gérard Roussel, 80–84, 85–87, 88–89
  Institutes of the Christian Religion (1536), 77–79, 83–84, 89–90, 141, 158–59, 161–63, 230
  Institutes of the Christian Religion (1559), 98, 233–34, 235
  and Louis du Tillet, 80, 91–95
  as a pastoral theologian, 4–5, 7–9, 115, 128–29, 229, 235–37
  Petit traicté (1543), 109, 111, 112, 113–14, 121
  Response à un certain holandais (1562), 123–24
Campanus, John, 56–57
canon and civil law (classical), 5–6, 16–17, 20–21, 22–23, 33–34, 35–36, 39, 42–44, 46, 50–52, 231
Capito, Wolfgang, 42n.81, 53, 58–59, 70, 73, 74–75, 90–91, 92–93, 94–95, 96–99, 100, 101–2, 145–47, 154, 234–35
  De Pueris Instituendis Ecclesiae Argentinensis Isagoge (1527), 96
Caracciolo, Galeazzo, 177–78
Caroli, Pierre, 143–44
Castellio, Sebastian, 123–24, 123–24n.71
casuistry, 19n.14
Catholic (Roman) Church and Catholicism, 1–4, 9–10, 36–37, 40–41, 44, 49–50, 56–57, 72, 75–76, 82–84, 85–86, 87–88, 89–90, 93, 94–95, 98, 99–101, 129–30, 133–34, 151, 162–63, 221, 225–26, 228–29, 233–34
charity (neighbor-love), 6, 8, 34–35, 37–39, 40, 42–43, 45–46, 63–64, 66, 75, 87–88, 94–95, 96–97, 100, 107, 116–20, 122–23, 124–25, 133–35, 170, 186, 234–35, 236–37. *See also* rule of love
Charles V, Emperor, 38n.69, 41, 51n.4, 146–47
Charles Emmanuel I, 221
Chrisman, Miriam Usher, 52, 62, 69–70
Chrysostom, Saint John, 4n.10, 18n.7
civil rulers (magistrates), 6, 9–10, 11, 42, 43–44, 45–46, 49–50, 53, 58–59, 60, 63, 72, 73, 96–97, 100, 156, 195–96, 202–4, 205, 211–12, 213, 214–15, 216, 217, 221–22, 223, 224, 225, 226–27, 231, 235–36
Cochrane, Arthur, 146–47, 151
coercion (religious), 11, 27–28, 45–46. *See also* tolerance
confessions (of faith) and confessionalism, 3–5, 7–8, 9–12, 49–50, 56–57, 144, 156–57, 202, 206–7, 230–31, 234–35, 237
Coornhert, Dirk Volkerts, 123–28, 123–24n.71
Cop, Nicolas, 85–87
Cordier, Mathurin, 209–10
Corpus Iuris Civilis, 16–17
Council of Bern, 104–5. *See also* Bern (Switzerland)
Cyprian of Carthage, 18n.7

Daneau, Lambert, 208–9, 220–21
Daniel, François, 85–86, 88–89, 202
David, King, 22–23
De Bonnefoy, Ennemond, 214–15
De La Faye, Antoine, 220–21
De La Marck, Robert, 85
De Raemond, Florimond, 85–86
Diodati, Jean, 220–25
discipline (moral), 11–12, 53, 55, 56–57, 69–70, 202–3, 206–7, 214, 219, 228–30, 232
dissimulation and simulation, 75–76, 77–79, 80, 81–83, 85–86, 88–91, 96–97, 99–100, 102–3, 104–6, 107–8, 111, 112–13, 114, 116–24, 133–35, 169–70, 234–35. *See also* Nicodemites and (anti-)Nicodemism

Dougherty, M. V., 23
Duchemin, Nicolas, 80–81
Du Jon, François, 208–9
Du Tillet, Louis, 80, 85–86, 91–95

ecclesiastical rulers, 6, 9–10, 11, 27–28, 29–30, 45–46, 49–50, 62, 66–68, 69–70, 202–4, 205, 217, 235–36
Engelbrecht, Anton, 60–61, 63
equity, 6, 16
Erasmus, Desiderius, 3n.7, 36–39
Estienne, Robert, 204
evangelical(s), 42–44, 78–79, 80–81, 85–86, 93, 144–45, 177–78, 213
excommunication, 168, 196, 210
exegesis, 4–5, 119–20, 125–27, 147–48

Farel, Guillaume, 9–10, 11–12, 74–75, 77, 80–81, 84–85, 86–91, 95–97, 98–101, 102–3, 104–7, 116–18, 133, 139–43, 144, 157–58, 159–61, 162–65, 166, 167, 180–81, 206–7, 234–35
  Epistre exhortatoire (1544), 116–18
  Summary and Brief Exposition (1529/34), 141
Formula of Concord, 68–69
Francis I, King, 77–78, 80–81, 83–84, 88–90, 98
Franck, Sebastian, 54–56, 57–59, 64–65, 70–71, 100, 123–24, 125–26. *See also* Schwenckfeld, Caspar; Spiritualists
Frey, Claus, 61–62

Geneva, 3–4, 5–7, 8–9, 11–12, 91, 93, 94–95, 108–9, 123–24, 135, 139–44, 159–61, 162, 163–64, 166–71, 172–78, 179–81, 182, 183–84, 186, 188, 190–94, 195–96, 197, 198–201, 203–4, 205, 208–10, 213–14, 216–17, 219, 221, 228–30, 231–32, 234–36
  Academy of, 11–12, 202–12, 213–22, 223–24, 225–27, 234–35
  Articles concernant l'organisation de l'église et du culte a Genève, 139, 162
  Children of Geneva (*Enfants de Genève*), 195–96
  Company of Pastors, 9–10, 11–12, 135, 182–86, 190–92, 196, 199–200, 205–6, 211–12, 213–14, 216–17, 218–21, 222–24, 225, 226, 234–35
  Confession of Faith (1537), 9–10, 139–40, 139–40n.4, 141–43, 144–45, 157–60, 165, 203, 206–7, 208–9, 213, 216–17, 225–26
  Consistory, 9–10, 11–12, 168–82, 183, 184–85, 186–98, 199–201, 218–19, 223, 229–30, 231–32, 234–37
  Council of Two Hundred (*Deux Cents*), 198–99, 205–6
  Ecclesiastical Ordinances (1541), 168–69, 180–81, 183, 186, 198, 200–1, 205–6, 216, 222, 230
  General Council, 198–99, 205–6, 216
  magistrates, 9–10, 11–12, 135
  Register of the Company of Pastors, 182, 190–92
  Registers of the Consistory, 6–7, 9–10, 169–70
  Small Council, 139–40, 157–58, 162, 168, 169–75, 176–81, 182–86, 188–95, 196–201, 205–7, 212–13, 218–20, 223, 224–25, 231–32
Gentiles, 122–23
Germany, 1–2, 39, 42–43
Gesner, Conrad, 209–10
Gordon, Bruce, 85–86
gospel, 10, 45–46, 57–58, 72, 83–84, 86–87, 92–93, 96, 101–2, 105–6, 116, 118–19, 124–25, 162, 164–65, 177–78
Gratian, 18–19, 23, 23n.28, *See also* canon and civil law (classical)
  Decretum, 18–19, 21, 22–23, 42
Gregory, Brad, 164
Grey, Jonathan, 5–6
Grynaeus, Simon, 154

Haller, Jean, 210–11
Hedio, Caspar, 53, 63–64
Hemholz, R. H., 5–6, 17n.6
Henry of Navarre, 80–81
heretics and heresy, 28, 35–37, 70–71, 84, 217
Herod, King, 22–23, 37
Herodias. *See* Herod, King
Hoffman, Melchior, 54, 61–62

254 INDEX

Hotman, François, 209–10, 214–16, 224–25
Hubmaier, Balthasar, 54
Hugh of St. Victor, 32
humanist (Christian tradition), 35–36, 38–39

Isidore of Seville, 18–19
Ivo of Chartres, 28n.37, 32

Jerome, Saint, 18–19
Jews, 27–28, 82–83, 100–1, 122–23, 125–27
John the Baptist, 22–23, 37
Jonah, 166
Jonathan. *See* Saul, King
Jud, Leo, 62, 154
justification, 40, 44
Justinian, Emperor, 16–17, 25–26. *See also* canon and civil law (classical)
Digest, 16–17, 21

Karlstadt, Andreas, 45–46
Kingdon, Robert, 6–7, 177–78, 188–89

Lambert, Thomas, 6–7
Laurent, Gaspard, 219–20, 221–22
Lausanne (Switzerland), 105–6, 209–11, 214–15
  Academy of, 203, 209–11
Lausanne Disputation (1536), The, 73, 77, 87–89
law-gospel distinction, the, 6
Lecler, Joseph, 35–36, 55
Levy, Ian Christopher, 33–34
Lewis, Gillian, 206–7
liberties or freedoms (individual), 6, 9–10, 32, 37–38, 39, 43–44, 79, 96–97, 106–7, 119–20, 121–22, 133, 142–43, 145, 156, 158–59, 228–29, 232
libertines, 125–26
Lord's Supper, the, 85, 144–45, 146–47, 150, 160–61, 164–65, 172–73, 183, 192–97, 198–200, 210
Lot, 129–30
Louis XII, King, 80
Luther, Martin, 1–2, 36–37, 39–46, 49–50, 55, 57–58, 66–68, 67n.64, 113–14, 141, 146–47, 228–29, 231

Against the Storming Peasants (1525), 42–43
Galatians Commentary (1519), 40
Invocavit Sermons (1522), 45–46
Ninety-Five Theses (1517), 1–2
On Secular Authority (1523), 41
Sermon on the Sacrament of Penance (1519), 40
Lutherans and Lutheranism, 56–57, 80, 87–88, 144–45, 146–47, 154, 225–26

Maag, Karin, 203–4, 219–20
Manetsch, Scott, 6–7
Marguerite of Angoulême (Navarre), 80–81
Mass, Catholic, 73–74, 77, 81, 82–83, 85–86, 87–89, 95–96, 108–9, 120, 121–22, 131
Matheson, Peter, 100
McDonald, M. Wallace, 6–7
Meaux Group, 80–81, 87–88
Megander, Kaspar, 154
Melanchthon, Philip, 42n.81, 45–46, 97, 113–14
Myconius, Oswald, 139, 151, 154

Nabal. *See* David, King
Naphy, William, 6–7, 163–64
natural law, 7–8, 22–23, 29–30, 32, 235–36
  permissive, 16, 32–33
  and *perplexitas* (moral dilemma), 22–23, 23n.28, 27–28
Neuchâtel, 105–6, 180–81
Nicholas of Cusa, 35–36
Nicodemites and (anti-)Nicodemism, 11, 73–74, 75–80, 82–83, 84, 86–88, 89–91, 94–96, 97–98, 100, 101–3, 104–9, 111, 112, 113–14, 116–20, 121–22, 123–24, 128, 129–30, 131–35, 234–35. *See also* dissimulation or simulation
Nicodemus, 73–74, 114

Oaths and vows (swearing of), 3–7, 4n.10, 8, 9–12, 16–20, 21, 24–26, 27, 28, 33, 37–38, 46, 52–53, 73–74, 100, 101–2, 124–26, 131, 141–42, 143–44, 152–54, 156, 160, 161–63, 165, 169–71,

173–75, 178, 199–200, 219–20, 229, 231, 233–34, 235–36, 237
academic (matriculation), 11–12, 203–4, 208, 210–11, 213, 216, 217–18, 219–20, 225–26
citizen's, 95–96, 139–41, 174–75, 234–35
good faith (*bona fide*), 20, 21–22n.22, 27
and intention (*intentio*), 20, 21, 30–31, 186, 226
licit and illicit, 17, 19
marriage, 11–12, 186–92
ministerial, 223–25, 226–27
professorial, 207, 215, 224
and the *salus animarum* (health of the souls), 24–25
subscription, 3–4, 6–7, 10, 11–12, 125–26, 139–40, 203–4, 206–7, 210–11, 213, 216–17, 219–20, 225–26, 233–34

Oecalampadius, Johann, 139, 151
First Confession of Basel (1534), 139, 144, 151–54, 155, 157, 158–59
Old Covenant, 82–83, 100–1, 228–29

paillardise (illicit sexuality), 168–69, 171–72, 179
Paris, 15–16, 84, 85–86, 87–88, 213–14
Paul III, Pope, 154
Paul, the apostle, 40, 66, 74, 82–83, 100–1, 121–23, 126–27, 150, 155–56, 159, 177–78
Peace of Amboise, The (1563), 211–12
Peasants' War of 1525, The, 42–43
perjury, 16–17, 18–19, 20–21, 24–25, 168–69
Perrot, Charles, 214, 216–17
Peter, the apostle, 122–23
piety, 50–52, 55, 70, 74, 75–77, 79, 81, 90–91, 95–97, 100–2, 107–8, 111–13, 128, 131–32, 148–49, 154–55, 156, 202, 205, 229–30, 232, 233–37
pope, the, 39, 41, 87–88, 141
Prodi, Paolo, 5–6, 6n.14
profession (confession) of faith, 37, 45–46, 69–70, 73–78, 81, 83, 85, 95–96, 99–100, 101–2, 105–6, 108–9, 111, 112–13, 116–19, 120–21, 124–26, 127–28, 131–32, 133–34, 143–44, 160, 164–65, 169–70, 209–10, 230–31. *See also* confessions (of faith) and confessionalism
prudence, 16–17, 33, 34, 81, 90–91, 97, 112–13, 122–23, 128–29, 130–32, 165

Ratisbon (Regensburg), Diet of, 167
Reid, Jonathan, 77, 83
Renata, Duchess (Renée of France), 80, 120
Richardot, François, 120
Roussel, Gérard, 80–82, 83, 84–89, 90–91, 98–99, 104–5
rule of love, 43, 61–62, 63–64, 66–68, 96–97, 98–99, 100–3, 119–20, 121–23, 133–34, 142–43, 144, 147–49, 152–53, 154–55, 156, 157, 161–62, 175–76. *See also* charity (neighbor-love)

sacraments, 38–39, 42
Sadoleto, Cardinal, 166–67
Saint Bartholomew's Day Massacre (1572), 213–14
salvation, 9–10, 53. *See also* justification
sanctification, 9–10, 44
Sattler, Michael, 54
Saul, King, 21
Savoyard War. *See* Charles Emmanuel I
scandal, 31–32, 34–35, 78–79, 116–20, 121–22, 130–31, 168–69, 170, 174–75, 178, 180–81, 190–92, 230, 234–35
scandalum infirmorum, 34–35, 228–29 (*see also* Aquinas, Thomas; charity [neighbor love])
Schmalkald Articles, 146–47
Schola privita and *schola publica*. *See* Geneva: Academy of; Lausanne: Academy of
scholasticism (medieval), 27–28, 35–36, 37–38
Schwenckfeld, Caspar, 54–55, 57–59, 60–63, 64–66, 68–69, 70–71, 100, 123–24. *See also* Franck, Sebastian; Spiritualists
Scribner, Bob, 2–3

256　INDEX

Scripture, 1–2, 3–5, 8–10, 17–18, 21, 37–38, 41, 42, 44, 49–50, 55, 56–59, 60–62, 63, 66–68, 70–71, 82–83, 85–86, 90–91, 108, 110, 115, 119–21, 125, 126–28, 131–32, 133, 141–43, 145–46, 147–48, 149–50, 151–52, 154–55, 156, 157–58, 164, 165, 232–34, 237
Servetus, Michael, 123–24, 180–81
Simons, Menno, 123–24
Sodom and Gomorrah, 129–30
Sola fide, 1–2, 9–10. *See also* justification
Sola gratia, 9–10. *See also* justification
Sola scriptura. *See* Scripture
Sorbonne, 87–89
Spierling, Karen, 6–7
Spirit (Holy), 42
Spiritualists, 11, 49–50, 73, 123–24, 133, 234–35. *See also* Anabaptists
Stor, Martin, 61–62
Strasbourg, 50–53, 54–55, 56–59, 60–61, 63, 69–72, 73, 84, 90–91, 95–96, 97, 98–99, 100, 101–2, 108–9, 146–47, 154, 166, 234–36
　Ammeister, 52, 68–69
　General Synod of 1533, 58–60, 61–62, 63, 68–69, 71–72
　Kirchenpfleger, 58–59, 59n.34
　Rat, 52, 63–64, 68–69
Strauss, Gerald, 1–3
Sturm, Jacob, 53
Sturm, Jean, 86–87
Swiss Confederacy, 84

Thompson, John L., 7–8
Tierney, Brian, 32
Timothy, 122–23
Titus, 122–23
tolerance (religious), 1–2, 3n.7, 27–28, 35–37, 46, 55, 65n.58, 123–24. *See also* coercion (religious)
tradition (human), 2–5, 11–12, 16, 27, 28–29, 34, 37, 39–40, 42, 43–44, 45–46, 120–21, 141–43, 144, 145–46, 148, 149–50, 152, 153–54, 155, 156–57, 159–60, 165, 228–29, 233–34, 235
Trinity, the, 38–39, 208
Tronchin, Theodore, 220–21, 223–25, 223n.82
Tuininga, Matthew, 6
Tutino, Stefania, 5–6
two kingdoms, the, 6, 62, 65–66

Van Stam, Frans Peter, 77, 83, 87–88
Verkamp, Bernard, 45–46
Vermigli, Peter Martyr, 97, 104–7, 116, 121, 131, 133, 177–78, 234–35
　A treatise of the cohabitacyon of the faithfull with the unfaithfull (1555), 116
Viret, Pierre, 74–75, 87–91, 95–97, 100, 104–7, 112, 115–19, 122–23, 130–31, 133, 166–67, 180–81, 209–10, 234–35
　Admonition et consolation aux fideles (1547), 129–30
　Epistre envoyee aux fideles (1543), 112–14, 118–19, 122, 129–30

Watt, Jeffrey and Isabella, 6–7
William of Ockham, 30–32
William of Orange, 123–24
Witte, John, 6–7, 39, 188–89, 228–29
Worms, Diet of, 40–41
worship, 73–77, 81, 82–83, 85–86, 88–89, 90–91, 95–97, 100–3, 104–6, 111, 112–13, 116, 119–21, 123–24, 125–26, 127–28, 131–32, 133–35, 228–29, 230

Ziegler, Clement, 61–62
Zurich, 145, 177–78
Zwingli (and Zwinglianism), 56, 145–50, 225–26
　Sixty-seven Articles or *Conclusions* (1523), 145, 152, 156–57, 162–63